Gems of Theoretical Computer Science

Springer
Berlin
Heidelberg
New York
Barcelona
Budapest
Hong Kong
London
Milan
Paris
Singapore
Tokyo

Uwe Schöning   Randall Pruim

Gems of Theoretical Computer Science

Springer

Uwe Schöning
Abt. Theoretische Informatik
Universität Ulm
D-89069 Ulm, Germany

Randall Pruim
Dept. of Mathematics and Statistics
Calvin College
Grand Rapids, MI 49546, USA

Title of the Original German Edition:
Perlen der theoretischen Informatik
1995 © Spektrum Akademischer Verlag

Translated from the German, revised and expanded by Randall Pruim

Cip-Data applied for

Die Deutsche Bibliothek – CIP-Einheitsaufnahme

Schöning, Uwe:
Gems of theoretical computer science/Uwe Schöning; Randall Pruim. - Berlin; Heidelberg; New York; Barcelona; Budapest; Hong Kong; London; Milan; Paris; Singapore; Tokyo: Springer, 1998
Einheitssacht.: Perlen der theoretischen Informatik <engl.>
ISBN-13: 978-3-642-64352-1

ISBN-13: 978-3-642-64352-1 e-ISBN-13: 978-3-642-60322-8
DOI: 10.1007/978-3-642-60322-8

Softcover reprint of the hardcover 1st edition 1998

Typesetting: Randall Pruim
Cover Design: Künkel + Lopka, Werbeagentur, Heidelberg
Printed on acid-free paper SPIN 10674534 33/3142 – 5 4 3 2 1 0

Preface to Original German Edition

In the summer semester of 1993 at Universität Ulm, I tried out a new type of course, which I called *Theory lab*, as part of the computer science major program. As in an experimental laboratory – with written preparatory materials (including exercises), as well as materials for the actual meeting, in which an isolated research result is represented with its complete proof and all of its facets and false leads – the students were supposed to prove portions of the results themselves, or at least to attempt their own solutions. The goal was that the students understand and sense "how theoretical research is done." To this end I assembled a number of outstanding results ("highlights," "pearls," "gems") from theoretical computer science and related fields, in particular those for which some surprising or creative new method of proof was employed. Furthermore, I chose several topics which don't represent a solution to an open problem, but which seem in themselves to be surprising or unexpected, or place a well-known problem in a new, unusual context.

This book is based primarily on the preparatory materials and worksheets which were prepared at that time for the students of my course and has been subsequently augmented with additional topics. This book is not a text book in the usual sense. In a textbook one pays attention to breadth and completeness within certain bounds. This comes, however, at the cost of depth. Therefore, in a textbook one finds too often following the statement of a theorem the phrase: "The proof of this theorem would go beyond the scope of this book and must therefore be omitted." It is precisely this that we do not do here; on the contrary, we want to "dig in" to the proofs – and hopefully enjoy it. The goal of this book is not to reach an encyclopedic completeness but to pursue the pleasure of completely understanding a complex proof with all of its clever insights. It is obvious that in such a pursuit complete treatment of the topics cannot possibly be guaranteed and that the selection of topics must necessarily be subjective. The selected topics come from the areas of computability, logic, (computational) complexity, circuit theory, and algorithms.

Where is the potential reader for this book to be found? I believe he or she could be an active computer scientist or an advanced student (perhaps specializing theoretical computer science) who works through various topics as an independent study, attempting to "crack" the exercises and by this means learns the material on his or her own. I could also easily imagine portions of this book being used as the basis of a seminar, as well as to provide a simplified introduction into a potential topic for a *Diplomarbeit* (perhaps even for a *Dissertation*).

A few words about the use of this book. A certain amount of basic knowledge is assumed in theoretical computer science (automata, languages, computability, complexity) and for some topics probability and graph theory (similar to what my students encounter prior to the *Vordiplom*). This is very briefly recapitulated in the preliminary chapter. The amount of knowledge assumed can vary greatly from topic to topic. The topics can be read and worked through largely independently of each other, so one can begin with any of the topics. Within a topic there are only occasional references to other topics in the book; these are clearly noted. References to the literature (mostly articles from journals and conference proceedings) are made throughout the text at the place where they are cited. The global bibliography includes books which were useful for me in preparing this text and which can be recommended for further study or greater depth. The numerous exercises are to be understood as an integral part of the text, and one should try to find one's own solution before looking up the solutions in the back of the book. However, if one initially wants to understand only the general outline of a result, one could skip over the solutions altogether at the first reading. Exercises which have a somewhat higher level of difficulty (but are certainly still doable) have been marked with $^\diamond$.

For proof-reading (the original German text) and for various suggestions for improvement I want to thank Gerhard Buntrock, Volker Claus, Uli Hertrampf, Johannes Köbler, Christoph Meinel, Rainer Schuler, Thomas Thierauf, and Jacobo Torán. Christoph Karg prepared a preliminary version of Chapter 14 as part of a course paper.

Uwe Schöning

Preface to the English Edition

While I was visiting Boston University during the 1996–97 academic year, I noticed a small book, written in German, on a shelf in Steve Homer's office. Curious, I borrowed it for my train ride home and began reading one of the chapters. I liked the style and format of the book so much that over the course of the next few months I frequently found myself reaching for it and working through one chapter or another. This was my introduction to *Perlen der Theoretischen Informatik.*

A few of my colleagues had also seen the book. They also found it interesting, but most of them did not read German well enough to read more than small portions of it enjoyably. I hope that the English version will rectify this situation, and that many will enjoy (and learn from) the English version as much as I enjoyed the German version.

The front matter of this book says that it has been "translated, revised, and expanded." I should perhaps say a few words about each of these tasks. In translating the book, I have tried as much as possible to retain the feel of the original, which is somewhat less formal and impersonal than a typical text book yet relatively concise. I certainly hope that the "pleasure of the pursuit of understanding" has not gotten lost in the translation.

Most of the revisions to the book are quite minor. Some bibliography items have been added or updated; a number of German sources have been deleted. The layout has been altered somewhat. In particular, references now occur systematically at the end of each chapter and are often annotated. This format makes it easier to find references to the literature, while providing a place to tie up lose ends, summarize results, and point out extensions. Specific mention of the works cited at the end of each chapter is made informally, if at all, in the course of the presentation. Occasionally I have added or rearranged a paragraph, included an additional exercise, or elaborated on a solution, but for the most part I have followed the original quite closely. Where I spotted errors, I have tried to fix them; I hope I have corrected more than I have introduced.

While translating and updating this book, I began to consider adding some additional "gems" of my own. I am thankful to Uwe, my colleagues and Hermann Engesser, the supervising editor at Springer Verlag, for encouraging me to do so. In deciding which topics to add, I asked myself two questions: What is missing? and What is new? From the possible answers to each question I picked two new topics.

The introduction to average-case complexity presented in Topic 25 seemed to me to be a completion (more accurately, a continuation) of some of the ideas from Topic 8, where the term average-case is used in a somewhat different manner. It was an obvious "gap" to fill.

The chapter on quantum computation (Topic 26) covers material that is for the most part newer than the original book; indeed, several of the articles used to prepare it have not yet appeared in print. I considered covering Shor's quantum factoring algorithm – either instead or additionally – but decided that Grover's search algorithm provided a gentler introduction to quantum computation for those who are new to the subject. I hope interested readers will find Shor's algorithm easier to digest after having worked through the results presented here. No doubt, there are many other eligible topics for this book, but one must stop somewhere.

For reading portions of the text and providing various suggestions for improvement, I want to thank Drue Coles, Judy Goldsmith, Fred Green, Steve Homer, Steve Kautz, Luc Longpré, Chris Pollett, Marcus Schaefer, and Martin Strauss, each of whom read one or more chapters. I also want to thank my wife, Pennylyn Dykstra-Pruim, who in addition to putting up with my long and sometimes odd hours also proofread the manuscript; her efforts improved its style and reduced the number of typographical and grammatical errors. Finally, many thanks go to Uwe Schöning for writing the original book and collaborating on the English edition.

Randall Pruim
July, 1998

Table of Contents

Fundamental Definitions and Results 1

1. The Priority Method 9

2. Hilbert's Tenth Problem 15

3. The Equivalence Problem for LOOP(1)- and LOOP(2)-Programs 25

4. The Second LBA Problem 37

5. LOGSPACE, Random Walks on Graphs, and Universal Traversal Sequences 41

6. Exponential Lower Bounds for the Length of Resolution Proofs 49

7. Spectral Problems and Descriptive Complexity Theory ... 61

8. Kolmogorov Complexity, the Universal Distribution, and Worst-Case vs. Average-Case 71

9. Lower Bounds via Kolmogorov Complexity 77

10. PAC-Learning and Occam's Razor 85

11. Lower Bounds for the Parity Function 91

12. The Parity Function Again 101

13. The Complexity of Craig Interpolants 111

14. Equivalence Problems and Lower Bounds for Branching Programs 115

15. The Berman-Hartmanis Conjecture and Sparse Sets 123

16. Collapsing Hierarchies ... 131

17. Probabilistic Algorithms, Probability Amplification, and the Recycling of Random Numbers ... 141

18. The BP Operator and Graph Isomorphism ... 153

19. The BP-Operator and the Power of Counting Classes ... 163

20. Interactive Proofs and Zero Knowledge ... 175

21. IP = PSPACE ... 183

22. P $\neq$ NP with probability 1 ... 191

23. Superconcentrators and the Marriage Theorem ... 197

24. The Pebble Game ... 203

25. Average-Case Complexity ... 213

26. Quantum Search Algorithms ... 223

Solutions ... 237

Bibliography ... 309

Index ... 313

Fundamental Definitions and Results

Before we begin, we want to review briefly the most important terms, definitions, and results that are considered prerequisite for this book. More information on these topics can be found in the appropriate books in the bibliography.

General

The set of natural numbers (including 0) is denoted by $\mathbb{N}$, the integers by $\mathbb{Z}$, and the reals by $\mathbb{R}$. The notation log will always be used to indicate logarithms base 2, and ln to indicate logarithms base e.

If Σ is a finite non-empty set (sometimes referred to as the *alphabet*), then Σ^* denotes the set of all finite *strings* (sequences) from Σ, including the empty string, which is denoted by λ. A subset L of Σ^* is called a (formal) *language* (over Σ). The complement of L (with respect to some alphabet Σ) is $\bar{L} = \Sigma^* - L$. For a string $x \in \Sigma^*$, $|x|$ denotes the length of x; for a set A, $|A|$ denotes the cardinality of A. For any ordering of the alphabet Σ, the *lexicographical order* on Σ^* (induced by the order on Σ) is the linear ordering in which shorter strings precede longer ones and strings of the same length are ordered in the usual lexicographic way. For $\Sigma = \{0,1\}$ with $0 < 1$, this ordering begins

$$\lambda < 0 < 1 < 00 < 01 < 10 < 11 < 000 < \cdots$$

We assume that all finite objects (graphs, formulas, algorithms, etc) that occur in the definition of a language have been suitably encoded as strings over $\{0,1\}$. Such encodings are denoted by $\langle\cdot\rangle$.

A *polynomial* p in variables $x_1, \ldots, x_n$ is a function of the form

$$p(x_1, \ldots, x_n) = \sum_{i=1}^{k} \alpha_i x_1^{a_{1i}} x_2^{a_{2i}} \ldots x_n^{a_{ni}} ,$$

where $k, a_{ij} \in \mathbb{N}$. For our purposes, the coefficients, α_i, will usually also be integers (sometimes natural numbers). The largest occurring exponent a_{ij} (with $\alpha_i \neq 0$) is the *degree* of the polynomial p. The *total degree* of the polynomial p is the largest occurring value of the sum $a_{i1} + a_{i2} + \ldots + a_{in}$ (with $\alpha_i \neq 0$). A univariate polynomial of degree d is uniquely determined by specifying $d+1$ support points $(x_0, y_0), (x_1, y_1), \ldots, (x_d, y_d)$ with $x_0 < x_1 < \ldots < x_d$ (Interpolation Theorem).

Graph Theory

Graphs play a role in nearly all of our topics. A graph is a structure $G = (V, E)$ consisting of a finite sets V of *nodes* and E of *edges*. In the case of a directed graph, $E \subseteq V \times V$, and in the case of an undirected graph $E \subseteq \binom{V}{2}$, the set of all two-element subsets of V. A *path* (from v_1 to v_2) is a sequence of adjoining edges (which begins at v_1 and ends at v_2). If $v_1 = v_2$ and the path consists of at least one edge, then the path is called a *cycle*. A graph is *connected* if there is a path from any node in the graph to any other node in the graph; *acyclic* if it contains no cycles; and *bipartite* if the node set V can be partitioned into $V = V_1 \cup V_2$ in such a way that $V_1 \cap V_2 = \emptyset$, and every edge of the graph joins a node in V_1 with a node in V_2. The *degree* of a node is the number of other nodes that are joined to it by an edge. In directed graphs we speak further of the *in-degree* and *out-degree* of a node. A node without predecessors (in-degree 0) is called a *source*, a node without successors (out-degree 0) is called a *sink*.

Two graphs $G_1 = (V_1, E_1)$ and $G_2 = (V_2, E_2)$ are *isomorphic* if there is a bijective mapping $\varphi : V_1 \to V_2$ (which can be extended in the obvious way to edges) such that $e \in E_1 \iff \varphi(e) \in E_2$. We denote by $\varphi(G)$ the graph isomorphic to G that results from applying the permutation φ to the nodes and edges of G. The set of *automorphisms* of a graph G is the set of all isomorphisms between G and G, i.e., the set of all permutations φ such that $\varphi(G) = G$.

Boolean Formulas and Circuits

A *boolean function* is a function $f : \{0,1\}^n \to \{0,1\}$. Boolean functions can be represented as *boolean formulas*, *boolean circuits*, or *branching programs*. A boolean formula is built up in the usual way from the symbols $\wedge$, $\vee$, and $\neg$, the variables x_i, and parentheses. *SAT* denotes the (decision) problem of determining for a given boolean formula whether or not it is *satisfiable*, that is, whether there is an assignment for the variables in the formula that causes the formula to be evaluated as "true" (or 1).

A boolean circuit is a directed, acyclic, connected graph in which the input nodes are labeled with variables x_i and the internal nodes have in-degree either 1 or 2. Nodes with in-degree 1 are labeled with $\neg$ and nodes with in-degree 2 are labeled with either $\wedge$ or $\vee$. Each node in the graph can be associated with a boolean function in the obvious way by interpreting $\neg$ as the NOT-function, $\wedge$ as the AND-function, and $\vee$ as the NOT-function. The function associated with the output node of the graph is the function computed by (or represented by) the circuit. A formula can also be understood as a circuit in which every node has out-degree 1. The *size* of a circuit or a formula is the number of $\wedge$, $\vee$, and $\neg$ symbols that occur in it. For some of the topics, we will consider families of boolean circuits for which there is a polynomial $p(n)$ such that the size of the nth circuit is bounded by $p(n)$. In this case we will say that the family of functions has ***polynomial-size circuits.*** For some of the topics we will also consider circuits in which the AND- or OR-gates may have unbounded fan-in.

Branching programs will be introduced in Topic 14.

Quantifier Logic

Formulas with quantifiers occur in various contexts. In order to evaluate a formula of the form $\exists x F$, where F is a formula (containing function and predicate symbols in addition to boolean operations), one must first fix a ***structure***, which consists of a domain and interpretations of all occurring function and predicate symbols over that domain. The formula $\exists x F$ is ***valid*** if there exists some element of the domain such that if all free occurrences of x in F are replaced with that element, then the resulting formula is valid. Formulas with universal quantifiers are evaluated analogously.

In this book, the following variations occur: in a ***quantified boolean formula*** the domain for the variables is always considered to be the truth values 0 and 1, and no function or predicate symbols are permitted other than the boolean operations. The problem *QBF* is the problem of determining for a given quantified boolean formula with no free variables if it is valid (under this interpretation).

A ***predicate logic formula*** may have arbitrary function and predicate symbols as well the equality symbol. When such a formula F is valid in a given structure A, then we write $\mathsf{A} \models F$. In this case A is called a ***model*** for F. The formula F is ***satisfiable*** if it has at least one model. It is a ***tautology*** if for every suitable structure A, $\mathsf{A} \models F$. In this case we write $\models F$.

In an arithmetic formula only the two special functions symbols $+$ and $*$, the equality symbol, and the constant symbols 0 and 1 are allowed. Such formulas are interpreted in the special, fixed structure with domain $\mathbb{N}$, and $+$ and $*$ interpreted by the usual addition and multiplication in $\mathbb{N}$.

Probability

We will only consider finite or countable probability spaces Ω, so any subset of Ω can be an *event*. $Pr[E]$ is used to denote the probability of event E. It is always the case that $Pr[\emptyset] = 0$, $Pr[\Omega] = 1$, and $Pr[\Omega - E] = 1 - Pr[E]$. If $E_1, E_2, \ldots$ are pairwise mutually exclusive events, i.e., for any pair i and j, $E_i \cap E_j = \emptyset$, then $Pr[\cup_i E_i] = \sum Pr[E_i]$. The *inclusion-exclusion principle* holds for arbitrary events $E_1, \ldots, E_n$ and states that

$$\begin{aligned} Pr[\cup_i E_i] = & \textstyle\sum_i Pr[E_i] - \sum_{i<j} Pr[E_i \cap E_j] \\ & + \textstyle\sum_{i<j<k} Pr[E_i \cap E_j \cap E_k] - \cdots \pm \cdots Pr[E_1 \cap \ldots E_n] \,. \end{aligned}$$

In the equation above the first term on the right overestimates the correct value, the first two underestimate it, etc. Thus, the first term can be used as an upper bound and the first two terms as a lower bound for $Pr[\cup_i E_i]$.

By *conditional probability* $Pr[E_1|E_2]$ (read the probability of E_1 given E_2) we mean the quotient $Pr[E_1 \cap E_2]/Pr[E_2]$.

A set of events $\{E_1, \ldots, E_n\}$ is called *pairwise independent* if for every $i, j \in \{1, \ldots, n\}$ with $i \neq j$, $Pr[E_i \cap E_j] = Pr[E_i] \cdot Pr[E_j]$ and *completely independent* if for every non-empty set $I \subseteq \{1, \ldots, n\}$, $Pr[\cap_{i \in I} E_i] = \prod_{i \in I} Pr[E_i]$.

A *random variable* is a map from the set of events into the set $\mathbb{R}$. The *expected value* of a random variable Z is $E(Z) = \sum_a Pr[Z = a] \cdot a$ and its *variance* is $V(Z) = E((Z - E(Z))^2 = E(Z^2) - (E(Z))^2$. (The sum is over all values a that the random variable Z takes on with non-vanishing probability.) The expected value operator is linear: $E(aX + bY) = aE(X) + bE(Y)$. Occasionally we will make use of various inequalities when approximating probabilities.

Markov's inequality. If Z is a random variable that only takes on positive values, then $Pr[Z \geq a] \leq E(Z)/a$.

Chebyshev's inequality. $Pr[|Z - E(Z)| \geq a] \leq V(Z)/a^2$.

One frequently occurring probability distribution is the *binomial distribution*. In a binomial distribution a random experiment with two possible outcomes ("success" and "failure") is carried out n times independently. Let p be the probability of success in one of these trials, and let X be the random variable that "counts" the number of successes. Then

$$\begin{aligned} Pr[X = i] &= \binom{n}{i} p^i (1-p)^{(n-i)} \,, \\ E(X) &= np \,, \\ V(X) &= np(1-p) \,. \end{aligned}$$

Computability

The set of (partial) computable functions (over $\mathbb{N}$ or Σ^*, depending on the context) can be defined (among other ways) by means of Turing machines. One defines a *transition function* (or a transition relation if the Turing machine is *nondeterministic* instead of *deterministic*) on the set of *configurations* of a Turing machine, among which are the *start configurations*, which correspond uniquely to the possible values of the function argument x, and *end configurations*, from which one can derive the value of the function, $f(x)$. A configuration is a complete description of the Turing machine at a given time (consisting of state, head position(s), and contents of the work tape(s)). A sequence of configurations beginning with the start configuration corresponding to input x such that each successive configuration is determined according to the transition function of the machine is called a *computation* of the machine on input x. M_i denotes the ith Turing machine, which corresponds to the ith partial computable function φ_i and the ith computably enumerable language $W_i = L(M_i)$. A language L is *computable* (or *decidable*) if both the language and its complement are computably enumerable. (Equivalently, L computable if there is a Turing machine M such that $L = L(M)$ and M halts on all inputs.) Well-known undecidable problems (languages) include the *halting problem*:

$$H = \{\langle M, x\rangle \mid M \text{ halts on input } x\}$$

and the halting problem with empty tape:

$$H_0 = \{\langle M\rangle \mid M \text{ halts when started with an empty tape}\} .$$

Other models of computation that are equivalent to the Turing machine model include register machines (also called GOTO-programs), WHILE-programs, and μ-recursive functions. In each of these one can define similar undecidable halting problems. A further example of a language that is undecidable but still computably enumerable is the set of all tautologies in predicate logic. On the other hand, the set of all valid arithmetic formulas (in the structure $(\mathbb{N}, +, *)$) is not even computably enumerable. (One says that arithmetic is not axiomatizable.)

A language A is (many-one) *reducible* (written $A \leq_{\mathrm{m}} B$) if there is a total computable function f such that for all x, $x \in A \iff f(x) \in B$. The language A is *Turing-reducible* to B (written $A \leq_{\mathrm{T}} B$) if there is an oracle Turing machine M that halts on all inputs and for which $A = L(M^B)$, where $L(M^B)$ denotes the language accepted by M using B as oracle (i.e., as a "sub-routine"). If A is reducible to B by either of these types of reducibilities and B is decidable (or computably enumerable), then A is also decidable (computably enumerable, respectively).

Complexity Theory

A *complexity class* is formed by collecting together all languages that can be computed by Turing machines with similar restrictions on their resources or structure. The class P consists of all problems that can be solved with deterministic Turing machines whose running time is bounded by a polynomial in the length of the input. The class NP consists of all problems that are accepted by a nondeterministic Turing machine for which the "running time" (in this case the depth of the computation tree) is bounded by a polynomial in the length of the input. More generally, one can define the classes $\mathsf{DTIME}(f(n))$ and $\mathsf{NTIME}(f(n))$. The difference is that the running times of the corresponding Turing machines are no longer required to be bounded by some polynomial but instead must be bounded by some function that is $O(f(n))$. The classes $\mathsf{DSPACE}(f(n))$ and $\mathsf{NSPACE}(f(n))$ can be defined analogously, in which case the amount of space used on the work tape (but not the input tape) is bounded instead of the running time. PSPACE denotes the class $\bigcup\{\mathsf{DSPACE}(f(n)) \mid f \text{ is a polynomial}\}$.

We have the following inclusions:

$$\mathsf{DSPACE}(\log n) \subseteq \underbrace{\mathsf{NSPACE}(\log n) \subseteq \mathsf{P} \subseteq \mathsf{NP} \subseteq \mathsf{PSPACE}}_{\subsetneq}$$

Notice that at least the first two classes are strictly contained in the last. Sometimes L and NL are used to denote $\mathsf{DSPACE}(\log n)$ and $\mathsf{NSPACE}(\log n)$.

If f and F are two functions such that F is time constructible and grows significantly more rapidly than f, for example, if

$$\lim_{n\to\infty} \frac{f(n)\log f(n)}{F(n)} = 0,$$

then $\mathsf{DTIME}(f(n)) \subsetneq \mathsf{DTIME}(F(n))$. Analogous statements hold for DSPACE, NTIME, and NSPACE.

For a complexity class C, co$C$ denotes the set of all languages whose complements are in C. Some classes are known to be closed under complementation: $\mathsf{P} = \mathsf{coP}$, $\mathsf{PSPACE} = \mathsf{coPSPACE}$, $\mathsf{DTIME}(f(n) = \mathsf{coDTIME}(f(n)))$, $\mathsf{DSPACE}(f(n) = \mathsf{coDSPACE}(f(n))$, and $\mathsf{NSPACE}(f(n) = \mathsf{coNSPACE}(f(n))$ (see Topic 4). For other classes, closure under complement is not known and in fact doubtful: $\mathsf{NP} =?\mathsf{coNP}$.

A language L is called NP-*complete* if $L \in \mathsf{NP}$ and for all $A \in \mathsf{NP}$, $A \leq_{\mathrm{m}}^{\mathsf{P}} L$, where $\leq_{\mathrm{m}}^{\mathsf{P}}$ is defined analogously to $\leq_{\mathrm{m}}$ with the difference that the reduction function must be computable in time that is bounded by a polynomial in the length of the input. The language *SAT* is NP-complete. For every NP-complete language L we have

$$L \in \mathsf{P} \iff \mathsf{P} = \mathsf{NP}\,.$$

The definition of NP-completeness can be sensibly extended to other (larger) complexity classes. For example, the language *QBF* is PSPACE-complete. Just as $\leq_{\mathrm{m}}^{\mathsf{P}}$ is a polynomial time-bounded version of $\leq_{\mathrm{m}}$, $\leq_{\mathrm{T}}^{\mathsf{P}}$ can be defined as the polynomial time-bounded version of $\leq_{\mathrm{T}}$. Instead of $A \leq_{\mathrm{T}}^{\mathsf{P}} B$ we sometimes write $A \in \mathsf{P}(B)$ or $A \in \mathsf{P}^B$ (and say that A is computable in polynomial time *relative to* B). If in this definition we use a nondeterministic machine instead of a deterministic one, then we write $A \in \mathsf{NP}^B$. These notations can also be extended to classes of languages:

$$\mathsf{P}^C = \bigcup_{B \in C} \mathsf{P}^B, \quad \mathsf{NP}^C = \bigcup_{B \in C} \mathsf{NP}^B .$$

Algorithms and Programming Languages

For the representation of algorithms, we use a notation that resembles programming language MODULA; this language contains the usual assignment of variables, branching instructions of the form

IF ... **THEN** ... **ELSE** ... **END**

and the usual loop constructs:

FOR ... **TO** ... **DO** ... **END**
WHILE ... **DO** ... **END**
REPEAT ... **UNTIL** ... **END**

Occasionally we will use procedures, especially when describing recursive algorithms.

The programs are typically to be understood as informal descriptions of Turing machines, and from time to time we will expand the programming language to include additional keywords that describe operations specific to Turing machines. The instructions

INPUT ...
OUTPUT ...

express that the Turing machine is to read from its input tape or write to its output tape. The instructions

ACCEPT
REJECT

cause the Turing machine to halt in an accepting or rejection state.

Nondeterministic machines "guess" a string (from a finite set) and assign the guess to a program variable. The variable then takes on any one of the possible values. For this we write

GUESS $x \in S$

where S is a finite set.

Probabilistic (randomized) algorithms are similar to nondeterministic algorithms, but the various possibilities of a guess are assigned probabilities (always according to the uniform distribution, that is, each possibility is equally likely to be guessed). In this case we modify the instruction above to

GUESS RANDOMLY $x \in S$

After the execution of such an instruction, for every $s \in S$ it is the case that $Pr[x = s] = 1/|S|$.

1. The Priority Method

In the early years of computability theory, Emil Post formulated a problem which was first solved twelve years later independently by a Russian (Muchnik) and an American (Friedberg). The solution introduced a new method, the priority method, which has proven to be extremely useful in computability theory.

Let $W_0, W_1, W_2, \ldots$ be an enumeration of all computably enumerable languages. Such an enumeration can be obtained by enumerating all Turing Machines M_i and setting $W_i = L(M_i)$, the language accepted by M_i. In an analogous way we can also enumerate all oracle Turing Machines. For any language B, let $W_i^B = L(M_i^B)$ be the ith language that is computably enumerable relative to B (that is, with B as oracle).

A language A is Turing reducible to B (written: $A \leq_{\mathrm{T}} B$), if there is an oracle Turing Machine M that computes the characteristic function of A relative to B (i.e., with oracle B). In particular, this implies that M halts on every input (with oracle B).

The definition of $\leq_{\mathrm{T}}$ can also be written

$$A \leq_T B \Leftrightarrow (\exists i : A = W_i^B \text{ and } \exists j : \overline{A} = W_j^B) .$$

Two languages A and B are said to be *Turing equivalent* if $A \leq_{\mathrm{T}} B$ and $B \leq_{\mathrm{T}} A$, in which case we write $A \equiv_T B$.

"Post's Problem," as it has come to be known, is the question of whether there exist undecidable, computably enumerable sets that are not Turing equivalent to the halting problem. In particular the answer is yes if there are two computably enumerable languages A and B that are incomparable with respect to $\leq_{\mathrm{T}}$, i.e. such that $A \not\leq_{\mathrm{T}} B$ and $B \not\leq_{\mathrm{T}} A$.

If there are two such languages, then neither one can be decidable –

Exercise 1.1. Why? ◁

– nor can either one be equivalent to the halting problem.

Exercise 1.2. Why? ◁

So the picture looks like this:

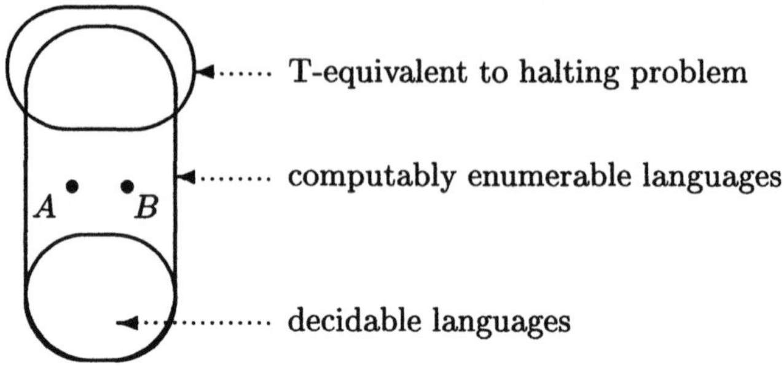

It is not difficult to define languages by diagonalization so that $A \not\leq_T B$ (in fact so that A and B are incomparable with respect to $\leq_T$). One selects for each i an x_i and arranges the definitions of A and B such that $x_i \in \overline{A} \iff x_i \notin W_i^B$, i.e. $x_i \in A \iff x_i \in W_i^B$. The input x_i is said to be a *witness* for the fact that $\overline{A}$ is not computably enumerable in B via W_i. In the known diagonalization constructions one can usually recognize easily that the function $i \mapsto x_i$ is in fact computable. This means that the witness x_i can be found *effectively* in i.

The problem with these constructions is that the languages A and B that they produce are not computably enumerable. In fact, it can be shown that it is impossible to construct two computably enumerable languages A and B for which $A \not\leq_T B$ and $B \not\leq_T A$ and such that the respective witnesses can be found effectively. Thus some new method, fundamentally different from the "usual" diagonalization technique, is needed to solve Post's Problem.

Before solving Post's Problem, however, we want to show that the claim just made is valid. Notice first that a computably enumerable language A is computable (in B) if and only if $\overline{A}$ is computably enumerable (in B). Therefore, we make the following definition: a language A is *effectively not Turing reducible to* B if there is a total computable function f such that for all i, $f(i) \in \overline{A} \not\Leftrightarrow f(i) \in W_i^B$, that is, $f(i) \in A \Leftrightarrow f(i) \in W_i^B$.

The following claim is then true:

Claim. If A and B are computably enumerable languages and A is effectively not Turing reducible to B, then B is computable.

Exercise 1.3. Why does it follow from the claim that if there are any computably enumerable languages that are incomparable with respect to Turing reducibility that this fact cannot be demonstrated *effectively*? ◁

Proof (of the claim). Since B is computably enumerable, it suffices to show that the hypothesis implies that $\overline{B}$ is computably enumerable. For each z, let M_z be the following oracle Turing machine:

```
INPUT x;
IF z ∈ ORACLE THEN REJECT
   ELSE ACCEPT
END
```

The function

$$g : z \mapsto \text{Coding of Machine } M_z$$

is clearly computable, and furthermore

$$W^B_{g(z)} = \begin{cases} \mathbb{N} & \text{if } z \notin B, \\ \emptyset & \text{if } z \in B. \end{cases}$$

By hypothesis there is a total computable function f such that

$$f(n) \in A \Leftrightarrow f(n) \in W^B_n.$$

Now consider $f(g(z))$ for arbitrary z. We obtain

$$\begin{aligned} f(g(z)) \in A &\Leftrightarrow f(g(z)) \in W^B_{g(z)} \text{ (by choice of } f) \\ &\Leftrightarrow W^B_{g(z)} = \mathbb{N} \text{ (by choice of } g) \\ &\Leftrightarrow z \notin B\,. \end{aligned}$$

That is, $\overline{B} = g^{-1}(f^{-1}(A))$. Since A is computably enumerable, it follows from this representation of $\overline{B}$ that $\overline{B}$ is computably enumerable. □

Exercise 1.4. Show that the preceding sentence is valid. ◁

On the basis of this observation, many researchers were of the opinion that Post's Problem could not be solved. There is, however, a solution. The languages A and B must be Turing incomparable in a certain non-effective way. The method by which this is possible is now referred to as the *priority method* and was developed independently by Friedberg (USA) and Muchnik (Russia) in 1956, roughly 12 years after Post originally posed the problem.

In 1983, at the Computational Complexity Conference in Santa Barbara P. Young considered these 12 years as the potential length of time needed to find a solution to the P-NP problem. Twelve years after its definition in 1971, the P-NP problem, unfortunately, remained unsolved, as it remains today.

* * * * *

Now we turn our attention to the solution of Post's Problem.

Theorem 1.1. *There exist computably enumerable languages A and B that are Turing incomparable.*

Proof. We present an enumeration procedure that enumerates A and B simultaneously, thereby showing that both are computably enumerable. The enumeration proceeds in stages: stage 0, stage 1, stage 2, etc. Each stage is subdivided into two phases, an A phase and a B phase. In an A phase, an element of A (and in a B phase, an element of B) can potentially be enumerated; that is, in each phase one element may be put into the appropriate language. In addition, we maintain during the construction two lists–L_A and L_B– the entries of which are all of the form (i,x). In these pairs i is the index of a Turing machine M_i, and x is an input for which we will try to guarantee that $x \in A \Leftrightarrow x \in W_i^B$ ($x \in B \Leftrightarrow x \in W_i^A$, respectively). Each entry in these lists is either 'active' or 'inactive'. Furthermore, x_A (x_B) will always be an input that is so large that it does not affect any of the preceding decisions.

Step 0 is used for initialization.

Step 0. (Phase A and B)
Let $A = B = L_A = L_B = \emptyset$ and $x_A = x_B = 0$

The actual construction then proceeds as follows:

- *Step* $n+1$. (Phase A)

```
L_A := L_A ∪ {(n, x_A)};  ((n, x_A) is 'active').
FOR all active (i, x) ∈ L_A in increasing order according to i DO
   IF M_i on input x and Oracle B (as constructed so far)
      accepts in n or fewer steps
      THEN A := A ∪ {x};  Declare (i, x) to be 'inactive';
              ⎧ Let y be the largest oracle query in
              ⎪                    the computation above;
              ⎪ x_B := max(x_B, y + 1);
              ⎪ j := 0;
          (*) ⎨ FOR (k, y) ∈ L_B, k ≥ i DO
              ⎪    L_B := L_B − {(k, y)} ∪ {(k, x_B + j)};  (*active*)
              ⎪    j := j + 1;
              ⎪ END;
              ⎩ x_B := x_B + j;
           GOTO Phase B;
   END;
END;
GOTO Phase B;
```

- *Step* $n+1$. (Phase B)

```
L_B := L_B ∪ {(n, x_B)};  (*active*)
FOR all active (i, x) ∈ L_B in increasing order according to i DO
   IF M_i on input x and Oracle A (as constructed so far)
      accepts in at most n steps
      THEN B := B ∪ {x};  Declare (i, x) to be 'inactive';
```

(*) {
Let y be the largest oracle query in the computation above;
$x_A := \max(x_A, y + 1)$;
$j := 0$;
FOR $(k, y) \in L_A,\ k > i$ **DO**
  $L_A := L_A - \{(k, y)\} \cup \{(k, x_A + j)\}$; (*active*)
  $j := j + 1$;
END;
$x_A := x_A + j$;
}
GOTO Step $n + 2$;
END;
END;
GOTO Step $n + 2$;

We claim that the languages A and B that are "enumerated" by the preceding construction have the desired properties, namely that $A \not\leq_T B$ and $B \not\leq_T A$, or more precisely that for all $i \in \mathbb{N}$ there exist x and x' with $x \in A \not\Leftrightarrow x \in W_i^B$ and $x' \in B \not\Leftrightarrow x' \in W_i^A$.

Notice that the entries (i, x) in the lists L_A and L_B can change and that such changes respect the following priority ordering: The entry $(0, ...)$ in List L_A has highest priority, then $(0, ...)$ in list L_B, then $(1, ...)$ in list L_A, then $(1, ...)$ in list L_B, etc. This means that if at stage n of the construction $(i, x) \in L_A$ and M_i accepts x with oracle B in at most n steps, then x is enumerated into A. To prevent subsequent changes to the oracle B that might alter this computation, all of the entries $(j, ...)$ in the list L_B that have lower priority than (i, x) are removed from the list and replaced by new entries which are "large enough" that they do not affect the computation. On the other hand, it can happen that a requirement "$x \in A \not\Leftrightarrow x \in W_i^B$" that at some point in the construction appears satisfied is later "injured." This happens if some x' is enumerated into B for the sake of some entry (i', x') of higher priority (i.e., for which $i' < i$). It is precisely the determination of these priorities that is carried out in section (*) of the construction.

What is important is that for each i the entry $(i, ...)$ in list L_A or L_B is changed only finitely many times ("finite injury"). This can be proven by induction on i.

Exercise 1.5. Carry out this induction. Also determine how often (at most) an entry $(i, ...)$ in L_A (L_B, respectively) can change. ◁

A picture is useful in understanding how the construction proceeds. One can imagine the construction taking place on the following "abacus":

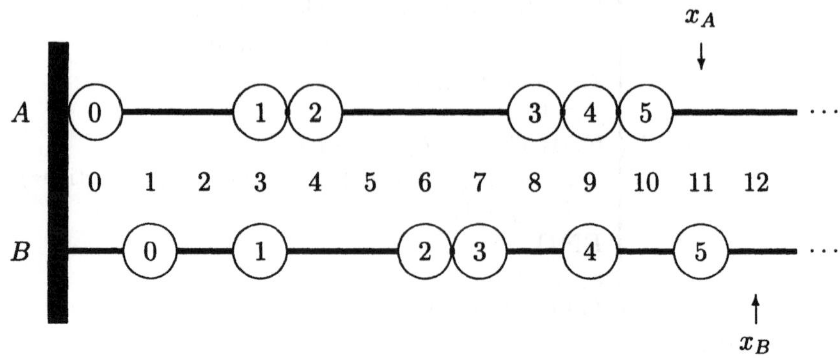

The active entries (i, n) in the lists L_A and L_B are represented by balls labeled with the number i and appearing in position n of the appropriate row. The arrows indicate the numbers x_A and x_B, respectively. If the values of entries in L_B (L_A) change, then this is caused by one of the balls labeled i in the A row (B row). In this case, all of the balls of lower priority (that is, with larger index) in the B row are slid to the right until they are beyond the arrow for x_B (x_A). After the balls have been slid to the right, the arrow x_B (x_A) is slid to the right beyond all of the balls.

We know that the entry (i, x) in L_A slides only finitely many times. Let (i, x) be the final entry in L_A, corresponding to the location in which ball i "comes to rest." There are two cases: $x \in A$ or $x \notin A$. If $x \in A$, then there is a step n such that during the A phase of stage n, x enters A. Since (i, x) is the final entry in L_A, it is not possible that at some later stage anything entered B (for the sake of some (i', x') of higher priority) that might have injured the requirement $x \in A \Leftrightarrow x \in W_i^B$.

If $x \notin A$, then $x \notin W_i^B$, since otherwise there would have been a stage n during which the THEN-clause for (x, i) would have been operative, in which case x would have been enumerated into A. So in this case it is also true that $x \in A \Leftrightarrow x \in W_i^B$.

By a symmetric argument, one can show that for all i there is a x' with $x' \in B \Leftrightarrow x' \in W_i^A$. □

References

- H. Rogers: *Theory of Recursive Functions and Effective Computability*, McGraw-Hill, 1967, Chapter 10.
- W.S. Brainerd, L.H. Landweber: *Theory of Computation*, Wiley, 1974, Section 8.4.
- R.I. Soare: *Recursively Enumerable Sets and Degrees*, Springer, 1980, Chapter VII.

2. Hilbert's Tenth Problem

Hilbert's Tenth Problem goes back to the year 1900 and concerns a fundamental question, namely whether there is an algorithmic method for solving Diophantine equations. The ultimate solution to this problem was not achieved until 1970. The "solution" was, however, a negative one: there is no such algorithm.

Among the 23 famous open problems posed by the mathematician David Hilbert in 1900 was one – problem number ten – which possesses an especially close connection to computability theory, (although this connection was only apparent later). This problem deals with *Diophantine equations* – named after Diophantus of Alexandria, 3rd century A.D. – which are equations of the form $f(x_1, \ldots, x_n) = 0$, where f is a polynomial with integer coefficients. Required is a method finding integer solutions $x_1, \ldots, x_n$ to such an equation (i.e., zeroes of f in $\mathbb{Z}$). This task is equivalent to the task of finding, given two polynomials f and g with integer coefficients, solutions to the equation $f = g$, since $f = g$ if and only if $f - g = 0$.

Exercise 2.1. For what values of $a, b \in \mathbb{Z} - \{0\}$ does the Diophantine equation

$$ax + by = 1$$

have integer solutions? ◁

A positive solution to Hilbert's tenth problem (by which we mean the existence of an algorithm to solve such equations) would have had many important consequences. Many open problems in Number Theory and also in some other areas of mathematics can be reformulated as Diophantine equations.

Hilbert's tenth problem was solved in 1970 by Y.V. Matijasevič after significant progress had been made by J. Robinson, H. Putnam and M. Davis. The solution was, however, of a much different sort than Hilbert had probably conjectured. The problem is *undecidable*, which means that there is no algorithm that takes as input a Diophantine equation and correctly decides whether it has an integer solution.

This result represents a significant sharpening of (a variant of) Gödel's Incompleteness Theorem, which says that the problem of testing an *arithmetic* *formula* for validity is undecidable. Arithmetic formulas are formulas that are built up from the basic operators $=, *, +$, boolean operations, constants and variables over the integers, as well as existential and universal quantifiers.

Example of an arithmetic formula:

$$\exists x\ \forall z\ \exists u\ (u * 2 = v) \wedge \neg(x * x + u * z = u * x + 5)$$

Diophantine equations can be seen as a special case of arithmetic formulas, namely those in which negation and universal quantifiers do not occur. (That is, all variables that occur are existentially quantified.) The following two exercises show how to eliminate the logical connectives AND and OR.

Exercise 2.2. Show that the problem of simultaneously solving a system of Diophantine equations

$$\begin{aligned} f_1(x_1, \ldots, x_n) &= 0, \text{ and} \\ f_2(x_1, \ldots, x_n) &= 0, \text{ and} \\ &\vdots \\ f_k(x_1, \ldots, x_n) &= 0 \end{aligned}$$

can be reduced to the case of a *single* Diophantine equation. ◁

Exercise 2.3. The last exercise demonstrated in a certain sense the existence of an AND-function for the solvability problem for Diophantine equations. Show that there is a corresponding OR-function, that is, show that the problem of solving

$$\begin{aligned} f_1(x_1, \ldots, x_n) &= 0, \quad \text{or} \\ f_2(x_1, \ldots, x_n) &= 0, \quad \text{or} \\ &\vdots \\ f_k(x_1, \ldots, x_n) &= 0 \end{aligned}$$

can be reduced to the solution of a *single* Diophantine equation. ◁

Exercise 2.4.° Let Dioph($\mathbb{Z}$) denote the (decision) problem of determining for a given Diophantine equation whether it has solutions in $\mathbb{Z}$ (i.e., precisely the problem we have been discussing up to this point). Analogously, let Dioph($\mathbb{N}$) denote the problem of determining if there are solutions in $\mathbb{N}$. (Note that there are equations G that are in Dioph($\mathbb{Z}$) but not it Dioph($\mathbb{N}$).)

Show: Dioph($\mathbb{Z}$) $\leq_T$ Dioph($\mathbb{N}$).

Show: Dioph($\mathbb{Z}$) $\leq_m$ Dioph($\mathbb{N}$). ◁

Exercise 2.5.° Show: Dioph($\mathbb{N}$) $\leq_m$ Dioph($\mathbb{Z}$).

Hint: By a theorem of Lagrange (1770) every natural number can be expressed as a sum of four squares. ◁

Now we turn our attention to the proof of undecidability. This will be done by first reducing the halting problem for register machines to the problem ExpDioph($\mathbb{N}$). The problem ExpDioph($\mathbb{N}$) differs from Dioph($\mathbb{N}$) in that exponential terms of the form x^y, where x and y are variables, are also allowed.

The second reduction that we need, the reduction from ExpDioph($\mathbb{N}$) to Dioph($\mathbb{N}$) is a gem of number theory, but has little to do with theoretical computer science. For this reason, we omit the proof. (See the references for places to find a proof.)

For the following it will be important that the so-called *dominance relation*, a partial order on $\mathbb{N}$ which we will denote by $\trianglelefteq$, can be expressed using exponential Diophantine equations. The relation $x \trianglelefteq y$ means that all the bits of the binary representation of x are less than or equal to the corresponding bits in the binary representation of y. (That is, if x has a 1 in a certain position, the y must have a 1 there, too.) We postpone for the moment the problem of expressing $\trianglelefteq$ by means of Diophantine equations and simply use the dominance relation in what follows.

For the undecidability proof we use the following model for *register machines*: A register machine has a finite number of registers $R_1, \ldots, R_k$, which can hold arbitrarily large natural numbers. A register program consists of a sequence of consecutively numbered instructions

$$\begin{aligned} 1 &: A_1 \\ 2 &: A_2 \\ &\vdots \\ m &: A_m \end{aligned}$$

The possible instructions are:

- INC R_j (respectively DEC R_j)
  Increases (decreases) the value in register R_j by one. Negative register values are not allowed.
- GOTO l
  Unconditional jump instruction: Jumps to instruction l, the computation proceeds from there.
- IF $R_j = 0$ GOTO l
  Conditional jump instruction: Jumps to instruction l if the value in register R_j is 0.
- HALT
  Ends the program.

One might wonder about the missing instructions "$R_j := 0$" or "$R_j := R_n$," which many authors allow in their GOTO programs, but it is easy to convince oneself that these instructions can be simulated by corresponding programs that use a kind of counting loop:

Exercise 2.6. Show that the instructions "$R_j := 0$" and "$R_j := R_n$" can be simulated using the given set of instructions. ◁

For the following proof, however, it turns out to be a significant simplification if only the set of instructions presented above is available. In addition, it is easy to see that without loss of generality we can assume:

- The last instruction of the program, A_m, is always the HALT instruction, and that it is the only HALT instruction in the program.
- Whenever the program stops due to the HALT instruction, all of the registers will have been previously set to 0.
- A DEC R_j instruction is never executed while the value of register j is 0. (This can be avoided using conditional jumps.)

Despite these various restrictions, this model of computation is computationally universal. Thus, the halting problem H for programs begun with all registers initialized to 0 is undecidable:

$$H = \{P \mid P \text{ is a program for a register machine and this machine stops when it is started with all registers initialized to } 0\} .$$

We will reduce this problem to ExpDioph(ℕ) by giving for each program P a set of (exponential) Diophantine equations which have a (simultaneous) solution if and only if $P \in H$. Using the methods discussed in Exercises 2.2 and 2.3, this set of equations can then be transformed into a single equation.

So let P be a program of the form

$$\begin{array}{c} 1: A_1 \\ 2: A_2 \\ \vdots \\ m: A_m \end{array}$$

and let the registers that are addressed in the program be $R_1, \ldots, R_k$. We assume without loss of generality that the previously mentioned restrictions are satisfied.

The system of Diophantine equations will contain a number of variables, the intended meaning of which we will give first. For the sake of readability, we will use capital letters for all variables. Certain of the variables are supposed to represent finite *sequences* of natural numbers $(n_0, n_1, \ldots, n_s)$. We represent such a sequence with the single number

$$\sum_{i=0}^{s} n_i B^i,$$

where B is a (sufficiently large) base number – also a variable. "Sufficiently large" will mean that in arithmetic operations we will be using (for example, adding two such sequence-numbers) we will never need to carry. In addition, B will be a power of 2. This will allow us to use the dominance relation to control individual bits of the binary representation of such a sequence-number.

Now we describe the most important variables and their intended meanings. (All of these variables are understood to be existentially quantified.)

B	the base number described above.
S	the number of steps in the computation (i.e., the number of instructions executed) until the HALT instruction is reached. The number S is the length of the sequences coded in the following variables.
W_j $(j = 1, \ldots, k)$	a sequence-number for each register, which represents the contents of that register at each step $0, 1, \ldots, s$ in the computation, where s is the value of S.
N_i $(i = 1, \ldots, m)$	a sequence-number for each instruction number, which represents for each step $0, 1, \ldots, s$ whether the instruction was (=1) or was not (=0) executed at that step.

Example. Suppose $B = 10$, $S = 5$, and the register R_1 takes on the values $0, 1, 2, 1, 1, 0$ as the computation runs. Then $W_1 = 11210$. If the first instruction is executed at steps 0 and 3, then N_1 codes the sequence $1, 0, 0, 1, 0, 0$, so $N_1 = 1001$.

Now we can give the required Diophantine equations that describe the halting problem. All the equations are conjunctively connected, so we can use the previous exercises to transform them into a single equation.

First, we have a requirement on the base number B, namely B must be a power of 2:

$$B = 2^K .$$

K is an additional (auxiliary) variable. In addition, B must be "sufficiently large":

$$B > k, \quad B > m, \quad B > 2 \cdot S .$$

The last condition implies that B will be more than twice as large as any register value that can be computed in S steps. (We will need this fact later.) These are not Diophantine equations, since we have made use of the less than symbol, but by introducing another auxiliary variable (Z), an expression like $X < Y$ can be easily expressed as an equation, namely $X + Z + 1 = Y$. (Another method would have been to define B large enough from the start, say $B = 2^{k+m+S}$.)

The next equations establish certain boundary conditions, for example that the sequence-numbers N_i consist solely of 0- and 1-components. For this (and also in the following) it is convenient to have available a variable T that consists solely of 1's, that is $T = \sum_{i=0}^{s} B^i$. T can be specified with the equation

$$1 + (B - 1) \cdot T = B^{s+1}.$$

The condition on the variables N_i can now be formulated as

$$N_i \trianglelefteq T \quad (i = 1, \ldots, m).$$

Since exactly one instruction is executed at each step of the computation, we have the condition

$$\sum_{i=1}^{m} N_i = T.$$

The next equations establish the start and end conditions for the register machine computation. The equation

$$1 \trianglelefteq N_1$$

forces the execution of the program to begin with the first instruction. The last instruction must be the HALT instruction, which we are assuming is instruction m:

$$B^s \trianglelefteq N_m .$$

Furthermore, initially all registers must be set to 0:

$$W_j \trianglelefteq B^{s+1} - B \quad (j = 1, \ldots, k).$$

Now we come to the significant equations, namely those which guarantee the correct transition behavior from one time step to the next. For each instruction of the form i : GOTO j we introduce an equation of the form

$$B \cdot N_i \trianglelefteq N_j.$$

The multiplication by B causes the 1's in N_i, which indicate the steps at which instruction i is executed, to be moved over one position, thus forcing instruction j to be executed in step $s + 1$ whenever instruction i is executed at step s.

In instructions of the forms i : INC R_j and i : DEC R_j there is also a "hidden" GOTO instruction, namely the jump to instruction $i + 1$. So in these cases we also introduce

$$B \cdot N_i \trianglelefteq N_{i+1} \; .$$

The actual function of INC and DEC instructions can be simulated with

$$W_j = B \cdot (W_j + \sum N_i - \sum N_{i'}) \quad (j = 1, \ldots, k),$$

where the first sum is over all i for which there is an instruction in the program of the form i : INC R_j, and the second sum is over all i', for which there is an instruction in the program of the form i' : DEC R_j. Once again the factor of B causes the effect of the instructions to take effect at the next time step.

The only remaining instructions are the conditional jumps. An instruction of the form i : IF $R_j = 0$ GOTO l implies that execution continues either with instruction l (if $R_j = 0$) or with instruction $i + 1$. So first we introduce the equation

$$B \cdot N_i \trianglelefteq N_l + N_{i+1} \; ,$$

which forces that the next instruction can only be instruction l or instruction $i + 1$. To test the condition $R_j = 0$ we use

$$B \cdot N_i \trianglelefteq N_{i+1} + B \cdot T - 2 \cdot W_j \; .$$

Exercise 2.7. Explain how this equation works. ◁

All that remains is to show that the dominance relation $\trianglelefteq$ can be expressed using exponential Diophantine equations. For this a theorem of Kummer (1852) and Lucas (1878) is helpful:

Theorem 2.1. *$x \trianglelefteq y$ if and only if $\binom{y}{x}$ is odd.* □

Exercise 2.8. Prove Theorem 2.1.
Hint: $\binom{y}{x} \pmod 2 = \binom{y_n}{x_n}\binom{y_{n-1}}{x_{n-1}} \cdots \binom{y_1}{x_1}\binom{y_0}{x_0} \pmod 2$, where $x_n \ldots x_0$ and $y_n \ldots y_0$ are the binary representations of x and y. ◁

Since the property "odd" can be easily expressed as a Diophantine equation (z is odd if and only if $z = 2 \cdot n + 1$ for some n) it only remains to show that binomial coefficients can be expressed using (exponential) Diophantine equations. For this we make use of the Binomial Theorem:

$$(1 + u)^n = \sum_{i=0}^{n} \binom{n}{i} u^i.$$

Provided $\binom{n}{i} < u$, this implies that $\binom{n}{i}$ is just the ith coefficient in the u-adic representation of $(1 + u)^n$. Since $\binom{n}{i} \leq 2^n$ it is sufficient to choose $u > 2^n$. So we can write

$$m = \binom{n}{k} \iff \exists u, v, w : u = 2^n + 1, \quad v < u^k, \quad m < u \text{ and}$$
$$(1+u)^n = wu^{k+1} + mu^k + v\ .$$

This completes the solution to Hilbert's Tenth Problem. □

The next two exercises present some variations on Hilbert's Tenth Problem that remain undecidable.

Exercise 2.9.◇ Show that the undecidability of Hilbert's Tenth Problem, i.e., the undecidability of Dioph($\mathbb{N}$) (or Dioph($\mathbb{Z}$)), implies the undecidability of the following problem:

> Given two n-variate polynomials f and g with *positive* coefficients, determine whether it is the case that $f(x) \leq g(x)$ *for all* $x \in \mathbb{N}^n$. ◁

Exercise 2.10.◇ Show that Hilbert's Tenth Problem is already undecidable if one restricts oneself to polynomial equations of the form $f(x_1, \ldots, x_n) = 0$ where the total degree of f (i.e., the degree of $f(x, x, \ldots, x)$) is *at most four*.

Hint: As in the reduction of *SAT* to 3*SAT* (see Garey and Johnson) one introduces for each sub-polynomial of f a new variable and then expresses the property that $f = 0$ through the conjunction of a set conditions of the form $f_1 = 0, \ldots, f_k = 0$. Each polynomial f_i has total degree at most two and the equation $f_i = 0$ expresses that the ith new variable has the desired value. ◁

References

For the portions of the proof of Hilbert's Tenth Problem, the following literature was helpful:

- L. Adleman, K. Manders: Diophantine complexity, *Symposium on Foundations of Computing*, IEEE 1976, 81–88;
- J.L. Bell, M. Machover: A Course in Mathematical Logic, North-Holland, 1977.
- M. Davis, Unsolvable Problems, in J. Barwise, ed., *Handbook of Mathematical Logic*, North-Holland, 1977.
- P. van Emde Boas: Dominoes are forever, Technical Report 83-04, Dept. of Mathematics, University of Amsterdam, 1983.
- R.W. Floyd, R. Beigel: *The Language of Machines: An Introduction to Computability and Formal Languages*, Computer Science Press, 1994. (Exercise 2.10 appears here.)

- J.P. Jones, Y.V. Matijasevič: Proof of recursive unsolvability of Hilbert's tenth problem, *American Mathematical Monthly*, Oct. 1991, 689–709.
- G. Rozenberg, A. Salomaa: *Cornerstones of Undecidability*, Prentice-Hall, 1994.

The reduction of ExpDioph($\mathbb{N}$) to Dioph($\mathbb{N}$) can be found in the article by Jones and Matijasevič and also in

- M. Davis: *Computability and Unsolvability*, Dover, 1982.

Exercise 2.9 is from

- M. Hack: The equality problem for vector addition systems is undecidable, *Theoretical Computer Science* 2 (1976), 77–95.

The article above also presents further applications of the undecidability result to questions about Petri nets.

3. The Equivalence Problem for LOOP(1)- and LOOP(2)-Programs

In the 1960's, before the boom in complexity theory, several subrecursive classes of functions and languages were investigated extensively. One such hierarchy of functions (contained in the primitive recursive functions) considers the depth of nesting of (FOR) loops. It turns out that there is a decided difference in the complexity of the equivalence problems for LOOP(1)- and LOOP(2)-programs: the former is coNP-complete, but the latter is undecidable.

LOOP-programs form a very restricted class of programs for manipulating numbers in $\mathbb{N}$ (including 0), which are stored in registers. Registers in this model can hold arbitrarily large integers. The syntax of LOOP-programs is defined inductively: If X and Y are names of registers, then $X := Y$, $X := X + 1$ and $X := 0$ are LOOP-programs. Furthermore, if P and Q are LOOP-programs, then P;Q is a LOOP-program, as is `LOOP` X `DO` P `END`.

Regarding the semantics of LOOP-programs, that is, the manner in which they are to be executed, the following should be said: Assignment statements are executed in the obvious way so that the register values are changed in the appropriate fashion. A LOOP-program of the form $P; Q$ is executed by executing the program P first and then (with the values P leaves in the registers remaining intact) executing program Q. And a program of the form `LOOP` X `DO` P `END` executes program P as many times as the value of X *at the beginning of the loop.*

In addition to specifying the LOOP-program itself, it is necessary to specify which of the registers – which we will also refer to as *variables* – are to be understood as the input registers, and which as output registers. (Typically, there is only one output register.)

The function $f : \mathbb{N}^n \to \mathbb{N}^m$ computed by a LOOP-program (with n input registers and m output registers) is defined as follows: $f(a_1, \ldots, a_n)$, with $a_i \in \mathbb{N}$, is the vector of values in the output registers of the machine after the program is run with a_i in the ith input register and 0 in all other registers at the start of execution. It is known that the functions that are computable by LOOP-programs are precisely the *primitive recursive* functions.

Examples. Addition, in the sense of the assignment "$Z := X + Y$" can be done via

```
Z := Y;
LOOP X DO Z := Z + 1 END
```

where Z is the output register and X and Y are input registers. Multiplication can be done with the following program:

```
Z := 0;
LOOP X DO
  LOOP Y DO
    Z := Z + 1
  END
END
```

The loop-depth of a LOOP-program is the maximum occurring depth of nesting of the for loops in the program. (In our examples, the addition program has loop-depth 1 and the multiplication program has loop-depth 2.)

Exercise 3.1. Define loop-depth inductively on the formation of LOOP-programs. ◁

We call a LOOP-program with loop-depth n a LOOP(n)-program.

Exercise 3.2. Subtraction was not included in our set of instructions for LOOP-programs. Show that the instruction $X := X \dot{-} 1$ can be simulated by a LOOP(1)-program. Note: $x \dot{-} y$ is defined by

$$x \dot{-} y = \begin{cases} x - y & \text{if } x \geq y, \\ 0 & \text{if } x < y. \end{cases}$$

◁

Exercise 3.3. Show that the instruction "IF $X = 0$ THEN P END" can be simulated by a LOOP(1)-program. ◁

Exercise 3.4.° Show that if k is a *constant*, then the instruction "IF $X = k$ THEN P END" can be simulated by a LOOP(1)-program. ◁

The equivalence problem (for programs of a certain type) is the problem of determining for two given programs if they compute the same function. The equivalence problem for Turing machines is easily seen to be undecidable, since it is at least as difficult as the halting problem. On the other hand, the equivalence problem for finite automata is decidable. The question then is this: With respect to equivalence problems, where exactly is the boundary between undecidability and decidability? We want to investigate this question using LOOP-programs.

The result will be this: The equivalence problem for LOOP(1)-programs is *decidable*, but for LOOP(2)-programs it is *undecidable*, and hence also undecidable for LOOP(n)-programs where $n > 2$.

* * * * *

We will begin with the undecidability result. The halting problem for Turing machines is undecidable. GOTO-programs are equivalent to Turing machines, so the halting problem for GOTO-programs is also undecidable. In a GOTO-program, every line of the program is numbered consecutively beginning with 1 and contains one of the following instructions:

$X := Y$
$X := X + 1$
$X := 0$
GOTO i
IF $X = k$ THEN GOTO i
HALT

The semantics of each is self-explanatory.

We will focus on the special version of the halting problem for GOTO-programs where the programs are "run on themselves." Let $P_1, P_2, P_3, \ldots$ be a systematic enumeration of all GOTO-programs with one input register and one output register. Then the language

$$K = \{n \mid P_n(n) \text{ halts}\}$$

is undecidable. This problem can be reduced to a suitable version of the equivalence problem for LOOP-programs as follows:

$$\begin{aligned} n \in K &\Leftrightarrow P_n(n) \text{ halts} \\ &\Leftrightarrow \exists s\ P_n(n) \text{ halts in at most } s \text{ steps} \\ &\Leftrightarrow \exists s\ A_n(s) \neq B(s) \\ &\Leftrightarrow A_n \not\equiv B\ . \end{aligned}$$

Here B is a fixed LOOP(0)-program that, independent of its input, always outputs 0, and A_n is a LOOP-program that computes the following function:

$$A_n(s) = \begin{cases} 1 & \text{if } P_n(n) \text{ halts in at most } s \text{ steps,} \\ 0 & \text{otherwise.} \end{cases}$$

We will see that A_n belongs to LOOP(2). From this it follows immediately that the equivalence problem for LOOP(2)-programs is undecidable.

What remains then is to give a construction that for each n (i.e., for each GOTO-program P_n) effectively produces a LOOP(2)-program A_n with the desired property. As a first step, we define a LOOP-program D_n that can simulate individual transitions from one configuration of P_n to the next. We represent a configuration as a vector $(a, x, y, z_1, \ldots, z_k)$, where a is the number of the instruction about to be executed (or 0 if the program has halted), x is the value stored in the input register, X; y the value stored in the output register, Y; and $(z_1, \ldots, z_k)$ the values stored in the remaining registers $Z_1, \ldots, Z_k$ used by P_n. The desired program D_n works with the registers A, $X, Y, Z_1, \ldots, Z_k$ (and perhaps others) to represent such configurations. That is, D_n computes a function $f : \mathbb{N}^{k+3} \longrightarrow \mathbb{N}^{k+3}$, where $f(a, x, y, z_1, \ldots, z_k)$ is the successor configuration of $(a, x, y, z_1, \ldots, z_k)$.

Exercise 3.5. If one is given program D_n that behaves as described, how can one build the desired program A_n?

Program A_n must have loop-depth 2. What loop-depth must D_n have for this to be the case? ◁

Now we construct D_n. Let the instructions of the GOTO-program P_n be numbered 1 through r. Then D_n looks roughly like

IF $A = 1$ THEN ... END
IF $A = 2$ THEN ... END
⋮
IF $A = r$ THEN ... END

How the ellipses are filled in depends on the particular instructions of P_n: Assignment statements $X := Y$, $X := X + 1$, and $X := 0$ can be carried over directly with the addition of $A := A + 1$. The instruction HALT yields $A := 0$. For GOTO i we write $A := i$. For IF $X = k$ THEN GOTO i we write (at first)

IF $X = k$ THEN $A := i$ ELSE $A := A + 1$

Note that by using conjunction we can "program out" any nesting of IF statements that occur, so that we remain in LOOP(1). For example: IF B_1 THEN IF B_2 THEN P END END is equivalent to IF B_1 AND B_2 THEN P END, can be simulated by

"$Z_1 := B_1$";
"$Z_2 := B_2$";
"$Z_1 := Z_1 + Z_2$";
"$Z_1 := Z_1 \dot{-} 1$";
LOOP Z_1 DO P END

The instructions in quotation marks indicate LOOP(1)-programs, see the previous exercises.

Altogether, D_n is a LOOP(1)-program and A_n is a LOOP(2)-program, so we have

Theorem 3.1. *The equivalence problem for LOOP(2)-programs is undecidable.* □

* * * * *

Now we turn our attention to LOOP(1)-programs. In this case we shall see that the equivalence problem is decidable, in fact, it is coNP-complete. For this we need to characterize the LOOP(1)-programs precisely by giving a certain "normal form" for LOOP(1)-programs, so that we can decide if two LOOP(1)-programs are equivalent by considering only their normal forms.

Definition 3.2. *A function* $f : \mathbb{N}^m \longrightarrow \mathbb{N}$, $m \geq 0$, *is called* simple *if it can be built from the following components using composition:*

1. $s(x) = x + 1$,
2. $z^n(x_1, \ldots, x_n) = 0$,
3. $u_i^n(x_1, \ldots, x_n) = x_i$,
4. $x_1 + x_2$,
5. $x \dot{-} k$,
6. $w(x_1, x_2) = \begin{cases} x_1, & x_2 = 0, \\ 0, & x_2 > 0, \end{cases}$
7. x *DIV* k,
8. x *MOD* k.

where $k \in \mathbb{N}$ *is an arbitrary constant.*

We want to prove the following theorem:

Theorem 3.3. *A function is LOOP(1)-computable if and only if it is simple.*

For the direction from right to left, we observe first that functions (1)–(5) above are all clearly LOOP(1)-computable.

Exercise 3.6. Show that the function w in item (6) is LOOP(1)-computable. ◁

Exercise 3.7.° Show that for every $k \in \mathbb{N}$, the functions x DIV k and x MOD k are LOOP(1)-computable.

Hint: Note that k is a constant and not the value of an input register. This means that the number of registers used to compute x MOD k (or x DIV k) can depend on k. ◁

Now we must show the converse: every LOOP(1)-computable function is simple. Let P be a LOOP(1)-program. Then P has the form $P = P_1; P_2; \ldots; P_m$. The function computed by P is the composition of the functions computed by $P_1, P_2, \ldots, P_m$ in various registers. It is sufficient to show that each P_i computes a simple function in its registers.

If P_i is an assignment statement, this is clear. Now consider a for loop of the form

$$P_i = \texttt{LOOP}\ X\ \texttt{DO}\ Q\ \texttt{END}$$

where Q is a LOOP(0)-program.

Exercise 3.8. Show that Q can only compute functions of the form $(x_1, \ldots, x_n) \mapsto x_j + k$ or $(x_1, \ldots, x_n) \mapsto k$, where k is a constant. ◁

So the effect of the LOOP(0)-program can be described with the following equations:

$$\begin{aligned} Z_1 &= \alpha_1 y_{i_1} + k_1 \\ Z_2 &= \alpha_2 y_{i_2} + k_2 \\ &\vdots \\ Z_m &= \alpha_m y_{i_m} + k_m \end{aligned}$$

where for each i, Z_i is a program register, $\alpha_i \in \{0,1\}$, $k_i \in \mathbb{N}$, and y_i is the value of the register Z_i before execution the for loop.

Now we can define a directed graph corresponding to this representation. The set of vertices is $\{Z_1, \ldots, Z_m\}$ and the edges are

$$E = \{(Z_i, Z_j) \mid \alpha_j = 1 \text{ and } (i \neq j \text{ or } k_j > 0)\}\,.$$

That is, there is an edge from Z_q to Z_j if the variable Z_j is assigned the value of Z_q, perhaps increased by some constant k_j.

Example. The equations below

$$\begin{aligned} Z_1 &= y_2 \\ Z_2 &= y_4 + 5 \\ Z_3 &= y_1 \\ Z_4 &= y_1 + 3 \\ Z_5 &= y_2 + 2 \\ Z_6 &= y_6 + 7 \\ Z_7 &= y_7 \\ Z_8 &= y_6 + 1 \\ Z_9 &= 4 \end{aligned}$$

give rise to the following graph:

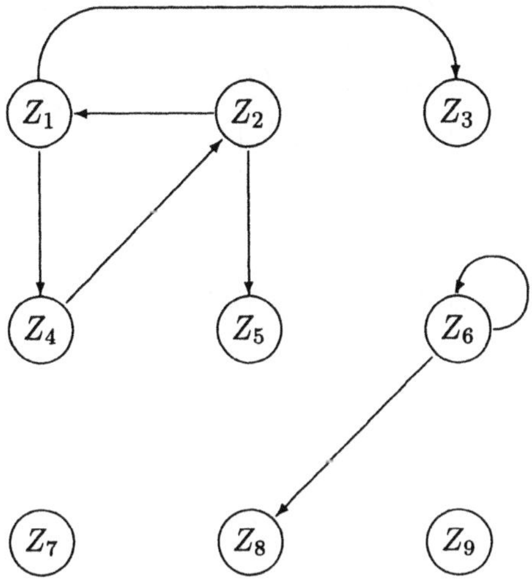

Isolated variables, i.e., variables that do not occur within a for loop, or that are independent of loops, are easily handled. In the example above, the for loop computes in variables Z_7 and Z_9 the following functions:

$$\begin{aligned} Z_7 &= y_7 \\ Z_9 &= (\text{IF } x = 0 \text{ THEN } y_9 \text{ ELSE } 4) \end{aligned}$$

These functions are clearly simple (see Exercise 3.9), and this example can be immediately generalized.

Exercise 3.9. Show how functions of the form

$$\text{IF } x = 0 \text{ THEN } f \text{ ELSE } g$$

can be expressed using the functions w and $+$. ◁

The remaining variables are either part of exactly one cycle or depend on exactly one cycle, since each vertex has at most one predecessor.

Now we introduce labels on the edges of the graph. These correspond exactly to the k_i's. (Note that Z_7 and Z_9 can be considered taken care of and omitted from the graph altogether.)

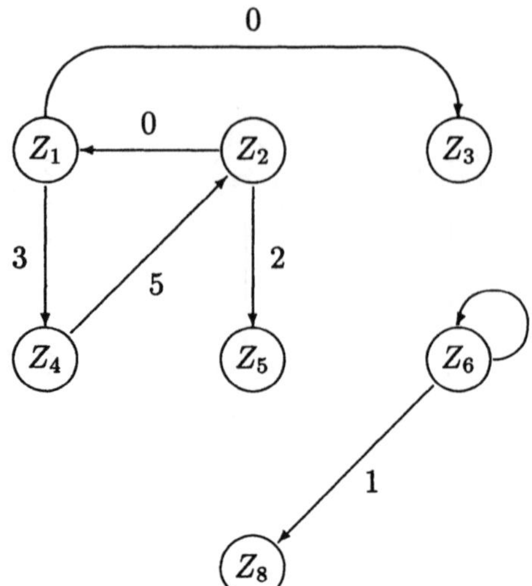

Suppose that variable Z is part of a cycle of length t, and that if we start from Z and traverse the cycle "backwards" then the edge labels are $k_1, k_2, \ldots, k_t$. Let $M = k_1 + \cdots + k_t$. If X (the register that determines the number of times the loop is executed) contains a multiple of t, i.e., $x = n \cdot t$ for some $n > 0$, then the function computed in register Z is $M \cdot n$ $(= n+n+\cdots+n$ (M times)). If $x = n \cdot t + l$, for some $l < t$, then $Z = M \cdot n + (k_1 + \cdots + k_l)$. The numbers n and l are just x DIV t and x MOD t, so the function that is computed in this case is

$$Z = (\text{IF } x = 0 \text{ THEN } z \text{ ELSE } M \cdot (x \text{ DIV } t) + (k_1 + \cdots + k_{(x \text{ MOD } t)}))$$

which is simple, since the numbers M, t, and k_i are constants.

Exercise 3.10. The argument for the simplicity of this function is still lacking with regards to the sub-function $(k_1 + \cdots + k_{(x \text{ MOD } t)})$. Fill in the missing details. ◁

Now consider the case of a variable Z that depends on a cycle, but is not itself in the cycle. If this variable is i steps from a cycle variable Z', then the function computed in register Z is equal to the function computed in register Z' (but on input $x \dot{-} i$) plus a constant, which can be read off of the path from Z to Z'. So such a function is also simple. This concludes the proof of Theorem 3.3. □

Now that we have described an effective procedure for obtaining a simple function from a LOOP(1)-program, the equivalence problem for LOOP(1)-programs is reduced to the equivalence problem for simple functions. A simple function is specified by describing in a systematic way how it is built up from the basic functions. This could be done, for example, by giving an "expression tree" with leaves given labels corresponding to the basic functions, or by providing a sufficiently parenthesized expression.

We now want to investigate to what extent a simple function is uniquely determined by specifying its values at certain "support points." For example, a polynomial (in one variable) of degree d is completely determined by specifying its value at any $d+1$ points. (This fact will also be important in Topic 14.) In the case of simple functions, however, the situation is a bit more complicated.

First, we introduce a relation on $\mathbb{N}^n$, i.e., on the set of potential input values for a LOOP-program. Let $M, K \in \mathbb{N}$. We say that the tuple $(x_1, \ldots, x_n)$ is (M,K)-*comparable* with $(x'_1, \ldots, x'_n)$ if for $i = 1, \ldots, n$ we have:

- $(x_i < M \text{ or } x'_i < M) \implies x_i = x'_i$, and
- $(x_i \geq M \text{ and } x'_i \geq M) \implies x_i \equiv x'_i \pmod{K}$.

We denote this by $(x_1, \ldots, x_n) \overset{M,K}{\equiv} (x'_1, \ldots, x'_n)$ and note that $\overset{M,K}{\equiv}$ is an *equivalence relation* on $\mathbb{N}^n$. Furthermore, we observe that

- if $M' \geq M$, then

$$(x_1, \ldots, x_n) \overset{M',K}{\equiv} (x'_1, \ldots, x'_n) \implies (x_1, \ldots, x_n) \overset{M,K}{\equiv} (x'_1, \ldots, x'_n) \,,$$

- and if K' is a multiple of K, then

$$(x_1, \ldots, x_n) \overset{M,K'}{\equiv} (x'_1, \ldots, x'_n) \implies (x_1, \ldots, x_n) \overset{M,K}{\equiv} (x'_1, \ldots, x'_n) \,.$$

Exercise 3.11. Determine the *index* of the equivalence relation $\overset{M,K}{\equiv}$, that is, the number of distinct equivalence classes. ◁

Lemma 3.4. *Every simple function f can be assigned numbers M and K such that f is a linear combination on equivalence classes of $\overset{M,K}{\equiv}$, i.e.,*

$$f(x_1, \ldots, x_n) = \beta_0 + \sum_{i=0}^{n} \beta_i \cdot x_i \,,$$

where each β_i is a rational constant that depends only on the equivalence class.

Proof. The proof proceeds by structural induction on the simple function. The argument for the base case is contained in the argument for the inductive step, so we will focus on the inductive step from the start.

1. Let f be a simple function that has already been shown to satisfy the statement of the lemma with constants M and K. Then the statement of the lemma is true also of $f(x_1, \ldots, x_n) + 1$ with the same constants M and K.

2. Upon applying the function $z^n(\cdots)$ the lemma holds with $M = 0$ and $K = 1$.
3. If $f_1, \ldots, f_m$ are simple functions that satisfy the lemma with the constants $M_1, K_1, \ldots, M_m, K_m$, then the function $u_i^m(f_1(\boldsymbol{x}), \ldots, f_m(\boldsymbol{x}))$ satisfies the lemma with the constants M_i, K_i.
4. If the functions f_1 and f_2 satisfy the lemma with the constants M_1, K_1, M_2, and K_2, then $f_1(\boldsymbol{x}) + f_2(\boldsymbol{x})$ satisfies the lemma with the constants $\max(M_1, M_2)$ and $K_1 \cdot K_2$.
5. If the function f satisfies the lemma with the constants M and K, then the function $f(\boldsymbol{x}) \dot{-} 1$ satisfies the lemma with $M + K$ and K.
6. If the functions f_1 and f_2 satisfy the lemma with constants M_1, K_1, M_2, and K_2, then the function $w(f_1(\boldsymbol{x}), f_2(\boldsymbol{x}))$ satisfies the lemma with constants $\max(M_1, M_2) + K_2$ and $K_1 \cdot K_2$.
7. If the function f satisfies the lemma with constants M and K, then $f(\boldsymbol{x})$ DIV k satisfies the lemma with the constants M and $k \cdot K$.
8. If the function f satisfies the lemma with constants M and K, then $f(\boldsymbol{x})$ MOD k satisfies the lemma with the constants M and $k \cdot K$. □

Exercise 3.12.° Fill in the details of the proof above by determining the constants β_i in cases 6 and 7. ◁

Now the decidability result is at hand. Simple functions can be completely specified by giving the appropriate values of M and K, and for each of the finitely many equivalence classes, the constants β_i. Therefore, they can also be compared on the basis of such specifications. But there is an even simpler way to compare simple functions:

Exercise 3.13.° Show that a simple function with constants K and M is completely specified by giving in addition to K and M the finitely many function values $\{f(\boldsymbol{x})\}_{\boldsymbol{x} \in Q}$, where $Q = \{(x_1, \ldots, x_n) \mid \text{for } i = 1, \ldots, n,\ x_i \leq M + 2K\}$. ◁

From this our theorem follows immediately:

Theorem 3.5. *The equivalence problem for LOOP(1)-programs is decidable.*

Proof. First one determines the constants M_1, K_1 and M_2, K_2 for the two programs, then one checks to see if the functions agree on the input values $\boldsymbol{x}$ that have $x_i \leq \max(M_1, M_2) + 2K_1K_2$ for all i. □

Exercise 3.14.° Justify the claims made in the previous proof. ◁

* * * * *

Now we want to determine more exactly the complexity of the equivalence problem for LOOP(1)-problems. We shall see that this problem is coNP-complete, which is the same as saying that the inequivalence problem is NP-complete. Most of the work in showing that this problem belongs to

NP has already been done. The required nondeterministic algorithm, given 2 LOOP(1)-programs as input, first determines the constants K_1, M_1 and K_2, M_2 for the two programs, then nondeterministically guesses an input vector $\boldsymbol{x}$ with $x_i \le \max(M_1, M_2) + 2K_1K_2$ for all i, and finally checks to see that $P_1(\boldsymbol{x}) \neq P_2(\boldsymbol{x})$.

To verify that this whole procedure is in NP, we must take a closer look at portions of the computation. The effective procedure that produces for a given LOOP(1)-program its associated simple function can clearly be carried out in deterministic polynomial time. An inspection of the proof of Lemma 3.4 shows that the constants M and K that are assigned to a simple function can be chosen in such a way that K is the product of all the constants previously occuring in DIV and MOD functions. (An empty product is considered to have the value 1.) The value of M can be determined by counting the occurrences of w and $\dot{-}\ 1$ functions that occur; if there are m such occurrences, then we can choose M to be $M = m \cdot K$. Notice that the number of bits in the binary representations of M and K is polynomial in the length of the original LOOP-program, so we can guess $\boldsymbol{x}$ in nondeterministic polynomial time. Finally, we need to evaluate the LOOP-programs on the input $\boldsymbol{x}$. A step-by-step simulation of the LOOP-program, however, does not work, since the simulation time could be linear in the *values* of the inputs, which would be exponential in the lengths of their binary representations. It is more efficient to make use of the representations as simple functions, since the functions $+$, $\dot{-}$, w, DIV, and MOD can be evaluated in polynomial time.

Theorem 3.6. *The inequivalence problem for LOOP(1)-programs is* NP-*complete.*

Proof. It remains to show that *SAT* can be reduced to this problem. Let F be a boolean formula with n boolean variables. We construct two LOOP(1)-programs such that the first one does nothing but output 0. The second program interprets the input x_i in such a way that $x_i = 0$ means FALSE and $x_i > 0$ means TRUE. Under this interpretation, the program evaluates F with the given assignment and outputs 1 if the assignment makes the formula true and 0 otherwise. Clearly the problems are inequivalent if and only if there is a satisfying assignment for F, i.e., $F \in SAT$. □

Exercise 3.15. Construct the second LOOP(1)-program mentioned above.

Hint: It is sufficient to show how to simulate the logical NOR-function with a LOOP(1)-program. ◁

Exercise 3.16. Show that the inequivalence problem for LOOP(1)-programs is already NP-complete if it is restricted to include only programs with *one* input variable. ◁

References

- V. Claus: The equivalence problem of loop-2-programs, Report No. 40/77, Abteilung für Informatik, Universität Dortmund.
- A.R. Meyer, D.M.Ritchie: Computation complexity and program structure, IBM Research Report RC 1817, 1967.
- D. Tsichritzis: The equivalence of simple programs, *Journal of the ACM* 17 (1970), 729–738.

4. The Second LBA Problem

The solution of the so-called second LBA problem came unexpectedly in 1987 and was discovered independently by an American (Immerman) and a Slovakian (Szelepcsényi). Among other things, this result says that the class of context sensitive languages is closed under complementation.

The two LBA problems were posed in 1964 by S.Y. Kuroda. The meaning of these problems (the formal definitions will be given shortly) were repeatedly brought up and discussed (see, for example, the article by Hartmanis and Hunt). In 1987 the time must have been "ripe"; the second LBA problem was solved completely independently by an American researcher, N. Immerman, and a Slovakian student, R. Szelepcsényi. The amazing part of these proofs is this: they are considerable easier than one would have expected of a problem that had remained unsolved for 23 years. Furthermore, the solution is precisely the opposite of the conjecture that was widely held prior to the proof.

What are the LBA problems? Kuroda showed in 1964 that the class of languages that are recognized by *nondeterministic* linear space-bounded Turing machines (LBAs, linear bounded automata) is the same as the class of context sensitive languages. This result is often presented in an undergraduate course on formal languages. In modern terminology, this result says that

$$\mathsf{NSPACE}(n) = \mathsf{CSL} ,$$

where CSL is the class of context sensitive languages. The *first LBA problem* is the question of whether deterministic and nondeterministic LBAs are equivalent:

$$\mathsf{NSPACE}(n) \stackrel{?}{=} \mathsf{DSPACE}(n) .$$

The result that comes closest to solving the first LBA problem is Savitch's Theorem which says that

$$\mathsf{NSPACE}(s(n)) \subseteq \mathsf{DSPACE}(s^2(n)) ,$$

for all $s(n) \geq \log n$. So in particular,

$$\mathsf{NSPACE}(n) \subseteq \mathsf{DSPACE}(n^2) .$$

The *second LBA problem* is the question of whether the class of languages accepted by nondeterministic LBAs is closed under complement:

$$\mathsf{NSPACE}(n) \stackrel{?}{=} \mathsf{coNSPACE}(n) .$$

A negative answer to the second LBA problem implies, of course, a negative answer to the first, since $\mathsf{DSPACE}(n)$ is closed under complement. But from a positive solution to the second LBA problem, there is no direct consequence regarding the first LBA problem.

The second LBA problem has now been solved (the first LBA problem remains open): $\mathsf{NSPACE}(n)$ is – contrary to the previously generally believed conjecture – closed under complementation. This solution to the second LBA problem is actually an instance of a more general result: From the proof it follows immediately that

$$\mathsf{NSPACE}(s(n)) = \mathsf{coNSPACE}(s(n)) ,$$

whenever $s(n) \geq \log n$.

Although the proof is actually relatively easy, at least in the case of Immerman, it appears at the end of a sequence of results which say that certain hierarchies, defined in terms of the class $\mathsf{NSPACE}(n)$, "collapse." In all of these results, a certain counting technique is employed which can be used to complement classes. An overview of these techniques was presented in an article by U. Schöning.

Exercise 4.1.$^\diamond$ Suppose that membership in a language A can be determined by some nondeterministic algorithm M (with certain resource bounds which do not interest us at the moment). Furthermore, suppose that the number of strings in A of a given length is given by an "easily computed" function $f : \mathbb{N} \to \mathbb{N}$.

Under these assumptions, give a nondeterministic algorithm for $\overline{A}$. $\lhd$

Exercise 4.2. Now suppose that in the previous exercise the the algorithm M has nondeterministic time complexity $t_M(n)$ and space complexity $s_M(n)$, and the the computation of f requires $t_f(n)$ time and $s_f(n)$ space. Determine upper bounds for the time- and space-complexity of the algorithm for $\overline{A}$ in the previous exercise. $\lhd$

Now suppose that $A \in \mathsf{CSL} = \mathsf{NSPACE}(n)$. If $f(n)$ can also be computed in linear space, then by the observations above, $\overline{A} \in \mathsf{NSPACE}(O(n)) = \mathsf{NSPACE}(n)$. So to finish the proof, we need to show how to compute f in linear space.

Exercise 4.3. For the computation of f in linear space, we will need to make use of nondeterminism. That is, we should be thinking of a nondeterministic linear space-bounded Turing machine that computes f.

For such nondeterministic machines, there are various imaginable models of what it means for them to compute functions (e.g., single-valued, multi-valued). Find a definition that is sufficient to work correctly in this context. ◁

Since A is context sensitive, there is a corresponding grammar G with variable set V and terminal alphabet Γ that generates A. For all $n, i \in \mathbb{N}$ define the subset T_i^n of $(V \cup \Gamma)^*$ as follows:

$$T_i^n = \{x \;:\; |x| \leq n, S \overset{i}{\Rightarrow}_G x\} ,$$

where $S \overset{i}{\Rightarrow}_G x$ means that x can be derived from the start symbol S in at most i steps according to the rules of grammar G. For all n, $T_0^n = S$. For any context sensitive grammar G, it is clear that for each n there is an m such that $T_m^n = T_{m+1}^n$. Let $g(n) = |T_m^n|$, where m is the number just mentioned. *Sketch:*

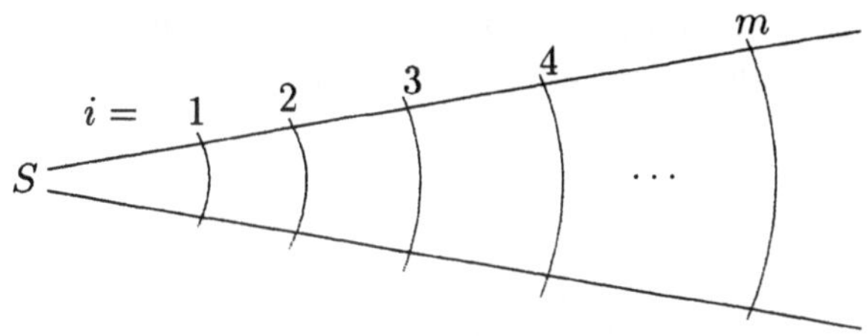

Exercise 4.4. Show that for the proof it suffices to show that g can be computed in the manner described in Exercise 4.3. ◁

Now we show that g can be computed in this nondeterministic sense in linear space. Herein lies the reason why this entire proof is often referred to as the *inductive counting method.* Our plan is to compute (nondeterministically) in order the numbers $1 = |T_0^n|, |T_1^n|, |T_2^n|, \ldots$ until for some m we have $|T_m^n| = |T_{m+1}^n|$ at which point we will output this number as $g(n)$. What we need then is a (nondeterministic) procedure that correctly computes $|T_{i+1}^n|$ under the assumption that the correct value of $|T_i^n|$ is known.

Exercise 4.5.$^\diamond$ Provide the algorithm for this.

Hint: In order to compute $|T_{i+1}^n|$ correctly, we must identify and count all the elements of T_{i+1}^n. For this we need to first generate (in an "inner loop") all the elements of T_i^n. We will be able to guarantee that we have generated all of T_i^n since we know how many elements are in the set. ◁

It should be noted that we have intentionally displaced the inductive counting argument of the preceding proof from its original context to the context of the sets T_i^n. The original proof uses instead the sets (and number) of configurations that are reachable from the start configuration of an LBA in at most i steps. The original proof is more easily generalized to other space bounds like $\log n$.

References

For background to the LBA problems see

- J. Hartmanis, H.B. Hunt: The LBA problem and its importance in the theory of computing, in R. Karp, ed.: *Complexity of Computation*, Vol. VII, SIAM-AMS Proceedings, 1973, 27–42.
- S.Y. Kuroda: Classes of languages and linear-bounded automata, *Information and Control* 7 (1964), 207–233.

Savitch's Theorem originally appeared in

- J. Savitch: Relationships between nondeterministic and deterministic tape complexities, *Journal of Computer and Systems Sciences* 4 (1970), 177–192.

The original solutions to the second LBA problem appeared in

- N. Immerman: NSPACE is closed under complement, *SIAM Journal on Computing* 17 (1988), 935–938.
- R. Szelepcsényi: The method of forced enumeration for nondeterministic automata, *Acta Informatica* 26 (1988), 279–284.

Since then, proofs of this result have found their way into the following textbooks, including:

- J. Balcázar, J. Diaz, J. Gabarró: *Structural Complexity II*, Springer, 1990.
- D.P. Bovet, P. Crescenzi: *Introduction to the Theory of Complexity*, Prentice-Hall, 1994.
- E. Gurari: *An Introduction to the Theory of Computation*, Computer Science Press, 1989.
- C. Papadimitriou: *Computational Complexity*, Addison-Wesley, 1994.
- R. Sommerhalder, S.C. van Westrhenen: *The Theory of Computability*, Addison-Wesley, 1988.

An overview of the applications of this sort of counting technique appears in

- U. Schöning: The power of counting, in A.L. Selman, ed., *Complexity Theory Retrospective*, Springer, 1990, 204–223.

5. LOGSPACE, Random Walks on Graphs, and Universal Traversal Sequences

There is a surprising, at first glance unexpected, difference in (space) complexity between the problems of finding a path from a start node to an end node in a directed graph and of doing so in an undirected graph. In an undirected graph this is easier to solve; in fact, in can be done using a random walk or a universal traversal sequence.

We denote by L the class of all decision problems that can be solved using algorithms that use only logarithmically much space, i.e., $\mathsf{L} = \mathsf{DSPACE}(O(\log(n))$. In this definition we only count the storage space used on the work tape, not on the (read-only) input tape. Similarly, one can define a nondeterministic version of this class: $\mathsf{NL} = \mathsf{NSPACE}(O(\log(n))$. Whether the inclusion $\mathsf{L} \subseteq \mathsf{NL}$ is strict is an open question. (It has, however, been shown that $\mathsf{NL} = \mathsf{coNL}$, see Topic 4.) Just as in the case of the $\mathsf{P} = \mathsf{NP}$ question, one can define a notion of completeness for dealing with these classes. But polynomial time reductions are meaningless in this case, since $\mathsf{NL} \subseteq \mathsf{P}$.

Exercise 5.1. Why is the running time of every halting NL-computation polynomially bounded? Why is $\mathsf{NL} \subseteq \mathsf{P}$? ◁

One must design the notion of reduction with the *smaller* of the two classes in mind (in this case, L). A problem A is said to be *log-reducible* to problem B (written $A \leq_{\log} B$) if there is a logarithmically space-bounded Turing machine with designated (read-only) input and (write-only) output tapes which are not considered when computing the space usage, such that for all x, $x \in A \iff M(x) \in B$.

Exercise 5.2. Show that log-reducibility is a transitive relation. ◁

A problem A_0 is called NL-complete if $A_0 \in \mathsf{NL}$ and for all $A \in \mathsf{NL}$, $A \leq_{\log} A_0$.

Consider the following algorithmic problem:

$$PATH = \{(G, a, b) \mid G \text{ is a directed graph and } a \text{ and } b \text{ are nodes in } G \text{ such that there is a path from } a \text{ to } b \text{ in } G\}.$$

Exercise 5.3. Show that *PATH* (sometimes called *GAP*, graph accessibility problem) is NL-complete.

Hint: The graph that represents the possible transitions from one configuration to the next in the NL-computation has polynomial size (in the length of the input). Solutions to this exercise and the previous one can be found in many books on complexity theory. ◁

Now one can ask about the situation with undirected graphs instead of directed graphs. We define

$$\textit{UPATH} = \{(G,a,b) \mid G \text{ is an undirected graph and } a \text{ and } b \text{ are nodes in } G \text{ such that there is a path from } a \text{ to } b \text{ in } G\}.$$

Often the directed and undirected version of a given problem about graphs are equivalent in the sense of complexity theory. For example, the Hamiltonian Circuit Problem is NP-complete for directed and for undirected graphs (see Garey and Johnson). The graph isomorphism problems for undirected and directed graphs are also equivalent under polynomial-time reductions (see Köbler, Schöning, Torán). In this case, however, there seems to be a difference: The NL-completeness proof above does not work for *UPATH*.

Exercise 5.4. Why not? ◁

It is still the case that *UPATH* ∈ NL, so it is possible that *UPATH* is an easier problem than *PATH*. We will show that a randomized version of *UPATH* is in L.

Let RL denote the class of problems that can be decided by algorithms that are simultaneously logarithmically space-bounded and polynomially time-bounded and are allowed to make use of random decisions in their computations. The use of these random decisions causes the output of the machine M to be a two-valued random variable. The computation of a problem A is to be understood in the following way:

$$x \in A \Rightarrow Pr[M \text{ accepts } x] \geq 1/2,$$
$$x \notin A \Rightarrow Pr[M \text{ accepts } x] = 0.$$

It is clear that $\mathsf{L} \subseteq \mathsf{RL} \subseteq \mathsf{NL}$.

Perhaps the reader is wondering why we had to require polynomial running-time in the definition. In the exercises above, we just showed that L- and NL-algorithms only need at most polynomial time. But this is not the case for randomized log-space machines:

Exercise 5.5.° Give a randomized, logarithmic space-bounded algorithm that has an exponential expected running time.

Hint: Have the algorithm repeatedly simulate a random experiment for which each trial succeeds with probability only 2^{-n} until there is a successful trial, then halt. ◁

In fact, it can be shown that the class of all languages accepted by randomized log-space algorithms (without the polynomial bound on running time) is exactly NL, so the restriction to polynomial running-time is significant.

The problems *UPATH* and *PATH* may not be in L, since a systematic search for a path from a to b would require keeping track of where one has been. If the input graph has n nodes, this would require at least n bits of stored information, too much for a log-space machine.

There is, however, a randomized algorithm that demonstrates that *UPATH* $\in$ RL. This algorithm carries out a random walk on the graph, starting at a. This is continued until, if ever, b is reached. A random walk requires less space than a systematic search of the graph: we only need enough space to store the number of the current node, i.e. $\log(n)$ bits. Of course, we can no longer avoid nodes being visited more than once.

Our random algorithm is the following:

```
INPUT (G, a, b);
v := a;
FOR i := 1 TO p(n) DO
    Randomly choose a node w adjacent to v using the uniform
    distribution;
    v := w;
    IF v = b THEN ACCEPT END;
END;
REJECT;
```

It remains to show that for an undirected graph G, the polynomial p can be chosen in such a way that the definition of *UPATH* $\in$ RL is satisfied, namely so that

$$(G,a,b) \in \mathit{UPATH} \Rightarrow Pr[M \text{ accepts } (G,a,b)] \geq 1/2,$$
$$(G,a,b) \notin \mathit{UPATH} \Rightarrow Pr[M \text{ accepts } (G,a,b)] = 0.$$

Exercise 5.6. Show that the given algorithm cannot work for directed graphs. That is, show that there are directed graphs G such that the node b in G is reachable by a random walk, but only with probability 2^{-n}. So the expected length of the random walk is 2^n, hence not polynomial.

Hint: This exercise is very similar to Exercise 5.5. ◁

By a *random walk on a graph G, started at a* we mean an infinite sequence $W = (v_1, v_2, v_3, \ldots)$ with $v_1 = a$ and v_{i+1} chosen randomly (under the uniform distribution) from among the nodes adjacent to v_i. (So $\{v_i, v_{i+1}\}$ must be an (undirected) edge in G.) Let W_i denote the finite subsequence consisting of the first i nodes in W. For a node v in G we compute the probability of the occurrence of v in W as

$$P_v = \lim_{n\to\infty} \frac{|\{i \leq n \mid v = v_i\}|}{n}.$$

From the theory of Markov chains it is clear (by the law of large numbers) that this limit exists and that for a connected graph G, $P_v > 0$ for all v. $1/P_v$ is the expected value of the distance between adjacent occurrences of the node v in W, that is, the mean number of steps it takes for a random walk starting at v to return to v.

For the moment we will treat each undirected edge $\{u, v\}$ like two directed edges (u, v) and (v, u). We claim that each of these directed edges occurs with probability $1/2e$ in a random walk on a connected graph G with e (undirected) edges. It is clear that the sum of these probabilities is 1.

If we extend the notation above to edges as well as nodes, then our claim becomes

$$P_{(u,v)} = \lim_{n\to\infty} \frac{|\{i \leq n \mid (v_i, v_{i+1}) = (u, v)\}|}{n} = 1/2e\ .$$

Suppose this is not the case. If the edges do not all occur with the same probability, then there must be an edge (u, v) that has a larger probability than the mean of the probabilities of its adjacent edges (via node v). That is,

$$P_{(u,v)} > \frac{1}{d(v)} \cdot \sum_{(v,w)\in G} P_{(v,w)}\ ,$$

where $d(v)$ is the degree of the node v.

Exercise 5.7. Justify that this inequality follows from the assumption that the edges do not all occur with equal probability. ◁

Thus if we can show that for all edges (u, v)

$$P_{(u,v)} = \frac{1}{d(v)} \cdot \sum_{(v,w)\in G} P_{(v,w)}\ ,$$

then by Exercise 5.7 we can conclude that $P_{(u,v)} = 1/2e$ for all edges (u, v). We can see that this is the case as follows: Consider the points in the random walk W when the edge (u, v) occurs:

$$W = (\ldots, u, v, \ldots, u, v, \ldots)\ .$$

After v must come an adjacent edge (v, w), and each such edge occurs with equal probability $1/d(v)$. So W looks like

$$W = (\ldots, u, v, w_1, \ldots, u, v, w_2, \ldots)\ ,$$

and the desired equality follows. Thus every directed edge (u, v) occurs with probability $1/2e$, and, therefore, every undirected edge $\{u, v\}$ with probability $1/e$.

Every edge of the form (u, v) leads to node v. Every such edge occurs with probability $1/2e$, so the node v occurs with probability $d(v)/2v$, i.e., $P_v =$

$d(v)/2e$. The mean length of a random walk starting at a random node until the node v occurs is, therefore, $1/P_v = 2e/d(v)$.

Exercise 5.8. Let X be a random variable that has an expected value and takes on only non-negative values. Show the following inequality: $Pr[X \geq a] \leq E(X)/a$.

Hint: Look in a book on probability under the topic "Markov's inequality." ◁

Now we only have the small step of showing that the length of the random walk can be bounded by a polynomial but that each node (in particular, our destination node b) will still occur with probability $\geq 1/2$. Furthermore, we will show that there are ***universal traversal sequences***, that is, polynomially long sequences of instructions of the form (right, left, left, right, left ...) which if followed will cause a walk to visit ***every*** node in ***any*** graph that has n nodes. (Frequent museum visitors will likely be very interested in this result.)

Let $E(i, j)$ denote the expected value of the number of steps in a random walk from node i to node j. We have already shown that the mean length of time from one occurrence of v to the next is $1/P_v = 2e/d(v)$. In this notation we can express this as $E(v, v) = 2e/d(v)$.

Exercise 5.9. Let (u, v) be an edge in G. Show that $E(u, v) \leq 2e$. ◁

Now we want an approximation for $E(a, b)$ for any nodes a and b, which are not necessarily adjacent. Let $E(a, G)$ denote the mean length of a random walk starting at a until all the nodes in G have been visited at least once. We assume that G is connected, so that all nodes in G are reachable from a. Then for any a and b in G we have $E(a, b) \leq E(a, G)$.

Let $(a = v_0, v_1, v_2, \ldots, v_k)$ be a path in G that starts at a and visits every node at least once.

Exercise 5.10. Show that in a connected graph with n nodes there is always such a path of length $k \leq 2n$. ◁

Now we can give a very rough approximation for $E(a, G)$ by considering the mean length of a random walk that first goes from a to v_1 (in one or more steps), then wanders to v_2, then v_3, etc and in this way eventually arrives at v_k. From this we get

$$E(a, G) \leq \sum_{i=1}^{k} E(v_{i-1}, v_i) \leq 2n \cdot 2e = 4en \ .$$

Exercise 5.11. Show that from this inequality it follows that the probability that a fixed node b in G is *not* visited in a random walk that starts at a and proceeds for $8e$ steps is at most $1/2$.

Hint: Use Exercise 5.8. ◁

Now we put everything together: On input (G, a, b), where G is an undirected graph with n nodes and e edges, we simulate a random walk of length $8e$. If there is no path from a to b, then this algorithm cannot possibly find one. If there is such a path, i.e., $G(a, b) \in UPATH$, then this algorithm finds one with probability at least $1/2$.

To reduce the probability that a path exists but is not found, this random experiment can be repeated or, equivalently, the the length of the random walk can be increased. If the length of the random walk is $m \cdot 8e$, (i.e., m repetitions of the experiment), then the probability of overlooking an existing path is reduced to at most 2^{-m}.

The ability to drastically increase the probability of success while maintaining a polynomially long random walk (often referred to as *probability amplification*) is the key to the existence of a *universal traversal sequence*. A *d-regular graph* is a connected graph in which each node has degree at most d. Clearly, any d-regular graph has $e \leq dn/2$ edges. We order the $\leq d$ edges leaving a given node arbitrarily and assign each a number $0, 1, \ldots, d-1$. (Note that each edge (u, v) has *two* numbers, one with respect to each of u and v.) By a universal traversal sequence (for d-regular graphs) we mean a sequence $I = (i_1, i_2, \ldots, i_k)$ with $i_j \in \{0, 1, \ldots, d-1\}$, such that for any of these graphs and any choice of starting nodes, the graph is traversed via I, in the sense that at each step the choice of the next node to visit is made according to I and the numbering of the edges leaving the current node, and that all nodes of the graph are visited.

A randomly chosen sequence $I = (i_1, i_2, \ldots, i_k)$ where each i_j is chosen independently at random under the uniform distribution on $\{0, 1, \ldots, d-1\}$ describes precisely a random walk. We have already seen that the probability that a random walk of length $k = m \cdot 8en \leq m \cdot 4dn^2$ does not completely traverse a graph G is at most 2^{-m}. So if g is the number of labeled d-regular graphs (with the labeling described above) and we choose m so large that $2^{-m} \cdot g < 1$, then the probability that a randomly chosen sequence is a universal traversal sequence is positive, which means at least one such sequences must *exist*. But how large must m be?

Exercise 5.12. Show that the number of labeled d-regular graphs is at most n^{dn}. ◁

Since

$$\begin{aligned} 2^{-m} \cdot g < 1 &\iff 2^{-m} \cdot n^{dn} < 1 \\ &\iff -m + dn \cdot \log n < 0 \\ &\iff m > dn \cdot \log n \, , \end{aligned}$$

there must exist a universal traversal sequence for all d-regular graphs with n nodes that has length $(dn \log n) 4dn^2 = O(n^3 \log n)$.

References

- R. Aleliunas, R.M. Karp, R.K. Lipton, L. Lovász, C. Rackoff: Random walks, universal traversal sequences, and the complexity of maze problems, *Proceedings of Symposium on Foundations of Computer Science*, IEEE, 1979, 218–223.
- M. Garey, D. Johnson: *Computers and Intractability*, Freeman, 1979.
- J. Köbler, U. Schöning, J. Torán: *The Graph Isomorphism Problem – Its Structural Complexity*, Birkhäuser, 1993.
- M. Sipser: *Lecture Notes*, 18.428, MIT, 1985.

6. Exponential Lower Bounds for the Length of Resolution Proofs

The resolution calculus is one of the most commonly used methods in theorem proving. For a long time an exponential lower bound for the length of such proofs was sought. In 1985 this was finally proven by Haken.

The *resolution calculus* operates on sets of clauses. A *clause* is a disjunction (OR) of literals. A *literal* is a variable or its negation. A set of clauses is understood to represent a conjunction (AND) of the clauses. Altogether this corresponds to a formula in *disjunctive normal form.*

Example. The set of clauses

$$\{\ \{x_1, \overline{x_2}, \overline{x_3}\},\ \{\overline{x_1}, \overline{x_2}\},\ \{\overline{x_2}, x_3\},\ \{x_2\}\ \}$$

corresponds to the formula

$$(x_1 \vee \overline{x_2} \vee \overline{x_3}) \wedge (\overline{x_1} \vee \overline{x_2}) \wedge (\overline{x_2} \vee x_3) \wedge x_2\ .$$

Exercise 6.1. Make a truth table for this formula. Is the formula satisfiable? ◁

In each resolution step of a resolution proof two (previously derived or given) clauses, K_1 and K_2, are combined to derive a new clause K_3. This is possible only if there is a variable x_i that occurs positively in one clause and negatively in the other. The resolvent K_3 is then $K_1 \cup K_2 - \{x_i, \overline{x_i}\}$. The notation for this is

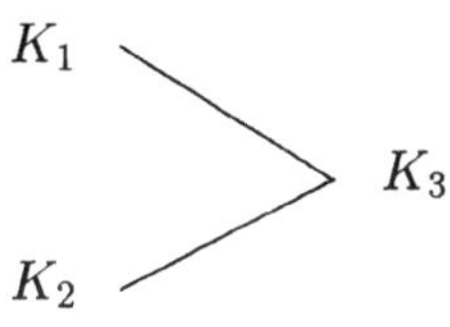

Example.

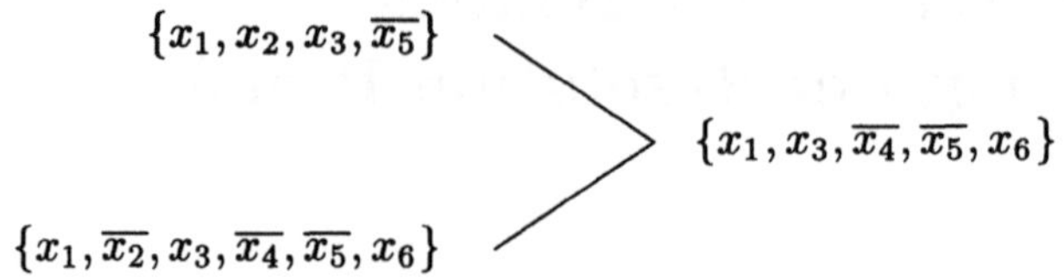

In the example above, the resolution is done on variable x_2, since x_2 occurs in the upper clause and $\overline{x_2}$ in the lower one. After resolution, x_2 does not occur in the resulting clause (but it may occur again later in the resolution).

Several resolution steps can be represented by an acyclic graph. The goal of the resolution proof is to derive $\emptyset$.

Example. (continued from above)

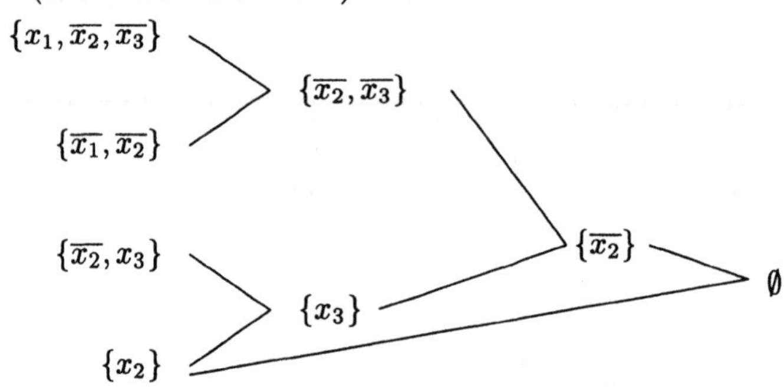

The resolution calculus is *sound* and *complete* for *refutation.* That is, if a set of clauses F has a resolution proof that leads to the empty clause, then F is unsatisfiable (soundness), and if F is unsatisfiable, then there is a resolution proof that leads to the empty clause (completeness).

Exercise 6.2.$^\circ$ Prove this.

Hint: The proof of soundness can be done by induction on the length of the resolution proof; the proof of completeness can be done by induction on the number of variables that occur in the clause. ◁

Now suppose we are given a resolution proof. Furthermore, let α be an arbitrary assignment of the variables that occur. Then α uniquely determines a path through the resolution proof – from one of the original clauses to the empty clause – so that for each clause K along this path, $\alpha(K) = 0$.

Example. Let $\alpha(x_1) = \alpha(x_2) = \alpha(x_3) = 1$. Then the path determined by α in the resolution proof above is indicated below.

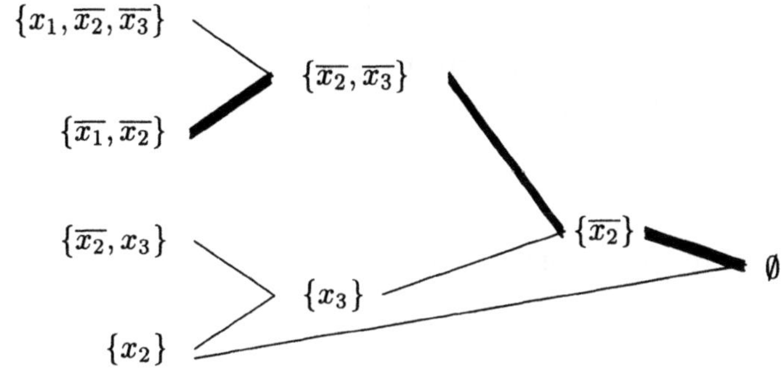

Exercise 6.3. Justify the claim that for each such α there is a path through the resolution proof from one of the original clauses to the empty clause and that this path is unique.

Hint: Construct the path by starting from the empty clause and working backwards toward one of the original clauses. ◁

A sound and complete proof system for refutation, like resolution, can be viewed as a nondeterministic algorithm that works in the following way:

INPUT F; (* the formula to refute *)
REPEAT
Nondeterministically choose one possible proof step and
add it to the proof that has been constructed so far;
UNTIL unsatisfiability of F is established by the proof;
OUTPUT unsatisfiable and accept;

where the test in the REPEAT-UNTIL loop is required to run in time that is polynomial in the length of the proof. Such an algorithm accepts (in the nondeterministic sense) precisely the set of unsatisfiable formulas, i.e. $\overline{SAT}$.

In the theory of NP-completeness, one defines the time complexity of a nondeterministic algorithm to be the least possible number of steps (under some choice of the nondeterministic decisions) in which the result (in this case establishing the unsatisfiability of a formula) can be reached. So in this case, the nondeterministic time complexity corresponds precisely to the length of the shortest possible proof in some calculus. We call a (sound and complete) proof system a SUPER proof system if there is a polynomial p so that the algorithm above on an input of length n makes (more exactly: can only make) at most $p(n)$ passes through the loop before arriving at a result. Or, formulated differently, a proof system is SUPER if for every unsatisfiable formula F of length n there is a proof of the unsatisfiability of F that is at most polynomially long (in n).

Exercise 6.4. Show that NP = coNP if and only if there is a SUPER proof system for refutation.

Hint: Use the fact that *SAT* is NP-complete. ◁

Is the resolution calculus a SUPER proof system? If so, then by the exercise above it would follow that NP = coNP, which would be spectacular and contradict most conjectures. On the other hand, if we can show that resolution is not a SUPER proof system, then this is an interesting result, but it does not have any immediate, direct implications for the NP =?coNP problem. In the remainder of this chapter we will prove this interesting result.

Theorem 6.1. *The resolution calculus is not a SUPER proof system.*

Proof. First we will define for each n a formula, i.e., a set of clauses, that expresses the pigeonhole principle: $n+1$ pigeons do not fit into n pigeonholes in such a way that no hole contains more than one pigeon.[1] The variable $x_{i,j}$ ($i \in \{1,\dots,n\}$ and $j \in \{1,\dots,n+1\}$) will be used to express that pigeon j is in pigeonhole i. The set of clauses PHP_n consists of:

- Type 1 clauses:
  $\{x_{1,1}, x_{2,1}, \dots, x_{n,1}\}, \{x_{1,2}, x_{2,2}, \dots, x_{n,2}\}, \dots, \{x_{1,n+1}, x_{2,n+1}, \dots, x_{n,n+1}\}$, and
- Type 2 clauses:

$$\{\overline{x_{1,1}}, \overline{x_{1,2}}\}, \{\overline{x_{1,1}}, \overline{x_{1,3}}\}, \dots, \{\overline{x_{1,1}}, \overline{x_{1,n+1}}\}, \{\overline{x_{1,2}}, \overline{x_{1,3}}\}, \dots, \{\overline{x_{1,n}}, \overline{x_{1,n+1}}\},$$
$$\{\overline{x_{2,1}}, \overline{x_{2,2}}\}, \{\overline{x_{2,1}}, \overline{x_{2,3}}\}, \dots, \{\overline{x_{2,1}}, \overline{x_{2,n+1}}\}, \{\overline{x_{2,2}}, \overline{x_{2,3}}\}, \dots, \{\overline{x_{2,n}}, \overline{x_{2,n+1}}\},$$
$$\vdots$$
$$\{\overline{x_{n,1}}, \overline{x_{n,2}}\}, \{\overline{x_{n,1}}, \overline{x_{n,3}}\}, \dots, \{\overline{x_{n,1}}, \overline{x_{n,n+1}}\}, \{\overline{x_{n,2}}, \overline{x_{n,3}}\}, \dots, \{\overline{x_{n,n}}, \overline{x_{n,n+1}}\}$$

The type 1 clauses express that each pigeon is in at least one hole. The type 2 clauses express that each hole contains at most one pigeon (literally, each hole does not contain a pair of distinct pigeons).

It is clear that for each n, PHP_n is unsatisfiable. Our goal is to show that every resolution proof of this fact must have length at least c^n for some constant $c > 1$. Since the number of variables in PHP_n is quadratic in n and the number of clauses is $O(n^3)$, it follows from this that the resolution calculus is *not* SUPER.

For the proof we use $n \times (n+1)$ matrices to represent the clauses in PHP_n and their resolvents. The n rows represent the n holes and the $n+1$ columns

[1] Translation note: In German, the pigeonhole principle is called the *Schubfachprinzip*, literally the drawer principle, and the original examples here included the pigeon example and the following: $n+1$ socks do not fit in n drawers in such a way that no drawer contains more than one sock. Also, the English expression "pigeonhole" probably does not refer to bird houses, but to a certain type of mail slots (common in many university department offices) which are also called pigeonholes. So that a better example would perhaps be to replace pigeons with letters, but we will continue with pigeons, as in the original.

the $n+1$ pigeons. We will place a $\oplus$ in position (i,j) if the literal $x_{i,j}$ occurs in the clause and a $\ominus$ in position (i,j) if the literal $\overline{x_{i,j}}$ occurs in the clause.

Exercise 6.5. Draw the representation of PHP_3 in this scheme. ◁

Analogously, we can represent assignments to variables in this rectangle notation scheme: we place a $b \in \{0,1\}$ in position (i,j) if the variable $x_{i,j}$ should have the value b. We will call an assignment ***critical*** if n of the $n+1$ pigeons have been assigned distinct holes, so that all n holes contain a pigeon. In other words, an assignment is said to be critical if for every i (hole) there is a j (pigeon) with $\alpha(x_{i,j}) = 1$ and also for every j there is at most one i with $\alpha(x_{i,j}) = 1$.

Exercise 6.6. Draw a 5×6 matrix that represents an arbitrary critical assignment. ◁

Exercise 6.7. Let n be fixed. How many critical assignments are there? ◁

In the matrix representation of a critical assignment there will be a column in which there are only 0's; we will call this column the *0-column* of the critical assignment.

Exercise 6.8. A critical assignment always satisfies all clauses of PHP_n except for one, which one? ◁

Assume we have a resolution proof that demonstrates the unsatisfiability of PHP_n, represented as an acyclic graph. Let α be a critical assignment. We apply the construction of Exercise 6.3, which produces for each such assignment a unique path connecting one of the original clauses with the empty clause such that for each clause K along this path $\alpha(K) = 0$.

Exercise 6.9. The path associated with α can only connect the empty clause with one of the original clauses in PHP_n. Which one? ◁

Now we put everything together. Every critical assignment α has a 0-column. The unique path through the resolution proof of PHP_n determined by α connects a clause of PHP_n with the empty clause. This clause in PHP_n must be the type 1 clause that has $\oplus$'s in the 0-column of α.

Consider a 4×5 example (so $n = 4$). Let α be the following critical assignment:

0	1	0	0	0
0	0	1	0	0
1	0	0	0	0
0	0	0	0	1
			↑	

The arrow indicates the 0-column of α.

The next diagram indicates the path in the resolution proof associated with α.

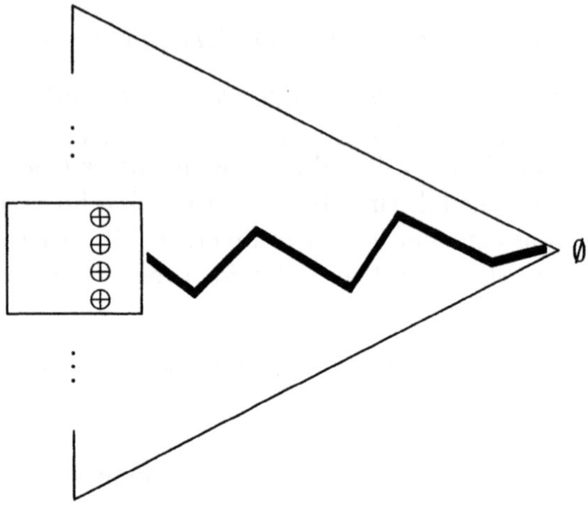

The leftmost clause contains n $\oplus$'s. The empty clause at the end has none. A resolution step can only eliminate at most one of these $\oplus$'s. So there must be a clause along this path that has *exactly* $n/2$ $\oplus$'s in the 0-column of α.

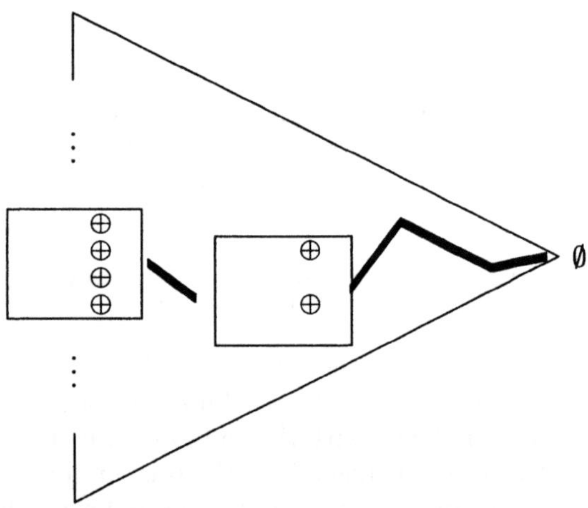

Of course, the remaining columns of this clause can (and must) also have changed, but for the moment we are only interested in the 0-column. So we have shown that for every critical assignment α there is a clause K in the resolution proof that has exactly $n/2$ $\oplus$'s in the 0-column of α and that $\alpha(K) = 0$.

Now imagine the clauses of the resolution proof to be linearly ordered in such a way that resolvents always occur later in the list than their parent clauses. (Such an ordering is a topological ordering of the acyclic graph of the proof). The last clause of this order must be the empty clause. For every critical assignment α, let $K_{[\alpha]}$ be the first clause K in this ordering that has exactly $n/2$ $\oplus$'s in the 0-column of α and for which $\alpha(K) = 0$. (This clause is not necessarily the clause constructed above in our proof of the existence of such a clause.)

Exercise 6.10. Show that the clause $K_{[\alpha]}$, which has $n/2$ $\oplus$'s in the 0-column of α, has no $\ominus$'s in this column. $\triangleleft$

Next we want to consider *partial* assignments, i.e., assignments that do not assign a value to all of the variables. We are only interested in partial assignments that can be extended to critical assignments. That is, the partial assignments that interest us cannot have two 1's in the same row or column. In what follows we will consider only partial assignments that in addition to being extendible to a critical assignment also have the property that *exactly* $n/8$ of the positions are assigned a 1. (For simplicity we will assume that n is divisible by 8.) In order to make these partial assignments notationally distinguishable from critical assignments, we will use capital letters for the partial assignments. Let S be a partial assignment (with the restrictions as mentioned). We let K^S denote the first clause in the proof sequence of the form $K_{[\alpha]}$ such that S can be extended to α. In this way, every partial assignment S is assigned a critical assignment α, namely one for which $K_{[\alpha]} = K^S$. From now on we will call the clauses of the form K^S *complex clauses*.

The proof strategy is now the following: We will show that if a resolution proof is "too short" then it must contain an error. Suppose there is a resolution proof P for PHP_n that is "too short," where for the length of the proof P we only count the number of complex clauses that occur. Suppose this number is less than c^n for some constant $c > 1$ to be determined later. Then a certain greedy algorithm, which we will give below, with the set of complex clauses in P as input will find a partial assignment S that satisfies all of these complex clauses. (That is, the $n/8$ 1's in S will be in positions such that for each of the complex clauses at least one of these positions contains a $\oplus$.) Starting with this partial assignment S, as described above, we produce a complex clause $K^S = K_{[\alpha]}$ in P for some α with $\alpha(K^S) = 0$. But this is a contradiction, since S makes all of the complex clauses in P true. Thus K^S represents an error in the proof, and all correct proofs must be "long enough."

In order to carry out this argument with our greedy algorithm, we must show that every complex clause must necessarily have, in addition to the $n/2$ $\oplus$'s in the 0-column, other $\oplus$'s in other columns. In fact, there must be so many that we can always assume that there are at least $\Omega(n^2)$ $\oplus$'s. The existence of this many $\oplus$'s simplifies the argument, that $n/8$ 1's can be fixed so that all complex clauses become true.

Consider an 8×9 example. A partial assignment S must in this case fix $n/8 = 1$. Assume that the 1 is in position $(1,1)$. Let $K^S = K_{[\alpha]}$ for some α that extends S. Furthermore, suppose that $\alpha(x_{2,2}) = 1, \ldots, \alpha(x_{n,n}) = 1$. The 0-column in this case is $n+1$. (Unspecified values in the diagram below are 0.)

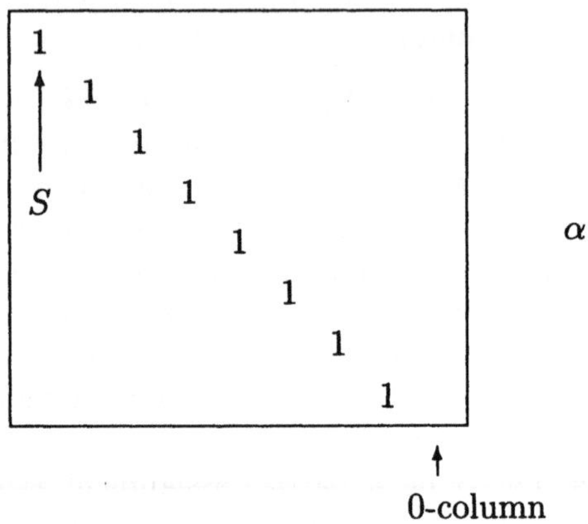

The corresponding complex clause $K^S = K_{[\alpha]}$ has exactly $n/2 = 4$ $\oplus$'s in column $n+1$. For simplicity, we draw them at the bottom:

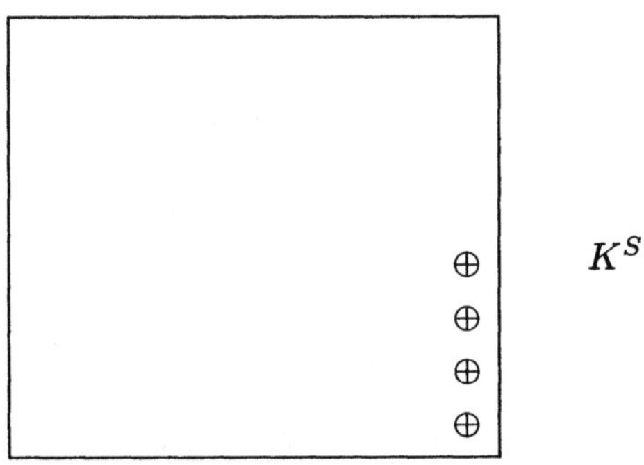

Exercise 6.11. Show that there must be at least $3n/8$ 1's in the diagram for α that are neither in the same row as a $\oplus$ in the 0-column of K^S nor fixed by S. $\triangleleft$

Now select an arbitrary 1 from among these $3n/8$ many and change α to 0 at this location. At the same time, change the 0 in the same row of the 0-column to a 1. The result is another critical assignment α^*, for which the 0-column is the column in which a 1 was changed to a 0. If we carry this procedure out using the 1 in column 4 of our example, we get the following transformation:

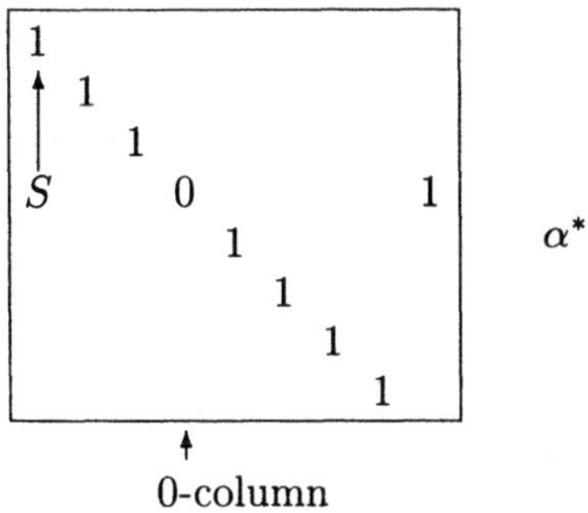

Claim. Now we claim that all $3n/8$ columns in which 1's of the type described in the last exercise occur are "good" columns. (In our example this would include, among others, column 4.) A good column is one in which either there is exactly one $\ominus$ or at least $n/2$ $\oplus$'s.

Proof (of the claim). First note that no column of K^S can contain two $\ominus$'s.

Exercise 6.12. Why? ◁

Now consider one of the $3n/8$ columns mentioned in the claim and suppose that this column is not good. Let this be column j. Then there must be no $\ominus$'s and fewer than $n/2$ $\oplus$'s in this column. In this case, the transformation from α to α^* (using this column) does not change the truth value; it is still the case that $\alpha^*(K^S) = 0$.

Exercise 6.13. Justify this. ◁

Now we can construct a path backwards from the clause K^S to one of the original clauses so that for each clause K along this path $\alpha^*(K) = 0$. As in Exercise 6.9, this path must lead to a clause of type 1 in which the column j is filled with $\oplus$'s. So at the end of this path we have a clause with more than $n/2$ $\oplus$'s. Somewhere strictly between there must be a clause with *exactly* $n/2$ $\oplus$'s in column j. This is a clause of the same form as $K_{[\alpha^*]}$ (perhaps $K_{[\alpha^*]}$). Since $K_{[\alpha^*]}$ is defined to be the first clause of this type that occurs in the proof P, $K_{[\alpha^*]}$ must come strictly before K^S. But since α^* is also an extension of S, and K^S was chosen to be at the first possible position in the proof, this is a contradiction; K^S should have been chosen to be $K_{[\alpha^*]}$. Thus every complex clause has at least $3n/8 + 1$ "good" columns (including the 0-column). □

Now suppose that P is a resolution proof for the unsatisfiability of PHP_n and $\{K_1, K_2, \ldots, K_t\}$ are the complex clauses that occur in P. We modify the sequence $\{K_i\}$ to a sequence K_i': in every column that contains a $\ominus$ (this will be a "good" column) we strike the $\ominus$ and fill the rest of the column (except for the position of the original $\ominus$) with $\oplus$. For any partial assignment S, if $S(K_i') = 1$, then $S(K_i) = 1$.

The sequence $(K_1', K_2', \ldots, K_t')$ is the input for the following greedy algorithm. This algorithm "tries" to construct a partial assignment S such that the $n/8$ 1's in S are sufficient to force that $S(K_i') = S(K_i) = 1$. In particular, this will also be the case for any extension of S to a critical assignment. But this would be a contradiction, since for each complex clause K^S (which is in the input list) there must be an α for which $K^S = K_{[\alpha]}$ and $\alpha(K^S) = 0$.

We will see that this contradiction always arises if t is "too small." Thus the number of complex clauses in P and, therefore, the length of P itself must be large enough.

```
PROCEDURE Greedy(M : Set of clauses): partial assignment;
VAR
    S : partial assignment;
    E : set of matrix positions;
    k, i, j : CARDINAL ;
BEGIN
    S := empty assignment;
    E := all positions;
    FOR k := 1 TO n/8 DO
        Find the positions (i, j) in E, where the most clauses
            in M have a ⊕;
        Expand S by (i, j);
        Strike from M those clauses that have ⊕ in position (i, j);
        Strike from E row i and column j;
    END;
    RETURN S;
END Greedy;
```

Now we analyze the algorithm. The initial situation is that M contains the t complex clauses given as input. By the discussion above, each of these complex clauses must have at least $(3n/8+1)\cdot(n/2)$ $\oplus$'s. E initially contains all $n\cdot(n+1)$ positions. This means that in the first step the fraction of clauses that are "taken care of" (i.e., for which their value under S is determined to be 1) is at least

$$\frac{(3n/8+1)\cdot(n/2)}{n\cdot(n+1)} \geq \frac{(3n/8)\cdot(n/2)}{n^2} = \frac{3}{16} \approx 0.1875 .$$

Exercise 6.14. Justify this. ◁

Of course, the fraction of clauses that can be "taken care of" decreases with each step, since row i and column j are stricken. After k passes through the loop, the ratio of remaining $\oplus$'s to the size of E is

$$\frac{(3n/8+1-k)\cdot(n/2-k)}{(n-k)\cdot(n+1-k)} \geq \frac{(3n/8-k)\cdot(n/2-k)}{(n-k)^2} .$$

This quotient is smallest at the last pass through the loop. We get a lower bound by taking only this last ratio, when $k = n/8$:

$$\frac{(3n/8 - n/8) \cdot (n/2 - n/8)}{(n - n/8)^2} = \frac{6}{49} \approx 0.1224\,.$$

Let M_i be the set of remaining clauses in M after the ith pass through the loop. Then

$$|M_i| \leq |M_{i-1}| - \frac{6}{49} \cdot |M_{i-1}| = \frac{43}{49} \cdot |M_{i-1}|\,.$$

This yields the approximation $|M_i| \leq (\frac{43}{49})^i \cdot |M_0|$. Now we hope that the line of argumentation outlined above actually works, i.e., that $|M_{n/8}| = 0$. It is sufficient to show that $|M_{n/8}| < 1$, since $|M_{n/8}|$ is an integer. This is the case provided $(\frac{43}{49})^{n/8} \cdot |M_0| < 1$, or equivalently if $|M_0| < [(\frac{49}{43})^{1/8}]^n = c^n$ where $c = 1.01646...$

In summary, if the number of complex clauses that are given as input to the greedy algorithm is less than c^n, then the algorithm succeeds after $n/8$ passes through the loop in constructing a partial assignment S that makes all clauses in the input true. However, we have also seen that starting with this partial assignment we can find a complex clause that does not have the value 1 under S, since there is an extension α of S that makes the clause false. This contradiction implies that all resolution proofs of PHP_n must have at least c^n complex clauses. □

* * * * *

A computer generated proof of PHP_3 appears at the end of this chapter. In its search for a proof, the computer generated 1006 clauses (including the input clauses 1–22), 91 of which are required for the proof.

References

The notion of a SUPER proof system and its relationship to the NP =?coNP problem originated with

- S. Cook, R. Reckhow: The relative efficiency of propositional proof systems, *Journal of Symbolic Logic* 44 (1979), 36–50.

After the problem had been worked on since the 70's, the proof of an exponential lower bound for the resolution calculus was first achieved in 1985:

- A. Haken: The Intractability of Resolution, *Theoretical Computer Science* 39 (1985), 297–308.

The proof given here follows a somewhat more elegant technique of

- S. Cook and T. Pitassi: A Feasible Constructive Lower Bound for Resolution Proofs, *Information Processing Letters* 34 (1990), 81–85.

but improves on the lower bound stated there.

```
   -------- PROOF ---------
   1 -p11 | -p12.
2 -p11 | -p13.
3 -p11 | -p14.
4 -p12 | -p13.
5 -p12 | -p14.
6 -p13 | -p14.
7 -p21 | -p22.
8 -p21 | -p23.
9 -p21 | -p24.
10 -p22 | -p23.
11 -p22 | -p24.
12 -p23 | -p24.
13 -p31 | -p32.
14 -p31 | -p33.
15 -p31 | -p34.
16 -p32 | -p33.
17 -p32 | -p34.
18 -p33 | -p34.
19 p11 | p21 | p31.
20 p12 | p22 | p32.
21 p13 | p23 | p33.
22 p14 | p24 | p34.
23 [res:19,3] p21 | p31 | -p14.
24 [res:19,2] p21 | p31 | -p13.
25 [res:19,1] p21 | p31 | -p12.
26 [res:19,9] p11 | p31 | -p24.
27 [res:19,8] p11 | p31 | -p23.
30 [res:19,14] p11 | p21 | -p33.
32 [res:20,5] p22 | p32 | -p14.
33 [res:20,4] p22 | p32 | -p13.
34 [res:20,1] p22 | p32 | -p11.
41 [res:21,6] p23 | p33 | -p14.
42 [res:21,4] p23 | p33 | -p12.
43 [res:21,2] p23 | p33 | -p11.
52 [res:22,3] p24 | p34 | -p11.
53 [res:22,12] p14 | p34 | -p23.
54 [res:22,11] p14 | p34 | -p22.
55 [res:22,9] p14 | p34 | -p21.
57 [res:22,17] p14 | p24 | -p32.
60 [res:23,8] p31 | -p14 | -p23.
77 [res:25,14] p21 | -p12 | -p33.
82 [res:26,13] p11 | -p24 | -p32.
84 [res:27,15] p11 | -p23 | -p34.
97 [res:32,10] p32 | -p14 | -p23.
98 [res:32,7] p32 | -p14 | -p21.
107 [res:33,7] p32 | -p13 | -p21.
113 [res:34,11] p32 | -p11 | -p24.
114 [res:34,10] p32 | -p11 | -p23.
160 [res:41,16] p23 | -p14 | -p32.
161 [res:41,14] p23 | -p14 | -p31.
181 [res:43,16] p23 | -p11 | -p32.
265 [res:52,18] p24 | -p11 | -p33.
277 [res:53,17] p14 | -p23 | -p32.
289 [res:54,15] p14 | -p22 | -p31.
298 [res:55,18] p14 | -p21 | -p33.
299 [res:55,17] p14 | -p21 | -p32.
337 [res:60,13] -p14|-p23|-p32.
888 [res:337,277] -p23 | -p32.
889 [res:337,160] -p14 | -p32.
890 [res:337,97] -p14 | -p23.
891 [res:888,181] -p32 | -p11.
894 [res:888,114] -p23 | -p11.
897 [res:889,299] -p32 | -p21.
899 [res:889,57] -p32 | p24.
900 [res:889,98] -p14 | -p21.
903 [res:890,53] -p23 | p34.
904 [res:890,161] -p14 | -p31.
907 [res:891,113] -p11 | -p24.
909 [res:891,82] -p32 | -p24.
914 [res:894,43] -p11 | p33.
915 [res:894,84] -p23 | -p34.
918 [res:897,107] -p21 | -p13.
923 [res:900,298] -p21 | -p33.
932 [res:904,289] -p31 | -p22.
939 [res:907,265] -p11 | -p33.
944 [res:909,899] -p32.
946 [res:944,20] p12 | p22.
953 [res:915,903] -p23.
954 [res:953,42] p33 | -p12.
955 [res:953,21] p13 | p33.
957 [res:918,24] -p13 | p31.
959 [res:923,77] -p33 | -p12.
960 [res:923,30] -p33 | p11.
975 [res:939,914] -p11.
995 [res:959,954] -p12.
997 [res:995,946] p22.
1001 [res:997,932] -p31.
1002 [res:1001,957] -p13.
1003 [res:1002,955] p33.
1004 [res:960,1003] p11.
1006 [res:1004,975] .

   ------- end of proof --------
```

7. Spectral Problems and Descriptive Complexity Theory

This chapter begins with a question from predicate logic, namely to determine the set of all (sizes of) finite models of a given formula. It turns out that there is an amazingly close relationship between this question and the world of P and NP.

In this chapter we want to discuss formulas in predicate logic. These formulas are built up from *atomic formulas*. There are two kinds of atomic formulas. One type has the form $P(x_1, \ldots, x_k)$, where P is a *predicate symbol* with arity k, and each x_i is a *variable*. The other possibility for an atomic formula is a formula of the form $x_i = x_j$.

Atomic formulas are the simplest formulas. More complex formulas are built up from the atomic formulas. Given two formulas G and H, we can form boolean combinations, for example

$$(G \wedge H), \quad (G \vee H), \quad (G \rightarrow H), \quad (G \leftrightarrow H), \quad (\neg G) .$$

Let x be a variable, then by (existential or universal) quantification over x we obtain from G the new formulas

$$\exists x\, G, \quad \forall x\, G .$$

An occurrence of the variable x in a formula G is called *bound* if it occurs in a subformula of F of the form $\exists x\, G$ or $\forall x\, G$. Otherwise an occurrence of the variable x is said to be *free*. In this topic we are only interested in formulas in which all occurrences of x are bound. Such formulas are called *sentences*.

A sentence can be assigned a truth value by "interpreting" the sentence in a given *structure* A. A structure (suitable for interpreting the sentence F) consists of a non-empty set (the *universe*) of values for the variables that occur in F, and concrete predicates for each predicate symbol that occurs in F, i.e., relations on the universe of the appropriate arity. The truth value $\mathsf{A}(F)$ of the formula F is determined recursively on the structure of the formula:

- If the formula is a boolean combination of subformulas G and H, then one determines recursively the truth values $\mathsf{A}(G)$ and $\mathsf{A}(H)$ and combines these values according to the usual boolean operations (i.e., truth tables).

- If F has the form $\exists x\, G$ then $\mathsf{A}(F)$ is true if and only if there is a value w in the universe such that G, interpreted under A with x interpreted as w, is assigned the value true. (See the instructions below regarding assigning truth values to atomic formulas for more about the substitution of w for x.)
  If the formula F has the form $\forall x\, G$ then we replace "there exists" with "for all" in the instructions above.
- If the formula is an atomic formula, then in general it contains variables. (Note that this case does not occur for sentences themselves, since all variables in a sentence are bound by quantifiers, but it occurs "inside the recursion" – in fact, it is the base case of the recursion.) In the previously executed recursive steps, each variable in a sentence will have been assigned a value from the universe. Therefore we can evaluate this atomic formula directly using the interpretations of the predicates given by A. (The equals sign is always interpreted as identity on the universe.)

If $\mathsf{A}(F)$ is true we write $\mathsf{A} \models F$. In this case A is said to be a *model* for F. A particular structure is denoted in tuple form: $\mathsf{A} = (M; R_1, \ldots, R_m)$, where M is the universe and each R_i is a relation on the universe which is used to interpret the predicate P_i. A formula can have finite or infinite models (or none at all), where the size of a model is measured by the size of the universe, $|M|$. We let $|\mathsf{A}| = |M|$ denote the size of a model A with universe M. In what follows, we are interested in the set of all (sizes of) *finite* models for a given formula. Let

$$Spectrum(F) = \{n \in \mathbb{N} \mid \text{ there is a model } \mathsf{A} \text{ with } |\mathsf{A}| = n \text{ and } \mathsf{A} \models F\}\,.$$

In 1952, H. Schulz posed the problem (the so-called *spectral problem*) of characterizing the set of all such spectra. And in 1955, G. Asser posed the question of whether the class of all spectra is closed under complement.

Example. Let F be a predicate logic formula that formalizes the axioms for a field. (In the usual definition of a field, a field is specified by its underlying set and two functions on that set. Since we have not allowed function symbols in our language, we must modify the usual definition slightly. Candidates for a field are structures $\mathsf{A} = (M; R_*, R_+)$, where R_*, R_+ are each 3-ary relations expressing the equations $x * y = z$ and $x + y = z$, respectively.) A subformula of F that formalizes the associative law for field multiplication would then be

$$\forall x \forall y \forall z \forall u \forall v \forall w_1 \forall w_2 \;\; (R_*(x,y,u) \wedge R_*(u,z,w_1) \wedge R_*(y,z,v) \wedge R_*(x,v,w_2)) \\ \rightarrow w_1 = w_2\,.$$

Other subformulas of F would have to express the other field axioms as well as the fact that the relations R_* and R_+ are functions, i.e., that the values of the field operations are unique. The set of all models of F would then be the set of all fields. From algebra we know that there is a finite field of size n if and only if n is a prime power. So

$$Spectrum(F) = \{n \mid n \text{ is a prime power }\} .$$

Exercise 7.1. Give a formula for which $Spectrum(F) = \mathbb{N} - \{0\}$. ◁

Exercise 7.2. Give a formula for which $Spectrum(F) = \{3\}$. ◁

Generalizing the previous exercise we see immediately that every finite subset of $\mathbb{N}$ is the spectrum of some sentence.

A finite structure can be coded as a string, just as is commonly done in complexity theory with other types of objects (e.g., graphs). For example, the structure $\mathsf{A} = (M; R_1, \ldots, R_m)$, with $|\mathsf{A}| = |M| = n$, can be coded as

$$1^n 0 r_1 r_2 \ldots r_m ,$$

where r_i is a 0-1 string of length n^k and R_i is the interpretation of a k-ary predicate P_i. This string describes the relation R_i "bit for bit" (as a characteristic sequence) on the universe. Note that we have not coded in the arity of the predicates – it is implicit in the syntax of the formulas – but this could be easily done.

Exercise 7.3.° Use the recursive description for evaluation of $\mathsf{A}(F)$ to give for every sentence F an algorithm that on input A determines in polynomial time whether $\mathsf{A} \models F$. (In other words, show that for all sentences F in first-order predicate logic, the set $Models(F) = \{\mathsf{A} \mid \mathsf{A} \models F \text{ and } \mathsf{A} \text{ is finite}\}$ is in P.) ◁

On the other hand, one can ask if for every language $L \in \mathsf{P}$ there is a formula F so that the models of F are precisely the strings $x \in L$. But this is not the case; there are languages in P that cannot be described in this sense by sentences in first-order predicate logic. In fact, Immerman has shown that the class of languages described by sentences of first-order predicate logic (under certain additional technical assumptions) is precisely the class AC^0. Symbolically this is expressed as $\mathsf{FO} = \mathsf{AC}^0$. ($\mathsf{FO}$ stands for *first-order*. For more information about the class AC^0 see Topics 11 and 12.)

It follows immediately from Exercise 7.3 that for every formula F the set $Spectrum(F)$ over the alphabet $\{0\}$ (i.e., with all numbers *coded in unary*) is in NP. If we code the numbers in binary then the strings are only logarithmically as long, so in this case $Spectrum(F) \in \mathsf{NEXP} = \bigcup_{c>0} \mathsf{NTIME}(2^{cn})$.

Exercise 7.4. Justify the last statement. ◁

The set $Spectrum(F)$ codes the information about the sizes of models for F. This is very crude information about F. In what follows we want to use a language that expresses somewhat more information about F. Observe first that F has a model $\mathsf{A} = (M; R_1, \ldots, R_m)$ (where $P_1, \ldots, P_m$ are the predicate symbols that occur in F) if and only if the formula

$$G = \exists P_1 \ldots \exists P_m\, F$$

has (M) – a model consisting only of a universe, only the size of which really matters – for a model. The formula $\exists P_1 \ldots \exists P_m\, F$ is a formula in *second-order predicate logic*, which means that we may quantify not only over variables but also over predicate symbols, and hence over relations on the universe. The semantics of such a formula are defined in the expected way: relations corresponding to the predicate symbols P_i must exist over the universe that make the formula F true. Since the predicate symbols are now bound by the quantification, they no longer require interpretations as part of the model A for G.

Now we modify the formula (and the underlying question about the existence of models) in the following way: some of the predicate symbols may be bound by quantifiers, others (for simplicity we will consider just one) may occur freely in G:

$$G = \exists P_1 \ldots \exists P_m\, F(P, P_1, \ldots, P_m) \,.$$

The notation $F(P, P_1, \ldots, P_m)$ is intended to indicate that exactly the predicate symbols $P, P_1, \ldots, P_m$ occur in F. A model for G now must have the form $\mathsf{A} = (M; R)$, where R is a relation over the universe M of the appropriate arity. We assign to this formula G the set of all of its models

$$\mathit{Models}(G) = \{\mathsf{A} \mid \mathsf{A} \models G \;\&\; \mathsf{A} \text{ is finite}\} \,,$$

which is sometimes called the *generalized spectrum* of G.

Exercise 7.5. We want to consider the question of what complexity the language $Models(G)$ has for this type of second-order formula G, where the second-order quantifiers are only existential (and occur before all first-order quantifiers).

Show that $Models(G) \in \mathsf{NP}$.

Hint: Make a small modification to the observation above that $Spectrum(F)$ – coded in unary – is in NP. ◁

As we will show below, this time the converse is also true: A language L is in NP if and only if there is such a (second-order, existentially quantified) formula G such that $L = \{x \mid \mathsf{A}_x \models G\}$. For this we assign to each string x a structure A_x which codes x in a certain way. In this sense – ignoring issues of coding – the set of all models of second-order existential formulas *is* the class NP. This fact is expressed succinctly as NP = SO∃. The amazing thing about this result is that it gives an exact characterization of the class NP solely in terms of expressibility in a certain logic. There is no mention of

Turing machines, computations, running times or polynomials. *Descriptive complexity theory* deals with the question of which complexity classes can be characterized in such a way and whether it may be possible to prove that two such classes are distinct using only methods from model theory.

It is instructive (and for what follows useful) to reprove the previous exercise ($\mathsf{SO}\exists \subseteq \mathsf{NP}$) in a different way, namely via a polynomial reduction to *SAT*. For this we must reduce an arbitrary structure $\mathsf{A} = (M; P)$ (appropriate for a formula G) in polynomial time to a boolean formula α. The construction will, of course, make use of G. But note that G is fixed and A is the input, so the algorithm must only be polynomial in $|\mathsf{A}|$. Let $G = \exists P_1 \ldots \exists P_m\, F(P, P_1, \ldots, P_m)$, and let $\mathsf{A} = (M; P)$ be a suitable structure. The first-order part of G is the formula F, where the predicate symbols $P, P_1, \ldots, P_m$ occur. The interpretation of P is given by A, but the existence of predicates $\{P_i\}$ that make F true is the question. Let $M = \{1, 2, \ldots, n\}$. We replace step by step every subformula of F of the form $\exists x\, F'$ with $F'(x/1) \vee \cdots \vee F'(x/n)$, where $F'(x/i)$ denotes that for every free occurrence of x in F' we replace x with i. (This is a purely syntactic process.) Similarly, every subformula of the form $\forall x\, F'$ is replaced by $F'(x/1) \wedge \cdots \wedge F'(x/n)$. The resulting formula (a substitute for the formula F) contains no quantifiers or variables; all of the variables have been replaced by constants. The atomic formulas in the new formula have three possible forms:

$$
\begin{array}{rl}
P(i_1, \ldots, i_l) & \quad (*) \\
(i = j) & \quad (*) \\
P_i(i_1, \ldots, i_k) &
\end{array}
$$

(l and k are the arities of the predicate symbols involved.) The atomic formulas of the forms marked with $(*)$ can be evaluated directly using the structure A. This can be used to simplify the formula. Furthermore, every atomic formula of the form $P_i(i_1, \ldots, i_k)$ can be made true or false independently of every other one. So each $P_i(i_1, \ldots, i_k)$ can be considered as a name for a ***boolean*** variable. Now we are just looking for a satisfying assignment to a boolean formula, which will exist if and only if $\mathsf{A} \models G$. Since the construction requires only polynomial time, what we have described is nothing other than a reduction to *SAT*.

What is interesting here is that the structure of the formula F is reflected in a certain way in the resulting formula α. If we assume that the formula F has the form $F = \forall x_1 \ldots \forall x_l\, H$, where H is quantifier free and a *Horn formula* (i.e., H is in conjunctive normal form and each clause contains at most one positive literal), then the formula α given by the reduction is also a Horn formula.[1] For Horn formulas, the satisfiability problem is known to be solvable in polynomial time: $SAT \cap Horn \in \mathsf{P}$. So

[1] In fact, it is sufficient in this context if only the portions of the formula consisting of the literals $P_i(i_1, \ldots, i_k)$ form a Horn formula but the input predicate or the order relation do not.

$$\mathsf{SO}\exists \cap Horn \subseteq \mathsf{P}\,.$$

* * * * *

Now we want to turn our attention to the reverse direction, which strongly resembles the proof of Cook's theorem. Let L be a language in NP. So there is a nondeterministic Turing machine M that accepts the language L in polynomial time. Let the number of nondeterministic steps needed by M on inputs of length n be bounded by the polynomial n^k. Without loss of generality we can assume that the machine never visits tape cells to the left of the input. Let Σ be the work alphabet of the Turing machine, and let the input alphabet be $\{0, 1, \sqcup\} \subseteq \Sigma$. Furthermore, let Z be the set of states. Then configurations of M can be described as strings of length n^k over the alphabet $\Gamma = \Sigma \cup (Z \times \Sigma)$: The string

$$a_1\, a_2\, \ldots\, a_{i-1}\, (z, a_i)\, a_{i+1}\, \ldots\, a_{n^k}$$

codes that the tape contents of M at a given time are precisely $a_1 \ldots a_{n^k}$, the head is located at position i and the state is z. An accepting computation of M on input x with $|x| = n$ and $x = x_1 \ldots x_n$, can be represented by an $n^k \times n^k$ matrix with entries from Γ:

(z_0, x_1)	x_2	x_3	$\cdots$	x_n	$\sqcup$	$\cdots$	$\sqcup$
$\vdots$							$\vdots$
$(z_e, \sqcup)$	a_2	a_3	$\cdots$	a_n	a_{n+1}	$\cdots$	a_{n^k}

The first row represents the start configuration. In the last row the halting state z_e has been reached, and we will assume that this only happens when the read-write head is at the left most position and reading a blank tape cell.

The symbol in position $(i + 1, j + 1)$ depends only on the three symbols in positions (i, j), $(i, j + 1)$, and $(i, j + 2)$, and the nondeterministic choices of the machine.

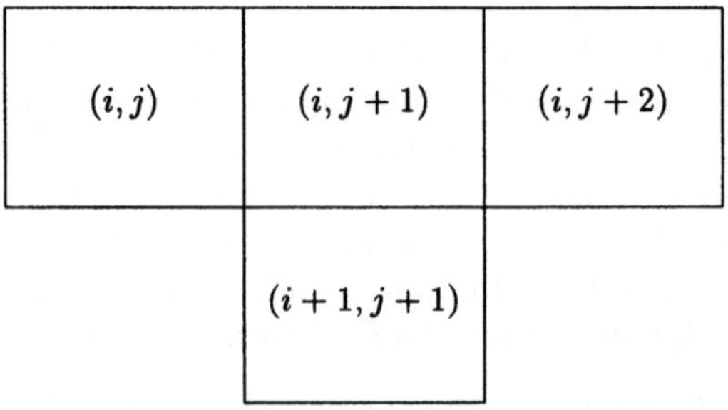

If we assume that at each step there are always two nondeterministic choices available, then we can describe this with two finite 4-ary relations, Δ_0, Δ_1, which "list" all possible allowable tuples: $\begin{bmatrix} a\ b\ c \\ d \end{bmatrix} \in \Delta_0$ (or $\in \Delta_1$), Δ_0 "listing" one choice; Δ_1, the other.

Now we set about describing a formula G so that $x \in L$ if and only if for a certain structure A_x, $\mathsf{A}_x \models G$. The simplest structure that can be used to represent a binary string (for the moment) is $\mathsf{A}_x = (\{1, \ldots, n\}, E)$, where $E(i)$ is true if and only if $x_i = 1$. But if we use this encoding, we have the following problem: All structures that are isomorphic to A_x will be indistinguishable to the formula G (which we have yet to give). So we must add to the structure an order relation $<$ on the universe, which represents our intended ordering of the universe (which we have already indicated by saying that our universe is $\{1, 2, \ldots, n\}$). The unique structure A_x describing x is now

$$\mathsf{A}_x = (\{1, \ldots, n\}, <, E) .$$

The fact that G can make use of an ordering of the universe will be seen to be very useful. A first component of G, based on $<$, will be used to describe a successor relation S on k-tuples. In this way we will in a certain sense be able to count to n^k (and not just up to n). The $2k$-ary predicate S will be existentially quantified in G: $G = \exists S \ldots$. Later in G we will "axiomatize" the desired properties of the predicate S. We will define the portion of G used to specify the properties of S recursively, defining S_1, S_2, ... $S_k = S$, where each S_i is a $2i$-ary predicate defining an ordering on i-tuples:

$$\begin{aligned} S_1(x, y) = \quad & (x < y) \land \forall z \left((x < z) \land (y \neq z) \to (y < z)\right) \\ S_{i+1}(x_1, & \ldots, x_i, y_1, \ldots, y_i) \ , \\ = \quad & \Big(S_1(x_1, y_1) \land \textstyle\bigwedge_{j=2}^{i} (x_j = y_j)\Big) \\ & \lor \Big(\mathrm{Max}(x_1) \land \mathrm{Min}(y_1) \land S_{i-1}(x_2, \ldots, x_i, y_2, \ldots, y_i)\Big) \ . \end{aligned}$$

The two additional predicates used above, Min and Max, identify the largest and smallest elements of the universe. Min can be defined via

$$\exists\,\mathrm{Min}\,\forall x \Big(\mathrm{Min}(x) \leftrightarrow \forall y \left((x = y) \lor (x < y)\right)\Big) .$$

Max can be defined similarly.

For every symbol a in Γ we introduce a new $2k$-ary predicate symbol P_a which we use to represent the computation of machine M on input x as described above. In particular, $P_a(\boldsymbol{x}, \boldsymbol{y})$ will be true if and only if the symbol a is in position $(\boldsymbol{x}, \boldsymbol{y})$ in the matrix given above. We are using $\boldsymbol{x}$ as an abbreviation for $(x_1, \ldots, x_k)$.

So the final formula G will have the form

$$G = \exists S\, \exists\,\mathrm{Min}\, \exists\,\mathrm{Max}\, \exists P_{a_1} \ \ldots\ \exists P_{a_m}\, \exists C\ F \ ,$$

where $\Gamma = \{a_1, \ldots, a_m\}$. The k-ary predicate C expresses (through its truth value) for each time step which of the two nondeterministic choices was made. The Formula F consists of the axiomatization of S, Min, and Max given above, and the following conditions on the predicates P_a.

Let's get right to the heart of the formula G: the transition relation for the machine M. This can be expressed as

$$\forall \boldsymbol{x}, \boldsymbol{x}', \boldsymbol{x}'', \boldsymbol{y}, \boldsymbol{y}' \bigwedge_{\substack{a,b,c,d \in \Gamma \\ (a,b,c,d) \in \Delta_1}} \Big(P_a(\boldsymbol{x}, \boldsymbol{y}) \wedge P_b(\boldsymbol{x}, \boldsymbol{y}') \wedge P_c(\boldsymbol{x}, \boldsymbol{y}'') \wedge S(\boldsymbol{x}, \boldsymbol{x}') \wedge S(\boldsymbol{y}, \boldsymbol{y}') \wedge S(\boldsymbol{y}', \boldsymbol{y}'') \wedge C(\boldsymbol{y}) \rightarrow P_d(\boldsymbol{x}', \boldsymbol{y}') \Big) .$$

We will also need the same formula with Δ_0 in place of Δ_1 and $\neg C(\boldsymbol{y})$ in place of $C(\boldsymbol{y})$. (Note: this is the only formula in the construction that is not a Horn formula.)

In a similar way we can express the transition relation for the column at the far right and left edges of the matrix.

Exercise 7.6.° Give a formula that correctly describes the first row of the matrix, i.e., the start configuration of the machine. ◁

Exercise 7.7. Give a formula that expresses that at no time and at no location can more than one of the predicates P_a be true. ◁

Exercise 7.8. Give a formula for the last row of the matrix, that is, one that checks for an appropriate end configuration. ◁

The desired existentially quantified, second-order formula G now consists of the conjunction of all of the formulas generated in the construction. The models of this formula characterize precisely the strings x that the Turing machine M accepts. So we have

Theorem 7.1. *(Fagin's Theorem)* $\mathsf{NP} = \mathsf{SO}\exists$. □

This result can be immediately generalized to the polynomial hierarchy, PH (cf. Topic 16). Let SO denote the set of all models of arbitrary second-order formulas (universal quantification is allowed now), then

Corollary 7.2. *(Stockmeyer)* $\mathsf{PH} = \mathsf{SO}$. □

Let's return now to the spectral problem. Here we do not have an input encoding like A_x and, therefore, also no order relationship on the universe. Only the question of the sizes of the models is relevant. In this context there can be *any arbitrary* ordering of the universe – not just the one that corresponds to the intended order of the input string – that causes the construction to work. The input is coded in unary as 1^n. For this reason we can extend the construction above to existentially "guess" an ordering and fix it with additional axioms: $G = \exists <$ (Axioms for $<$) $\wedge \ldots$.

Exercise 7.9. Give a formula that characterizes $<$ as a total ordering. That is, every model for the formula must interpret $<$ as a strict total ordering of the universe. ◁

From this we get

Theorem 7.3. *(Bennett, Rödding, Schwichtenberg; Jones, Selman; Fagin) The set of spectra of first-order formulas (coded in unary) is exactly the class of* NP*-languages over a one-element alphabet (*NP_1*).*

Corollary 7.4. *The set of spectra of first-order formulas in closed under complement if and only if* NP_1 *is closed under complement if and only if* NEXP *is closed under complement.*

Exercise 7.10. Justify the last part of the corollary: NP_1 is closed under complement if and only if NEXP is closed under complement. ◁

In the construction above there was only one place where we made use of a formula that was not a Horn formula in the sense described on page 65 (see also the footnote there). If the Turing machine is deterministic, then we no longer need the predicate C, which simulated the nondeterministic choices of the nondeterministic machine, or the distinction between Δ_0 and Δ_1. The result is a Horn formula. This gives the following result:

Theorem 7.5. *(Grädel)* $\mathsf{P} = \mathsf{SO}\exists \cap Horn$. □

We note only that once again it is important for this last result that an order relation on the universe be available, either in the form of the input encoding or, as it is often done, by enriching the logical language to include a built-in $<$ symbol with a fixed interpretation. The axioms for the ordering cannot be expressed as a purely Horn formula. (The problem is the totality condition.)

References

More detailed discussion of predicate logic can be found in many introductory books on logic, including

- H. Enderton: *A Mathematical Introduction to Logic*, Academic Press, 1972.
- H.J. Keisler, J. Robbin: *Mathematical Logic and Computability*, McGraw-Hill, 1996.

For a proof that $SAT \cap Horn \in \mathsf{P}$, see

- C.H. Papadimitriou: *Computational Complexity*, Addison-Wesley, 1994, page 78.

The results presented here can be found in

- E. Börger: Decision problems in predicate logic, in G. Lolli, *Florence Logic Colloquium 82*, North-Holland.
- C.A. Christen: Spektralproblem und Komplexitätstheorie, in E. Specker, V. Strassen: *Komplexität von Entscheidungsproblemen*, Lecture Notes in Computer Science 43, Springer, 1974, 102–126.
- R. Fagin: Generalized first-order spectra and polynomial-time recognizable sets, in R. Karp, ed., *Complexity of Computation*, SIAM-AMS Proceedings, Volume 7, 1974, 43–73.
- R. Fagin: Finite-model theory – a personal perspective, *Theoretical Computer Science* 116 (1993), 3–31.
- E. Grädel: The expressive power of second-order Horn logic, *Proceedings of the 8th Symposium on Theoretical Aspects of Computer Science*, Lecture Notes of Computer Science 480, Springer, 1991, 466–477.
- E. Grädel: Capturing complexity classes by fragments of second order logic, *Proceedings of the 6th Structure in Complexity Theory Conference*, IEEE, 1991, 341–352.
- Y. Gurevich: Toward logic tailored for computational complexity, in M.M. Richter et al, *Computation and Proof Theory*, Lecture Notes in Mathematics 1104, Springer, 1984, 175–216.
- N. Immerman: Expressibility as a complexity measure: results and directions, *Proceedings of the 2nd Structure in Complexity Theory Conference*, IEEE, 1987, 194–202.
- N. Immerman: Descriptive and computational complexity, in J. Hartmanis, ed., *Computational Complexity Theory*, AMS Applied Mathematics Proceedings, Vol. 38, 1989, 75–91.
- N.D. Jones, A.L. Selman: Turing machines and the spectra of first-order formulas, *The Journal of Symbolic Logic* 39, No. 1 (1974), 139–150.
- C.H. Papadimitriou: *Computational Complexity*, Addison-Wesley, 1994.
- L.J. Stockmeyer: The polynomial-time hierarchy, *Theoretical Computer Science* 3 (1977), 1–22.

8. Kolmogorov Complexity, the Universal Distribution, and Worst-Case vs. Average-Case

An algorithm can exhibit very different complexity behavior in the worst case and in the average case (with a "uniform" distribution of inputs). One well-known example of this disparity is the QuickSort algorithm. But it is possible – by means of Kolmogorov Complexity – to define a probability distribution under which worst-case and average-case running time (for *all* algorithms simultaneously) are the same (up to constant factors).

What is the difference between the following two bit sequences?

010101010101010101010101010101

110101000011100100100101111111

The first sequence exhibits a certain pattern which is easy to notice and which makes the sequence easy to describe: it consists of 15 repetitions of '01'. The second sequence does not have such an obvious pattern. In fact, the second sequence was generated by flipping a coin. If a pattern were detectable in the second sequence, this would be merely coincidence. In this sense, the second sequence is "more random" than the first. On the other hand, in the sense of probability theory, each sequence is an equally likely result of flipping a coin 30 times, namely, each occurs with probability 2^{-30}. Thus, probability theory does not provide the correct framework within which to talk meaningfully about a random sequence.

But consider now algorithms that generate each sequence: In the first case:

FOR $i := 1$ **TO** 15 **DO OUTPUT** '01' **END**

and in the second case:

OUTPUT '110101000011100100100101111111'

If we abstract away the specific length of our examples, namely 30, and imagine instead an arbitrary value n, then the length of the first program (as text) is $O(1) + \log(n)$, since we need $\log(n)$ bits to represent the number $n/2$. The second program, on the other hand, has length $O(1)+n$. That is, in order to describe this "random" sequence, we are essentially forced to write down the entire sequence, which takes n bits. On the basis of this intuition we will define a sequence to be random if any description of the sequence requires essentially n bits.

We will also consider the following variation: Consider algorithms that take an input y and produce an output x. The minimal length of such a program that generates x from y is a measure of the relative randomness of x with respect to y; or said another way, it describes how much information about x is contained in y. If in the examples above we let n, the length of the sequence to be generated, be the input to the program rather than a constant within the program, for example,

INPUT n; **FOR** $i := 1$ **TO** $n/2$ **DO OUTPUT** '01' **END**

then the first program has length only $O(1)$, while the second program is still of length $O(1) + n$.

Now fix a universal programming language (say MODULA or Turing machine). Then $K(x \mid y)$ denotes the length of the shortest program (in this fixed programming language) that on input y outputs x in finite time. $K(x \mid y)$ is the *conditional Kolmogorov complexity* of x with respect to y. The (absolute) Kolmogorov complexity of x is $K(x) = K(x \mid \lambda)$.

Returning to our first example above, we obtain $K(\underbrace{01}_{n/2\text{-times}}) \leq \log n + c$ and $K(\underbrace{01}_{n/2\text{-times}} \mid n) \leq c$, where c is a constant independent of n. (The constant c depends on the choice of programming language.)

In many cases, the information y from which x is to be generated will be precisely the length of x, as in our example. This has the following intuitive explanation: a string x contains two kinds of information – its inner irregularity or randomness, and its length. If we reveal the information about the length of x "for free," then we can concentrate solely on the randomness of x. If $n = |x|$, then $K(x \mid n)$ is called the *length-conditioned Kolmogorov complexity* of x.

Exercise 8.1. Show that there are constants c and c' such that for all strings x and y, $0 \leq K(x \mid y) \leq K(x) + c$ and $K(x) \leq |x| + c'$. ◁

Exercise 8.2. Show that there is a constant c such that for all x, $K(x \mid x) \leq c$. ◁

Exercise 8.3. Let π_n be the sequence consisting of the first n binary digits in the representation of the irrational number π. How large is $K(\pi_n \mid n)$? ◁

Since the choice of programming language seems to be arbitrary, one must consider how this choice affects the definition. In any universal programming language one can write an interpreter u (a universal Turing machine) which on input $p'y$ behaves just like program p' (in programming language P') on input y. Let K_P ($K_{P'}$) denote the Kolmogorov complexity with respect to the programming language P (P'). If we assume that p' is the shortest program that generates x from y, then $K_{P'}(x \mid y) = |p'|$. Since $u(p'y) = x$, we get $K_P(x \mid p'y) \leq |u|$, and since $K_P(p') \leq |p'| + c$ (see Exercise 8.1), we get

$$K_P(x \mid y) \leq |p'| + c + |u| = K_{P'}(x \mid y) + c + |u| = K_{P'}(x \mid y) + O(1) .$$

So values of K with respect to two different programming languages differ by at most an *additive* constant. As long as we are willing to ignore constant additive factors, we can consider the definition of Kolmogorov complexity to be robust and speak of *the* Kolmogorov complexity of a string x.

There can't be too many strings of low Kolmogorov complexity. There are at most 2^k programs of length k, so there can be at most 2^k strings with $K(x) = k$. (The same is true of $K(x \mid y) = k$ for any y.) Altogether we see that the 2^n strings of length n are partitioned as follows:

at most 1 string has K-complexity $= 0$,
at most 2 strings have K-complexity $= 1$,
at most 4 strings have K-complexity $= 2$,
⋮
at most 2^{n-1} strings have K-complexity $= n - 1$.

In general, the number of strings with K-complexity $\leq k$ is at most $1 + 2 + \cdots + 2^k = 2^{k+1} - 1$. Considered the other way around this means that

at least 1 string has K-complexity $\geq n$,
more than half of the 2^n strings have K-complexity $\geq n - 1$,
more than 3/4 of the 2^n strings have K-complexity $\geq n - 2$,
more than 7/8 of the 2^n strings have K-complexity $\geq n - 3$,
⋮

Exercise 8.4.° Give a lower bound for the expected value of the K-complexity of a string chosen uniformly at random from among all strings of length n. ◁

Exercise 8.5.° Show that the function $x \mapsto K(x)$ is not computable. ◁

Now we want to define the ***universal probability distribution***, at least on strings of length n. That is, for each length n we define a probability distribution μ so that $\mu(x)$ is the probability of selecting the string x from among the strings of length $n = |x|$. In order for this to be a probability distribution, of course, it must be the case that $\sum_{\{x:|x|=n\}} \mu(x) = 1$. We want to define μ in such a way that $\mu(x)$ is proportional to $2^{-2K(x|n)}$, i.e., for some constant c, $\mu(x) = c \cdot 2^{-2K(x|n)}$. This is possible as long as $\sum_{\{x:|x|=n\}} 2^{-2K(x|n)} = d$ for some constant d, since then we can set $c = 1/d$. So it suffices to show that $\sum_{\{x:|x|=n\}} 2^{-2K(x|n)}$ is bounded above by some constant. (The 2 in the exponent is there to give us convergence.)

Exercise 8.6.◇ Show this. ◁

Many algorithms exhibit different behavior in the worst case than in the average case, at least when average-case is interpreted under the uniform distribution of strings of a given length. A naive implementation of the QuickSort algorithm is an example: in the worst case it requires $\Omega(n^2)$ time, but on average it requires only $O(n \log n)$. Now we want to study the average-case complexity of QuickSort (or any other algorithm) under the probability distribution μ.

An interesting detail in the case of QuickSort is that the worst-case occurs when the input list is sorted in ascending or descending order. Let the numbers to be sorted be $\{1, 2, \ldots, n\}$. $K((1,2,\ldots,n) \mid n) = O(1)$, so under the distribution μ, the probability of a sorted list is especially large, in fact, it is a constant independent of n: $\mu((1,2,\ldots,n)) = c2^{-2K((1,2,\ldots,n)|n)} = c2^{-O(1)} =:$ α. From this it follows that the expected running time for QuickSort under the probability distribution μ is:

$$\sum_{\{x:|x|=n\}} \mu(x) T_{\text{QuickSort}}(x) \geq \mu((1,2,\ldots,n)) T_{\text{QuickSort}}((1,2,\ldots,n))$$

$$= \alpha \cdot \Omega(n^2) = \Omega(n^2) .$$

where $T_A(x)$ denotes the running time of algorithm A on input x and x is a permutation of $\{1, 2, \ldots, n\}$. So under the probability distribution μ, the average running time of QuickSort is as bad as the worst case, namely $\Omega(n^2)$. We shall see that the probability distribution μ exhibits this same malevolent behavior towards all algorithms, namely that the average-case running time is within a constant factor of the worst-case.

In the counting arguments given above to bound the number of strings x with $K(x) \geq n - k$ or $K(x \mid y) \geq n - k$ we focused our attention on strings of only one length n. Now we want to generalize this into the following very useful and generally applicable theorem.

Exercise 8.7.◇ Let M be an arbitrary set of strings and let $m = |M|$. Show that for every number k and every string y, there are at least $m(1 - 2^{-k}) + 1$ strings x in M for which $K(x \mid y) \geq \log m - k$. ◁

Next we want to discuss the properties of a *Kolmogorov random* string x, i.e., a string for which $K(x \mid |x|) \geq |x|$. We expect a random string (in the usual sense of probability theory) to have roughly the same number of zeroes and ones. This is also the case for a Kolmogorov random string:

Exercise 8.8.◇ Explain why a Kolmogorov random string (if it is sufficiently long) cannot consist of $\frac{3}{4}n$ ones and $\frac{1}{4}n$ zeroes.

Hint: How would this situation provide a means of describing the string (algorithmically) with fewer than n bits? ◁

Now let's take another look at the universal probability distribution and our QuickSort example. QuickSort was intended to be understood as a representative for an arbitrary algorithm, in particular, for one where the average-case and worst-case running times differ (under the uniform distribution). The only important property of the sequence $(1, 2, \ldots, n)$ for that argument was that it is an input – in fact, the lexicographically least input – on which the algorithm exhibits its worst-case behavior ($\Omega(n^2)$ in the case of QuickSort).

Now let A be an arbitrary algorithm that halts on all inputs. Consider the following program, which on input n, describes (i.e., outputs) a certain string of length n.

INPUT n;
$w := 0$;
FOR (all y with $|y| = n$, in lexicographical order) **DO**
  $v :=$ (Running time of A on input y)
  IF $v > w$ **THEN** $w := v$; $x := y$ **END**;
END;
OUTPUT x;

This algorithm has a fixed length (independent of the input n but dependent on the algorithm A); let's call it c. For every n, let x_n be the output of A on input n. Then $K(x_n \mid n) \leq c$ and so $\mu(x_n)$ is proportional to $2^{-2K(x_n|n)} \geq 2^{-2c}$. This means that for some constant α, independent of n, $\mu(x_n) \geq \alpha$. Furthermore, by the construction of the algorithm for generating x_n, the running time of A on input x_n is maximal among inputs of length n. That is, A exhibits its worst-case complexity on input x_n.

Exercise 8.9. Now finish the proof that under the universal probability distribution μ on inputs of length n, *every* algorithm that halts on all inputs has an average-case complexity that is (up to constant factors) identical to its worst-case complexity. ◁

References

The idea of Kolmogorov complexity first appeared in the 1960's in papers by Kolmogorov, Solomonoff and Chaitin. A comprehensive overview is given in

- M. Li and P. Vitányi: *An Introduction to Kolmogorov Complexity and Its Applications, 2nd edition*, Springer, 1997.

The use of the universal probability distribution – originally defined by Levin and Solomonoff – to analyze the complexity of algorithms comes from

- M. Li and P. Vitányi: Average-case complexity under the universal distribution equals worst-case complexity, *Information Processing Letters* 42 (1992), 145–149.

∘ M. Li and P.M.B. Vitányi: A theory of learning simple concepts and average case complexity for the universal distribution. *Proceedings of the 30th Symposium on Foundations of Computer Science*, IEEE, 1989.

Further results can be found in

∘ P.B. Miltersen: The complexity of malign ensembles. *SIAM Journal on Computing* 22 (1993), 147–156.

9. Lower Bounds via Kolmogorov Complexity

The concept of Kolmogorov complexity can be used to prove complexity lower bounds. In many cases the proofs obtained in this way are much more "elegant," or at least shorter, than the original proofs. In a few cases, the lower bounds were first achieved by means of Kolmogorov complexity.

The method of using Kolmogorov complexity to establish lower bounds works as follows: Suppose we want to prove a lower bound on the running time of a Turing machine to perform a certain task – or a lower bound on the size of some other mathematical or computational object. Let x be a sufficiently long Kolmogorov random string, i.e., $K(x) \geq |x|$. Now we assume that the lower bound we are seeking is violated, e.g., there is a Turing machine that performs the given task more quickly than the stated bound. Then perhaps there is a way to use this Turing machine – and possibly some additional information – to describe the Kolmogorov random string x with fewer than $n = |x|$ bits. This would, of course, be a contradiction and establish the lower bound.

Our first example of this approach comes from number theory rather than computer science, but the result has implications for computer science as well. We will use Kolmogorov complexity to prove that there are infinitely many prime numbers. In fact, the argument we will give can even be extended to prove a weak form of the Prime Number Theorem.

So suppose that there are only finitely many prime numbers, say $p_1, p_2, \ldots, p_k$. Let n be a sufficiently large number so that the Kolmogorov complexity of the binary representation of n is not compressible, i.e., $K(bin(n)) \geq |bin(n)| = \log n$.[1] Every natural number has a unique prime factorization, i.e., $n = p_1^{n_1} p_2^{n_2} \ldots p_k^{n_k}$. So the numbers $n_1, n_2, \ldots, n_k$ (coded as bit strings) constitute a unique description of n, and thus n – or rather $bin(n)$ – can be reconstructed from the sequence $n_1, n_2, \ldots, n_k$.

---

[1] For simplicity in this example we will do computations assuming that $|bin(n)| = \log n$. The exact value is actually $|bin(n)| = \begin{cases} 1, & n = 0 \\ \lfloor \log_2 n \rfloor + 1, & n > 0 \end{cases}$. But since additive constants do not play a role in this context, this simplification does not change the validity of the argument.

Exercise 9.1. Use the observations just made to determine an upper bound on $K(bin(n))$ that contradicts the choice of n made above and thus completes the proof that there are infinitely many primes. ◁

This argument can be pushed farther. The *Prime Number Theorem* is a famous and hard theorem in number theory which says that $\pi(n)$, the number of prime numbers $\leq n$, is asymptotic to $n/\ln n$, that is

$$\pi(n) \sim \frac{n}{\ln n} .$$

With significantly simpler arguments – using Kolmogorov complexity – we will show that for infinitely many n a lower bound of

$$\pi(n) \geq \frac{n}{\log^2 n}$$

holds. This lower bound is sufficient for many applications.

Let p_m be the mth prime number. It is sufficient to show that for infinitely many m, $p_m \leq m \log^2 m$.

Exercise 9.2. Show that this is indeed sufficient. ◁

Now let n be a sufficiently large natural number such that $K(bin(n)) \geq \log n$. Let p_m be the largest prime number that divides n. The number n can be (algorithmically) reconstructed from m and n/p_m. So a bit string that codes these two numbers is a sufficient description of n.

Exercise 9.3. Give an algorithm that reconstructs n from the numbers m and $k = n/p_m$. ◁

Thus

$$\log(n) \leq K(bin(n)) \leq |\text{encoding of } m \text{ and } n/p_m| .$$

The problem is that we cannot simply write down the binary representations of m and n/p_m one after the other, since then we would not know where one number ended and the other began. We must sacrifice some additional (and in this case very costly) bits to make our encoding such that it can be correctly decoded.

For a string $w = a_1a_2 \ldots a_{n-1}a_n \in \{0,1\}^*$ let $\overline{w} = a_1 0 a_2 0 \ldots a_{n-1} 0 a_n 1$. By means of this encoding of w, the end of the code for w can be recognized by the final '1'. Such a code is called *self-terminating*. More formally, an encoding scheme is self-terminating if it can "recognize its own end" in the following sense: From any string of the form code$(w)v$, where v is arbitrary, it is possible to recover code(w) algorithmically.

We could code the pair of numbers as $\overline{bin(m)}bin(n/p_m)$. But since $|\overline{w}| = 2|w|$, this would cost $2\log m + \log(n/p_m)$ bits. Plugging this into the approximation above would yield: $\log n \leq K(bin(n)) \leq 2\log m + \log n - \log p_m$, so $p_m \leq m^2$, i.e., $\pi(n) \geq \sqrt{n}$. So this method of coding wastes too many bits.

If, however, we let

$$\text{code}(w) = \overline{bin(|w|)}w ,$$

then we get another coding of w that is also self-terminating.

Exercise 9.4. Justify the claim just made. Furthermore, compute the length of code(w) as a function of w. Use this to show that $p_m \le m \log^2 m$. ◁

Exercise 9.5. The improvement from $\overline{w}$ to code(w) can be iterated. What self-terminating code does one get in this way? What improved lower bound for $\pi(n)$ does this yield? ◁

It is interesting to note that any improvement in the length (or, rather, shortness) of self-terminating codes can be translated directly into a sharper bound in our 'Weak Prime Number Theorem.'

Exercise 9.6. Show that if n is a sufficiently large number and its binary representation has high Kolmogorov complexity, (i.e., $K(bin(n)) \ge \log n$), then n cannot be a prime number.

Hint: Use $\pi(n) \sim n/\ln n$. ◁

* * * * *

This Kolmogorov method can also be used in the context of circuit complexity. Consider a boolean function f from $\{0,1\}^n$ to $\{0,1\}$. The circuit complexity of such a function is the smallest number of boolean gates that suffice to build a circuit that has n (binary) input gates and computes the function f. Since a truth table for such a function has 2^n rows, by giving a binary string of length 2^n (the evaluation vector) such a function can be uniquely characterized.

Now we select an especially "difficult" boolean function, f, for which the Kolmogorov complexity of this string is high, i.e., $K \ge 2^n$. What is the circuit complexity of the associated boolean function f? Since a boolean circuit completely characterizes a function (and, in turn, its encoding as a binary string), we have the following inequality for the Kolmogorov complexity of the binary string for f:

$$K \le |\text{the shortest description of the circuit}| + O(1) .$$

How many bits do we need to represent a circuit consisting of g gates? The circuit can be described by listing all its gates. Each gate is described by giving its type (i.e., which boolean operation it computes) and the numbers of the gates (or inputs) that feed into the gate. This requires $c + 2\log(g+n)$ bits for each gate.

Exercise 9.7. Let size(f) be the circuit complexity of f, that is, the smallest number of gates that can be used to compute f. Show that size$(f) = \Omega(2^n/n)$. ◁

Exercise 9.8.$^\diamond$ A formula is a circuit in which every gate has fan-out 1. Show that the smallest formula for f has size $\Omega(2^n/\log n)$.

Hint: A formula can be encoded especially compactly, without the use of any parentheses, in "reverse Polish notation." ◁

* * * * *

Finally, we want to use the Kolmogorov method to prove that any one-tape Turing machine that accepts the language

$$L = \{w0^{|w|}w \mid w \in \{0,1\}^*\}$$

requires at least quadratic ($\Omega(n^2)$) time. From this it follows (or at least is provable with only slight modifications) that the languages

$$\{ww \mid w \in \{0,1\}^*\}$$

and

$$\{ww^R \mid w \in \{0,1\}^*\}$$

also require quadratic time. In the latter, a^R is the reversal of a:

$$(a_1 \dots a_n)^R = a_n \dots a_1 .$$

We use the concept of a crossing sequence. Let M be a Turing machine and let i be some fixed boundary between two adjacent cells on the tape. On a given input x, the crossing sequence for x and i is the sequence of states in which the Turing machine finds itself as its read-write head crosses point i on the tape. We denote this crossing sequence by $CS_M(x,i)$. $CS_M(x,i)$ is an element of Z^*, where Z is the set of states for the Turing machine.

Example.

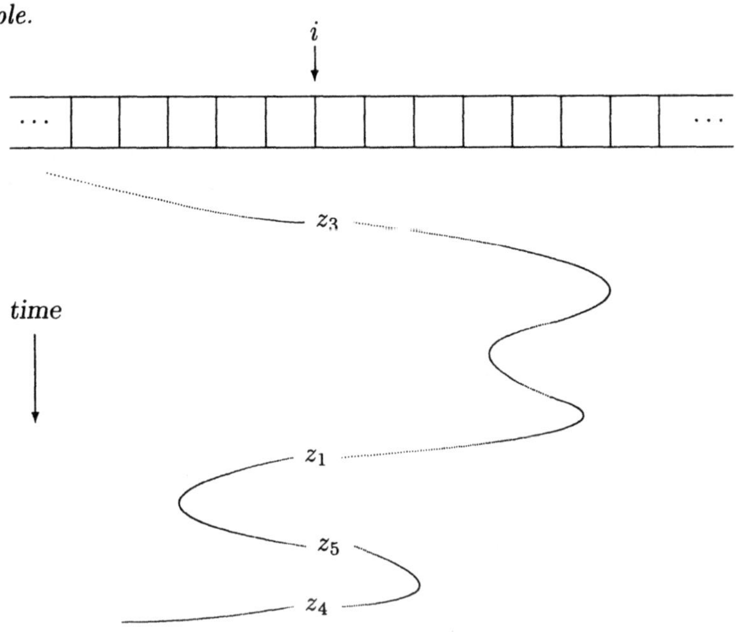

$$CS = z_3 z_1 z_5 z_4$$

Exercise 9.9. Why is

$$\sum_{i=-\infty}^{\infty} |CS_M(x,i)| = time_M(x) \; ?$$

($time_M(x)$ is the running time of M on input x.) ◁

By Exercise 9.9, in order to show that $time_M(x) = \Omega(n^2)$, it is sufficient to show that a number of crossing sequences $CS_M(x,i)$ for x (specifically $\Omega(n)$ of them) each have length at least $\Omega(n)$. We will restrict our attention to the crossing sequences that occur in the middle $n/3$ positions of the input, where n is the total length of the input. This is the portion that on input $w0^{|w|}w$ consists entirely of 0's.

Without loss of generality, we can assume that all of our Turing machines only enter the halting state when their read-write head is on cell 0 of the tape.

Exercise 9.10.° Prove the following lemma:

Let $|x| = i$. If $CS_M(xy,i) = CS_M(xz,i)$, then $xy \in L(M)$ if and only if $xz \in L(M)$. ◁

Exercise 9.11. At what point in the proof of the previous exercise do we make use of the "WLOG" assumption above? ◁

Exercise 9.12.$^\circ$ Prove the following lemma:
If $i = |x| = |x'|$ and $c = CS_M(xy, i) = CS_M(x'y', i)$, then $c = CS_M(xy', i) = CS_M(x'y, i)$. ◁

Now let M be a Turing machine that accepts L. Let $w0^{|w|}w$ be an input for M and let $|w| \le i \le 2|w|$. By the previous lemma we know that for distinct w and w' with $|w| = |w'|$, the crossing sequences $CS_M(w0^{|w|}w\,,\,i)$ and $CS_M(w'0^{|w'|}w'\,,\,i)$ must also be distinct.

Exercise 9.13. Why? ◁

Exercise 9.14. Describe an algorithm that on inputs M, $m \in \mathbb{N}$, $i \in \mathbb{N}$, $m \le i \le 2m$ and crossing sequence c (all coded in binary), outputs the string w of length m for which $CS_M(w0^{|w|}w\,,\,i) = c$. (By the previous observation, w, if it exists, must be unique.) ◁

We conclude, therefore, that the Kolmogorov complexity of w must satisfy $K(w) \le O(\log |w|) + |c|$. If w is chosen to be Kolmogorov random – here's where the Kolmogorov argument comes in – then $K(w) \ge |w|$, so $|c| \ge |w| - O(\log n)$.

Exercise 9.15. Complete the proof that for every one-tape Turing machine M that accepts L, $time_M(x) = \Omega(|x|^2)$. ◁

As an aside, we mention that the argument above actually works not only for a string w that is Kolmogorov random but also for any "typical" string w. The expected value (under the usual uniform distribution) for the Kolmogorov complexity is $E(K(w)) \ge |w| - 2$ (cf. Topic 8). So even in the "average" case, $time_M(x) = \Omega(|x|^2)$.

References

For more on the Prime Number Theorem see a book on number theory, for example,

- I. Niven, H.S. Zuckerman: *An Introduction to the Theory of Numbers*, Wiley, 1960.

The following references contain examples of using Kolmogorov complexity to obtain lower bounds:

- W.J. Paul: Kolmogorov complexity and lower bounds, *Foundations of Computation Theory*, Akademie-Verlag, Berlin, 1979.
- W.J. Paul, J.I. Seiferas, J. Simon: An information-theoretic approach to time bounds for on-line computation, *Journal of Computer and System Sciences* 23 (1981), 108–126.

- M. Li, P. Vitányi: Applications of Kolmogorov complexity in the theory of computation, in A.L. Selman, ed., *Complexity Theory Retrospective*, Springer, 1990, 147–203.
- M. Li, P. Vitányi: *An Introduction to Kolmogorov Complexity and its Applications, 2nd edition*, Springer, 1997.

10. PAC-Learning and Occam's Razor

Many (algorithmic) learning theories have been developed. The one which is now most often considered originated with L. Valiant (1984) and is called PAC-learning. In this chapter we show an interesting connection between PAC-learning and the principal known as "Occam's Razor."

The philosopher and logician Wilhelm von Occam (1285–1349) is credited with the following principle, which is usually referred to as Occam's Razor:

> If there are several hypotheses that each explain an observed phenomenon, then it is most reasonable to assume the simplest of them (i.e., the one most succinctly formulated).

With this "razor," Occam cut out all superfluous, redundant explanations. (This was directed in particular at the scholastics.)

If looked at dynamically, the process of formulating a hypothesis that explains previously made observations is very much like *learning*; upon presentation with additional observations, it may be necessary to revise the previously held hypothesis and replace it with a new one (which explains the new observations as well as the old), and so on. More precisely, we are interested in learning a concept by means of observations or examples which are provided by a *teacher* "at random" along with a statement about whether or not the examples belong to the class that is to be learned.

The process can be understood as the principle of finding a hypothesis in the natural sciences: "Nature" is directed "internally" by a function f which is unknown to humans. Furthermore, examples $x_1, x_2, \ldots$ are generated according to some (equally unknown) probability distribution $\mathbf{P}$. As an outsider, one can only observe the pairs $(x_1, f(x_1)), (x_2, f(x_2)), \ldots$. After a while, one forms a hypothesis h, which explains the observations made *up until time* m, i.e., $h(x_1) = f(x_1), \ldots, h(x_m) = f(x_m)$.

Sketch:

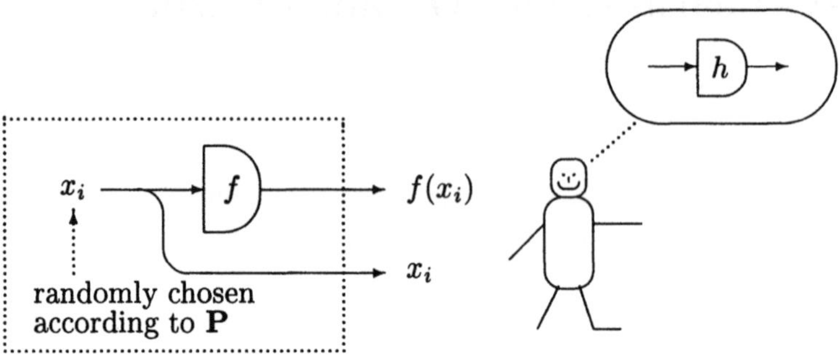

The principle of Occam's Razor suggests that one should choose h to be the simplest possible hypothesis. "Simple" could be understood in the sense of Kolmogorov complexity, i.e., choose h so that $K(h)$ is minimal. A "good" hypothesis h is one that proves to be valuable for future observations as well: $Pr[h(x) = f(x)]$ should be close to 1, where x is chosen randomly according to **P**. The quintessence of the following investigations will be that it is worth looking for a simple hypothesis (in the sense of Occam's Razor) since with high probability such a hypothesis will also be a good hypothesis.

Now we want to formalize these ideas and capture them with a definition. The x_i's will simply be 0-1-strings of a suitable length n. The concept to be learned, f, and the hypotheses h will then be n-place boolean functions.

Definition 10.1 (Valiant). *Let $n > 0$. A* hypothesis space *H_n is a subset of the set of* all *n-place boolean functions. A* concept *to be learned is any function $f \in H_n$. Let **P** be a probability distribution on $\{0,1\}^n$. A* set of examples *is a finite set of pairs $((x_1, f(x_1)), \dots, ((x_m, f(x_m))$, where the x_i's are independently chosen according to the distribution **P**. A* hypothesis *$h \in H_n$ is* consistent *with a set of examples if $h(x_1) = f(x_1), \dots, h(x_m) = f(x_m)$. The function $h \in H_n$ differs from the concept f by at most ε if $Pr[h \triangle f] \le \varepsilon$, where $h \triangle f = \{x \mid h(x) \neq f(x)\}$ and x is chosen randomly according to **P**. An algorithm A that on input of a finite set of examples produces a consistent hypothesis is called a* learning algorithm.

A family of hypothesis spaces $(H_n)_{n>0}$ is called PAC-learnable *if there is a learning algorithm A and a polynomial m – in the arguments n, $1/\varepsilon$, and $1/\delta$ – such that for every $n > 0$, every concept $f \in H_n$, every probability distribution **P** on $\{0,1\}^n$, every $\varepsilon > 0$ and every $\delta > 0$, A on input of an example set with $m(n, 1/\varepsilon, 1/\delta)$ elements (chosen at random according to **P**) produces a hypothesis $h \in H_n$ that with probability $1 - \delta$ differs from h by at most ε.*

The abbreviation PAC stands for "probabilistically approximately correct."

Sketch:

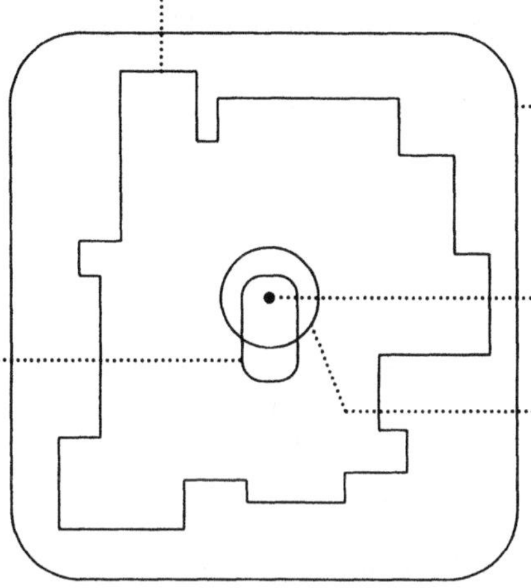

Exercise 10.1. Let A be a learning algorithm that on input of a (sufficiently large) example set with probability $\geq 1 - \delta$ produces a hypothesis h that differs from f, the concept being learned, by at most ε.

If a set of examples and a value $x \in \{0,1\}^n$ are chosen at random (independently and according to $\mathbf{P}$), what is the probability that the hypothesis h produced by A on this example set agrees with the concept being learned, i.e., with what probability is $h(x) = f(x)$? ◁

In the diagram, a small oval represents the set of all hypotheses that are consistent with a fixed example set. Such an example set, consisting of m examples, is chosen at random according to $\mathbf{P}$. The concept f is, of course, always among the consistent hypotheses. We will see that the larger m is, the more likely it is that *all* consistent hypotheses lie in the ε-neighborhood of f, so that in the diagram, the oval is entirely contained in the circle. In this case, *any* learning algorithm has a high probability of producing a hypothesis that differs from f by no more than ε, since by definition, a learning algorithm always produces a consistent hypothesis.

Let's approximate the probability p that after a random choice of an example set of size m there is a consistent hypothesis that is *not* in the ε-neighborhood of f:

$$
\begin{aligned}
p &\leq \sum_{\substack{h \in H_n, \\ Pr[h \triangle f] > \varepsilon}} Pr[h \text{ is consistent}] \\
&\leq \sum_{\substack{h \in H_n, \\ Pr[h \triangle f] > \varepsilon}} (1-\varepsilon)^m
\end{aligned}
$$

$$\leq |H_n| \cdot (1-\varepsilon)^m .$$

Exercise 10.2. Under the assumption that **P** is the uniform distribution on $\{0,1\}^n$, give an upper bound for the number of $h \in H_n$ with $Pr[h \triangle f] \leq \varepsilon$. ◁

If $\delta \leq |H_n| \cdot (1-\varepsilon)^m$, then we are guaranteed that every learning algorithm (on example sets of size m) has probability at least $1-\delta$ of producing a hypothesis that differs from f by at most ε. We can re-express this as a condition on m:

$$\delta \leq |H_n| \cdot (1-\varepsilon)^m$$
$$\Updownarrow$$
$$m \geq \tfrac{1}{-\log(1-\varepsilon)}(\log |H_n| + \log(1/\delta)) \ .$$

To satisfy this inequality, since $\ln(1-x) \leq -x$, it is sufficient to choose m so that

$$m \geq \frac{\ln 2}{\varepsilon}(\log |H_n| + \log(1/\delta)) \ .$$

This term is polynomial in $1/\varepsilon$, $1/\delta$ and $\log |H_n|$. The dominant term is $\log |H_n|$. If H_n is the set of all n-place boolean functions on $\{0,1\}$, then $|H_n| = 2^{2^n}$, so $\log |H_n| = 2^n$. For the polynomial bounds that are required in the definition it is necessary to restrict the set of (relevant) hypotheses.

In cases that occur in practice it is often the case that there are many fewer than 2^{2^n} potential possible hypotheses. Sometimes it is the case that the learning algorithm is guaranteed to produce a hypothesis that is shorter than the typical hypothesis, which has length 2^n, as if it were following Occam's razor. In order to speak of the length of a hypothesis, we must fix some encoding scheme, for example boolean circuits. In "pure form" we can identify the length of the hypothesis with its Kolmogorov complexity.

Definition 10.2. *(Blumer, Ehrenfeucht, Haussler, Warmuth) A learning algorithm is said to be an* Occam algorithm, *if for every $n > 0$ with respect to the hypothesis space H_n, on input of an example set of (sufficiently large) size m, the hypothesis produced by the algorithm always has length $\leq p(n) \cdot m^{1-\alpha}$, where p is a polynomial and $\alpha > 0$.*

This means that we can restrict our hypothesis space to include only hypotheses of length $\leq p(n) \cdot m^{1-\alpha}$, and this set has size $2^{p(n) \cdot m^{1-\alpha}}$. The term $m^{1-\alpha}$ in this expression has an interesting interpretation: an Occam algorithm must perform a certain form of information compression so that the number of examples, m, is sub-linear in the size of the hypothesis space.

Exercise 10.3.° Show that from $|H| \leq 2^{p(n) \cdot m^{1-\alpha}}$, it follows that for PAC-learnability it is sufficient to choose m to be polynomial in n, $1/\varepsilon$, $1/\delta$. ◁

So we have shown

Theorem 10.3. *(Blumer, Ehrenfeucht, Haussler, Warmuth) If for a family $H = \{H_n : n\}$ of hypothesis spaces there is an Occam-algorithm, then H is PAC-learnable.* □

We want to explain this concept using an example from the literature (cf. Valiant). Let $DNF_{n,k}$ denote the set of all formulas in disjunctive normal form in the variables $x_1, \ldots, x_n$, such that all of the monomials consist of at most k literals. That is, a formula f in $DNF_{n,k}$ has the form:

$$f(x_1, \ldots, x_n) = \bigvee_{i=1}^{m} \bigwedge_{j=1}^{k} z_{ij} \quad \text{with} \quad z_{ij} \in \{x_1, \ldots, x_n, \overline{x_1}, \ldots, \overline{x_n}, 1\},$$

where $z_{ij} = 1$ denotes that position j of clause i remains unfilled, so that clause j contains fewer than k literals. In what follows we will identify formulas with the functions they define.

Exercise 10.4. Show that in $DNF_{n,k}$ there are at most $2^{(2n+1)^k}$ different functions. ◁

The number of functions in the hypothesis space $H = DNF_{n,k}$ is drastically less than 2^{2^n}; the function $\log|H|$ is bounded by the polynomial $(2n+1)^k$. By the preceding discussion, to demonstrate the PAC-learnability of $DNF_{n,k}$ it is sufficient to give *any* learning algorithm and to choose the size of the example set to be $m \geq \frac{1}{\varepsilon}((2n+1)^k + \log(1/\delta))$. The only thing that remains, then, is to give an algorithm that for any example set produces a *consistent* hypothesis.

Although the PAC-learnability of $DNF_{n,k}$ is often discussed in the literature in connection with Occam's Razor, this example is really too simple. The hypothesis space is so small that the length of every hypothesis h satisfies $K(h) \leq (2n+1)^k \leq p(n) \cdot m^{1-\alpha}$ with $p(n) = (2n+1)^k$ and $\alpha = 1$. So *every* learning algorithm (i.e., any algorithm as long as it is merely able to produce something consistent with the examples) is an Occam algorithm. The requirement that the hypothesis have length sub-linear in m does not play a role at all.

Here is a simple learning algorithm:

INPUT example set $\{(x_1, f(x_1)), \ldots, (x_m, f(x_m))\}$;
$h :=$ set of all monomials with $\leq k$ literals;
FOR $i := 1$ **TO** m **DO**
    IF $f(x_i) = 0$ **THEN**
        $h := h - \{m \mid m \text{ is a monomial in } h \text{ with } m(x_i) = 1\}$;
    END;
END;
OUTPUT h;

Exercise 10.5. Show that this algorithm always produces a hypothesis that is consistent with the example set. ◁

In this example, it is important that the function f is also in the hypothesis space H_n, even though all of the definitions and theorems and the algorithm are applicable even when $f \notin H_n$. For example, let f be the parity function. The results in Topic 12 will imply that this function cannot be approximated by a low-degree polynomial. So the naive algorithm just given must necessarily produce an inconsistent hypothesis when applied to the parity function.

* * * * *

It should be noted that in the literature, the complexity of the learning algorithm (relative to the size of the input example set) is also an issue and is usually included in the definition. The learning algorithm should run in polynomial time, just as it does in our example. Since the complexity of the learning algorithm is irrelevant for Theorem 10.3, we left this out of our definition.

In a further departure from the literature, we have implicitly assumed that the hypotheses are boolean functions. This seemed to us to be consistent with the usual practice in complexity theory where every finite mathematical object is coded as a 0-1-string.

References

- L.G. Valiant: A theory of the learnable, *Communications of the ACM* 27 (1984), 1134–1142.
- A. Blumer, A. Ehrenfeucht, D. Haussler, M.K. Warmuth: Occam's Razor, *Information Processing Letters* 24 (1987), 377–380.
- A. Blumer, A. Ehrenfeucht, D. Haussler, M.K. Warmuth: Learnability and the Vapnik-Chervonenkis dimension, *Journal of the ACM* 36 (1989), 929–965.
- R. Board, L. Pitt: On the necessity of Occam algorithms, *Proceedings of the 22nd Symposium on Theory of Computing*, ACM, 1990, 54–63.
- D. Angluin: Computational learning theory: survey and selected bibliography, *Proceedings of the 24th Symposium on Theory of Computing*, ACM, 1992, 351–369.
- B. Natarajan: *Machine Learning*, Morgan Kaufmann, 1991.
- M. Anthony, N. Biggs: *Computational Learning Theory*, Cambridge University Press, 1992.
- M. Li, P. Vitányi: *An Introduction to Kolmogorov Complexity and its Applications, 2nd edition*, Springer, 1997.

11. Lower Bounds for the Parity Function

In their pioneering work of 1984, Furst, Saxe and Sipser introduced the method of "random restrictions" to achieve lower bounds for circuits: The parity function cannot be computed by an AND-OR circuit of polynomial size and constant depth.

By the *parity function*, PARITY, we mean the infinite sequence of functions $par_n : \{0,1\}^n \to \{0,1\}$, $n = 1, 2, 3, \ldots$ with

$$par_n(x_1, \ldots, x_n) = \left(\sum_{i=1}^{n} x_i\right) \bmod 2 \,.$$

The question of existence or non-existence of combinatorial circuits for the parity function has been investigated for a long time. This is because many other functions can be expressed in terms of the parity function.

We are interested here in circuits of a specific kind, namely circuits that consist of AND- and OR- gates with *unbounded fan-in* and have inputs labeled with variables x_i or their negations $\overline{x_i}$.

Example.

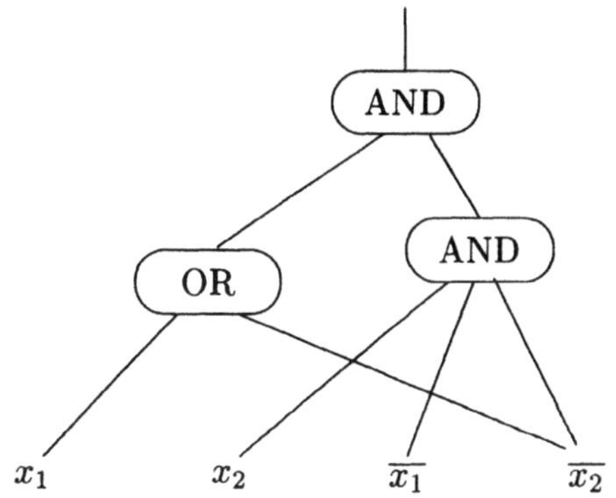

Gates of the same type that follow one directly after the other can be combined into a single gate without changing the function computed by the circuit. For example, the circuit above is equivalent to the following circuit:

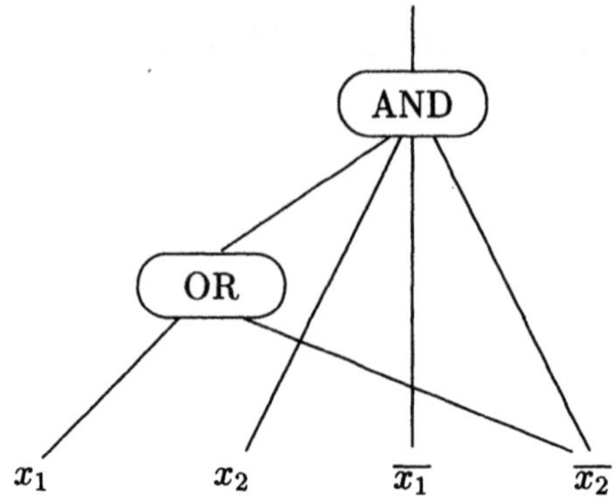

So circuits of this type can be put in a certain normalized (leveled) form by artificially filling in with gates of fan-in 1:

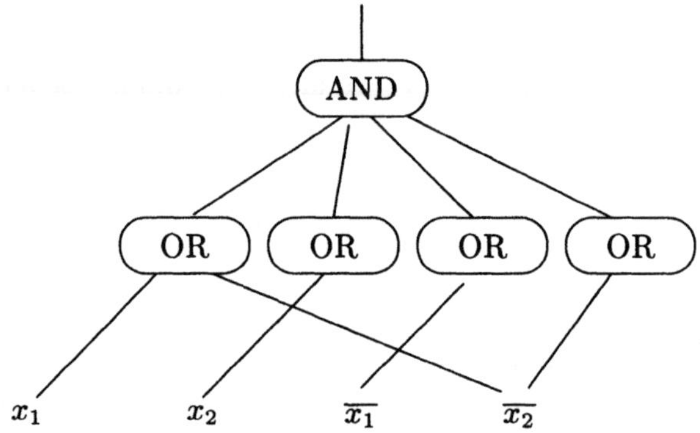

Now we have on the first level only OR-gates, on the second level only AND-gates, and, if necessary, we can continue alternating between levels of OR- and AND-gates.

Exercise 11.1. Why can all boolean functions on n variables be computed by a circuit with only 2 levels (a *depth 2* circuit)? What is the size (number of gates) of such a circuit in general? ◁

The distributive laws for boolean algebra state that

$$x \wedge (y \vee z) = (x \wedge y) \vee (x \wedge z) ,$$

$$x \vee (y \wedge z) = (x \vee y) \wedge (x \vee z) .$$

Exercise 11.2. Use the distributive laws to transform the depth 2 AND-OR circuit above into a depth 2 OR-AND circuit. ◁

Exercise 11.3. Suppose we have a depth 2 AND-OR circuit in which all the OR-gates in the first level have fan-in c and the AND-gate in the second level has fan-in d. After using the distributive laws to transform such a circuit into a depth 2 OR-AND circuit, what is the fan-in of the OR gate? What is the fan-in of the AND-gates? ◁

Note that the condition "fan-in = d" for the AND-gate in the previous exercise can be replaced by the condition that "the number of variables upon which the value of the AND-gate depends is at most d."

Exercise 11.4. Suppose we have a circuit for the complement of parity ($\overline{par_n}$) that has depth t and size g. Show that there is a circuit with t levels and g gates that computes par_n. ◁

Exercise 11.5. Suppose we have a circuit for par_n. Now set some of the x_i's to 0, others to 1, and leave the remaining ones as variables. Any OR-gate that now has an input with value 1 (or any AND-gate with an input with value 0) can be eliminated and replaced with 1 (or 0), etc. Show that the resulting reduced circuit again computes either parity or its complement (on a smaller number of variables). ◁

Now we want to investigate whether PARITY can be computed with circuits of *constant depth* and *polynomial size.* In other words, the question is: Is there a constant t and a polynomial p such that for all n the boolean function par_n can be computed with a depth t circuit that has at most $p(n)$ gates? Note that t is not allowed to grow with increasing values of n but must remain constant.

For $t = 2$, at least, we can show that this is not possible:

Exercise 11.6.◇ Prove that PARITY cannot be computed by polynomial-size, depth-2 OR-AND circuits.

Hint: First show that every AND-gate on level 1 in such a circuit must have exactly n inputs. From this conclude that the circuit must have at least 2^{n-1} AND-gates. ◁

Exercise 11.7. Show that PARITY can be computed by polynomial-size circuits of depth $O(\log n)$.

Hint: As a first step, construct a polynomial-size, $O(\log n)$ depth circuit of XOR-gates. ◁

We denote by AC^k the class of all boolean functions that can be computed by polynomial-size, depth $O((\log n)^k)$ circuits with AND- and OR-gates of unbounded fan-in. Exercise 11.7 shows that PARITY $\in \mathsf{AC}^1$. We want to show that PARITY $\notin \mathsf{AC}^0$. (Note that $O((\log n)^0) = O(1)$). Exercise 11.6 is a first step in that direction, the base case of an induction.

The proof of this is due to Furst, Saxe and Sipser, who made use of (at least in this context) a new technique of "random restrictions," which has since been used repeatedly even in other contexts. The result was later improved from "not polynomial size" to "at least exponential size" by Yao and then by Håstad, whose proof is regarded as the significant breakthrough.

We will discuss here the weaker Furst-Saxe-Sipser version because it is somewhat simpler and provides a good opportunity to work through the technique of random restrictions. For this we will need a bit of probability theory. If we conduct a random experiment in which there are two possible outcomes, success and failure, which occur with probability p and $q = 1 - p$, and if we repeat this experiment n times independently, then the probability of obtaining exactly k successes is just $\binom{n}{k} p^k q^{n-k}$. This is the binomial distribution.

Exercise 11.8. Let X be a random variable that "counts" the number of successes in n trials. Compute (or look up in a book on probability theory) the expected value $E(X)$ and the variance $V(X)$ for this random variable. ◁

Exercise 11.9. Prove Chebyshev's inequality:

$$Pr[\, |X - E(X)| \geq a \,] \leq V(X)/a^2 \; .$$

Hint: Use Markov's inequality. (See Exercise 5.8.) ◁

Exercise 11.10. Suppose $n = 100$ and $p = 0.3$. Use Chebyshev's inequality to give an upper bound for $Pr[X \leq 17]$. ◁

Exercise 11.11. Prove another inequality for the binomial distribution:

$$Pr[X \geq a] \leq p^a \cdot 2^n \; ,$$

where X is as above. (This inequality is only useful when the right side is less than 1.) ◁

* * * * *

In order to show that PARITY cannot be computed by polynomial-size, constant-depth circuits, it is sufficient to prove the following claim:

Claim 1. $\forall t \, \forall c \, \forall$polynomials p PARITY cannot be computed using a depth t circuit of size $p(n)$ that has input fan-in $\leq c$ (i.e., constant fan-in on level 1).

Theorem 11.1. PARITY $\notin$ AC^0.

Exercise 11.12. Why does this theorem follow directly from Claim 1? ◁

Proof (of Claim 1). Claim 1 was proven in Exercise 11.6 for the case $t = 2$. There it was shown that the input fan-in cannot be constant nor can the size of the circuit be polynomial.

Suppose the claim is false. Then there is some $t > 2$ such that parity can be computed by polynomial-size, depth t circuits with constant fan-in on level 1. Let t be the least such. Let k be strictly larger than the degree of the polynomial that bounds the size of the circuits, and let c be the constant that bounds the input fan-in. We will use this to show that there is also a polynomial-size circuit family of depth $t-1$ with constant input fan-in that computes parity. (It is worth noticing that both the degree of the polynomial bounding the size and the constant bounding the input fan-in will increase when we reduce the depth.) This will contradict the minimality of t and establish the claim.

The strategy for producing the new circuits is the following: Let $S_1, S_2, S_3, \ldots$ be the supposed depth t circuit family for PARITY. We will construct S'_n (a new depth $t-1$ circuit in the circuit family $S'_1, S'_2, S'_3, \ldots$ for PARITY) by taking an element of the S-sequence with more than n variables (say S_{4n^2}) and then as in Exercise 11.5 replacing (the appropriate) $4n^2 - n$ of the variables with the constants 0 and 1, leaving a circuit with n input variables. This circuit will be constructed in such a way that we can use the distributive laws (Exercises 11.2 and 11.3) to reverse the order of the AND- and OR-gates on levels 1 and 2 *without increasing the size of the circuit exponentially*, as happens in general (see Exercise 11.3). For this it is sufficient to show that each gate on level 2 depends on only a constant number of input variables. This guarantees that after application of the distributive laws, the new circuits will have constant input fan-in (see Exercise 11.3). After this transformation, the new circuit will have the same type of gates on levels 2 and 3, so these can be collapsed to a single level, leaving a depth $t-1$ circuit. The size of the resulting circuit S'_n will be quadratic in the original size, so the degree of the polynomial that bounds the size doubles.

The word "appropriate" in the preceding paragraph is loaded. Just how are we to find an "appropriate" constant substitution? Here is the new idea: try a random substitution (usually called a *random restriction*). If we can show that the probability of getting an appropriate substitution is positive, then we can conclude that one exists.

We use the following random restriction: For each variable x_i, independent of the others, we perform the following random experiment, which has three possible outcomes:

- with probability $1/\sqrt{n}$ the variable x_i remains,
- with probability $\frac{1-1/\sqrt{n}}{2}$ the variable x_i is set to 0.
- with probability $\frac{1-1/\sqrt{n}}{2}$ the variable x_i is set to 1.

How does one arrive at these probabilities? A boundary condition is that the probabilities for 0 and 1 must be equal so that in the following discussion we will be able to exchange the roles of AND and OR (by symmetry). In addition, it turns out to be useful to set the probability that a variable remains as small as possible. On the other hand, this probability can only be polynomially smaller than n for reasons which we will discuss below.

Let r denote a random restriction and let x_i^r be the result of this restriction on x_i, so $x_i^r \in \{x_i, 0, 1\}$. Let S^r denote the circuit S after applying the random restriction r. By Exercise 11.5 it is clear that S^r is once again a parity function – or the complement of parity – on fewer variables. In any case, by Exercise 11.4 there is a circuit for parity with the same depth and size.

By Exercise 11.8 the expected value of the number of variables in S_n^r is $n \cdot \frac{1}{\sqrt{n}} = \sqrt{n}$. The variance is $n \cdot \frac{1}{\sqrt{n}} \cdot (1 - \frac{1}{\sqrt{n}}) \leq \sqrt{n}$. The number of variables actually remaining must be in inverse polynomial relationship to the original number of variables and not decrease exponentially, otherwise we will not be able to bound the size of the resulting circuit with a polynomial in the number of remaining variables. The following exercise shows that this happens with high probability.

Exercise 11.13. Use Chebyshev's inequality (see Exercises 11.9 and 11.10) to show that $Pr[\text{ there are fewer than } \sqrt{n}/2 \text{ variables in } S_n^r] = O(\frac{1}{\sqrt{n}})$. ◁

This means that with high probability there are at least $\sqrt{n}/2$ variables remaining. In what follows, we are only interested in random restrictions that leave at least that many variables.

Exercise 11.14. At first glance it is not yet clear how to produce a new sequence $S_1', S_2', S_3', \ldots$ *without any gaps.* For every n the random restriction applied to the circuit S_{4n^2} produces a circuit that has on average $2n$ inputs and with high probability at least n inputs. Explain how to convert the results of this process into a sequence $S_1', S_2', S_3', \ldots$ without any gaps. ◁

Next we will give upper bounds for the probabilities that our random restriction has certain undesirable properties. If we succeed in showing, as in Exercise 11.13, that each of these probabilities can be bounded above by a function that approaches 0 as $n \to \infty$, then the probability that a random restriction has any of these (finitely many) properties will (for large enough n) be less than 1. From this it follows that for every large enough n there must exist a restriction that has only desirable properties.

First we show that with high probability the gates on level 2 (after the restriction) depend on only a constant number of inputs. For this argument we can assume that the gates on the first level are OR-gates and thus the gates on the second level are AND-gates. (If the situation is reversed, then by duality we can repeat the argument given below exchanging AND and OR, 0 and 1, and x_i and $\overline{x_i}$.)

For our probability approximations we will take an arbitrary, fixed AND-gate on level 2 and show that the random restriction has an undesirable effect

– in this case, dependence on too many variables – with probability at most $O(\frac{1}{n^k})$. Since altogether there are only $O(n^{k-1})$ gates, it follows that the probability of this undesirable effect occurring at *any* AND-gate on level 2 is at most $O(\frac{1}{n^k} \cdot n^{k-1}) = O(\frac{1}{n})$. So with high probability *all* of the AND-gates on level 2 have the desired property after the random restriction.

Now we use induction to prove the following claim:

Claim 2. For every AND-OR circuit that has input fan-in (at the OR-gates) at most c, there is a constant $e = e_c$ (depending only on c) such that the probability that the AND-gate after a random restriction depends on more than e variables is at most $O(\frac{1}{n^k})$.

Proof (of Claim 2). The proof of Claim 2 is by induction on c. The base case is when $c = 1$. In this case, there are no OR-gates, only the one AND-gate. We distinguish two cases, depending on whether the AND-gate has large or small fan-in.

Case B1. The fan-in of the AND-gate is at least $4k \cdot \ln n$.

In this case it is very likely that there is at least one input to the AND gate that has been set to 0 by the random restriction, in which case the AND-gate does not depend on any of the variables that remain after the random restriction.

Exercise 11.15.$^\diamond$ Show that in this case

$$Pr[\text{AND-Gate is not set to } 0] = O(\tfrac{1}{n^k}) . \qquad \triangleleft$$

Case B2. The fan-in of the AND-gate is less than $4k \cdot \ln n$.

In this case it is very likely that the random restriction sets all but constantly many variables to constants. This is at least plausible, since the expected value $E(X)$ for the number of remaining variables satisfies $E(X) \leq (4k \ln n) \cdot (1/\sqrt{n}) \to 0$ as $n \to \infty$ (see Exercise 11.11).

Exercise 11.16.$^\diamond$ Show that in this case

$$Pr[\text{the AND-Gate depends on more than ... inputs}] = O(\frac{1}{n^k}) .$$

Note that it does not matter what constant is inserted in place of ..., and that this may depend on k.

Hint: Our solution works with the constant $18k$. Use Exercise 11.11. $\triangleleft$

Now we come to the induction step. We assume that e_{c-1} exists and show that e_c exists. Once again there are two cases. The inductive hypothesis only plays a role in the second case.

Case I1. Before the random restriction, the AND-gate on level 2 has at least $d \cdot \ln n$ OR-gates below it with *disjoint input variables*, where $d = k \cdot 4^c$.

In this case we will show that it is very likely that after the random restriction one of the OR-gates will have had all of its inputs set to 0, which causes the AND-gate to also have the value 0. In this case the AND-gate does not depend on any inputs, and the claim is established.

Exercise 11.17.◇ Show that in this case

$$Pr[\text{the AND-Gate is not } = 0] = O(\frac{1}{n^k}) .$$

Hint: Remember that all of the OR-gates on level 1 have, by assumption, at most c inputs. Also, the following relationships might be useful: $a^{\ln b} = b^{\ln a}$ and $\ln(1-x) \le -x$. ◁

Case I2. Before the random restriction, the AND-gate on level 2 has less than $d \cdot \ln n$ OR-gates below it with *disjoint input variables*, where $d = k \cdot 4^c$.

In this case, choose a maximal set of OR-gates with disjoint variables. Let H be the set of variables that occur in these OR-gates.

Exercise 11.18. How large can $|H|$ be? ◁

It is important to note that in each of the OR-gates at least one variable from H occurs.

Exercise 11.19. Why is this the case? ◁

There are $l = 2^{|H|}$ assignments for the variables in H. If we plug any one of these assignments into the original AND-OR circuit, then at least one input to each OR-gate disappears. So after such plugging in, all of the OR-gates have fan-in at most $c-1$. Now we can apply the induction hypothesis. Let $A_1, \ldots, A_l$, be the l circuits that arise in this way (one for each assignment to the variables in H). The probability that the function value of A_j^r (i.e., after the random restriction) depends on more than e_{c-1} variables is bounded above by $O(\frac{1}{n^k})$.

The function f computed by the AND-OR circuit can be completely specified in terms of the A_j's. As an easy example, suppose that $H = \{x_1, x_2\}$, so $l = 4$, then

$$f = (\overline{x_1} \cdot \overline{x_2} \cdot A_1) \vee (\overline{x_1} \cdot x_2 \cdot A_2) \vee (x_1 \cdot \overline{x_2} \cdot A_3) \vee (x_1 \cdot x_2 \cdot A_4) .$$

From this it follows that the probability that f depends on more than $l \cdot e_{c-1}$ variables is bounded above by $l \cdot O(\frac{1}{n^k})$.

Instead of using the AND-OR circuit to determine the dependency of f (after the random restriction) on the input variables, we find it advantageous to work with the equivalent representation in terms of the A_j's just given. With high probability, after the random restriction, H will only consist of constantly many variables, so that the number of remaining terms in our expression for f will also be constant. Let h be the random variable that indicates the number of remaining variables in H after the random restriction. Once again we are dealing with a binomial distribution with $p = 1/\sqrt{n}$, and we can approximate as we did in case 2 of the base case of the induction:

Exercise 11.20.$^\diamond$ Show that $Pr[h > 4cd + 2k] = O(\frac{1}{n^k})$.

Hint: Feel free to use a larger constant if necessary. This size of the constant is not at issue. Use Exercise 11.11. ◁

Thus with high probability, $h \leq 4cd + 2k$, and when this is the case, then our representation of f consists of at most $2^h \leq 2^{4cd+2k} =: m$ terms that are not identically 0. Now we put together all the probability approximations: If we let $e_c = m \cdot e_{c-1}$, then we get

$$\begin{aligned}
&Pr[f \text{ depends on more than } e_c \text{ variables }]\\
&\leq Pr[h > 4cd + 2k]\\
&\quad + m \cdot Pr[\text{a fixed } A_j \text{ depends on more than } e_{c-1} \text{ variables}]\\
&\leq O(\frac{1}{n^k}) + m \cdot O(\frac{1}{n^k})\\
&= O(\frac{1}{n^k})\ .
\end{aligned}$$

This completes the proof of Claim 2. □

Now the proof of Claim 1 is complete as well: There must *exist* a restriction that leaves enough variables; however, each AND-OR circuit on levels 2 and 1 depends on only constantly many of these variables. So with only constant cost, we can apply the distributive laws and get the second level to be an OR-level and the first level an AND-level. But now the adjacent ORs on levels 2 and 3 can be combined, leaving us with a circuit of polynomial size, depth $t - 1$, and constant input fan-in, contrary to our assumption that t is the minimal depth for which this was possible. □

References

- Furst, Saxe, Sipser: Parity, circuits, and the polynomial-time hierarchy, *Mathematical Systems Theory* 17 (1984) 13–27.
- Håstad: Almost optimal lower bounds for small depth circuits, *Proceedings of the 18th Annual Symposium on Theory of Computing*, ACM, 1986, 6–12.

12. The Parity Function Again

The lower bound theory for circuits received an additional boost through algebraic techniques (in combination with probabilistic techniques) that go back to Razborov and Smolensky.

The result of Furst, Saxe, and Sipser that the parity function cannot be computed by AC^0 circuits (AND- and OR-gates, constant depth, unbounded fan-in, and polynomial size) was later proven in a completely different way by A. Razborov and R. Smolensky. Now we want to work through their method of proof and some related results. The technique is algebraic in nature but also uses a probabilistic argument. The argument works as follows:

1. First we show that every function f computed by AC^0 circuits can be approximated by a polynomial p of very low degree. Approximation in this case means that for "almost all" n-tuples $(a_1, \ldots, a_n) \in \{0,1\}^n$, $f(a_1, \ldots, a_n) = p(a_1, \ldots, a_n)$.
2. Then we show that the parity function cannot be approximated in this sense by a polynomial of low degree.

We begin with step 1. Clearly the AND-function

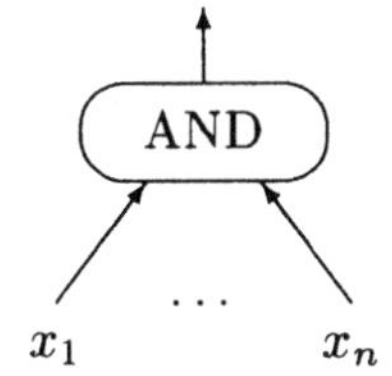

can be represented as the polynomial $x_1 \cdots x_n = \prod_{i=1}^{n} x_i$.

Exercise 12.1. Using $1 - x$ to represent the NOT-function and DeMorgan's laws, give a polynomial representation of the OR-function. ◁

The problem with this is that in general the polynomials have degree n; that is, they contain monomials that mention all of the x_i's. This can be greatly improved by a probabilistic method that goes back to Valiant and Vazirani. We construct a random polynomial as follows: Let $S_0 = \{1, \ldots, n\}$. Furthermore, let $S_{i+1} \subseteq S_i$ be chosen randomly so that each element $j \in S_i$

is in S_{i+1} with probability 1/2. Now consider a sequence $S_0, S_1, \ldots, S_{\log n+2}$ generated as just explained. Let q_i denote the random polynomial $\sum_{j\in S_i} x_j$, which has degree 1.

Now if $\mathrm{OR}(x_1,\ldots,x_n) = 0$, this means that all x_i's have the value 0. Thus all the q_i's are also 0, and, therefore, the polynomial $1-p$, where $p = \prod_{i=0}^{\log n+2}(1-q_i)$, is also 0. This polynomial has degree $O(\log n)$.

If, on the other hand, $\mathrm{OR}(x_1,\ldots,x_n) = 1$, then there is at least one $x_i = 1$. We will show that in this case, the probability is $\geq 1/2$ that one of the polynomials q_i has the value *exactly* 1. So in this case $Pr(1-p=1) \geq 1/2$.

Example.

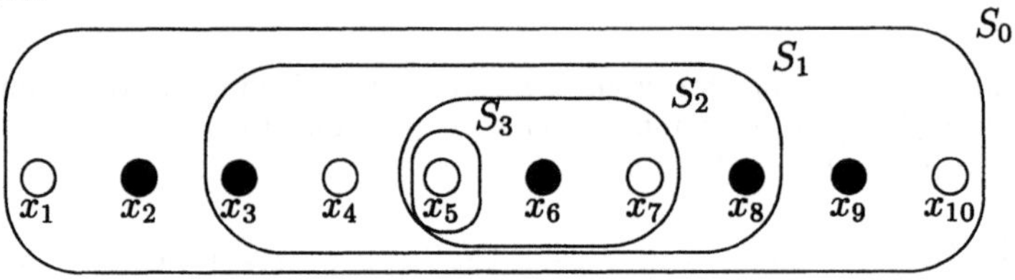

In this example we have 10 variables, 5 of which $(x_2, x_3, x_6, x_8, x_9)$ have the value 1. One possible realization of the random subsets S_i is indicated. Note that in our example, S_3 has *exactly* one variable with the value 1.

So the polynomial $1-p$ approximates the OR-function in a certain sense. The success rate is still not very high, however; it is only 1/2. But this can be significantly improved by using new, independent random numbers to generate additional polynomials p, say $p_1, p_2, \ldots, p_t$, and then using the polynomial $1 - p_1p_2\cdots p_t$ – which has degree $O(t \log n)$ – for our approximation.

Exercise 12.2. What is the error probability of the polynomial $1-p_1p_2\cdots p_t$? How large must t be to get an error probability below a given constant ε? ◁

Exercise 12.3. Construct the corresponding polynomial for the AND-function. ◁

We still need to show that for any choice of a non-empty subset T of S_0 (corresponding to the variables that are true) the probability is at least 1/2 that there is at least one $i \in \{0,1,\ldots,\log n+2\}$ such that the size of $T\cap S_i$ is *exactly* 1. To approximate this probability, we partition the event space into various cases and then compute the probability separately for each case.

Case 1. For all $i \in \{0,1,\ldots,\log n+2\}$, $|T\cap S_i| > 1$.

Exercise 12.4. Give an upper bound for this (for us bad) case. ◁

Case 2. There is an $i \in \{0, 1, \ldots, \log n + 2\}$ with $|T \cap S_i| \leq 1$.

Case 2A. $|T \cap S_0| = |T| = 1$.

Case 2B. $|T \cap S_0| = |T| > 1$ and there is an $i \in \{1, \ldots, \log n + 2\}$ with $|T \cap S_i| \leq 1$.

Under the assumption that we are in case 2B, let i be such that $|T \cap S_{i-1}| > 1$ and $|T \cap S_i| \leq 1$. The probability for $|T \cap S_i| = 1$ under the condition that $|T \cap S_i| \leq 1$ and $|T \cap S_{i-1}| =: t > 1$ is

$$\frac{\binom{t}{1}2^{-t}}{\binom{t}{0}2^{-t} + \binom{t}{1}2^{-t}} = \frac{t}{t+1} \geq \frac{2}{3} .$$

Exercise 12.5. Show that it now follows that

$$Pr(\text{there is an } i \text{ with } |T \cap S_i| = 1) \geq 1/2 . \qquad \lhd$$

Next we want to show how to simulate an AC^0 circuit with size s and depth t using our polynomials so that the error probability is at most ε. For this we use the polynomials above for the gates, but with error probability for each gate $\leq \varepsilon/s$.

Exercise 12.6. What is the degree of the resulting polynomial, as a function of ε, s, and t? (O-notation suffices.) If s is polynomial in n and ε a constant, what sort of function is this? (constant, logarithmic, polylogarithmic, linear, polynomial, exponential, etc.) $\lhd$

* * * * *

In summary, for every boolean function f that can be computed by AC^0 circuits, a polynomial p can be randomly generated that has very small degree and such that for any $(a_1, \ldots, a_n) \in \{0,1\}^n$ the probability is at least $1 - \varepsilon = 0.9$ (for example) that $f(a_1, \ldots, a_n) = p(a_1, \ldots, a_n)$. From this we conclude that there must be at least one choice of a *fixed* polynomial p for which $f(a_1, \ldots, a_n) = p(a_1, \ldots, a_n)$ for all $(a_1, \ldots, a_n) \in S$, where $|S| \geq 0.9 \cdot 2^n$.

Exercise 12.7. Justify the last claim. $\lhd$

Now we want to consider more carefully the possible representations of the boolean values TRUE and FALSE. In the polynomial approximations above we have tacitly identifying TRUE with 1 and FALSE with 0, as is usually done. For what we are about to do, it will be more advantageous to use the so-called Fourier representation which identifies TRUE with -1 and FALSE with 1.

Exercise 12.8. Find a linear function that maps 0 to 1 and 1 to -1. What is its inverse? $\lhd$

If we apply this function to our polynomial p, we get a polynomial $q(y_1, \ldots, y_n) = 1 - 2 \cdot p((1-x_1)/2, \ldots, (1-x_n)/2)$ that for $0.9 \cdot 2^n$ strings in $\{-1,+1\}^n$ correctly simulates f (transformed to use $\{-1,+1\}$) and has the same degree as p.

Suppose now that the parity function is in AC^0. Then there must be such a function q for parity. So for $0.9 \cdot 2^n$ strings in $\{-1,+1\}^n$, $q(y_1, \ldots, y_n) = \prod_{i=1}^n y_i$. That is, after this transformation, the parity function corresponds exactly to *multiplication.*

Exercise 12.9. Why? ◁

Now we prove the following

Lemma 12.1. *There is no polynomial of degree $\sqrt{n}/2$ that correctly represents the function $\prod_{i=1}^n y_i$ for $0.9 \cdot 2^n$ strings in $\{-1,+1\}^n$.*

Corollary 12.2. $\mathsf{PARITY} \notin \mathsf{AC}^0$. □

Proof (of the lemma). Let $q(y_1, \ldots, y_n)$ be a polynomial of degree $\sqrt{n}/2$ that correctly represents the function $\prod_{i=1}^n y_i$ for $0.9 \cdot 2^n$ strings in $\{-1,+1\}^n$. Let $S = \{(y_1, \ldots, y_n) \in \{-1,+1\}^n \mid \prod_{i=1}^n y_i = q(y_1, \ldots, y_n)\}$. So $|S| \geq 0.9 \cdot 2^n$. We can assume that the polynomial q is *multi-linear*, that is, no variable has an exponent larger than 1.

Exercise 12.10. Why? ◁

The vector space $L(S)$ (over $\mathbb{R}$), which consists of all linear combinations of vectors in S, has dimension $|S|$. Similarly, $\mathcal{POL}$, the set of all n-variate multi-linear polynomials of degree $(n+\sqrt{n})/2$, is a vector space with the usual polynomial addition (which does not increase the degree) and multiplication by scalars in $\mathbb{R}$. A basis for this vector space is the set of all monomials $\prod_{i \in T} x_i$ with $|T| \leq (n+\sqrt{n})/2$. Thus the dimension of this vector space is $\sum_{i=0}^{(n+\sqrt{n})/2} \binom{n}{i}$.

Exercise 12.11.° Show that this sum is strictly smaller than $0.9 \cdot 2^n < |S|$. ◁

Now we show that $L(S)$ can be embedded by a linear transformation h (a vector space homomorphism) as a subspace of $\mathcal{POL}$. It is sufficient to show how the basis vectors in $L(S)$ – the elements of S – are mapped by h. Let $s \in S$ and let T be the set of indices in s where a -1 occurs. If $|T| \leq n/2$, then $h(s)$ is the monomial $\prod_{i \in T} y_i$. if $|T| > n/2$, then $h(s)$ is the polynomial $q(y_1, \ldots, y_n) \prod_{i \notin T} y_i$, which has degree at most $(n+\sqrt{n})/2$ and, therefore, is in $\mathcal{POL}$.

Exercise 12.12. Convince yourself that for all $(y_1, \ldots, y_n) \in S$

$$\prod_{i \in T} y_i = q(y_1, \ldots, y_n) \prod_{i \notin T} y_i \,.$$

Therefore, the polynomials $h(s)$ are linearly independent in $\mathcal{POL}$. $\triangleleft$

Since the polynomials $h(s)$ are linearly independent in $\mathcal{POL}$, $\dim(\mathcal{POL}) \geq \dim(L(S))$. This yields the contradiction

$$0.9 \cdot 2^n \leq \dim(L(S)) \leq \dim(\mathcal{POL}) < 0.9 \cdot 2^n$$

and completes the proof of Lemma 12.1. $\square$

Exercise 12.13. Improve the result that PARITY $\notin$ AC^0 to show that any polynomial-size circuit for par_n must have depth at least $\Omega(\frac{\log n}{\log\log n})$. $\triangleleft$

* * * * *

We can use the result that parity is not in AC^0 to show that this is also the case for other boolean functions, for example for *majority*. For this we introduce a notion of reducibility that is tailored to the definition of the class AC^0.

A family of boolean functions $F = (f_1, f_2, f_3, \ldots)$, where $f_n : \{0,1\}^n \to \{0,1\}$, is ***$AC^0$-reducible*** to a family $G = (g_1, g_2, g_3, \ldots)$, if there is a constant d and a polynomial p such that for every n, there are circuits for f_n that have depth at most d and size at most $p(n)$ that may consist of AND-gates and OR-gates (with unbounded fan-in) and also g_i gates (i arbitrary).

It should be clear that if F is AC^0-reducible to G and $G \in \mathsf{AC}^0$, then $F \in \mathsf{AC}^0$ as well.

Exercise 12.14. Why? $\triangleleft$

Examples for such families of functions are

$$\mathsf{PARITY} = (par_1, par_2, par_3, \ldots)$$

and

$$\mathsf{MAJORITY} = (maj_1, maj_2, maj_3, \ldots)\ ,$$

where $maj(x_1, \ldots, x_n) = 1$ if and only if for at least $n/2$ of the inputs x_i we have $x_i = 1$.

Exercise 12.15. Show that PARITY is AC^0-reducible to MAJORITY. $\triangleleft$

From this it follows immediately that

Theorem 12.3. MAJORITY $\notin$ AC^0. $\square$

In fact, we can use this same technique to show that every *symmetric boolean function* is reducible to MAJORITY. A symmetric function is one that is invariant under permutations of the input variables; that is, its value depends only on the *sum* of the input variables, $\sum_{i=1}^n x_i$. Such a function can be completely specified by a value vector of the form $(f_0, f_1, \ldots, f_n)$, where each f_k gives the value of the function when $\sum_{i=1}^n x_i = k$. (So there are only 2^{n+1} distinct symmetric functions of n variables.)

Furthermore, one can show that all symmetric functions are in NC^1 and that majority is not AC^0-reducible to parity. In other words, majority cannot be computed by circuits with constant depth, polynomial size, and unbounded fan-in over $\{\wedge, \vee, \oplus\}$.

The following sketch shows the situation:

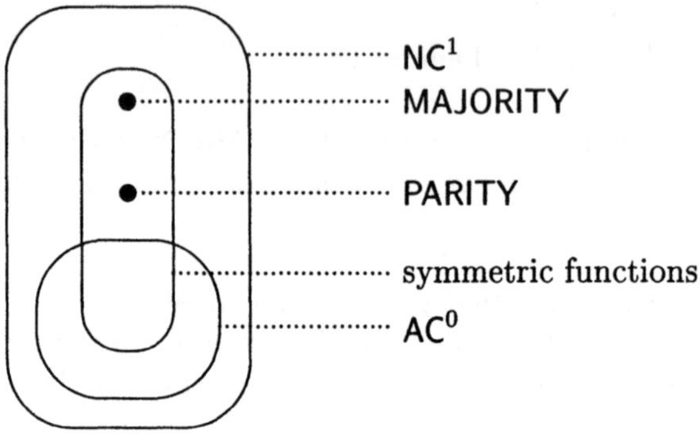

* * * * *

The proof method in which a circuit (in this case a so-called perceptron) is described via a polynomial and the degree of this polynomial is compared with the least possible degree of a polynomial that represents the parity function (in order to show that the proposed circuit cannot compute parity) was first used by Minsky and Papert. By a *perceptron* we mean a depth-2 circuit that has a threshold gate (also called a *McCulloch-Pitts neuron*) for its output gate. This means (for now) that the gates on the first level may compute *any* boolean functions of the inputs. From the binary output values, $a_i \in \{0,1\}$, of these functions a weighted sum is then computed, each input to the threshold gate being assigned the weight $w_i \in \mathbb{R}$. Finally, this weighted sum is compared with a threshold value $t \in \mathbb{R}$. If the sum is at least as large as the threshold, then the perceptron outputs 1, otherwise it outputs 0. That is, the value of the perceptron's output is given by

$$\begin{cases} 1 & \text{if } \sum_i w_i a_i \geq t, \\ 0 & \text{otherwise.} \end{cases}$$

The threshold gate can have an unbounded number of inputs.

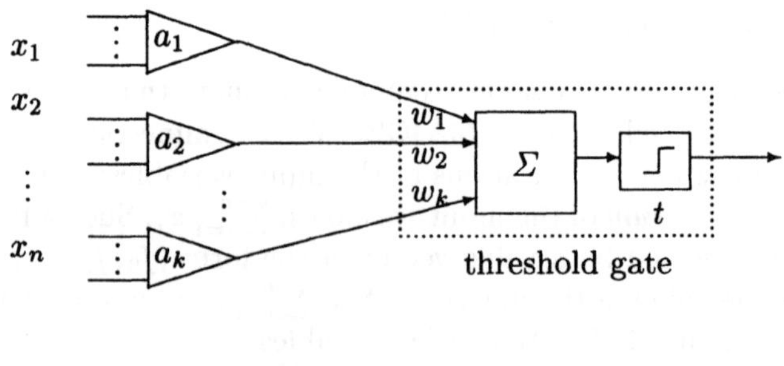

The intended application of such circuits as classifiers in the area of pattern recognition and the biological model of a neuron makes it reasonable to consider the case where the gates on level 1 do not depend on all of the inputs $x_1, \ldots, x_n$ but only on a strict (possibly very small) subset of the inputs. The perceptron is also attractive since one had hoped that by successively varying the weights, such circuits could "learn" any boolean function. Minsky and Papert showed, however, that such circuits are not capable of computing parity on $x_1, \ldots, x_n$. It is this result that we consider next. This result has been credited with bringing to a halt research (or at least funding of research) in the area of neural nets, which in the 60's had just begun to flourish. This lasted for about 20 years, until recently when – despite this negative result – the value of neural nets was again recognized.

Exercise 12.16. Convince yourself that the model just described is equivalent to a model in which all gates on the first level are AND-gates, but in addition to the input variables $x_1, \ldots, x_n$, their negations are also available. The number of inputs to an AND-gate is still required to be less than n.

Sketch:

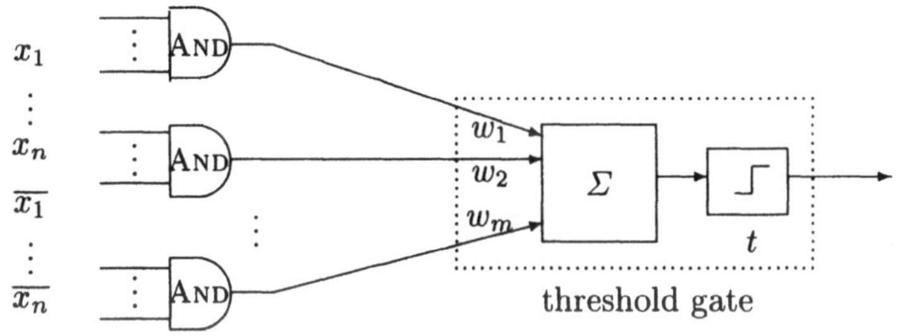

◁

Every AND-gate can be described as a polynomial over $\{0,1\}$, namely the product of terms that are x_i if the variable x_i is an input to the gate and $(1 - x_i)$ if its negation is an input to the gate.

Example. The AND-gate that conjuncts x_1, $\overline{x_2}$, and $\overline{x_3}$ is represented by the polynomial

$$x_1(1 - x_2)(1 - x_3) = x_1 - x_1x_2 - x_1x_3 + x_1x_2x_3 \ .$$

It is clear that on inputs from $\{0,1\}$, this multi-linear polynomial represents precisely the correct value of the AND-gate. Furthermore, the total degree of this polynomial corresponds to the number of inputs to the AND-gate, and must, therefore, be less than n. Let f_i $(i = 1, \ldots, m)$ be the polynomial that represents the ith AND-gate of a perceptron. These polynomials are then added (weighted according to the threshold gate):

$$\sum_{i=1}^{m} w_i f_i \, .$$

This is a multi-linear polynomial in all variables $x_1, \ldots, x_n$, and still has total degree $< n$ (i.e., no monomial in the sum can mention n literals). If such a circuit were capable of computing parity, then there would be some real constant t such that

$$\sum_{i=1}^{m} w_i f_i \geq t \iff \mathit{par}_n(x_1, \ldots, x_n) = 1 \, .$$

In other words, the sign of the polynomial p with

$$p(x_1, \ldots, x_n) = \sum_{i=1}^{m} w_i f_i - t$$

determines the parity of the input bits $x_1, \ldots, x_n$.

The next step makes use of the fact that parity is symmetric. This means that for any permutation π,

$$\mathit{par}_n(x_1, \ldots, x_n) = \mathit{par}_n(\pi(x_1), \ldots, \pi(x_n)) \, .$$

Now we build the polynomial

$$q(x_1, \ldots, x_n) = \sum_{\pi} p(\pi(x_1), \ldots, \pi(x_n)) \, .$$

This is a multi-linear polynomial of total degree $< n$, the sign of which also represents the parity function. The sum is over all permutations π of the n-element set $\{x_1, \ldots, x_n\}$. Furthermore, all monomials that have the same number of variables must occur with the same coefficients.

Exercise 12.17. Justify the last sentence. ◁

So the polynomial q can be written as

$$q(x_1, \ldots, x_n) = \sum_{i=0}^{s} \alpha_i t_i \, ,$$

where $s < n$, $\alpha_0, \ldots, \alpha_s$ are appropriate coefficients, and the terms t_i sum up all monomials with i variables:

$$t_i = \sum_{\substack{S \subseteq \{x_1, \ldots, x_n\} \\ |S| = i}} \prod_{j \in S} x_j \, .$$

By the previous exercise, the polynomial q depends only on $x_1 + \cdots + x_n$, and not on the particular tuple $(x_1, \ldots, x_n)$. Let r be a polynomial in one variable defined by

$$r(x_1 + \cdots + x_n) = q(x_1, \ldots, x_n) .$$

Since t_i is just $\binom{x_1+\cdots+x_n}{i}$,

$$r(k) = \sum_{i=0}^{s} \alpha_i \binom{k}{i} .$$

This is a univariate polynomial of degree $s < n$ with the property that $r(k) > 0$ exactly when k is even (for $k \in \{0, 1, \ldots, n\}$).

Sketch for $n = 4$:

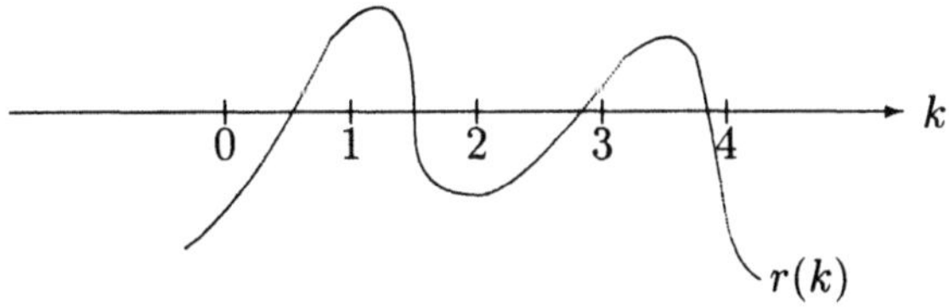

But such a polynomial that has n zeroes must have degree at least n. This is a contradiction, which proves that no perceptron can compute parity. □

References

- Valiant, Vazirani: NP is as easy as detecting unique solutions, *Theoretical Computer Science* 47 (1986), 85–93.
- A. Razborov: Lower bounds on the size of bounded depth networks over a complete basis with logical addition, *Mathematical Notes of the Academy of Sciences of the USSR* 41 (1987), 333–338.
- R. Smolensky: Algebraic methods in the theory of lower bounds for Boolean circuit complexity, *Proceedings of the 19th Annual Symposium on Theory of Computing*, ACM, 1979, 77–82.
- N. Alon, J.H. Spencer: *The Probabilistic Method*, Wiley, 1992, Chapter 11.
- R. Beigel: The polynomial method in circuit complexity, *Structure in Complexity Theory Conference*, IEEE, 1993.
- M.L. Minsky, S.A. Papert: *Perceptrons*, MIT Press, 1969.
- J. Aspnes, R. Beigel, M. Furst, S. Rudich: The expressive power of voting polynomials, *Combinatorica* 14 (1994) 135–148.

13. The Complexity of Craig Interpolants

> The Craig Interpolation Theorem (1957) was placed in the context of the $\mathsf{P} \stackrel{?}{=} \mathsf{NP}$ and $\mathsf{NP} \stackrel{?}{=} \mathsf{coNP}$ questions in a paper by Mundici (1984).

The *Craig Interpolation Theorem* of propositional logic states that for any two formulas F and G in propositional logic such that $F \to G$ there is a formula H which uses only variables occurring in both formulas such that $F \to H$ and $H \to G$. The formula H is called an interpolant of F and G.

Exercise 13.1.$^\diamond$ Prove the Craig Interpolation Theorem. ◁

If the formulas F and G have length n, then the question arises: How long must H be? It turns out that the answer is influenced by how the formulas are represented and that the method of encoding can have a decided impact on the result. Branching programs and boolean circuits are two length efficient representations of boolean functions as formulas.

For a given boolean function F, let size(F) be the size (number of gates) of the smallest circuit (over $\neg, \wedge, \vee$) that computes F. For formulas F and G of length n let H be an interpolant of minimal circuit size. So size(H) is the *interpolant complexity* of F and G, which we denote by $\text{int}(F, G)$. For every n let $\delta(n)$ be defined as

$$\delta(n) = \max\{\text{int}(F, G) \mid |F| = |G| = n\} \; .$$

Not much is known about the growth rate of $\delta(n)$. From the fact that formulas of length n can have (almost) n variables (more exactly $O(n/\log n)$ variables) and the proof of the previous exercise, we get an upper bound for $\delta(n)$ of $O(2^n)$.

Exercise 13.2. Why can't a formula of (coding-) length n contain more than $O(n/\log n)$ many variables? ◁

The interesting (open) question is whether perhaps $\delta(n)$ has only a polynomial rate of growth. A positive answer would have an interesting consequence for the class $\mathsf{NP} \cap \mathsf{coNP}$:

Theorem 13.1. *If $\delta(n)$ is polynomially bounded, then all languages in* $\mathsf{NP} \cap \mathsf{coNP}$ *have polynomial-size circuits.*

For more on polynomial circuit complexity see Topics 9, 16, and 17.

At first glance, this result seems very surprising. How does the proof work? Recall the proof of Cook's Theorem (that *SAT* is NP-complete, see the book by Garey and Johnson for a proof). The proof contains a construction that given any language $A \in \mathsf{NP}$ and $n \in \mathbb{N}$ produces in polynomial time a boolean formula $F_n(x_1, \ldots, x_n, y_1, \ldots, y_{p(n)})$ (where p is a polynomial), which we will call $F_n(x, y)$, so that for all $x \in \{0,1\}^n$,

$$x \in A \iff \exists y \, F_n(x, y) = 1 \, .$$

Now let $A \in \mathsf{NP} \cap \mathsf{coNP}$. Then for every n there is a Cook formula $F_n(x, y)$ for $A \in \mathsf{NP}$ and a corresponding formula $G_n(x, z)$ for $\overline{A} \in \mathsf{NP}$. Note that y and z are distinct variables, but that the x-variables are common to both formulas.

Exercise 13.3. Show that $F_n \to \neg G_n$. ◁

By the Craig Interpolation Theorem there must be an interpolant H_n so that $F_n \to H_n$ and $H_n \to \neg G_n$. Let C_n be the smallest circuit that computes the boolean function H_n. If $\delta(n)$ is polynomially bounded, then for some polynomial q and all n, $|C_n| \leq q(n)$.

Exercise 13.4. Show that C_n is a circuit for the characteristic function of A on strings of length n. Since the size of C_n is polynomial in n, this implies that all languages in $\mathsf{NP} \cap \mathsf{coNP}$ have polynomial-size circuits. ◁

Now one can ask if the proof can be modified to better reveal its "quintessence." In particular, we want to generalize the right side of the implication as much as possible while maintaining the truth of the statement. By inspecting the proof carefully, we arrive at the following formulation:

Theorem 13.2. *If the function $\delta(n)$ is polynomially bounded then any disjoint pair of* NP *languages A_1 and A_2 is* PC*-separable. (This means that there is a language C with polynomial-size circuits such that $A_1 \subseteq C$ and $C \subseteq \overline{A_2}$).*

Exercise 13.5. Why is Theorem 13.1 a (simple) corollary to Theorem 13.2? ◁

Exercise 13.6. Prove Theorem 13.2. ◁

Exercise 13.7. Show that at least one of the following statements is true:

1. $\mathsf{P} = \mathsf{NP}$,
2. $\mathsf{NP} \neq \mathsf{coNP}$,

3. An interpolant of F and G with $F \to G$ is *not*, in general, computable in time polynomial in $|F| + |G|$. $\lhd$

Exercise 13.8.$^\diamond$ Show that the hypothesis that every NP language has polynomial-size circuits (cf. Topic 16) implies that $\delta(n)$ is polynomially bounded. $\lhd$

So if one could show that $\delta(n)$ is not polynomially bounded, one would have shown that P $\neq$ NP!

References

A proof of Cook's Theorem can be found in many books, including

- M. Garey, D. Johnson: *Computers and Intractability – A Guide to the Theory of NP-Completeness*, Freeman, 1979.

The Craig Interpolation Theorem is from

- W. Craig: Three uses of the Herbrand-Gentzen theorem in relating model theory and proof theory, *Journal of Symbolic Logic* 44 (1957) 36–50.

Further results about interpolants can be found in

- E. Dahlhaus, A. Israeli, J.A. Makowsky: On the existence of polynomial time algorithms for interpolation problems in propositional logic, *Notre Dame Journal on Formal Logic* 29 (1988), 497–509.
- Y. Gurevich: Toward logic tailored for computational complexity, in M.M. Richter et al, *Computation and Proof Theory*, Lecture Notes in Mathematics 1104, Springer, 1984, 175–216.
- D. Mundici: Tautologies with a unique Craig interpolant, uniform vs. nonuniform complexity, *Annals of Pure and Applied Logic* 27 (1984), 265–273.
- D. Mundici: NP and Craig's interpolation theorem, in G. Lolli, G. Longo, A. Marja, ed., *Logic Colloquium 82* North-Holland, 1984.

From the assumption that $\delta(n)$ is polynomially bounded, it also follows that the class UP has polynomial-size circuits. (UP is the class of all NP languages A for which if $x \in A$, there is exactly one witness for this; cf. the definition of FewP in Topic 19.)

- U. Schöning, J. Torán: unpublished manuscript.

Exercise 13.8 was communicated by J. Torán.

14. Equivalence Problems and Lower Bounds for Branching Programs

Branching programs are a computational model for boolean functions which, in comparison to circuits, have a somewhat restricted "expressibility." For a certain (further restricted) model of branching programs, the equivalence problem is solvable in probabilistic polynomial time. For this model, explicit exponential lower bounds have also been proven.

An interesting algorithmic problem is to determine whether two differently constructed circuits are equivalent. Do these circuits compute the same function even though they are wired differently? In this case, we could replace the more complicated of the two circuits with the simpler one.

It would be ideal, of course, if this problem could be solved efficiently (say in polynomial time) on a computer. But it is well-known that the satisfiability problem (for boolean formulas or for circuits) is NP-complete, and there is no known algorithm for any NP-complete language that runs in polynomial time. Testing two circuits for equivalence is similarly hard, since the *in*equivalence problem is NP-complete. The naive method of trying out all possible assignments to the variables requires exponential time. But is there some alternative method that is cleverer and faster?

In order to investigate this question, we will leave the world of circuits and consider a new representation of boolean functions, namely branching programs (also called binary decision trees, or BDDs).

Definition 14.1 (Branching Program). *A* branching program *B with boolean variables $x_1, x_2, \ldots, x_n$ is a directed, acyclic graph $G = (V, E)$ with the following types of nodes:*

- computation nodes: *Every computation node b has exactly two out-going edges k_0 and k_1, where k_0 is labeled with "$\overline{x_i}$" and k_1 with "x_i" (for some $i \in \{1, \ldots, n\}$).*
- terminal nodes: *Nodes with out-degree 0 are called terminal nodes. Terminal nodes are divided into two categories:* accepting *and* rejecting.

There is one distinguished computation node with in-degree 0 which is called the start node *and denoted v_{start}.*

Given an assignment $x_1, \ldots, x_n \in \{0, 1\}$, the graph of B is traversed starting with the start node until a terminal node is reached. During this *traversal, edges may only be used if their labels agree with the assignment to the corresponding variable. If the computation ends in an accepting terminal node, then* $B(x_1,\ldots,x_n) = 1$*, otherwise* $B(x_1,\ldots,x_n) = 0$.

We say that a branching program B computes *the n-place boolean function f, if for all* $x_1,\ldots,x_n \in \{0,1\}$

$$B(x_1,\ldots,x_n) = f(x_1,\ldots,x_n)\ .$$

A branching program B is one-time-only *if in every path from the start node to a terminal node, each variable occurs at most once.*

Two branching programs B and B′ are equivalent *if for all assignments* $x_1,\ldots,x_n$,

$$B(x_1,\ldots,x_n) = B'(x_1,\ldots,x_n)\ .$$

Exercise 14.1. Show that for every boolean function f that is computable by a branching program of size s, there is a circuit of size $O(s)$ that computes f. ◁

The problem of determining whether two differently constructed circuits compute the same boolean function can now be translated to the world of branching programs. We define the language *BP-INEQ* as follows:

$$\textit{BP-INEQ} = \{\langle B, B'\rangle \mid B \text{ and } B' \text{ are not equivalent branching programs}\}\ .$$

Unfortunately, *BP-INEQ* is NP-complete. This greatly decreases our chances of finding an efficient algorithm for *BP-INEQ*. If we were to succeed, we would have shown that P = NP.

Exercise 14.2.° Show that *BP-INEQ* is NP-complete.

Hint: Reduce the satisfiability problem *SAT* to *BP-INEQ*. ◁

One special subproblem of *BP-INEQ* is *BP1-INEQ*, in which pairs of one-time-only branching programs are compared:

$$\textit{BP1-INEQ} = \{\langle B, B'\rangle \mid B \text{ and } B' \text{ are not equivalent one-time-only branching programs}\}\ .$$

Testing two one-time-only branching programs for equivalence appears to be simpler; we will show that *BP1-INEQ* ∈ RP. (For more on the class RP see Topic 17.) So *BP1-INEQ* is contained in a class that is "below" NP. This means that one-time-only branching programs must have a simpler structure than is generally the case. (One should check that in the proof of the NP-completeness of *BP-INEQ*, it is significant that no one-time-only branching programs are constructed.)

The basic idea of the proof that *BP1-INEQ* ∈ RP is to guess the assignment to the n variables. The values assigned to the variables, however, are not chosen from $\{0,1\}$; rather they are chosen from the larger set $\{1,\ldots,2n\}$.

Since branching programs are only set up to handle boolean functions, we need a procedure for turning a branching program into a function (preferably a polynomial) that can take n-tuples of integers as inputs. Of course, the actual information, the boolean function that the branching program is supposed to be computing, should not be lost in this process.

So the goal is to associate with any branching program B a polynomial p_B, such that for all $x_1, \ldots, x_n \in \{0,1\}$ we have $B(x_1, \ldots, x_n) = p_B(x_1, \ldots, x_n)$. To this end we construct for every node of B a polynomial that is built from the polynomials of its predecessors:

1. For the start node v_{start}, $p_{v_{\text{start}}} = 1$.
2. For a node v with predecessors $v_1, \ldots, v_l$,

$$p_v = \sum_{i=1}^{l} \alpha_i \cdot p_{v_i}, \text{ where } \alpha_i = \begin{cases} x_j & \text{if } (v_i, v) \text{ is labeled, with } x_j \\ 1 - x_j & \text{otherwise.} \end{cases}$$

3. Finally, the polynomial p_B is the sum of the polynomials for the accepting terminal nodes:

$$p_B = \sum_v p_v ,$$

where the sum is over accepting nodes v.

Exercise 14.3.◇ Let B be the following branching program:

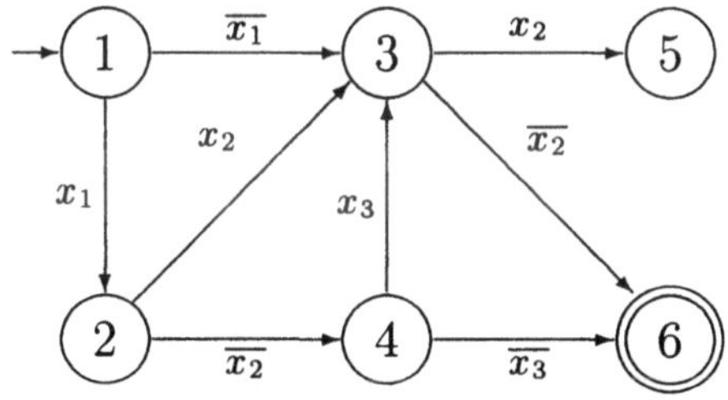

Construct the polynomial p_B and check if $p_B(x_1, x_2, x_3) = B(x_1, x_2, x_3)$ for all $x_1, x_2, x_3 \in \{0,1\}$. (Use a truth table.)

Now show that the polynomial constructed in this way from *any* branching program has the same value as the underlying branching program for any assignment $x_1, \ldots, x_n \in \{0,1\}$

Hint: Prove the following claim (by induction on m):

Let $x_1, \ldots, x_n \in \{0,1\}$ and let V_m be the set of all nodes in B that are reachable from v_{start} in exactly m steps. Then for all $v \in V_m$,

$$p_v(x_1, \ldots, x_n) = \begin{cases} 1 & v \text{ is reachable on the } m\text{th step of } B(x_1, \ldots, x_n), \\ 0 & \text{otherwise.} \end{cases}$$

◁

When we speak of the polynomial of a branching program, we will always assume that it has been constructed by the procedure described above. Note that it is easy to efficiently evaluate such a polynomial p_B on a particular input $(x_1, \ldots, x_n)$. In contrast, it is much more difficult to multiply out such a polynomial symbolically to compute its coefficients.

By the previous exercise, two branching programs B and B' are equivalent if and only if for all $x_1, \ldots, x_n \in \{0,1\}$, $p_B(x_1, \ldots, x_n) = p_{B'_n}(x_1, \ldots, x_n)$.

Exercise 14.4. Show that it is not possible (in the case of general branching programs) to conclude from this that for all $x_1, \ldots, x_n \in \mathbb{N}$, $p_B(x_1, \ldots, x_n) = p_{B'_n}(x_1, \ldots, x_n)$. ◁

* * * * *

Now comes the question, how many points must be tested for equality in order to know whether two such polynomials are identical? How many (distinct) support points of a polynomial with n variables and degree ≤ 1 (a *multi-linear polynomial*) determine the polynomial uniquely.

We are aided here by the following theorem:

Theorem 14.2. *If p and q are different multi-linear polynomials in n variables, and $S \subseteq \mathbb{R}$ is an arbitrary finite set with $|S| > 1$, then there are at least $(|S| - 1)^n$ points $(x_1, \ldots, x_n) \in S^n$ for which $p(x_1, \ldots, x_n) \neq q(x_1, \ldots, x_n)$.*

Exercise 14.5.° Prove Theorem 14.2 by induction on n. ◁

Corollary 14.3. *If the n-variate, multi-linear polynomials p and q agree on the 2^n points $(0,0,\ldots,0,0)$, $(0,0,\ldots,0,1)$, $\ldots$,$(1,1,\ldots,1,1)$, then p and q are identical.*

Exercise 14.6. Why is this a consequence of Theorem 14.2 ◁

So if B and B' are equivalent one-time-only branching programs, then the polynomials p_B and $p_{B'}$ are identical.

Exercise 14.7. Why? ◁

We have now gathered the necessary tools to show that *BP1-INEQ* is contained in the class RP.

Theorem 14.4. *BP1-INEQ* $\in$ RP.

Proof. Let B and B' be one-time-only branching programs with associated multi-linear polynomials p_B and $p_{B'}$. A probabilistic Turing-machine M for *BP1-INEQ* functions as follows:

1. For every variable x_i, $1 \leq i \leq n$, a value from $S = \{1, \ldots, 2n\}$ is chosen at random under the uniform distribution.
2. If $p_B(x_1, \ldots, x_n) \neq p_{B'}(x_1, \ldots, x_n)$, then M accepts, otherwise the input is rejected.

If $\langle B, B'\rangle \notin$ *BP1-INEQ*, then B and B' are equivalent. In this case $Pr[M(\langle B, B'\rangle)$ accepts$] = 0$

Exercise 14.8. Why? ◁

On the other hand, if $\langle B, B'\rangle \in$ *BP1-INEQ*, then for at least half of the assignments to $x_1, \ldots, x_n$,

$$B(x_1, \ldots, x_n) \neq B'(x_1, \ldots, x_n) .$$

Exercise 14.9.° Prove this.

Hint: Use Theorem 14.2. ◁

This concludes the proof that *BP1-INEQ* $\in$ RP. □

* * * * *

Next we want to compare the complexity of various statements regarding branching programs. The equivalence problem for general branching programs is coNP-complete, as we have argued above. In contrast, the corresponding equivalence problem for one-time-only branching programs is in coRP, since *BP1-INEQ* $\in$ RP.

A related, but potentially more difficult problem for a class of (branching) programs is the *inclusion problem*: given two branching programs, decide if the boolean functions f_1 and f_2 they represent satisfy $f_1(x_1, \ldots, x_n) \leq f_2(x_1, \ldots, x_n)$ (equivalently: $f_1(x_1, \ldots, x_n) \Rightarrow f_2(x_1, \ldots, x_n)$).

If the inclusion problem can be solved efficiently, then so can the equivalence problem. Thus the inclusion problem is harder: if the equivalence problem does not have an efficient solution, then the inclusion problem does not either. This follows from the fact that $f_1 = f_2$ if and only if $f_1 \Rightarrow f_2$ and $f_2 \Rightarrow f_1$.

For general branching programs, the inclusion problems remains coNP-complete. This follows from the NP-completeness proof for the inequivalence problem given above.

There are, however, situations in which there is a difference between the complexity of the inclusion problem and the complexity of the equivalence problem for a class. For example, the inclusion problem for deterministic context-free languages is undecidable. The status of the equivalence problem for deterministic context-free languages is an open question and may even be decidable.

We showed above that the equivalence problem for one-time-only branching problems is in coRP. The inclusion problem, on the other hand, is coNP-complete:

Theorem 14.5. *The inclusion problem for one-time-only branching problems is* coNP*-complete.*

Exercise 14.10.° Prove Theorem 14.5. ◁

* * * * *

Finally, we want to give an exponential lower bound for one-time-only branching programs with respect to an explicitly given boolean function. Note that it is not the exponential lower bound itself that is of interest – this follows, for example, from Exercise 9.7 – rather it is the explicit presentation of such a function.

Let n be a prime number. Then the algebraic structure

$$\mathrm{GF}(n) = (\{0, \ldots, n-1\}, *_{\text{mod } n}, +_{\text{mod } n})$$

is a finite field. Let $\mathcal{POL}$ be the set of all polynomials in one variable over $\mathrm{GF}(n)$ with degree $< n/3$. There are exactly $n^{\lceil n/3 \rceil}$ polynomials in $\mathcal{POL}$. By the Interpolation Theorem, since $\mathrm{GF}(n)$ is a field, specifying $\lceil n/3 \rceil$ zeroes uniquely determines the polynomial.

Now we define our explicit boolean function $f : \{0,1\}^{n^2} \longrightarrow \{0,1\}$. The graph of every polynomial on $\mathrm{GF}(n)$ can be represented by an argument tuple $x = (x_{0,0}, \ldots, x_{n-1,n-1})$ in the following way: $x_{i,j} = 1$ if and only if $p(i) = j$.

Example. Let $n = 7$. The first square below represents the polynomial $p(x) = x + 3$; the second represents the function $p(x) = 2x^2 + 3x - 1$. (A black circle represents the boolean value 1.)

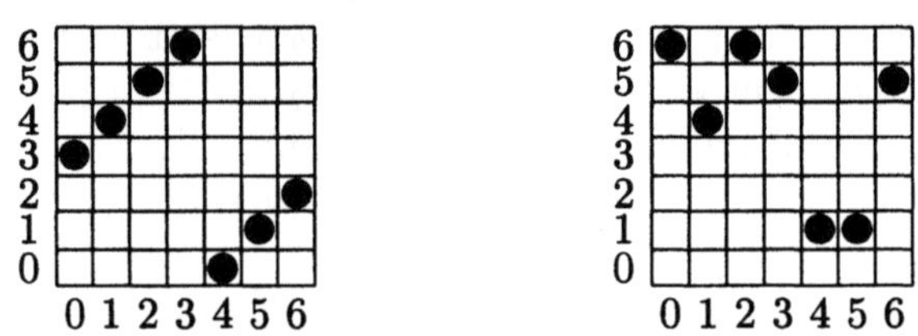

Of course, some tuples x do not represent any polynomial. Our boolean function $f : \{0,1\}^{n^2} \to \{0,1\}$ is defined by

$$f(X) = 1 \iff X \text{ represents a polynomial in } \mathcal{POL}\,.$$

Suppose that B is a one-time-only branching program that computes f. Along every path from the start node to a terminal node, each variable is queried at most once.

Exercise 14.11. Show that along every path from the start node to an accepting node, every variable is also queried *at least* once. ◁

Every boolean vector x induces a path through the branching program. We will call this path the x-path. Let x be given with $f(x) = 1$. So x represents a polynomial in $\mathcal{POL}$. Along the x-path there must be exactly n variables for which the query is answered 1, since there are exactly n 1's in

x. Let $k(x)$ be the node where on the x-path where for the $(n/2)$th time the query is answered with a 1.

The following picture sketches the branching program with the x-path, the node $k(x)$, and other nodes of the form $k(x')$ indicated.

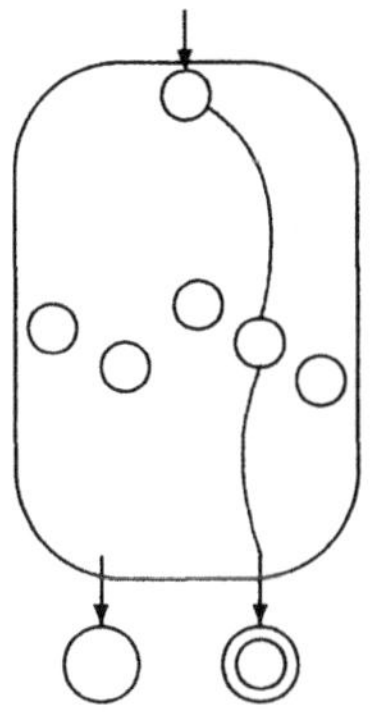

Exercise 14.12.° Show that for distinct x and x' with $f(x) = f(x') = 1$, $k(x) \neq k(x')$.

Hint: Use the Interpolation Theorem for polynomials and a "cut-and-paste" argument to construct a new path $\hat{x}$ from x and x'. ◁

From this it follows that in B there are $n^{n/3}$ distinct nodes of the form $k(X)$ with $f(X) = 1$, since there are that many polynomials in $\mathcal{POL}$. So $n^{n/3} = 2^{\Omega(n)}$ is a lower bound for the size of a one-time-only branching program that computes f. Since the number of input values is $m = n^2$, this bound, expressed in terms of m is $2^{\Omega(m^{1/2})}$.

References

For the proof that *BP1-INEQ* $\in$ RP see

- M. Blum, A. Chandra, M. Wegman: Equivalence of free boolean graphs can be decided probabilistically in polynomial time, *Information Processing Letters* 10, No. 2 (1980), 80–82.
- D. Kozen: *The Design and Analysis of Algorithms*, Springer, 1992, Lecture 40.

For the coNP-completeness of the inclusion problem for one-time-only branching programs see

- S. Fortune, J. Hopcroft, E.M. Schmidt: The complexity of equivalence and containment for free single variable program schemes, *Proceedings of the Symposium on Mathematical Foundations of Computer Science*, Lecture Notes in Computer Science 62, Springer, 1978, 227–240.

- J. Gergov, C. Meinel: On the complexity of analysis and manipulation of Boolean functions in terms of decision graphs, *Information Processing Letters* 50 (1994) 317–322.

The proof of the exponential lower bound given here is new. The "cut-and-paste" technique was used in

- S. Žák: An exponential lower bound for one-time-only branching programs, *Symposium on Mathematical Foundations of Computer Science*, Lecture Notes in Computer Science 176, Springer, 1984, 562–566.
- M. Krause, C. Meinel, S. Waack: Separating the eraser Turing machine classes L_e, NL_e, co-NL_e and P_e, *Theoretical Computer Science* 86 (1991), 267–275.

The definition of our boolean function, is patterned after a function in

- N. Nisan, A. Wigderson: Hardness versus randomness, *Journal of Computer and System Sciences* 49 (1994), no. 2, 149–167.

15. The Berman-Hartmanis Conjecture and Sparse Sets

If all NP-complete languages were P-isomorphic to each other, then it would follow that P $\neq$ NP. This "Isomorphism Conjecture" has been the starting point of much research, in particular into sparse sets and their potential to be NP-complete.

In computability theory it is well known that all complete problems for the class of computably enumerable sets (under many-one reductions) are actually computably isomorphic to each other. This means that between any two such problems, there is a computable bijection that provides the reduction.

Led by the idea that the classes P and NP are "polynomial-time analogs" of the classes of computable and computably enumerable languages (in the definitions of computable and computably enumerable, "finitely many steps" is replaced by "polynomial in the input length many steps") it is natural to ask whether a similar "isomorphism theorem" is true for NP-complete languages as well. Precisely this was conjectured by L. Berman and J. Hartmanis in 1977:

Berman-Hartmanis Conjecture (Isomorphism Conjecture)
All NP-complete languages are pairwise polynomial-time isomorphic (P-isomorphic) to each other.

Two languages A and B are said to be P-isomorphic if there is a polynomial-time computable bijection f that is polynomial-time invertible (i.e., f^{-1} is also polynomial-time computable) and is a many-one reduction from A to B. (This implies that f^{-1} is also a many-one reduction from B to A.)

The analogy to computability theory suggests that the conjecture should hold. But even if it is true, it will probably be hard to prove, since

$$\text{Berman-Hartmanis Conjecture holds} \implies \mathsf{P} \neq \mathsf{NP} .$$

Exercise 15.1. Prove the claim just made. ◁

In their paper, Berman and Hartmanis showed that all the then-known NP-complete problems were pairwise P-isomorphic. For this they showed that all the known NP-complete languages (including SAT) have a certain property P, and that any language that is NP-complete and has property P is

P-isomorphic to SAT and, therefore, to every other NP-complete language with property P. See the following sketch:

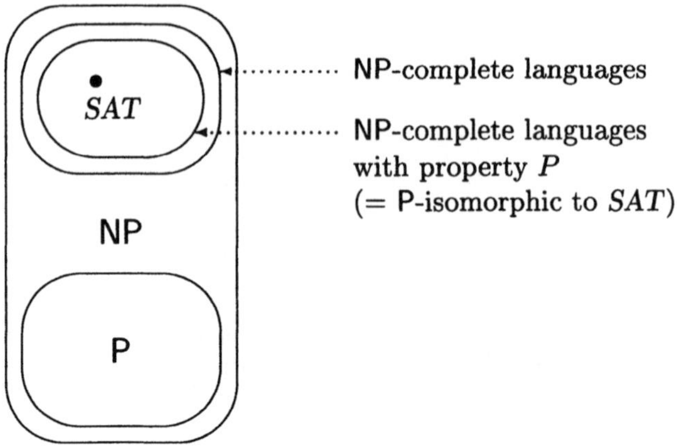

So the Berman-Hartmanis Conjecture is equivalent to the question: Do *all* NP-complete languages have property P? If they do, then they are all P-isomorphic, and we will say that the many-one degree (maximal set of many-one equivalent languages) of an NP-complete language *collapses* to its isomorphism degree (which is the isomorphism degree of SAT).

So what is this property P? Roughly, it says that all inputs x can be systematically extended with some "irrelevant" information y in such a way that (non-) membership is not altered. Furthermore, the information y can be easily recovered from the version of x that has been "padded" with y. The following definition makes this precise.

Definition 15.1. *A language $A \subseteq \Sigma^*$* has property P *if there are two polynomial-time computable functions $p_A : \Sigma^* \times \Sigma^* \to \Sigma^*$ and $d_A : \Sigma^* \to \Sigma^*$ such that*

- *p_A does not alter (non-) membership in A, i.e., $x \in A \Leftrightarrow p_A(x,y) \in A$,*
- *p_A is length-increasing, i.e., $|p_A(x,y)| > |x| + |y|$,*
- *p_A is injective, and*
- *d_A is the inverse of p_A with respect to the second argument, i.e.,*

$$d_A(z) = \begin{cases} y & \textit{if } z = p_A(x,y), \\ * & \textit{otherwise.} \end{cases}$$

Note: the function p_A is often referred to as a *padding function.*

Although this definition appears to be quite technical and involved, it turns out that for (typical) NP-complete languages this property is easily established.

Exercise 15.2.$^\diamond$ Show that SAT has property P. ◁

Next, we consider two lemmas which establish conditions under which many-one reductions can be converted into 1-1 reductions; and 1-1 reductions, into isomorphisms.

Lemma 15.2. *Let A and B be languages that each have property P and are polynomial-time many-one reducible to each other ($A \leq_m^{\mathrm{P}} B$ and $B \leq_m^{\mathrm{P}} A$). Then each of A and B can be reduced to the other via a polynomial-time computable injective function (1-1 reducibility) that is length-increasing (i.e., $|f(x)| > |x|$) and has a polynomial-time computable inverse.* □

Exercise 15.3.$^\diamond$ Prove Lemma 15.2.

Hint: Construct the injective function using a suitable composition of the many-one reduction and the padding function. ◁

Lemma 15.3. *Let A and B be languages that are polynomial-time many-one reducible to each other ($A \leq_m^{\mathrm{P}} B$ and $B \leq_m^{\mathrm{P}} A$) via reductions that are injective and length-increasing and have polynomial-time computable inverses. Then there is a polynomial-time computable bijection between A and B that has a polynomial-time computable inverse. In other words, the languages A and B are* P*-isomorphic.* □

Exercise 15.4.$^\diamond$ Prove Lemma 15.3. ◁

Combining these two lemmas and the observation that *SAT* has property P, we get the following theorem:

Theorem 15.4. *Every* NP*-complete language with property P is* P*-isomorphic to SAT.* □

* * * * *

From today's standpoint, the evidence seems to indicate that the Isomorphism Conjecture is probably false. (See the paper by P. Young.) But aside from the status of the conjecture itself, the Isomorphism Conjecture seems to be even more significant for the number of important investigations and results to which it led. In particular, this is the case in regard to *sparse* sets.

Definition 15.5. *A set A is called* sparse *if there is a polynomial p such that for all $n \in \mathbb{N}$, $|\{x \in A : |x| \leq n\}| \leq p(n)$.*

So in a sparse language, of the exponentially many possible strings of length less than n, only polynomially many belong to the language.

Exercise 15.5. Show that *SAT* is not sparse by showing that there are constants $\varepsilon > 0$ and $\delta > 0$ such that there are at least $\varepsilon 2^{\delta n}$ strings of length at most n in *SAT*. ◁

Exercise 15.6. Show that no sparse language can be P-isomorphic to *SAT*. ◁

In light of the previous exercise, one can formulate the following weaker version of the Isomorphism Conjecture:

Second Berman-Hartmanis Conjecture. If $P \neq \mathsf{NP}$, then no sparse language can be NP-complete.

The notion of NP-completeness in this conjecture (as in the original Isomorphism Conjecture) is polynomial-time many-one reducibility. But it is also interesting to investigate this question with respect to polynomial-time Turing reducibility.

After important first steps by P. Berman and by S. Fortune, and with one eye on a technique used by R.M. Karp and R.J. Lipton, the Second Berman-Hartmanis Conjecture was finally proven in 1980 by S. Mahaney.

For a long time, this result could only be marginally improved. An important breakthrough to more general reducibilities (namely to bounded truth-table reducibility) came in a 1991 paper by M. Ogiwara and O. Watanabe. A somewhat more streamlined proof of this result was given by S. Homer and L. Longpré. Finally, based on the technique of Homer and Longpré, the most comprehensive result was achieved by V. Arvind et al.

We present here the original result of Mahaney using the techniques of Ogiwara-Watanabe and Homer-Longpré.

Theorem 15.6. *If* $\mathsf{P} \neq \mathsf{NP}$, *then no* NP*-complete language can be sparse.*

Proof. Suppose there is a sparse language S with $SAT \leq_m^{\mathsf{P}} S$. Let p be the polynomial that witnesses the sparseness of S and let f be the reduction. We must somehow algorithmically exploit the fact that exponentially many strings in *SAT* of length at most n must be mapped onto only polynomially many strings in S to show that $SAT \in \mathsf{P}$ (so $\mathsf{P} = \mathsf{NP}$).

If we determine that for some pair of strings x and y, $f(x) = f(y)$, then the status of x and y with respect to membership in *SAT* must be the same: either they are both in *SAT* or neither of them is. And for strings x and y in *SAT* we expect that this situation (namely, that $f(x) = f(y)$) occurs frequently.

An important step in the proof consists of using a variant of *SAT* rather than *SAT* itself for the rest of the proof. Let $\lhd$ be the lexicographical ordering on the set of all strings of length at most n. For example, for $n = 3$ we have

$$\lambda \lhd 0 \lhd 00 \lhd 000 \lhd 001 \lhd 01 \lhd 010 \lhd \cdots \lhd 111 .$$

Now we define

$$LeftSAT = \{(F, a) \mid F \text{ is a boolean formula with } n \text{ variables, } a \in \{0,1\}^i,\ i \leq n, \text{ and there is a satisfying assignment } b \in \{0,1\}^n \text{ for } F \text{ with } a \lhd b\,\}$$

Imagine the set of all 0-1 strings of length at most n arranged in a tree. Let $b \in \{0,1\}^n$ be the largest (with respect to $\lhd$) satisfying assignment for F. Then for all strings a in the striped region below, $(F, a) \in LeftSAT$:

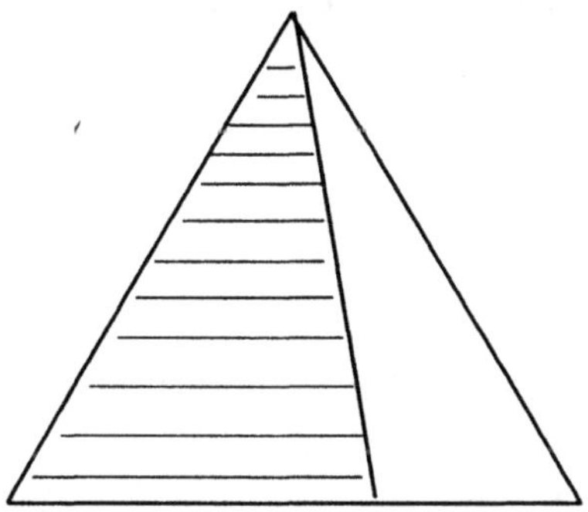

Exercise 15.7. Show that $SAT \leq^{\mathrm{P}}_{\mathrm{m}} LeftSAT$ and $LeftSAT \leq^{\mathrm{P}}_{\mathrm{m}} SAT$. $\lhd$

So $LeftSAT \leq^{\mathrm{P}}_{\mathrm{m}} S$, say via the reduction g. Let q be a polynomial such that $|g((F,a))| \leq q(|F|)$. Now we design an algorithm for SAT that exploits this reduction from $LeftSAT$ to S.

INPUT F;
{ Let n be the number of variables in F }
$T := \{ \lambda \}$;
FOR $i := 1$ **TO** n **DO** $T :=$ *Extend*(T) **END**;
FOR each $b \in T$ **DO**
  IF $F(b) = 1$ **THEN ACCEPT END**
END;
REJECT

In the function Extend, the set T of partial assignments is extended in such a way that after n extensions, all strings in T have length n. In order for this to be a polynomial-time algorithm, it is important that calls to Extend do not increase the size of T exponentially but only polynomially. In order for the algorithm to be correct, at the end of the algorithm, T must contain a satisfying assignment for F if there is one. For this it will be important that T always contain a string a that can be extended to the largest (with respect to $\lhd$) satisfying assignment b. Then at the end of the algorithm b must be in the set T.

Here is the procedure Extend:

PROCEDURE Extend (T : `Set_Of_Strings`):
  `Set_Of_Strings`;
VAR U: `Set_Of_Strings`;

```
BEGIN
   U := ∅;
   FOR each a ∈ T DO U := U ∪ {a0, a1} END;
   FOR each a, a' ∈ U, a ◁ a' DO
      IF g((F, a)) = g((F, a')) THEN U := U − {a} END
   END;
   { Now let U = {a_1, ..., a_k}, where i < j ⇒ a_i ◁ a_j. }
   { Let m = p(q(|F|)). }
   IF k > m THEN U := {a_1, ..., a_m} END;
   RETURN U
END Extend
```

First every string in T is extended by both 0 and 1. Thus U has twice as many strings as T. Two processes are then used to reduce the size of U: If a g-value occurs twice, then the smaller of the two strings giving rise to this value is removed from U. If U still has too many elements (more than m) then only the smallest m are kept. Since m is polynomial in n (it is the maximum possible number of strings $g(F, a)$ for $F \in SAT$), it is clear that the algorithm runs in polynomial time.

Correctness is established by the following exercise. □

Exercise 15.8.$^\diamond$ Suppose F is satisfiable. Let $b = b_1 \dots b_n$ be the largest satisfying assignment for F. Show that after each application of Extend, the initial segment $b_1 \dots b_i$ of b is in T.

Hint: Be sure you understand the effects of Extend in terms of the tree of assignments. ◁

Finally, we note that the proof just given can be fairly easily extended from many-one reductions to more general reductions (such as bounded truth-table reductions or conjunctive reductions, for example). Furthermore, we did not make use of the property that $S \in \mathsf{NP}$, so we have actually proven a somewhat stronger theorem, namely

Theorem 15.7. *If* $\mathsf{P} \neq \mathsf{NP}$, *then there is no sparse language that is* NP*-hard (with respect to many-one reducibility).* □

References

For more information about computability theory and proofs of the isomorphism result in that setting see

- M. Machtey, P. Young: *An Introduction to the General Theory of Algorithms*, North-Holland, 1978.
- P. Odifreddi: *Classical Recursion Theory*, North-Holland, 1989.

- H. Rogers: *Theory of Recursive Functions and Effective Computability*, McGraw-Hill, 1967.

The original statement of the Isomorphism Conjecture appeared in

- H. Berman and J. Hartmanis: On isomorphism and density of NP and other complete sets, *SIAM Journal on Computing* 6 (1977), 305–323.

For an overview of some of the work that was generated by this conjecture as well as an indication why the conjecture is most likely false see

- P. Young: Juris Hartmanis: Fundamental contributions to the isomorphism problem; in A. Selman, ed., *Complexity Theory Retrospective*, Springer, 1990, 28–58).

The proof of the Second Berman-Hartmanis Conjecture built on results found in

- P. Berman: Relationship between density and deterministic complexity of NP-complete languages, *Symposium on Mathematical Foundations of Computer Science*, Lecture Notes in Computer Science 62, Springer, 1978, 63–71.
- S. Fortune: A note on sparse complete sets, *SIAM Journal on Computing* 8 (1979), 431–433.
- R.M. Karp and R.J. Lipton: Some connections between nonuniform and uniform complexity classes, *Proceedings of the 12th Annual Symposium on Theory of Computing*, ACM, 1980, 302–309.

and appeared in

- S. Mahaney: Sparse complete sets for NP: solution of a conjecture of Berman and Hartmanis, *Journal of Computer and System Sciences* 25, 130–143.

Extensions of Mahaney's theorem can be found in

- V. Arvind et al: Reductions to sets of low information content, in K. Ambos-Spies, S. Homer, U. Schöning, ed., *Complexity Theory: Current Research*, Cambridge University Press, 1993, 1–45.
- S. Homer and L. Longpré: On reductions of NP sets to sparse sets, *Proceedings of the 6th Structure in Complexity Conference*, IEEE, 1991, 79–88.
- M. Ogiwara and O. Watanabe: On polynomial-time bounded truth-table reducibility of NP sets to sparse sets, *SIAM Journal on Computing* 20 (1991), 471–483.

16. Collapsing Hierarchies

> The polynomial hierarchy can be defined in exact analogy to the arithmetic hierarchy of computability theory, but it is not known if the polynomial hierarchy is a strict hierarchy of language classes. In fact, under certain assumptions about the class NP, this hierarchy "collapses."

NP is the class of all languages that can be defined using existential quantification over a polynomial-time predicate. The "search space" of the existential quantifier must, however, be bounded to include only strings of length polynomial in the length of the input. In the following formal definition, NP is precisely the class Σ_1^P of the *polynomial-time hierarchy*, which is usually abbreviated PH.

Definition 16.1. *A language L is in the class Σ_i^P of the polynomial-time hierarchy if L can be defined via a language $A \in \mathsf{P}$ and a polynomial q as follows:*

$$L = \{x \mid \exists^q y_1 \forall^q y_2 \ldots Q^q y_i \ \langle y_1, y_2, \ldots, y_i\rangle \in A\}\ .$$

In this definition $Q = \forall$, if i is even and $Q = \exists$ if i is odd. Furthermore, all quantifiers are polynomially bounded in the following sense:

$$\exists^q\ z\ \varphi(z) \iff \exists z\ [|z| \le q(|z|)\ \wedge\ \varphi(z)]\ ,$$
$$\forall^q\ z\ \varphi(z) \iff \forall z\ [|z| \le q(|z|) \Longrightarrow \varphi(z)]\ .$$

The classes Π_i^P are defined to include all languages L such that $\overline{L} \in \Sigma_i^P$. Finally, $\mathsf{PH} = \bigcup_i \Sigma_i^P$. □

Usually we will drop the superscripts on our quantifiers when it is clear from context that they are polynomially bounded.

The following diagram shows the inclusion structure of the classes in the polynomial hierarchy. (For more details see the books by Balcázar, Diaz, and Gabarro; Garey and Johnson, Köbler, Schöning and Torán; or Bovet and Crescenzi.)

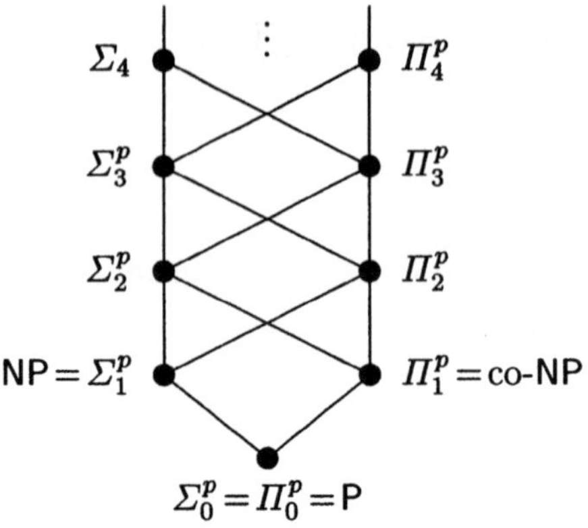

It is not known whether or not the polynomial-time hierarchy is a *strict* hierarchy (i.e., whether or not $\Sigma_0^P \subsetneq \Sigma_1^P \subsetneq \Sigma_2^P \subsetneq \cdots$). The analogously defined *arithmetic hierarchy* $\Sigma_0^0, \Sigma_1^0, \ldots$ from computability theory is a strict hierarchy. (The difference is that in the arithmetic hierarchy, the quantifiers do not have a polynomial length bound. So Σ_1^0 is the class of all computably enumerable languages.)

Exercise 16.1. Show that the statements $\Sigma_i^P = \Sigma_{i+1}^P$, $\Sigma_i^P = \Pi_i^P$, and $\mathsf{PH} = \Sigma_i^P$ are all equivalent. (This implies a "downward separation" property: If for some i, $\Sigma_i^P \neq \Sigma_{i+1}^P$, then $\Sigma_0^P \subsetneq \Sigma_1^P \subsetneq \cdots \subsetneq \Sigma_i^P$). ◁

The following diagram shows the inclusion structure of the polynomial-time hierarchy under the (unlikely) assumption that it "collapses" to the class Σ_3^P.

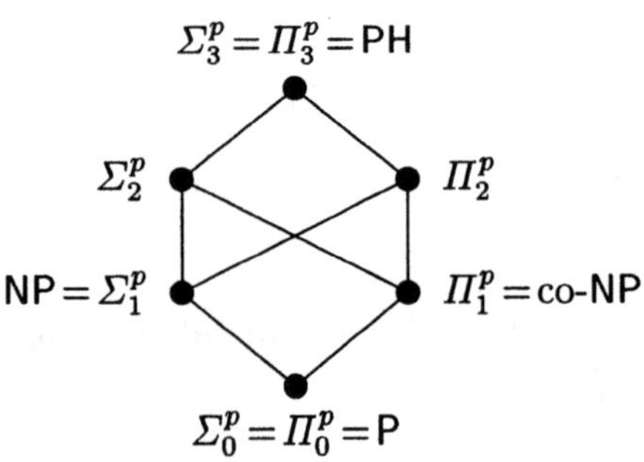

It is absolutely plausible, to take $\mathsf{P} \neq \mathsf{NP}$ as a working hypothesis and to prove theorems under this "Cook Hypothesis." The hypothesis $\mathsf{P} \neq \mathsf{NP}$, in terms of the polynomial-time hierarchy, means that $\Sigma_0^P \neq \Sigma_1^P$. Furthermore, by the previous exercise, the hypothesis $\mathsf{NP} \neq \text{co-}\mathsf{NP}$ is equivalent to $\Sigma_1^P \neq \Sigma_2^P$. This second hypothesis is stronger than the first. Altogether, the polynomial-time hierarchy provides an infinite reservoir of (plausible) hypotheses which could represent the working hypothesis of some theorems.

$$\boxed{\mathsf{PH} \neq \Sigma_k^p \text{ for all } k}$$

$$\Downarrow$$

$$\vdots$$

$$\Downarrow$$

$$\boxed{\mathsf{PH} \neq \Sigma_3^p}$$

$$\Downarrow$$

$$\boxed{\mathsf{PH} \neq \Sigma_2^p}$$

$$\Downarrow$$

$$\boxed{\mathsf{PH} \neq \Sigma_1^p} \qquad (\mathsf{NP} \neq \text{co-}\mathsf{NP})$$

$$\Downarrow$$

$$\boxed{\mathsf{PH} \neq \Sigma_0^p} \qquad (\mathsf{P} \neq \mathsf{NP})$$

The *circuit complexity* of a language L is a function $cc_L : \mathbb{N} \to \mathbb{N}$ such that $cc_L(n)$ gives the minimal necessary number of boolean gates (of the types AND, OR, and NOT) that can be used to build a circuit that computes the characteristic function of L on strings of length n. If the NP-complete languages are not computable via a (deterministic) polynomial time-bounded algorithm (i.e., $\mathsf{P} \neq \mathsf{NP}$), then it could still be the case that they have polynomial-size circuits. This would be a very interesting situation: It would be possible with a certain (exponential) expenditure to build a circuit with, for example, $n = 1000$ inputs that is only modestly sized (polynomial in n) and is capable of efficiently solving all instances of SAT of length (up to) 1000. This means that although it would require exponentially much work done as a preprocess – but then never repeated – one could design a fast "chip" for SAT.

We want to investigate this question and eventually link this situation with the (unlikely) collapse of the polynomial-time hierarchy.

Exercise 16.2. Show that there are languages that are not in P but do have polynomial-size circuits. ◁

Exercise 16.3.° Show that a language L has polynomial-size circuits if and only if there is a sparse set S such that $L \in \mathsf{P}^S$ (i.e., L can be computed in polynomial time relative to some sparse oracle). ◁

Instead of $L \in \mathsf{P}^S$, we can also write $L \leq_T^{\mathsf{P}} S$ and consider this as a (polynomial-time Turing) reduction of L to S. By means of the previous exercise we can express the question of whether all languages in NP have polynomial-size circuits equivalently as the question of whether all languages in NP (or just the NP-complete languages) are reducible to sparse sets. In this way, this question is related to the questions surrounding the Berman-Hartmanis Conjecture of the previous topic.

A language L in $\mathsf{NP} = \Sigma_1^P$ has the form

$$L = \{x \mid \exists y\ \langle x, y\rangle \in A\}$$

for some $A \in \mathsf{P}$ and a polynomially bounded existential quantifier. For every $x \in L$ there must be at least one y with $\langle x, y\rangle \in A$. We call such a y a *witness* or a *proof* for the fact that $x \in A$. (For example, a satisfying assignment for a formula F is a witness that $F \in SAT$.)

We want now to consider circuits that have not just a single output bit (which expresses whether or not $x \in L$) but which also have (suitably many) additional output gates by means of which the circuit provides a witness y for $x \in L$ (when this is the case). We will call such a circuit for a language in NP a *witness circuit.*

Exercise 16.4.° Show that if SAT has polynomial-size circuits, then SAT also has polynomial-size witness circuits (which produce in certain output gates a satisfying assignment for the boolean formula if it is satisfiable).

Hint: Use the self-reducibility of SAT. ◁

Now there is only a small step remaining to prove the following result of R.M. Karp and R.J. Lipton:

Theorem 16.2. *If all languages in* NP *have polynomial-size circuits then the polynomial-time hierarchy collapses to its second level* ($\mathsf{PH} = \Sigma_2^P$).

Proof. Let L be a language in Π_2^P. It suffices to show that from the hypothesis it follows that $L \in \Sigma_2^P$. Let A be a language in P such that

$$L = \{x \mid \forall y \exists z\ \langle x, y, z\rangle \in A\}\ .$$

Then the language

$$L' = \{\langle x, y\rangle \mid \exists z\ \langle x, y, z\rangle \in A\}$$

is in NP. Since SAT is NP-complete, L' can be reduced to SAT by a polynomial-time computable function f, i.e. $f^{-1}(SAT) = L'$. This implies that

$$L = \{x \mid \forall y\ \langle x, y\rangle \in L'\} = \{x \mid \forall y\ f(\langle x, y\rangle) \in SAT\}\ .$$

We claim now that the following characterization of L is possible, which shows that $L \in \Sigma_2^P$:

$$L = \{x \mid \exists c \forall y\ [\ c \text{ is a witness circuit and } c(f(\langle x, y\rangle)) \text{ produces a satisfying assignment for the formula } f(\langle x, y\rangle)\ ]\}\ .$$

Exercise 16.5. Prove that this representation of L is correct. ◁

This completes the proof of Theorem 16.2 (with a much simpler proof than was originally given). □

* * * * *

The *boolean hierarchy* (over NP), similar to the polynomial-time hierarchy, arises from the fact (or conjecture) that NP is not closed under complement. The class BH is the smallest class that contains NP and is closed under the boolean operations of intersection, union and complement.

A hierarchy of classes between NP and BH can be formed by beginning with NP and systematically adding unions and intersections with coNP languages.

Definition 16.3. *The classes* $\mathsf{BH}_1, \mathsf{BH}_2, \dots$ *of the boolean hierarchy over* NP *are defined as follows:*

$$\begin{aligned} \mathsf{BH}_1 &= \mathsf{NP}\,, \\ \mathsf{BH}_{2i} &= \{A \cap \overline{B} \mid A \in \mathsf{BH}_{2i-1}, B \in \mathsf{NP}\} \quad (i \geq 1)\,, \\ \mathsf{BH}_{2i+1} &= \{A \cup B \mid A \in \mathsf{BH}_{2i}, B \in \mathsf{NP}\} \quad (i \geq 1)\,. \end{aligned}$$

Exercise 16.6.$^\diamond$ Show that $\mathsf{BH} = \bigcup_i \mathsf{BH}_i$. ◁

The inclusion structure for the boolean hierarchy is similar to that for the polynomial-time hierarchy:

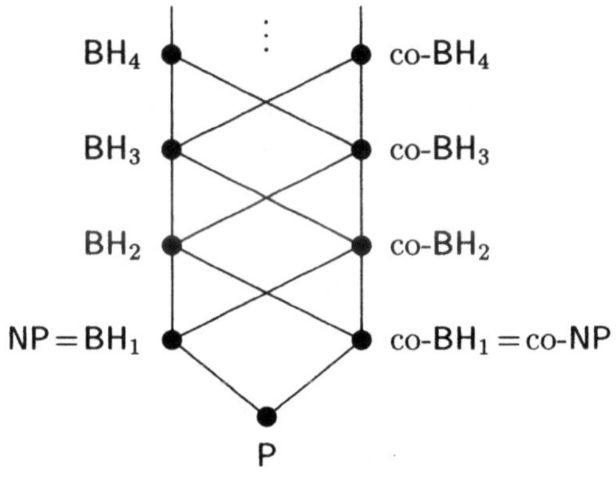

The boolean hierarchy is contained in the class $\mathsf{P}^{\mathsf{NP}} \subseteq \Sigma_2^P \cap \Pi_2^P$. We say that the boolean hierarchy *collapses to the kth level* if $\mathsf{BH}_k = \text{co-}\mathsf{BH}_k$. The following result due to J. Kadin was a sensation at the 1987 *Structure in Complexity Theory Conference* held at Cornell University:

Theorem 16.4. *If the boolean hierarchy collapses at* any *level, then the polynomial hierarchy collapse at the* third *level. More precisely, in this case the polynomial-time hierarchy collapses to the boolean closure of* Σ_2^P, *which in turn is contained in* Σ_3^P.

Proof. It is possible to systematically define complete languages for the levels of the boolean hierarchy. We sketch this below for the first few levels:

$$
\begin{aligned}
L_1 &= SAT \\
L_2 &= \{\langle F_1, F_2\rangle \mid F_1 \in L_1 \land F_2 \in \overline{SAT}\} \\
L_3 &= \{\langle F_1, F_2, F_3\rangle \mid \langle F_1, F_2\rangle \in L_2 \lor F_3 \in SAT\} \\
L_4 &= \{\langle F_1, F_2, F_3, F_4\rangle \mid \langle F_1, F_2, F_3\rangle \in L_3 \land F_3 \in \overline{SAT}\} \\
&\ \vdots
\end{aligned}
$$

It is easy to show that L_i is complete for BH_i (and so $\overline{L_i}$ is complete for coBH_i). If $\mathsf{BH}_i = \text{co-}\mathsf{BH}_i$, then L_i can be reduced to $\overline{L_i}$ and vice versa. This is the starting point for the proof. We will give the proof for the case $i = 2$. The general case contains the same basic argument but is technically somewhat more involved.

Suppose $L_2 \leq_m^P \overline{L_2}$, so there is a polynomial-time computable function f that maps pairs of boolean formulas (F_1, F_2) to pairs (G_1, G_2) with the property that

$$F_1 \in SAT \land F_2 \in \overline{SAT} \iff G_1 \in \overline{SAT} \lor G_2 \in SAT\ .$$

As a first step, we will try to show that $\overline{SAT} \in \mathsf{NP}$. We will not be successful, but will very nearly achieve this goal. How do we design a nondeterministic algorithm for $\overline{SAT}$? The following would be one attempt:

INPUT F;
Nondeterministically guess a formula F' with $|F'| = |F|$,
  and a satisfying assignment for F', so $F' \in SAT$;
Compute $(G_1, G_2) := f(F', F)$;
IF $G_2 \in SAT$ **THEN ACCEPT END**

This nondeterministic algorithm accepts a certain subset of $\overline{SAT}$, namely the unsatisfiable formulas F for which there is a satisfiable formula F' of the same length, so that $f(F', F) = (G_1, G_2)$ with $G_2 \in SAT$. We will call this algorithm the *easy* algorithm, and the formulas that it accepts will be called *easy formulas*. Clearly easy formulas are unsatisfiable, but perhaps they do not make up all unsatisfiable formulas. We will call a formula *hard* if it is unsatisfiable but not easy. So

$$
\begin{aligned}
F \text{ is hard} \iff\ & F \in \overline{SAT} \\
& \land \forall F'[|F'| = |F| \Longrightarrow f(F', F) = (G_1, G_2) \land G_2 \in \overline{SAT}]\ .
\end{aligned}
$$

We note at this point that the property of being hard can be described with a Π_1^P predicate.

But how do we get the hard formulas? The fact that they are hard is the key. Fix an arbitrary hard formula $\hat{F}$ of length n. With the aid of this one formula, we can correctly nondeterministically accept all other unsatisfiable formulas of this length by means of the following algorithm:

INPUT F;
Compute $(G_1, G_2) := f(F, \hat{F})$;
IF $G_1 \in SAT$ **THEN ACCEPT END**

Why is this algorithm correct? Since $\hat{F}$ is hard, $f(F, \hat{F})$ produces a pair of formulas (G_1, G_2) such that $G_2 \in \overline{SAT}$. Since $\hat{F} \in \overline{SAT}$, we have the following equivalence:

$$F \in SAT \iff G_1 \in \overline{SAT} \ ,$$

or equivalently,

$$F \in \overline{SAT} \iff G_1 \in SAT \ .$$

This demonstrates that the algorithm is correct. This algorithm is unusual in that first we need to be given n bits of information ($\hat{F}$), but then parameterized with this information (called *advice*), the algorithm is correct for all formulas of length n. For a given hard formula $\hat{F}$ we will call this algorithm the $\hat{F}$-algorithm.

We have come very close to demonstrating that $\overline{SAT} \in \mathsf{NP}$, but have fallen just short (because of the need for advice in the previous algorithm). Nevertheless, what we have done is sufficient to show a collapse to the polynomial-time hierarchy to $\Sigma_3^P \subseteq \mathsf{P}^{\Sigma_2^P}$. Let $L \in \Sigma_3^P$. L can be represented as

$$L = \{x \mid \exists u \forall v \exists w \ \langle x, u, v, w \rangle \in A\}$$

for some language $A \in \mathsf{P}$. Let

$$L' = \{\langle x, u, v \rangle \mid \exists w \ \langle x, u, v, w \rangle \in A\} \ .$$

$L' \in \mathsf{NP}$, so there exists a reduction g from L' to SAT. So L can be written as

$$L = \{x \mid \exists u \forall v \ g(\langle x, u, v \rangle) \notin \overline{SAT}\} \ .$$

If we could replace the reference to $\overline{SAT}$ with some NP-predicate (this would amount to $\overline{SAT} \in \mathsf{NP}$) then we would have a Σ_2^P characterization of L. As we have said, we are not able to achieve this. But consider the following language:

$$B = \{1^n \mid \text{there is a hard formula of length } n\} \ .$$

The language B is in Σ_2^P. Furthermore, let

$$C = \{x \mid \exists u \forall v \ [g(\langle x, u, v \rangle) \text{ is not accepted by the easy algorithm }]\} \ .$$

Then $C \in \Sigma_2^P$. Now consider

$$D = \{x \mid \exists \hat{F} \ [\hat{F} \text{ is hard } \wedge \exists u \forall v \ [g(\langle x, u, v \rangle) \text{ is not accepted by the } \hat{F}\text{-algorithm}]]\} \ .$$

D is also in Σ_2^P. The language L can now be recognized by the following deterministic oracle algorithm using the languages B,C, and D as oracles. In this algorithms, m is a suitable polynomial in $|x|$ that gives the length of $g(\langle x, u, v\rangle)$.

INPUT x;
IF $1^{m(|x|)} \in B$ **THEN**
  IF $x \in D$ **THEN ACCEPT END**
ELSE
  IF $x \in C$ **THEN ACCEPT END**
END;
REJECT

This oracle machine asks exactly two of the three oracle questions $1^{m(|x|)} \in B$, $x \in D$, and $x \in C$. Since this is a constant number of oracle queries, the language L is in the boolean closure of the class Σ_2^P. □

References

For general information about the polynomial-time hierarchy see

- L.J. Stockmeyer: The polynomial-time hierarchy, *Theoretical Computer Science* 3 (1977), 1–22.
- C. Wrathall: Complete sets and the polynomial-time hierarchy, *Theoretical Computer Science* 3 (1977), 23–33.

Theorem 16.2 was originally proved in

- R.M. Karp, R.J. Lipton: Some connections between nonuniform and uniform complexity classes, *Proceedings of the 12th Symposium on Theory of Computer Science*, ACM, 1980, 302–309.

Since then, the point of collapse has been improved from Σ_2^P to $\mathsf{ZPP}^{\mathsf{NP}}$; see

- N.H. Bshouty, R. Cleve, S. Kannan, C. Tamon: Oracles and queries that are sufficient for exact learning, *COLT* 1994.

(For more about the class ZPP see Topic 17.)

For a more detailed exposition of the boolean hierarchy see

- Cai, Gundermann, Hartmanis, Hemachandra, Sewelson, Wagner, Wechsung: The Boolean hierarchy I & II, *SIAM Journal on Computing* 17 (1989), 1232–1252 and 18 (1989), 95–111.

Theorem 16.4 appeared in

- Kadin: The polynomial hierarchy collapses if the Boolean hierarchy collapses, *SIAM Journal on Computing* 17 (1988), 1263–1282.

See also

∘ R. Chang, J. Kadin: The Boolean hierarchy and the polynomial hierarchy: a closer connection, *Proceedings of the Structure in Complexity Theory Conference*, IEEE, 1990, 169–178.

17. Probabilistic Algorithms, Probability Amplification, and the Recycling of Random Numbers

Probabilistic algorithms require (stochastically independent and uniformly distributed) random numbers, and in general the smaller the probability of error is supposed to be, the more random numbers are required. Here we introduce a method, whereby random numbers already used by an algorithm can be "recycled" and then reused later in the algorithm. In this way it is possible to drastically reduce the number of random numbers required to obtain a specific bound on the error probability.

A probabilistic algorithm can make decisions depending on chance. This can be modeled by a Turing machine in which each configuration may have several (but only finitely many) "next" configurations, each of which is chosen with equal probability. By introducing probability the decision and running time of an algorithm (accept or reject, 0 or 1) on input x become random variables.

The concept of acceptance is defined here differently than it is for nondeterministic machines. A string x is accepted by a probabilistic algorithm if the probability that the algorithm accepts x is $> 1/2$. More generally, one can fix an arbitrary threshold probability value $\alpha \in (0,1)$ and say that a string x is accepted if the probability of acceptance is greater than α.

Definition 17.1. *A language L is in the complexity class* PP *(probabilistic polynomial time) if there is a polynomial time-bounded probabilistic algorithm and a threshold value $\alpha \in (0,1)$ such that L consists of precisely those strings that are accepted with probability $> \alpha$.*

An algorithm that demonstrates that a language belongs to PP will be called a PP-algorithm.

The notion of a polynomial time-bound in the definition above means that for *every* realization of the random variables, $T(x)$ (the running time of the algorithm on input x) is bounded by $p(|x|)$, where $p(n)$ is some fixed polynomial.

In this topic, we are primarily interested in probabilistic algorithms that exhibit a "probability gap" between the accepted and rejected strings. This means that not only is the probability $> \alpha$ when $x \in L$ and $\leq \alpha$ when $x \notin L$, but in fact, the algorithm fulfills a stronger condition: If $x \in L$, then the probability of acceptance is $\geq \alpha + \varepsilon/2$, and if $x \notin L$ then the probability is

$\leq \alpha - \varepsilon/2$ (for some $\varepsilon > 0$). So there is a gap of ε between the probabilities of acceptance for the strings $x \in L$ and the strings $x \notin L$.

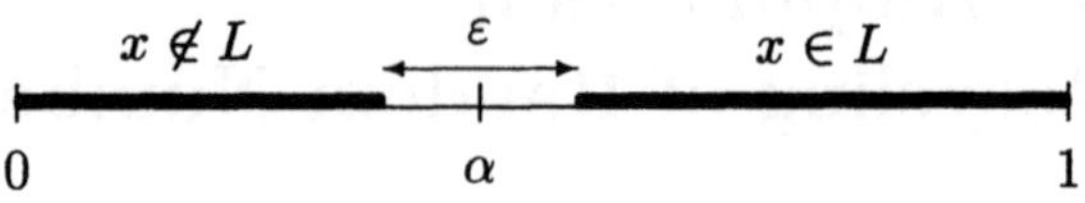

Definition 17.2. *A language L is in the class* BPP *(bounded-error probabilistic polynomial time), if there is a* PP*-algorithm for L with threshold probability α, and a probability gap ε, such that the condition above is satisfied. That is, L is accepted in the sense of a* PP*-algorithm, and the probability that a string x is accepted is never in the range* $(\alpha - \varepsilon/2, \alpha + \varepsilon/2)$.

A probabilistic algorithm that fulfills the definition above is called a BPP-algorithm. It is clear that P $\subseteq$ BPP $\subseteq$ PP.

Definition 17.3. *A language L is in the class* RP *if there is a* BPP*-algorithm for L such that $\varepsilon = 2\alpha$. That is, if $x \notin L$, then the probability that the algorithm accepts on input x is 0.*

Sketch:

This acceptance criterion is a strengthening of the requirement for an NP language, so it is clear that P $\subseteq$ RP $\subseteq$ NP and P $\subseteq$ RP $\subseteq$ BPP. The inclusion relationship between NP and BPP is an open question. We will come back to this relationship shortly; in particular, the inclusion NP $\subseteq$ BPP is unlikely, since it implies a collapse of the polynomial hierarchy (cf. Topic 16).

Definition 17.4. *A language L is in the class* ZPP *(zero error probabilistic polynomial time) if and only if $L \in$* RP *and $\overline{L} \in$* RP. *That is,* ZPP = RP $\cap$ coRP.

Exercise 17.1. The name "zero error" comes from the fact that for the languages $L \in$ ZPP, one can give a polynomial time-bounded probabilistic algorithm and a constant ε so that on input x with probability $p > \varepsilon$, the algorithm answers correctly ($x \in L$ or $x \notin L$) and with probability $1 - p$ the algorithm answers "I don't know." So in contrast to the class BPP, the algorithm never outputs a wrong assertion.

Show that for any language $L \in$ ZPP there is such an algorithm with three output values (accept, reject, don't know). ◁

Exercise 17.2.° Prove that ZPP is precisely the class of languages that possess probabilistic algorithms of the following type: the algorithm *always* outputs the correct answer (accept or reject, never "don't know") and the *expected* running time is polynomial. ◁

The following diagram indicates the inclusion structure of these probabilistic classes in comparison to P and NP:

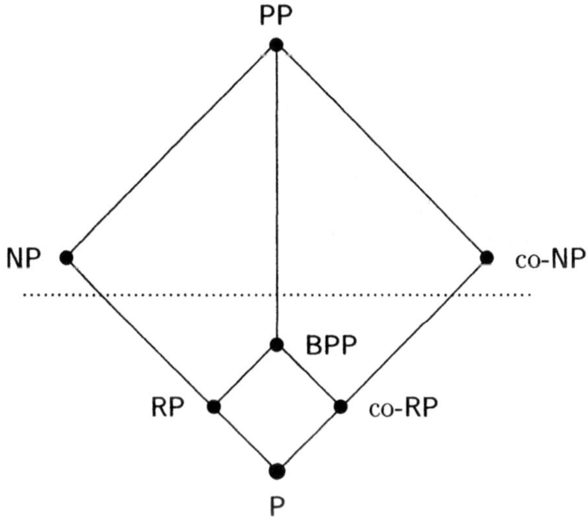

The problems below the dotted line can be considered efficiently solvable "for all practical purposes." In particular, all of them have polynomial-size circuits. The main reason for this is related to the fact that all of them permit "probability amplification." This will be our next topic of discussion.

* * * * *

The probability gap that exists in the definitions of the classes BPP, RP and ZPP plays an important role with regard to *probability amplification.* This means that with only a polynomial increase in running time, we can modify our algorithms, for example in the case of BPP, so that strings in the language are "almost always" accepted, and strings not in the language are "almost never" accepted.

Sketch:

In the case of the class RP – and hence also for ZPP – the probability amplification is relatively easy to obtain. Accepting computations are always correct, so in this case we know that $x \in L$. We only need to mistrust the rejecting computations. Suppose we have been given an RP-algorithm for a language L. This algorithm accepts strings in the language with a certain probability $\geq \varepsilon$. By running the algorithm several times on the same input, each time with new random numbers, so that the individual results of this experiment are independent, and accepting only if *at least one* of the individual results was an accepting computation, we obtain an algorithm with a significantly larger probability gap.

Exercise 17.3. How large is the probability gap after t trails? To get an error probability of $\leq 2^{-n}$, how many times must the algorithm be repeated? ◁

The situation is not quite so easy for BPP-algorithms. Here we must mistrust both the accepting computations and the rejecting computations, since both results can be wrong some of the time. Although neither result is a certain criterion for $x \in L$ or $x \notin L$, each offers a certain amount of evidence, evidence which can mount in favor of one decision or the other with repeated trials. Let M be a BPP-algorithm with threshold value α and probability gap ε. The following algorithm yields the desired probability amplification (i.e., a larger probability gap):

```
INPUT x;
s := 0;
FOR i := 1 TO t DO
    Simulate M on x; let the result be y;
    IF y="accept" THEN s := s + 1 END;
END;
IF s > αt THEN ACCEPT
    ELSE REJECT END
```

This is a Bernoulli experiment since a random experiment with a certain probability p of success is repeated independently t times. In our case $p \geq \alpha + \varepsilon/2$ if $x \in L$, and $p \leq \alpha - \varepsilon/2$ if $x \notin L$. So the probability that this algorithm gives a "false reject" when $x \in L$ is at most

$$\sum_{i=0}^{\alpha t} \binom{t}{i} \cdot \gamma^i \cdot (1-\gamma)^{t-i} ,$$

where $\gamma = \alpha + \varepsilon/2$.

Exercise 17.4.° Show that this function is exponential in $1/t$. How large must t be chosen to bring the probability of error under 2^{-n}? Give a similar approximation of the error for the case that $x \notin A$.

Hint: Use Chernoff bounds or Bernstein's law of large numbers. ◁

So as in the simpler case of RP, we get a linear relation between t and n if the goal is an exponentially small probability of error.

In summary, for every language $L \in$ BPP and for every polynomial p there is a BPP-algorithm M for the language L with threshold value α and a probability gap of $1 - 2^{-p(n)}$, where n is the length of the input. This means that the probability of error on input x is less than $2^{-p(|x|)}$.

So, for example, if one chooses $p(n) = 2n$, the probability of error is already so small that for most random choices z made by the algorithm, the algorithm is always correct with this fixed z for all x of length n. That is, this z serves as "advice," from which membership of all strings of length n can be correctly decided (cf. Topic 16).

Exercise 17.5. From this it follows that all languages in the class BPP have polynomial-size circuits (cf. Topics 16 and 13). Justify this claim. ◁

With the results of Topic 16, we now get the following theorem immediately:

Theorem 17.5. *If* NP $\subseteq$ BPP, *then the polynomial hierarchy collapses to* Σ_2^P.

Exercise 17.6.$^\diamond$ Show the following result: If NP $\subseteq$ BPP, then NP = RP.

Hint: It suffices to show that $SAT \in$ RP. Use a BPP-algorithm for SAT to with small error rate and the self-reducibility of SAT to find a potential satisfying assignment for the input formula. If the probabilistically generated assignment is not a satisfying assignment, then reject. ◁

* * * * *

In the last section we saw that in order to improve the probability gap from $\varepsilon > 0$ (for example, $\varepsilon = 1/2$) to $\varepsilon = 1 - 2^{-\Omega(k)}$, we needed to repeat the algorithm $O(k)$ times and then make a decision based on majority vote. This shrinks the probability of error to $2^{-\Omega(k)}$. If the underlying probabilistic algorithm requires r random bits, then our new algorithm requires $O(rk)$ random bits.

If one takes the perspective that not only computation time and memory use are costly resources to be minimized, but also the number of random bits, then one could attempt to achieve the probability amplification with the smallest possible number of random bits. It seems plausible that the number of random bits could be reduced when one considers that each block of r random bits used by the algorithm really only serves to get 1 bit of information, namely whether the probabilistic algorithm accepts some input with those r random bits. That is, the relative entropy of r bits on a given decision of the probabilistic algorithm is still very high. We just need to find a way to "recycle" (better re-prepare) the r random bits so that no (significant) dependency results. That this is possible is essentially due to the method of "universal hashing" and an analysis presented in the "Leftover Hash Lemma" below.

The solution to the problem will look like this: After using the r random bits, we will use a hash function h to obtain $s < r$ "recycled" bits, which are then augmented with $r - s$ "fresh" random bits to form r random bits for the next trial. This process is then iterated for each trial.

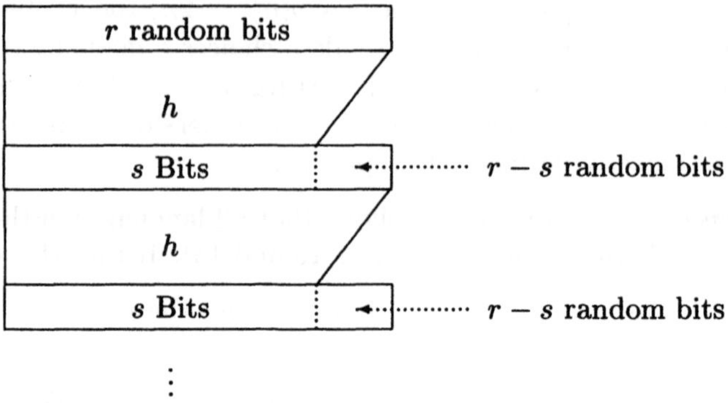

The sequence of r-bit "pseudo-random" numbers that arises in this way can then be used in place of the original k independently chosen random numbers.

Now we approximate the number of actual random bits used. We need r bits for the first random number and $r - s$ for each subsequent (pseudo-random) number. The function h will be chosen randomly from a class of so-called universal hash functions. We will see that the selection of h can be done with $O(r)$ bits. Altogether we need $r + O(r) + (r - s) \cdot (k - 1)$ random bits. We will see that $r - s$ can be chosen so that $r - s = O(k)$. So we need $O(r + k^2)$ random bits. (In fact, it is possible – by other methods – to further reduce the number of random bits required to $O(r + k)$.) This is a drastic improvement over our original probability amplification algorithm which required $O(rk)$ random bits.

Definition 17.6. *A class H of hash functions from $\{0,1\}^r$ to $\{0,1\}^s$ $(s < r)$ is called* universal, *if for every $x, y \in \{0,1\}^r$ with $x \neq y$,*

$$Pr[h(x) = h(y)] = 1/2^s \ .$$

The probability above is over h chosen uniformly at random from H. (In this case the probability of a collision is the same as if $h(x)$ and $h(y)$ are chosen uniformly at random from $\{0,1\}^s$).

A class H of hash functions from $\{0,1\}^r$ to $\{0,1\}^s$ $(s < r)$ is called almost universal, *if for every $x, y \in \{0,1\}^r$ with $x \neq y$,*

$$Pr[h(x) = h(y)] = 1/2^s + 1/2^r \ .$$

Let's try the following class of hash functions. Let $p \geq 2^r$ be a prime number with bit-length $O(r)$. The hash functions in H are specified by giving two numbers $a, b \in [0, p-1]$. The hash function $h = h_{p,a,b}$ is defined so that $h(x)$ is the s least significant bits of the number $(ax + b) \bmod p$. This can be expressed as

$$h_{p,a,b}(x) = ((ax + b) \bmod p) \bmod 2^s \ .$$

It is clear that for any $x \neq y$ and randomly chosen values a and b, the value $((ax+b) \bmod p) \cdot ((ay+b) \bmod p)$ is uniformly distributed in $[0, p-1] \times [0, p-1]$.

(This uses the fact that GF(p) is a field.) So this class of functions would be universal.

The restriction to the last s bits, however, destroys the uniformity of the distribution, and, therefore, the universality of the hash functions.

Exercise 17.7.$^\diamond$ Show that the class H defined above is an almost universal class of hash functions. $\triangleleft$

Definition 17.7. *Let D and D' be probability distribution on a finite set S. We say that D and D' are* ε-similar *if for every subset $X \subseteq S$,*

$$|D(X) - D'(X)| \leq \varepsilon .$$

Here $D(X)$ is the probability of X under the distribution D, so $D(X) = \sum_{x\in X} Pr_D(x)$.

A distribution D is ε-almost uniformly distributed *if D and the uniform distribution on S are ε-similar.*

The collision probability *of a distribution D is the probability that two elements x and y, chosen independently according to D, are the same.*

The following lemma shows that for an (almost) universal class of hash functions an amazing amount of uniformity holds if we choose h randomly from H, but choose the argument x at random from an unknown but "large enough" set.

Lemma 17.8 (Leftover Hash Lemma). *Let X be an arbitrary subset of $\{0,1\}^r$ with $|X| \geq 2^l$. Let H be an almost universal class of hash functions from $\{0,1\}^r$ to $\{0,1\}^s$. Suppose $r \geq l > s$ and let $e = (l-s)/2$. Then the distribution of $(h, h(x))$ is $1/2^e$-almost uniform on the set $H \times \{0,1\}^s$.*

Proof. We show the proof in two steps:

Step 1. The collision probability of the distribution $(h, h(x))$ is at most $(1 + 2/2^e)/(|H|2^s)$.

Step 2. Let D be a distribution on a finite set S. If the collision probability of D is at most $(1+2\delta^2)/|S|$, then D is δ-almost uniformly distributed on S.

It is clear that the statement of the lemma follows immediately from Steps 1 and 2, which are proven below. $\square$

Exercise 17.8.$^\diamond$ Prove Step 1. $\triangleleft$

Proof (of Step 2). Suppose D is not δ-almost uniformly distributed. Then there is a subset Y of S with $D(Y) > |Y|/|S| + \delta$. Let $\beta > \delta$ be such that $D(Y) = |Y|/|S| + \beta$. The collision probability of D is given by $Pr[d_1 = d_2]$

where d_1 and d_2 are chosen at random according to D. We use Y to partition the probability space. The probability for $d_1 = d_2$ under the condition that $d_1, d_2 \in Y$ is at least $1/|Y|$; and the probability for $d_1 = d_2$ under the condition $d_1, d_2 \notin Y$ is at least $1/(|S| - |Y|)$. So the collision probability is at least

$$\frac{D(Y)^2}{|Y|} + \frac{(1-D(Y))^2}{|S|-|Y|} = \frac{1}{|S|} + \frac{\beta^2}{|Y|} + \frac{\beta^2}{|S|-|Y|},$$

which is obtained by substituting $|Y|/|S| + \beta$ for $D(Y)$ and simplifying. This expression is minimized when $|Y| = |S|/2$. In that case, the collision probability is at least $(1+4\beta^2)/|S| > (1+4\delta^2)/|S|$, which contradicts our assumption. □

Let M be a BPP-algorithm for a language L that requires exactly r random bits to process an n-bit input. Let the probability of error be somewhere between 1/4 and 1/3. (For technical reasons we must also place a lower bound on the error.) So we have

$$x \in L \Rightarrow \begin{cases} 2/3 \le Pr[M(x) = 1] \le 3/4\,, \\ 1/4 \le Pr[M(x) = 0] \le 1/3\,; \end{cases}$$

$$x \notin L \Rightarrow \begin{cases} 1/4 \le Pr[M(x) = 1] \le 1/3\,, \\ 2/3 \le Pr[M(x) = 0] \le 3/4\,. \end{cases}$$

Let $x_1, x_2, \ldots, x_k$ be the sequence of pseudo-random numbers generated by the method and hash functions described above. We want to study the probabilistic behavior of the algorithm that uses the x_i's as random bits in k simulations of M, and then decides based on a majority vote whether $x \in L$. The bit sequence $x_1 x_2 \ldots x_k$ is certainly not uniformly distributed $\{0,1\}^{rk}$, it isn't even almost uniformly distributed, since only $O(r + k^2)$ genuine random bits were used to generate it. So most of the 0-1 sequences cannot even occur, and thus have probability 0. What is important for us is that the bit-sequence $b(x_1)b(x_2)\ldots b(x_k)$, where

$$b(x_i) = \begin{cases} 1 & \text{if } M \text{ with random number } x_i \text{ accepts,} \\ 0 & \text{if } M \text{ with random number } x_i \text{ rejects.} \end{cases}$$

approximates the distribution that one gets by running the algorithm M k times using new random numbers for each simulation and noting the bit sequence $b_1 b_2 \ldots b_k$.

Without loss of generality, we may assume that the input $x \in L$, so $2/3 \le Pr[b_i = 1] = p \le 3/4$. Suppose there is a small number ε, so that the "real" sequence $b_1 b_2 \ldots b_k$ and the "simulated" sequence $b(x_1)b(x_2)\ldots b(x_k)$ are ε-similar.

Exercise 17.9.° If we use genuine random numbers we know that the probability of error of the majority voting algorithm is $2^{-\Omega(k)}$. Approximate how small the error bound ε must be (as a function of k) so that using pseudo-random numbers instead of genuine random numbers still results in an error probability of at most $2^{-\Omega(k)}$. ◁

Now we prove the following claim by induction.

Claim. For all $i \geq 0$, the distribution of $b(x_1)\dots b(x_i)hx_{i+1}$, where x_j is the jth pseudo-random number as described above, is ε_i-similar (for some ε_i yet to be determined) to the following distribution: The first i bits are chosen independently at random to be 1 with probability p and 0 with probability $1-p$; then h is chosen uniformly at random from H; this is followed by a string chosen uniformly at random from $\{0,1\}^r$.

Proof (of the claim). If $i = 0$, we only need to consider the distribution of hx_1. In this case, this is uniformly distributed, so $\varepsilon_0 = 0$.

We also consider the case where $i = 1$ separately, since it is instructive for the inductive step. Let x_1 be chosen at random from $\{0,1\}^r$. We must show that the distribution of $b(x_1)hx_2$ is ε_1-similar to a "correct" distribution (one as is described in the statement of the claim, with $i = 1$) for some small ε_1. It is sufficient to show that $b(x_1)hh(x_1)$ is similar to a distribution where the first bit is chosen according to the $(p, 1-p)$-distribution and h is chosen randomly from H and the last s bits are chosen uniformly at randomly from $\{0,1\}^s$ (independent of each other). Since x_1 is random, $b(x_1)$ is distributed according to $(p, 1-p)$. Under the assumption that $b(x_1) = a \in \{0,1\}$, we must show that $hh(x_1)$ is nearly uniformly distributed on $H \times \{0,1\}^s$. This is where the Leftover Hash Lemma helps. Under the given condition, we still have $p \cdot 2^r$ (or $(1-p)2^r$), so at least $2^r/4$ choices available for x_1. The statement of the lemma is satisfied if we put $l = r - 2$. The lemma then yields a bound of

$$\varepsilon_1 = 2^{-e} = 2^{-(l-s)/2} = 2^{-(r-s-2)/2} .$$

Now comes the induction step. By the inductive hypothesis, the claim is true for $i-1$, so the distribution of $b(x_1)\dots b(x_{i-1})hx_i$ is ε_{i-1}-similar to the correct distribution. We want to show the claim for i. We need to compare the distribution of $b(x_1)\dots b(x_i)hx_{i+1}$ with the correct distribution, which we represent as $b_1\dots b_ihz$. It suffices to show that $b(x_1)\dots b(x_i)hh(x_i)$ is similar to the distribution of $b_1\dots b_ihv$, where the b_j's are chosen independently according to the $(p, 1-p)$-distribution, h is chosen uniformly from H, and v is chosen uniformly from $\{0,1\}^s$. The following claim is useful:

> Let F, G, and H be random variables such that the distribution of F is δ_1-similar to the distribution of G. Furthermore, let t be a transformation such that the distribution of $t(G)$ is δ_2-similar to H. Then H and $t(F)$ are $\delta_1 + \delta_2$-similar.

Sketch:

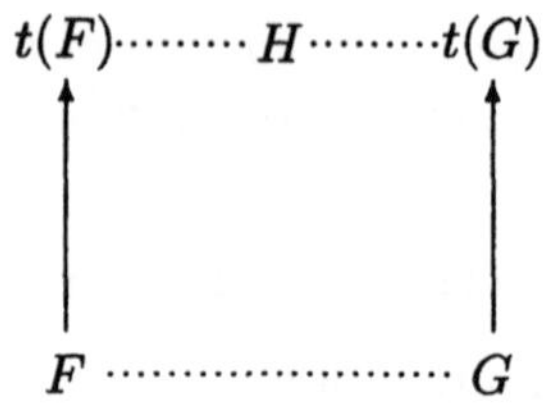

Exercise 17.10. Prove this claim. ◁

Now we put

$$\begin{aligned} F &= b(x_1)\dots b(x_{i-1})hx_i \ , \\ G &= b_1 \dots b_{i-1}hz \ , \\ H &= b_1 \dots b_{i-1}b_i hv \ . \end{aligned}$$

and define a transformation t by

$$t(b_1 \dots b_{i-1}hz) = b_1 \dots b_{i-1}b(z)hh(z) \ .$$

Then we get

$$\begin{aligned} t(G) &= b_1 \dots b_{i-1}b(v)hh(v) \ , \\ t(F) &= b(x_1)\dots b(x_{i-1})b(x_i)hh(x_i) \ . \end{aligned}$$

With this choice of F, G, H, and t; F and G are ε_{i-1}-similar (by the inductive hypothesis). Furthermore, $t(G)$ and H are ε_1-similar, as in the case $i = 1$. It follows that H and $t(F)$ are $(\varepsilon_1 + \varepsilon_{i-1})$-similar. But this is precisely the inductive claim, if we set $\varepsilon_i = \varepsilon_{i-1} + \varepsilon_1$, i.e., $\varepsilon_i = i\varepsilon_1$.

From the claim with $i = k$ it follows that the bits $b(x_1), \dots, b(x_k)$ are $k\varepsilon_1 = k/2^{(r-s-2)/2}$-similar to the distribution sets each bit to be 1 with probability p and 0 with probability $1 - p$.

All that remains is to determine the degrees of freedom s. We do this by setting $(r - s - 2)/2 = k$, so $s = r - 2k - 2$. Then we get a bound of $k/2^k = 2^{-\Omega(k)}$ on the similarity, which by Exercise 17.9 is good enough to obtain the desired probability amplification. □

Remarks. The proof above is still missing one detail: somehow we need to find the prime number p used in the definition of the hash function class H. This requires another probabilistic test (which was previously known). Furthermore, it is possible we may need to test several n-bit strings for primality before a suitable candidate is found. This seems to require an unavoidable number of random bits, which perhaps brings our upper bound on the number of random bits into question. Impagliazzo and Zuckerman, to whom this method of recycling random bits is due, actually used another class of hash functions that does not have this difficulty, but which is harder to analyze.

Another interpretation of the result presented here is that the sequence of pseudo-random numbers $x_1, \ldots, x_k$ appear to be genuinely random for every statistical test that can be performed in polynomial time: the sequence $b(x_1), \ldots, b(x_k)$ of "test results" differ in their probability distribution only minimally from the expected distribution $b(z_1), \ldots, b(z_k)$, where the z_i's are genuine random numbers. (The only boundary condition is that the test should not output 0 (or 1) too infrequently, cf. the Leftover Hash Lemma.)
Sketch:

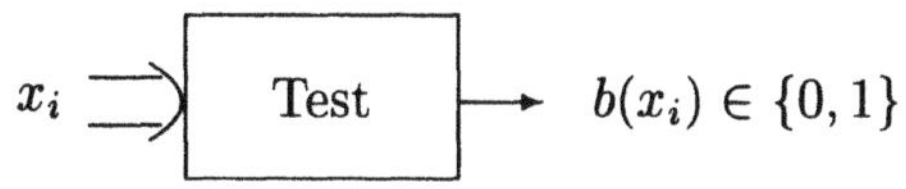

References

An introduction to probabilistic complexity classes appears in many text books, including books by the following authors: Balcázar, Diaz, and Gabarró; Brassard and Bratley; Bovet, and Crescenzi; Gurari; Welsh; Schöning (*Complexity and Structure*); and Köbler, Schöning, and Torán.

For more on universal hashing see

- Cormen, Leiserson, Rivest: *Introduction to Algorithms*, MIT Press, McGraw-Hill, 1990.

The method of recycling random numbers comes from

- R. Impagliazzo, D. Zuckerman: How to recycle random bits, *Symposium on Foundations of Computer Science*, IEEE, 1989, 248–253.

The elegant method used here to prove the induction step is thanks to J. Köbler.

Exercise 17.5 is from

- C.H. Bennett, J. Gill: Relative to a random oracle A, $P^A \neq NP^A \neq co\text{-}NP^A$ with probability 1. *SIAM Journal on Computing* 10 (1981), 96–113.

Exercise 17.6 is from

- K. Ko: Some observations on the probabilistic algorithms and NP-hard problems, *Information Processing Letters* 14 (1982), 39–43.

and the solution presented in the back of the book is from

- U. Schöning: *Complexity and Structure*, Lecture Notes in Computer Science 211, Springer 1986.

18. The BP Operator and Graph Isomorphism

> The following results suggest that the Graph Isomorphism problem is not NP-complete, since, unlike the known NP-complete problems, Graph Isomorphism belongs to a class that can be defined by means of the BP· operator, an operator that has proven useful in many other applications as well.

In this section we want to introduce a very useful operator notation that arises out of the observations about probabilistic algorithms made in Topic 17 and that will make possible the main result of this topic, namely that the graph isomorphism problem is not NP-complete unless the polynomial time hierarchy collapses. This result originally came out of a sequence of results in the area of interactive proof systems. We will not introduce these proof systems here (but see Topic 20); instead, we will prove this result along a more or less direct route using the BP· operator and some of its properties.

The transition from the class P to the class BPP (cf. Topic 17) amounts to the addition of probability but retains many of the essential features of the original class. We want to concentrate on this randomization step and formulate its essential characteristics with the help of an operator that can be applied to any class C to produce its probabilistic (or randomized) generalization.

Definition 18.1. *Let C be an arbitrary class of languages. We denote by* BP·C *the class of all languages A for which there is a language $B \in$ C, a polynomial p, and constants $\alpha \in (0,1)$ and $\varepsilon > 0$ such that for all strings x,*

$$x \in A \Longrightarrow Pr[\,\langle x,y\rangle \in B\,] \geq \alpha + \varepsilon/2\,,$$
$$x \notin A \Longrightarrow Pr[\,\langle x,y\rangle \in B\,] \leq \alpha - \varepsilon/2\,.$$

The probabilities are over all y with $|y| = p(|x|)$, chosen uniformly at random.

As in Topic 17, α will be called the *threshold value* and ε the *probability gap*. Furthermore, it is clear that BPP = BP·P. By applying the BP· operator to other complexity classes we can now form other classes as well, like BP·NP, for example.

Exercise 18.1. Formulate a condition on the class C so that $\mathsf{C} \subseteq \mathsf{BP}\cdot\mathsf{C}$. ◁

Now that we have generalized the BP· operator, we must rethink under what conditions probability amplification – as discussed in Topic 17 – is possible. This is possible if C possesses a certain closure property.

Exercise 18.2.◇ Formulate a condition on the class C that permits probability amplification (cf. Topic 17). More precisely, by probability amplification we mean that for every language $A \in \mathsf{BP}\cdot\mathsf{C}$ and every polynomial q there should be a language B in C such that

$$x \in A \Longrightarrow Pr[\,\langle x, y\rangle \in B\,] \geq 1 - 2^{-q(|x|)}\ , \text{ and}$$

$$x \notin A \Longrightarrow Pr[\,\langle x, y\rangle \in B\,] \leq 2^{-q(|x|)}\ .$$

Again, y is chosen uniformly at random from among all strings of some suitable polynomial length (in $|x|$).

Hint: Closure of the class C under polynomial time Turing reductions would certainly be a sufficient condition. But since we are particularly interested in the class BP·NP and would like to be able to amplify probabilities for that class, this condition is too strong: NP is probably not closed under Turing reductions since that would imply NP = coNP. So the task here is to find a sufficient but somewhat weaker condition than closure under Turing reductions that applies to the class NP (among other classes). ◁

Exercise 18.3. Let C be a class such that probability amplification is possible in the class BP·C. Show that BP·BP·C = BP·C. ◁

By applying probability amplification we are able to show the following result about swapping the order of two operations on a class of languages.

Lemma 18.2 (Swapping Lemma). *Let* Op *be an operator on complexity classes with the following property: If* D *is an arbitrary class and A is an arbitrary language in* Op·D, *then there is a polynomial p and a language $B \in$ D so that the property $x \in A$ depends only on the initial segment of B up to strings of length $p(|x|)$. Furthermore, let* C *be a class for which probability amplification is possible.*

Then $\mathsf{Op}\cdot\mathsf{BP}\cdot\mathsf{C} \subseteq \mathsf{BP}\cdot\mathsf{Op}\cdot\mathsf{C}$.

Exercise 18.4.◇ Prove Lemma 18.2. ◁

Such operators with a "polynomial dependency region" include, for example, co·, P(·), NP(·), and the polynomial quantifiers ∃ and ∀ used to define the classes Σ_i^P and Π_i^P in Topic 16. Since we will make use of the polynomial quantifiers again here, we repeat their formal definitions.

Definition 18.3. *For a class* C, ∃·C *denotes the class of all languages A for which there is a polynomial p and a language $B \in$* C *such that*

$$A = \{x \mid \exists y \ (|y| = p(|x|) \ \wedge \ \langle x, y\rangle \in B)\} .$$

The class $\forall\cdot\mathsf{C}$ *is defined analogously using universal quantification over strings of length* $p(|x|)$.

A few of the obvious properties of these operators include

$$\exists\cdot\mathsf{P} = \mathsf{NP}, \quad \mathsf{co}\text{-}\exists\cdot\mathsf{C} = \forall\cdot\mathsf{co}\text{-}\mathsf{C}, \quad \mathsf{co}\text{-}\forall\cdot\mathsf{C} = \exists\cdot\mathsf{co}\text{-}\mathsf{C} .$$

Now that we have studied a few properties of the $\mathsf{BP}\cdot$ operator, we want to become familiar with a natural problem that is in one of the $\mathsf{BP}\cdot$ classes. The problem is the graph isomorphism problem, *GI*: given two undirected graphs, determine whether or not they are isomorphic, that is, determine whether or not there is a permutation of the nodes (node numbers) such that when applied to the first graph it results in the second.

Example. The following two graphs are isomorphic. One possible isomorphism is $\binom{1\ 2\ 3\ 4\ 5}{3\ 4\ 1\ 5\ 2}$.

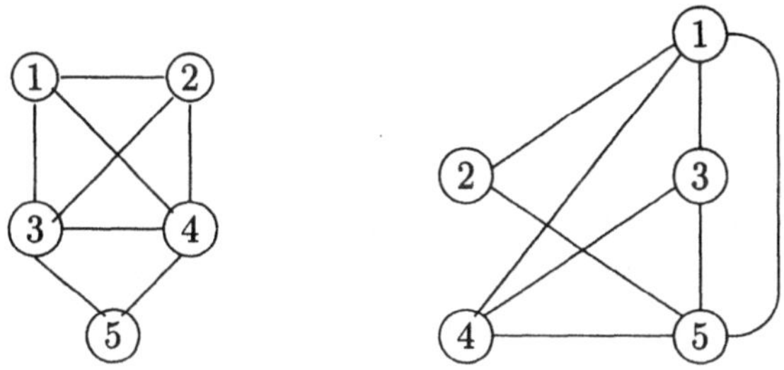

It is clear that this problem is in NP. Whether this problem is NP-complete remains an open question, but most likely it is not. (See for example a discussion of this problem in the book by Garey and Johnson.) On the other hand, no polynomial time algorithm is known for this problem either. So *GI* is a candidate for a problem that is in NP but neither NP-complete nor in P. (If $\mathsf{P} \neq \mathsf{NP}$, it can be proven that such problems exists, but it will probably be difficult to prove that any "natural" problem has this property.)

Our proof of the following theorem, unlike the original proof, will be the result of a more or less "direct attack."

Theorem 18.4. *The complement of the graph isomorphism problem* ($\overline{GI}$) *is in* $\mathsf{BP}\cdot\mathsf{NP}$.

Proof. We begin with a pair of elementary observations about isomorphism of graphs. Let $Aut(G)$ be the set (a group) of isomorphisms of a graph G, that is, the set of all permutations of the nodes that map the graph to itself. For example, $\binom{1\ 2\ 3\ 4\ 5}{2\ 1\ 4\ 3\ 5}$ is an automorphism of the first graph in the example above.

Exercise 18.5. If the graph G has exactly n nodes and $m = |Aut(G)|$, how many different graphs are isomorphic to G? ◁

Exercise 18.6.◇ Given two graphs G_1 and G_2, each having n nodes, define a set $X = X(G_1, G_2)$ of objects such that the objects in X can be generated nondeterministically from the graphs G_1 and G_2 in polynomial time and

$$G_1 \text{ and } G_2 \text{ are isomorphic} \Longrightarrow |X| = n!$$
$$G_1 \text{ and } G_2 \text{ are not isomorphic} \Longrightarrow |X| = 2(n!)$$

◁

By forming the cross-product

$$Y = X \times X,$$

we can increase the difference between these two numbers.

$$G_1 \text{ and } G_2 \text{ are isomorphic} \Longrightarrow |Y| = (n!)^2$$
$$G_1 \text{ and } G_2 \text{ are not isomorphic} \Longrightarrow |Y| = (2n!)^2 = 4 \cdot (n!)^2$$

Next we need a class $H = H_n$ of universal hash functions. This class of hash functions should map elements from a set U (for example, 0-1 strings) with $Y \subseteq U$ to the elements of the set $M = [4(n!)^2] = \{0, 1, \ldots, 4(n!)^2 - 1\}$. We require of this class of hash functions, H, the following:

- *Uniformity.* For every $y \in U$ and $a \in M$, if a hash function h is chosen at random from H, then

$$Pr[\, h(y) = a\,] = 1/|M|\,.$$

- *Pairwise independence.* For all $y, y' \in U$ with $y \neq y'$ and all $z \in M$, if a hash function h is chosen at random from H then

$$Pr[\, h(y) = z \wedge h(y') = z\,] = 1/|M|^2\,.$$

- *Efficient computation.* The random selection of a hash function h from $H = H_n$ and the evaluation of h on an input y should be possible in polynomial time with polynomially many random bits.

In what follows we will be interested in (an approximation to) the probability that for a randomly selected h, $0 \in h(Y)$. Let G_1 and G_2 be two input graphs with n nodes each. If they are isomorphic, then $|Y| = (n!)^2$ and in this case

$$\begin{aligned} Pr[\, 0 \in h(Y)\,] &= Pr[\, \exists y \in Y : \ h(y) = 0\,] \\ &\leq \sum_{y \in Y} Pr[\, h(y) = 0\,] \\ &= |Y|/|M| = 1/4\,. \end{aligned}$$

If the graphs are not isomorphic, then $|Y| = 4 \cdot (n!)^2 = |M|$. In this case we can give a lower bound for the probability by using the first two terms of the inclusion-exclusion principle (cf. Kozen, page 194):

$$\begin{aligned} Pr[\,0 \in h(Y)\,] &\geq \sum_{y \in Y} Pr[\,h(y) = 0\,] - \sum_{\{y,z\} \subseteq Y} Pr[\,h(y) = 0 \wedge h(z) = 0\,] \\ &= |Y|/|M| - \binom{|Y|}{2}/|M|^2 \\ &\geq 1 - 1/2 \;=\; 1/2\,. \end{aligned}$$

In summary,

$$G_1 \text{ and } G_2 \text{ are isomorphic} \Longrightarrow Pr[\,0 \in h(Y)\,] \leq 1/4\,,$$
$$G_1 \text{ and } G_2 \text{ are not isomorphic} \Longrightarrow Pr[\,0 \in h(Y)\,] \geq 1/2\,.$$

Since the predicate "$0 \in h(Y)$" is in NP – guess a y, verify nondeterministically that $y \in Y$, check that $h(y) = 0$ – this representation shows that the complement of graph isomorphism is in BP·NP. (The constants are $\alpha = 3/8$ and $\varepsilon = 1/4$.)

We have yet to discuss the class of hash functions required. We could use the class of hash functions introduced in Topic 17, but that choice brings with it a number of technical difficulties, since it requires a nondeterministic check for primality (which is possible) and because $|M|$ is not necessarily prime.

We can define another class of hash functions H from $\{0,1\}^a$ to $\{0,1\}^b$ as follows: A hash function $h \in H$ is described by a boolean $a \times b$ matrix (h_{ij}). Let $x = x_1 \dots x_a$ be a 0-1 string of length a. Then the jth bit of $h(x)$ is defined to be

$$\bigoplus_{i=1}^{a} (h_{ij} \wedge x_i), \quad 1 \leq j \leq b\,.$$

Each of the 2^{ab} such hash functions h can be chosen uniformly at random from H, so ab bits are required to specify a hash function.

Exercise 18.7.$^\diamond$ Show that this class H has the pairwise independence property, i.e., for all $y, y' \in \{0,1\}^a$ with $y \neq y'$ and for all $z \in \{0,1\}^b$, if h is chosen uniformly at random, then $Pr[\,h(y) = z \wedge h(y') = z\,] = 2^{-2b}$. ◁

A small technical problem is now that size of the range of the functions is a power of 2. This relaxation of the desired number $|M|$ is acceptable if we first further increase the difference in the possible values of $|Y|$ (for isomorphic vs. non-isomorphic pairs of graphs). Once this has been done, the proof follows easily from what we have done above. □

* * * * *

Since the complement of the graph isomorphism problem is in BP·NP, $GI \in$ coBP·NP = BP·coNP, so it is "almost" in coNP. The following diagram shows the relative position of GI.

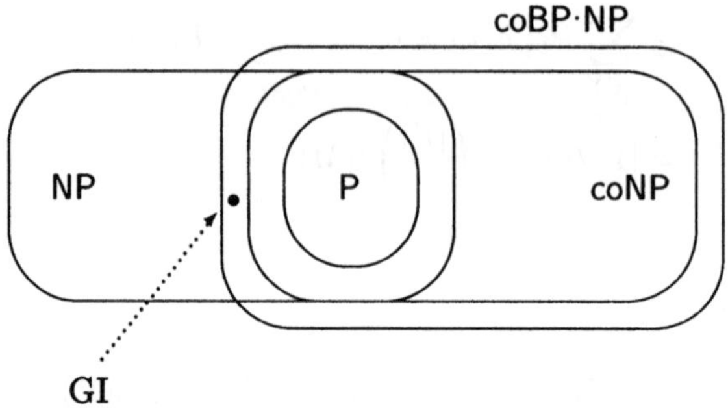

The diagram suggests that GI is probably not NP-complete, since the NP-complete problems should be thought of as being at the far left of the diagram, as far away from P as possible.

Just as no NP-complete language can be in coNP unless NP = coNP (that is, PH collapses to Σ_1^P), we will show now that if there is an NP-complete language in coBP·NP, then PH collapses to Σ_2^P. So if GI is NP-complete, then PH = Σ_2^P.

For this we need a method of simulating the BP· operator with sequences of $\exists$ and $\forall$.

Lemma 18.5. *Let* C *be a class of languages that is closed under the operator* Pos *(see page 285), so that in particular,* BP·C *permits probability amplification. Then* BP·C $\subseteq \exists\cdot\forall\cdot$C *and* BP·C $\subseteq \forall\cdot\exists\cdot$C.

Proof. Let A be in BP·C. We choose a language B in C so that for all x

$$x \in A \Longrightarrow Pr[\,\langle x,y\rangle \in B\,] \geq 1 - 2^{-n}\,,$$
$$x \notin A \Longrightarrow Pr[\,\langle x,y\rangle \in B\,] \leq 2^{-n}\,,$$

where y is chosen uniformly at random from $\{0,1\}^{p(|x|)}$ and p is a suitable polynomial.

With the help of the following claim, the proof proceeds easily:

Claim. Let $E, F \subseteq \{0,1\}^{p(n)}$ with $|E|, |F| \geq (1-2^{-n})2^{p(n)}$. Then

1. $\exists u_1, \ldots, u_{p(n)}\ \forall v\ [u_1 \oplus v \in E \vee \cdots \vee u_{p(n)} \oplus v \in E]$, and
2. $\forall u_1, \ldots, u_{p(n)}\ \exists v\ [u_1 \oplus v \in F \wedge \cdots \wedge u_{p(n)} \oplus v \in F]$.

All strings u_i and v above have length $p(n)$ and $\oplus$ is the bitwise XOR-function.

Let $G = \{y \mid \langle x,y\rangle \in B\}$. Then we can apply the claim to either G or $\overline{G}$, depending on whether $x \in A$ or $x \notin A$, to prove the lemma:

$$x \in A \Rightarrow (1) \qquad\qquad \text{with } E = G = \{y \mid \langle x,y\rangle \in B\}\ ,$$
$$x \notin A \Rightarrow (2) \Rightarrow \neg(1) \text{ with } F = \overline{G} = \{y \mid \langle x,y\rangle \notin B\}\ ;$$

and

$$x \in A \Rightarrow (2) \qquad\qquad \text{with } F = G = \{y \mid \langle x,y\rangle \in B\}\ ,$$
$$x \notin A \Rightarrow (1) \Rightarrow \neg(2) \text{ with } E = \overline{G} = \{y \mid \langle x,y\rangle \notin B\}\ .$$

The statements $[u_1 \oplus v \in E \vee \cdots \vee u_{p(n)} \oplus v \in E]$ and $[u_1 \oplus v \in E \wedge \cdots \wedge u_{p(n)} \oplus v \in E]$ with $E = \{y \mid \langle x,y\rangle \in B\}$ are in Pos(C), and C is closed under Pos, so $A \in \exists\cdot\forall\cdot\mathsf{C}$ and $A \in \forall\cdot\exists\cdot\mathsf{C}$.

This completes the proof of Lemma 18.5, modulo the proof of the claim, which is done in the next two exercises. □

Exercise 18.8.[◇] Prove part (1) of the claim.

Hint: Show the existence of $u_1, \ldots, u_{p(n)}$ by means of a probabilistic construction; that is, show that a random choice of u_i's has the desired property with non-zero probability, therefore, such u_i's must *exist*. ◁

Exercise 18.9.[◇] Prove part (2) of the claim.

Hint: Use an indirect proof and a combinatorial counting argument. ◁

Several inclusion relations are now immediate consequences of this result.

Theorem 18.6. BPP $\subseteq \Sigma_2^P \cap \Pi_2^P$.

Proof. BPP $=$ BP·P $\subseteq \exists\cdot\forall\cdot\mathsf{P} \cap \forall\cdot\exists\cdot\mathsf{P} = \Sigma_2^P \cap \Pi_2^P$. □

Theorem 18.7. BP·NP $\subseteq \Pi_2^P$.

Proof. BP·NP $\subseteq \forall\cdot\exists\cdot\mathsf{NP} = \forall\cdot\mathsf{NP} = \Pi_2^P$. □

The following lemma, along with Theorem 18.4, is the key to the main result of this section, namely that *GI* is "almost surely" not NP-complete.

Lemma 18.8. *If* coNP $\subseteq$ BP·NP *then* PH $= \Sigma_2^P = \Pi_2^P =$ BP·NP.

Exercise 18.10. Prove Lemma 18.8. ◁

Corollary 18.9. *If GI is* NP*-complete, then the polynomial hierarchy collapses to the second level.*

Proof. If *GI* is NP-complete, then $\overline{GI}$ is coNP-complete. By Theorem 18.4 it follows that coNP $\subseteq$ BP·NP. From this the collapse follows by Lemma 18.8. □

References

For background on probabilistic complexity classes and the BP· operator see

- U. Schöning: Probabilistic complexity classes and lowness, *Journal of Computer and System Sciences* 39 (1989), 84–100.
- S. Zachos: Probabilistic quantifiers, adversaries, and complexity classes: an overview, *Proceedings of the 1st Structure in Complexity Theory Conference*, Lecture Notes in Computer Science 223, Springer, 1986, 383–400.

More background on the graph isomorphism problem and its (structural) properties can be found in

- C.M. Hoffmann: *Group-Theoretic Algorithms and Graph Isomorphism*, Springer, 1982.
- J. Köbler, U. Schöning, J. Torán: *The Graph Isomorphism Problem: Its Structural Complexity*, Birkhäuser, 1993.

The original proof of Theorem 18.4 was very indirect and followed from results in

- O. Goldreich, S. Micali, A. Wigderson: Proofs that yield nothing but their validity and a methodology of cryptographic protocol design, *Proceedings of the Symposium on Foundations of Computer Science*, IEEE, 1986, 174–187.
- S. Goldwasser, M. Sipser: Private coins versus public coins in interactive proof systems, in S. Micali, ed., *Advances in Computing Research, Vol. 5: Randomness and Computation*, JAI Press, 1989, 73–90.

Theorem 18.6 is due to

- C. Lautemann: BPP and the polynomial hierarchy, *Information Processing Letters* 14 (1983), 215–217.

which includes the technique we used to prove Lemma 18.5, and

- M. Sipser: A complexity theoretic approach to randomness, *Proceedings of the 15th Symposium on Theory of Computing*, ACM, 1983, 330–335.

Theorem 18.7 is from

- L. Babai: Trading group theory for randomness, *Proceedings of the 17th Symposium on Theory of Computing*, ACM, 1985, 421–429.

where the result was expressed in terms of Babai's class AM (Arthur-Merlin games), which is a special version of interactive proof systems. AM has been shown to be equivalent to BP·NP.

For Lemma 18.8 and its implications for *GI* see

- R.B. Boppana, J. Håstad, S. Zachos: Does co-NP have short interactive proofs? *Information Processing Letters* 25 (1987), 27–32.
- U. Schöning: Graph isomorphism is in the low hierarchy, *Journal of Computer and System Sciences* 37 (1988), 312–323.
- U. Schöning: Probabilistic complexity classes and lowness, *Journal of Computer and System Sciences* 39 (1989), 84–100.

19. The BP-Operator and the Power of Counting Classes

With the help of the BP· operator, Toda (1989) achieved an astonishing result: the classes ⊕P and #P are, in a sense, at least as expressive as the entire polynomial hierarchy.

The class ⊕P (read "parity-P") consists of all languages L for which there is a nondeterministic polynomial time-bounded machine M (so far this sounds just like the definition of NP) with the following property:

$$x \in L \iff \text{the number of accepting computations of } M \text{ on input } x \text{ is } \textit{odd}.$$

The difference between this and the class NP is that the number of accepting paths is required to be odd rather than merely non-zero.

This class represents a rudimentary form of counting (of the number of accepting computations). In the full counting task, which we will discuss shortly, one would like to know all of the bits of (the binary representation of) this number; the languages in the class ⊕P are defined solely in terms of the lowest order bit, i.e., the parity.

What can one begin to do with this parity information? Or in other words: How powerful is the class ⊕P? It is clear that P is in ⊕P and that ⊕P is closed under complement.

Exercise 19.1. Why? ◁

But how does this class compare with the class NP? The only immediate conclusion is that $\mathsf{P} \subseteq \mathsf{NP} \cap \text{co-}\mathsf{NP} \cap \oplus\mathsf{P}$. The relationship between NP and ⊕P is unclear. Most likely they are incomparable.

Sketch:

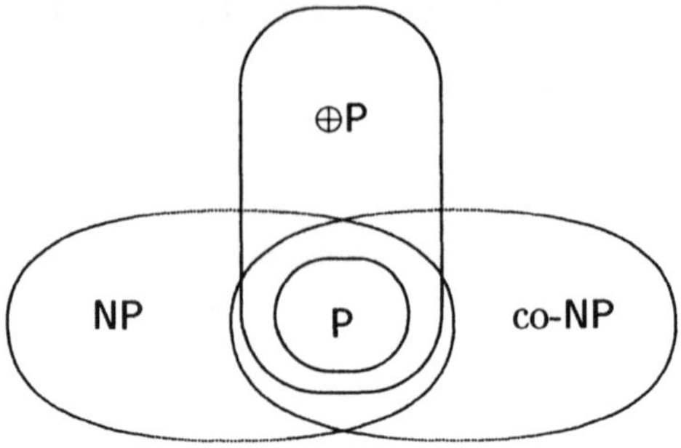

Each positive instance of an NP-problem can have a different number (in general up to exponentially many) "witnesses" for membership in the language. (More concretely, for a satisfiable boolean formula F, i.e., $F \in SAT$, there can be exponentially many satisfying assignments.) If we now restrict NP to the languages for which each positive instance has at most polynomially many witnesses, we obtain the class FewP. That is, a language L is in FewP if there is an NP-machine that accepts the language L and has the additional property that for each input x, there are at most $p(|x|)$ accepting paths, where p is a suitable polynomial.

Clearly, $\mathsf{P} \subseteq \mathsf{FewP} \subset \mathsf{NP}$. It is not clear how much of a restriction it is to require "few witnesses." We do, however, have the following result:

Theorem 19.1. $\mathsf{FewP} \subseteq \oplus\mathsf{P}$.

Exercise 19.2. Prove this theorem.

Hint: Let m be the correct number of accepting computations of the FewP-machine. Then $\sum_{i=1}^{m} \binom{m}{i} = 2^m - 1$ is odd if and only if $m > 0$. ◁

Sketch:

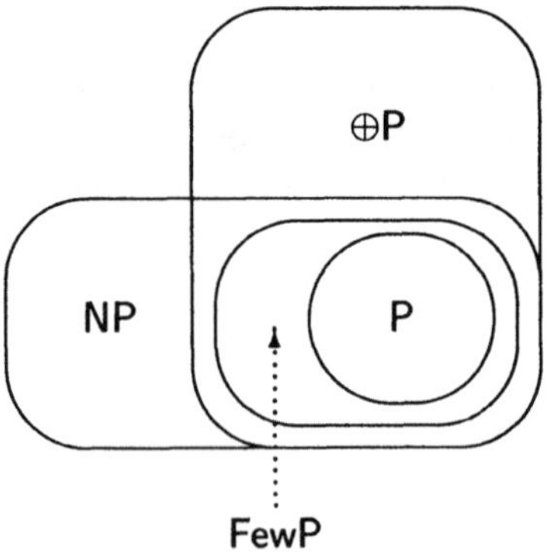

It is an interesting coincidence that in the examples known to this point, such as the prime number problem or the equivalence problem for tournaments (see the book by Köbler, Schöning, and Torán), the property of belonging to $\oplus$P seems to be connected with the property that faster algorithms are known, with upper bounds something like $O(n^{\log n})$, than are known for the NP-complete languages. (For the problems just mentioned it is not clear whether they are in P.) It is unknown if there is a causal link between $\oplus$P and the complexity $O(n^{\log n})$.

In this sense one can interpret $\oplus$P has a "low" complexity class. In the last chapter we applied the BP$\cdot$ operator to various complexity classes such as P and NP and interpreted this as merely a certain probabilistic generalization which did not significantly alter the properties of the underlying complexity classes. The intuition that therefore BP$\cdot\oplus$P is a "low" class is, however, completely incorrect: Valiant and Vazirani showed that NP $\subseteq$ BP$\cdot\oplus$P, and Toda extended this to show that even PH $\subseteq$ BP$\cdot\oplus$P. This will be the main result of this chapter.

We begin with a few observations about the class $\oplus$P. This class has complete languages (under polynomial-time many-one reductions), for example,

$$\oplus SAT = \{F \mid F \text{ is a boolean formula with an odd number of satisfying assignments}\}\ .$$

This follows from Cook's Theorem, which demonstrates the NP-completeness of SAT, and the observation that the Cook formula has the same number of satisfying assignments as the underlying Turing machine has accepting computations.

We say that a language L has AND-functions if there is a polynomial time computable function f such that

$$x_1 \in L \text{ and } \ldots \text{and } x_n \in L \iff f(\langle x_1, \ldots, x_n \rangle) \in L\ .$$

Analogously, we can define the notion of an OR-function and a NOT-function for a language.

Exercise 19.3. Show that SAT has AND-functions and OR-functions. Furthermore, SAT has NOT-functions if and only if NP = coNP. $\lhd$

What is the situation with $\oplus SAT$? We will see that $\oplus SAT$ has AND-, OR- and NOT- functions. The AND-function for $\oplus$P is demonstrated (as for SAT) by the function $f(\langle F_1, \ldots, F_n \rangle) = F_1 \wedge \cdots \wedge F_n$, where the formulas F_i have disjoint sets of variables. Let a_i be the number of satisfying assignments for F_i. Then the number of satisfying assignments for the formula $F_1 \wedge \cdots \wedge F_n$ is precisely $\prod_{i=1}^n a_i$, which is odd exactly when every a_i is odd.

A NOT-function can be obtained by adding on a "dummy" satisfying assignment: $g(F) = (F \wedge y) \vee (x_1 \wedge \cdots \wedge x_n \wedge \overline{y})$, where $x_1, \ldots, x_n$ are the variables that occur in F and y is a new variable. The formula $g(F)$ clearly has exactly one more satisfying assignment than the original formula F.

By combining these two formulas and using DeMorgan's laws we immediately obtain an OR-function:

$$h(x_1, \ldots, x_n) = g(f(g(x_1), \ldots, g(x_n))).$$

Theorem 19.2. NP $\subseteq$ BP$\cdot\oplus$P.

Proof. It is sufficient to show that *SAT* is in a certain sense probabilistically reducible to $\oplus SAT$. More precisely, each input formula F can be transformed by a probabilistic, polynomial-time algorithm into a formula F' with the property that:

$$F \in SAT \Longrightarrow Pr[F' \in \oplus SAT] > \frac{1}{p(|F|)} ,$$
$$F \notin SAT \Longrightarrow F' \notin \oplus SAT ,$$

for some polynomial p.

Exercise 19.4. Show that Theorem 19.2 follows from the preceding statement.

Hint: For the required probability amplification use the fact that the language $\oplus SAT$ has OR-functions. ◁

Let the input formula F have n variables $x_1, \ldots, x_n$. Let S be a random subset of $\{1, \ldots, n\}$, i.e., S is specified by n random bits, the ith bit determining whether $i \in S$. We denote by $[S]$ the boolean formula $\bigoplus_{i \in S} x_i$. That is, $[S]$ is a formula that is true precisely when there are an odd number of $i \in S$ for which $x_i = 1$. The probabilistic algorithm now transforms F as follows:

INPUT F;
GUESS RANDOMLY $k \in \{0, \ldots, n-1\}$;
GUESS RANDOMLY subsets $S_1, \ldots, S_{k+2} \subseteq \{1, \ldots, n\}$;
OUTPUT $F' = F \wedge [S_1] \wedge \cdots \wedge [S_{k+2}]$.

Intuitively, with each addition of a subformula of the form $[S]$ to the conjunction the number of satisfying assignments is approximately halved since for each assignment b the probability is $1/2$ that $b([S]) = 0$ (and $1/2$ that $b([S]) = 1$). (Without loss of generality assume that $b \neq 00\ldots0$.) These events are, however, not completely independent but only pairwise independent. This makes the analysis of the probabilities somewhat more difficult. But it seems at least plausible that after one of these halving steps there will be a non-negligible probability of having *exactly one* satisfying assignment left.

It is clear that if F is unsatisfiable, then F' is also unsatisfiable and therefore has an even number (namely, 0) of satisfying assignments, so that $F' \notin \oplus SAT$. Now suppose that F has $m \geq 1$ satisfying assignments. With probability at least $1/n$, k will be chosen so that $2^k \leq m \leq 2^{k+1}$. Now we show that with this choice of k, the probability that F' has *exactly one* satisfying assignment is at least $1/8$. Thus the probability that $F' \in \oplus SAT$ is at least $(1/n)(1/8) = 1/8n$.

Let b be a fixed satisfying assignment of F. Since the subsets S_i ($i = 1, \ldots, k+2$) are chosen independently, the probability that b is also a satisfying assignment of F' (i.e., that it "survives" each halving) is $1/2^{k+2}$. Under the condition that b survived, the probability of any other satisfying assignment b' for F also survives is also $1/2^{k+2}$. Thus the probability that b survives but none of the other $m-1$ satisfying assignments for F survive is at least

$$\frac{1}{2^{k+2}} \cdot (1 - \sum_{b'} \frac{1}{2^{k+2}}) = \frac{1}{2^{k+2}} \cdot (1 - \frac{m-1}{2^{k+2}}) \geq \frac{1}{2^{k+2}} \cdot (1 - \frac{2^{k+1}}{2^{k+2}}) = 1/2^{k+3} \, .$$

So the probability that there is such a b that is the *only* satisfying assignment for F' is at least

$$\sum_{b} 1/2^{k+3} = m/2^{k+3} \geq 2^k/2^{k+3} = 1/8.$$

With that Theorem 19.2 has been proven. □

Exercise 19.5. Show the following generalization of the preceding theorem:

$$\exists\cdot\oplus\mathsf{P} \subseteq \mathsf{BP}\cdot\oplus\mathsf{P}. \qquad \lhd$$

The preceding proof (and exercise) actually show not only that $\mathsf{NP} \subseteq \mathsf{BP}\cdot\oplus\mathsf{P}$ ($\exists\cdot\oplus\mathsf{P} \subseteq \mathsf{BP}\cdot\oplus\mathsf{P}$, respectively) but that for any polynomial q with a suitable choice of a $\oplus\mathsf{P}$-language, L, the probability that $F \in SAT$ but $F' \notin L$ can be made less than $2^{-q(n)}$.

Toda showed that this inclusion can be significantly strengthened:

Theorem 19.3. $\mathsf{PH} \subseteq \mathsf{BP}\cdot\oplus\mathsf{P}$.

Proof. We show by induction on k that the following claim holds:

Claim. For all $k \geq 0$, $\Sigma_k^P \cup \Pi_k^P$ is contained in $\mathsf{BP}\cdot\oplus\mathsf{P}$, and the error probability can be made to be less than $2^{-q(n)}$ for any polynomial q.

The base case when $k = 0$ is trivial. Now we show the claim holds for $k+1$ under the assumption that the claim holds for k. It suffices to show that Σ_{k+1}^P is contained in BP·⊕P, since BP·⊕P is closed under complement. Let L be an arbitrary language in $\Sigma_{k+1}^P = \exists\cdot\Pi_k^P$, let p be the polynomial that bounds the length of the existentially quantified strings, and let q be an arbitrary polynomial which gives the error rate, $2^{-q(n)}$, that must be achieved. By the inductive hypothesis, $L \in \exists\cdot$BP·⊕P, and an error rate of at most $2^{-(q(n)+p(n)+1)}$ may be assumed. The BP· operator can be pulled to the front (see previous chapter) so we get $L \in$ BP·∃·⊕P with an error rate now of at most $2^{-(q(n)+1)}$. The previous exercise implies that $L \in$ BP·BP·⊕P, and that the error rate of the second BP· operator can be chosen to be at most $2^{-(q(n)+1)}$. Now we can combine both BP· operators into one. In the worst case, the error rates add. So we get that $L \in$ BP·⊕P with an error rate of at most $2^{-q(n)}$, as was desired. □

As a corollary to this result in combination with techniques from the previous chapter we get the following immediately:

Corollary 19.4. *If* ⊕P *is contained in the polynomial time hierarchy,* PH, *then* PH *collapses.* □

Exercise 19.6. Prove Corollary 19.4.

Hint: Use the fact that ⊕P has complete languages (like $\oplus SAT$, for example). ◁

Exercise 19.7. Prove that the class BP·⊕P has complete languages. (This seems to be unusual for a BP·-class, although, for example, BP·PSPACE = PSPACE and, of course, PSPACE also has complete languages.)

Hint: Use the facts that ⊕P(⊕P) = ⊕P (which we have already implicitly shown) and that Theorem 19.3 relativizes, that is, for all classes C, PH(C) ⊆ BP·⊕P(C). From this we can conclude that BP·⊕P ⊆ ∀·∃·⊕P ⊆ PH(⊕P) ⊆ BP·⊕P(⊕P) = BP·⊕P. ◁

* * * * *

Let acc_M be a function from Σ^* to $\mathbb{N}$ that gives for each input $x \in \Sigma^*$ the number of accepting computations of M when run with input x. Let #P be the set of all functions of the form acc_M for some NP-machine M.

We want to investigate the question of whether one can compute languages in the polynomial time hierarchy using the information given by a #P-function. In fact, we will show that

Theorem 19.5. BP·⊕P ⊆ P(#P).

From this it follows that $\mathsf{PH} \subseteq \mathsf{P}(\#\mathsf{P})$. Indeed, for any language $A \in \mathsf{BP}\cdot\oplus\mathsf{P}$ we will show how to construct an NP-machine M such that from the value of $\mathsf{acc}_M(x)$ we can determine whether or not $x \in A$ by means of a simple arithmetic computation (in polynomial time). Consider the following example: $A \in \mathsf{BP}\cdot\oplus\mathsf{P}$ means that

$x \in A \Longrightarrow$ for "many" strings y there is an odd number of strings z such that $\langle x, y, z\rangle \in B$,

$x \notin A \Longrightarrow$ for only "a few" strings y is there an odd number of strings z such that $\langle x, y, z\rangle \in B$,

where B is a language in P. For the sake of concreteness let's assume that there are 4 potential y-strings and 2 potential z-strings. "Many" could mean in this case 3 or 4, "few" 0 or 1. Then the following tree represents a situation where $x \in A$. (An 'a' in the diagram represents that $\langle x, y, z\rangle \in B$.)

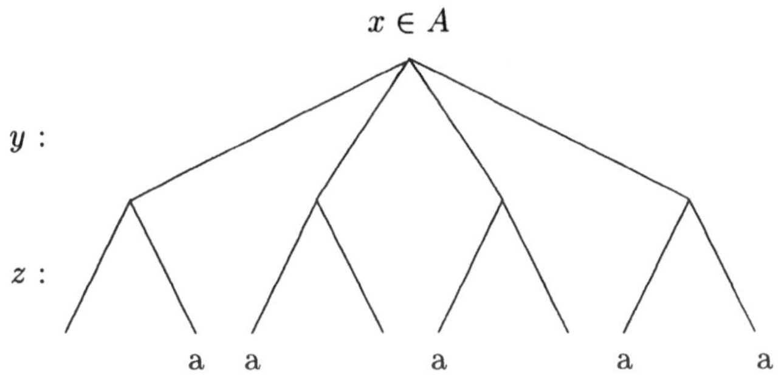

In this case there are 3 y's with an odd number of z values.

In the next picture there is only *one* such y, so $x \notin A$:

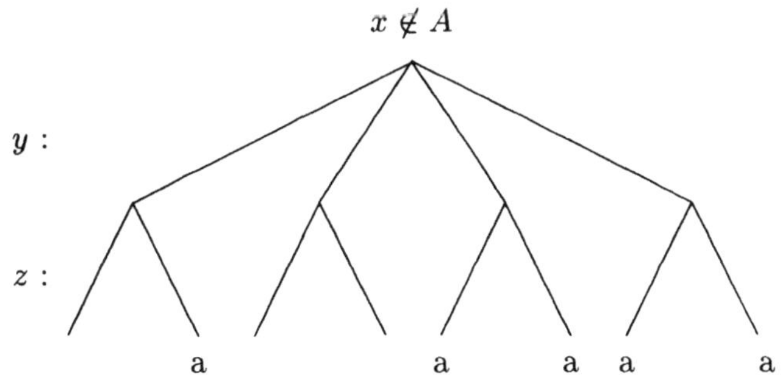

If we were to ignore the structural difference between y and z, however, and view the entire tree as an NP-machine M with input x, then we could not learn anything from the number of accepting paths, $\mathsf{acc}_M(x)$, since in both cases $\mathsf{acc}_M(x) = 5$.

Now we want to modify the z-subtrees to z'-subtrees in such a way that the following holds:

$$\text{Odd number of } z\text{'s} \Longrightarrow \text{the number of } z' \text{ is congruent to } 0 \pmod 8,$$

$$\text{Even number of } z\text{'s} \Longrightarrow \text{the number of } z' \text{ is congruent to } 1 \pmod 8.$$

The number 8 was chosen in this case because $8 > 4$ and 4 is the number of potential y's. In addition it simplifies matters to choose a power of 2.

In the first example above we now get:

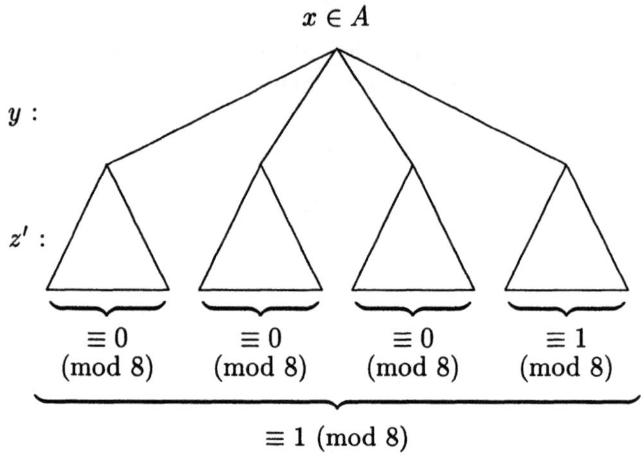

And in the second case:

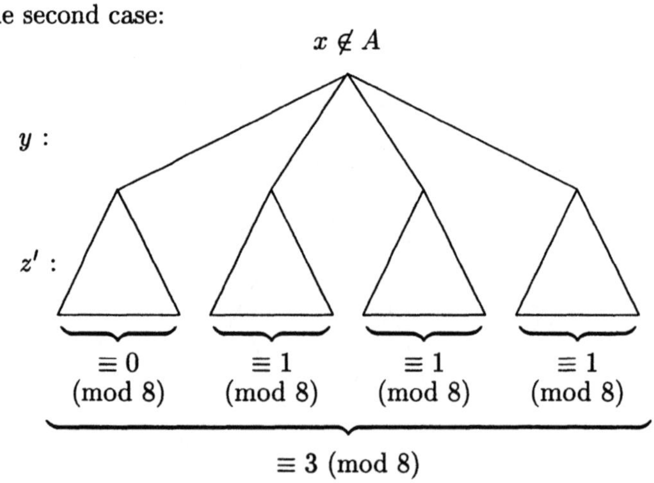

Now the total number g of accepting computations is sufficient to differentiate the two cases: $x \in A$ if $g \equiv 0$ or $g \equiv 1 \pmod 8$ and $x \notin A$, if $g \equiv 3$ or $g \equiv 4 \pmod 8$. In general: $x \in A$ if and only if $g < 2^{p(|x|)}/2 \pmod{2^{p(|x|)}}$, where p is a large enough polynomial and g is the total number of accepting computations. For an appropriate machine N, $g = \mathsf{acc}_N(x)$. So it turns out that the determination of whether $x \in A$ depends only on *a single bit* of the binary representation of $\mathsf{acc}_N(x)$, a $\#\mathsf{P}$-function. (Note: the proof of inclusion $\mathsf{BP}{\cdot}\oplus\mathsf{P} \subseteq \mathsf{P}(\#\mathsf{P})$ does not depend on the fact that the $\mathsf{BP}{\cdot}$ operator has a "gap" between the accepting and rejecting probabilities or that this gap can be amplified; the inclusion would also be true if we had defined the $\mathsf{BP}{\cdot}$ operator without this gap – see the previous chapter.)

Our goal has now been reached, provided we can transform an arbitrary NP-machine M into an NP-machine M' such that for some (sufficiently large) polynomial p we have:

$$\begin{aligned} \mathsf{acc}_M(x) \text{ odd} &\Longrightarrow \mathsf{acc}_{M'}(x) \equiv 0 \pmod{2^{p(|x|)}} , \\ \mathsf{acc}_M(x) \text{ even} &\Longrightarrow \mathsf{acc}_{M'}(x) \equiv 1 \pmod{2^{p(|x|)}} . \end{aligned}$$

The polynomial p depends on the number of y in the preceding example. ($2^{p(n)}$ should be larger than the number of potential y, i.e., $p(n)$ must be larger than the maximum possible length of such a y.) In order to fulfill this property, it suffices to give a general construction that works *for every polynomial p*.

For this consider the following "magic formula" (let $p = p(|x|)$):

$$(\mathsf{acc}_M(x)^p + 1)^p .$$

Now we run through each case ($\mathsf{acc}_M(x)$ even or odd):

Case 1. $\mathsf{acc}_M(x)$ even.

$$\underbrace{\Big(\underbrace{\underbrace{\underbrace{\mathsf{acc}_M(x)}_{\substack{\equiv 0 \\ (\mathrm{mod}\ 2)}}{}^{p}}_{\substack{\equiv 0 \\ (\mathrm{mod}\ 2^p)}} + 1}_{\substack{\equiv 1 \\ (\mathrm{mod}\ 2^p)}}\Big)^{p}}_{\substack{\equiv 1 \\ (\mathrm{mod}\ 2^p)}}$$

Case 2. $\mathsf{acc}_M(x)$ odd.

$$\underbrace{\Big(\underbrace{\underbrace{\underbrace{\mathsf{acc}_M(x)}_{\substack{\equiv 1 \\ \pmod 2}}{}^{p}}_{\substack{\equiv 1 \\ \pmod 2}} + 1}_{\substack{\equiv 0 \\ \pmod 2}}\Big)^{p}}_{\substack{\equiv 0 \\ \pmod{2^p}}}$$

In each case the chain of implications is understood to go from top to bottom.

Exercise 19.8. In both cases we used the implications

$$a \equiv 0 \pmod b \Longrightarrow a^p \equiv 0 \pmod{b^p},$$
$$a \equiv 1 \pmod b \Longrightarrow a^p \equiv 1 \pmod b.$$

Prove them. ◁

Exercise 19.9. Let M be an NP-machine. Show that the function

$$f(x) = (\mathsf{acc}_M(x)^{p(|x|)} + 1)^{p(|x|)}$$

is in #P. ◁

This completes the proof that $\mathsf{PH} \subseteq \mathsf{BP}\cdot\oplus\mathsf{P} \subseteq \mathsf{P}(\#\mathsf{P})$. □

The diagram below summarizes the known inclusion relationships. The language class PP, which appears in the diagram, is closely related to the function class #P. Let M be an NP-machine and p be a polynomial such that every computation on every input of length n runs in time $p(n)$. Then there are $2^{p(n)}$ different possible computations on each input of length n. A language A is in PP if there is such a machine M and polynomial p for which $x \in A \Longleftrightarrow \mathsf{acc}_M(x) > 2^{p(|x|)}/2$, i.e., at least half of the computations on input x are accepting. It is easy to see that $\mathsf{NP} \subseteq \mathsf{PP}$, $\mathsf{P}(\#\mathsf{P}) = \mathsf{P}(\mathsf{PP})$, and PP is closed under complementation.

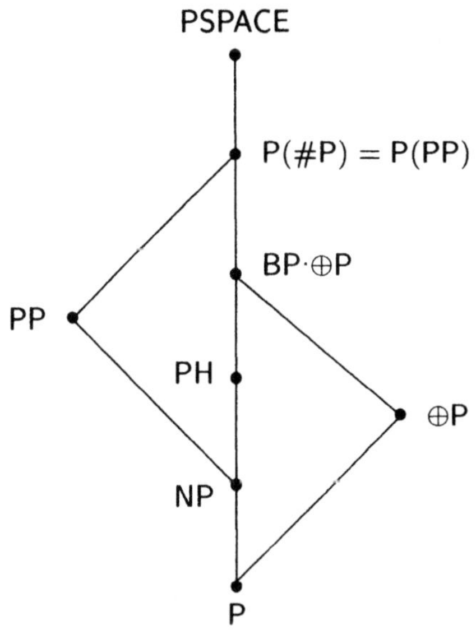

References

The class ⊕P was introduced by C.H. Papadimitriou and S. Zachos:

- Two remarks on the power of counting, *Proceedings of the 6th GI Conference in Theoretical Computer Science*, Lecture Notes in Computer Science 145, Springer, 1983, 269–276.

There ⊕P(⊕P) = ⊕P is proven.

The class FewP originated with

- E. Allender: *Invertible Functions*, PhD thesis, Georgia Tech., 1985.

The inclusion FewP $\subseteq$ ⊕P appears in

- J. Cai, L.A. Hemachandra: On the power of parity polynomial time, *Proceedings of the Symposium on Theoretical Aspects of Computer Science*, Lecture Notes in Computer Science 349, Springer, 1989, 229–240.

The BP· operator was first defined in

- U. Schöning: Probabilistic complexity classes and lowness, *Journal of Computer and Systems Sciences* 39 (1989), 84–100.

The result NP $\subseteq$ BP·⊕P (formulated differently) is from

- L.G. Valiant, V.V. Vazirani: NP is as easy as detecting unique solutions, *Theoretical Computer Science* 47 (1986), 85–93.

The extension of this inclusion to PH and the inclusion $\mathsf{PH} \subseteq \mathsf{P}(\#\mathsf{P})$ was achieved by

- S. Toda: PP is as hard as the polynomial-time hierarchy, *SIAM Journal on Computing* 20 (1991), 865–877.

Our approximations of the probabilities in the proof of "$\mathsf{NP} \subseteq \mathsf{BP}\cdot\oplus\mathsf{P}$" come from

- C.H. Papadimitriou: *Computational Complexity*, Addison-Wesley, 1994, page 450.

Our "magic formula" is a simplified version of the formulas found in

- R. Beigel, J. Tarui: On ACC, *Proceedings of the Symposium on Foundations of Computer Science*, IEEE 1991, 783–792.
- J. Köbler, S. Toda: On the power of generalized MOD-classes, *Mathematical Systems Theory* 29 (1994), 33–46.

20. Interactive Proofs and Zero Knowledge

In 1986 Goldwasser, Micali, and Rackoff introduced the notion of an interactive proof system. Using these systems, probabilistic generalizations of the complexity class NP can be defined. A zero knowledge protocol is able to provide convincing evidence that a proof of a statement exists without disclosing any information about the proof itself.

In Topic 6, among other things, the relationship between efficient proofs and the class NP was discussed. As we noted there, the class NP can be viewed as the set of all languages that have polynomially long proofs in an appropriate proof calculus.

Exercise 20.1. Sketch a proof of this characterization of NP. (The definition of a proof calculus is intentionally omitted; fix it appropriately for the proof.) ◁

Here we want to consider such proofs more generally as a communication problem between a *prover* who knows the proof (the *prover*) and a *verifier* who does not know the proof but is supposed to be convinced of its correctness (or perhaps only of its existence).[1] In our previous considerations, i.e., in the definition of the class NP given above, the communication has been entirely one-sided: the prover gives the verifier a complete proof, which the verifier then checks in polynomial time.

We want to recast this now as a communication problem between two Turing machines – prover and verifier. The verifier will be a polynomial time-bounded Turing machine. Later we will also consider probabilistic verifiers (cf. Topic 17). The prover, on the other hand, will have no complexity restrictions, which in some sense corresponds to the existential quantifier in the definition of NP. These two machines communicate over a common communication channel (a Turing machine tape), and both machines also have access

---

[1] This idea follows the manner in which proofs were often written down in antiquity, namely in the form of a dialog between someone carrying out a proof and another party who doubts its validity. In more modern form, such "dialog-proofs" can be found, for example in

- P. Lorenzen: *Metamathematik*, Bibl. Inst., 1962.

to the input, which in some sense represents the statement to be proven. Furthermore, each machine has a "private" work tape for internal computations.

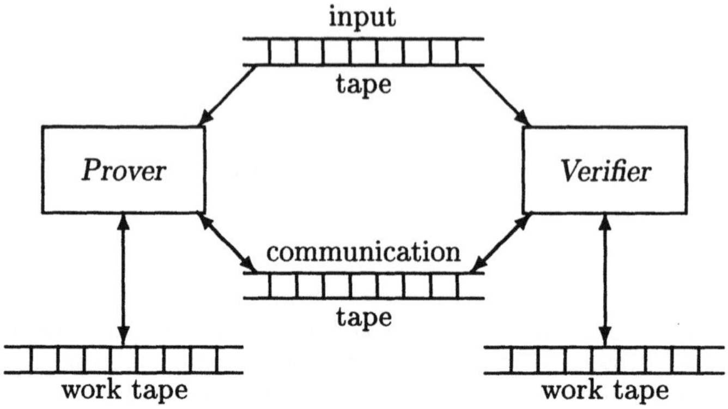

The computation proceeds in *rounds.* In each round, only one of the participants is active. A round begins with the reading of the information on the communication tape (or on the input tape) and ends – perhaps after some private computations – with writing at most polynomially much new information on the communication tape. The number of rounds is limited to be polynomial in the length of the input. Since both participants can in principle keep a complete log of all communication on their work tapes, the newly computed information at each round can be considered a function of the input and all previously communicated information. In the case of the verifier, this function must be computable in polynomial time. The (preliminary) definition of the language A that is represented by such an *interactive proof system* is the following: There must be a verifier-algorithm V so that for any $x \in A$, there is a prover-strategy so that the verifier eventually accepts. If $x \notin A$, then the verifier rejects, regardless of what strategy the prover uses. Note that we have made no restrictions on the complexity of the prover.

Exercise 20.2. Show that using this apparently more general interactive communication model, nothing more can be computed than the class NP. $\lhd$

The situation changes drastically (at least potentially) if the Turing machines (in particular the verifier) are allowed to work probabilistically. In this case, the participants can make the execution of their computations depend on the result of a random experiment. Furthermore, we relax the requirements for $x \in A$ (and $x \notin A$) somewhat. Our final definition goes as follows:

Definition 20.1. *A language A is in the class* IP *if there is a probabilistic, polynomial time-bounded Turing machine V (the verifier) such that for all x:*

$$x \in A \Rightarrow \exists \textit{Prover } P: \ Pr[\,(P,V)(x) = 1\,] > 2/3,$$

$$x \notin A \Rightarrow \forall \textit{Prover } P: \ Pr[\,(P,V)(x) = 1\,] < 1/3.$$

In the definition above, "$(P,V)(x) = 1$" means that the result for a given prover P and verifier V is that x is accepted. This definition was introduced by S. Goldwasser, S. Micali, and C. Rackoff.

The constants 2/3 and 1/3 are somewhat arbitrary. Because of the possibility of "probability amplification" in this model (cf. Topic 17), the exact values of the constants do not matter as long as the first one has the form $1/2 + \varepsilon$ and the second one the form $1/2 - \varepsilon$ for some constant $\varepsilon > 0$. In fact, one can choose the first "constant" to be $1 - 2^{-|x|}$ and the second to be $2^{-|x|}$.[2]

It is clear from the previous discussion that all NP-languages have interactive proofs. In fact, they have trivial ones in which all of the communication is from the prover to the verifier. So $\mathsf{NP} \subseteq \mathsf{IP}$. Since the verifier can compute the languages in BPP without any communication from the prover, it is also clear that $\mathsf{BPP} \subseteq \mathsf{IP}$.

Exercise 20.3.$^\diamond$ Show that $\mathsf{IP} \subseteq \mathsf{PSPACE}$. ◁

Exercise 20.4.$^\diamond$ A language A is ***provable by an oracle*** if there is a polynomial time-bounded, probabilistic Turing machine M such that for all x

$$x \in A \Rightarrow \exists \text{oracle } B : Pr[M^B(x) = 1] > 2/3,$$

$$x \notin A \Rightarrow \forall \text{oracle } B : Pr[M^B(x) = 1] < 1/3.$$

Show that $A \in \mathsf{IP}$ implies that A is provable by an oracle. Give an argument why the reverse direction might not be true. ◁

So just how large is the class IP? It is contained in PSPACE and contains NP. How much more of PSPACE is in IP? A well-known example of a problem in IP that is not known to be in NP is the complement of graph isomorphism, $\overline{GI}$ (cf. Topic 17): given two graphs G_1 and G_2 prove (interactively) that they are *not* isomorphic. One interactive protocol that achieves this is the following:

Prover	communication	*Verifier*
		Randomly guess $i \in \{1,2\}$ and a permutation π of $\{1,\ldots,n\}$, where n is the number of nodes in the graphs G_1 and G_2. Compute the graph $H = \pi(G_i)$.
	$\longleftarrow H \longleftarrow$	
Determine $j \in \{1,2\}$, so that G_j and H are isomorphic.		
	$\longrightarrow j \longrightarrow$	
		Accept if $i = j$.

[2] In fact, even more is true. It can be shown that the first constant can be chosen to be 1; see the 1987 paper by Goldreich, Micali, and Sipser.

Now if G_1 and G_2 are not isomorphic, then a suitable prover algorithm can always answer with the correct j – remember the prover is not computationally limited, and so is able to find any isomorphisms that exist – so the verifier will always accept. That is,

$$G_1 \text{ not isomorphic to } G_2 \Rightarrow \exists\, \mathit{Prover}\ P: \mathit{Pr}[(P,V)(G_1,G_2)=1]=1\,.$$

On the other hand, if the two graphs are isomorphic, then the prover has at most a 50-50 chance of selecting the "correct" value $i = j$. So

$$G_1 \text{ isomorphic to } G_2 \Rightarrow \forall\, \mathit{Prover}\ P: \mathit{Pr}[(P,V)(G_1,G_2)=1]\leq 1/2\,.$$

Exercise 20.5. For which provers is the probability exactly 1/2? What is the probability in other cases? ◁

The definition of IP has not yet been satisfied, since the probability of error is 1/2, which is greater than 1/3.

Exercise 20.6. Modify the protocol above slightly (without changing the "communication protocol") so that probabilities 1 and 1/2 above are transformed to $1/2+\varepsilon$ and $1/2-\varepsilon$, for some $\varepsilon > 0$. ◁

Exercise 20.7. How can the protocol be modified so that instead of the probabilities 1 and 1/2 we get the probabilities 1 and 2^{-k}? ◁

So $\overline{GI} \in \mathsf{IP}$. It is important to note that the protocol described above uses only a *constant* number of rounds, namely 2. So $\overline{GI} \in \mathsf{IP}(2)$, where $\mathsf{IP}(k)$ is the subset of IP where only k rounds are allowed. If we really make use of the polynomially many rounds available, then we arrive at IP = PSPACE. This was first shown by A. Shamir and will be the subject of Topic 21.

It appears at first glance to be significant that the verifier makes his random choices (i and π) on the private work tape, "out of sight" of the prover. S. Goldwasser and M. Sipser showed (1986), however, that this secrecy is not necessary. Every IP-protocol, like the one above, can be transformed into one in which the verifier does nothing but generate random numbers and communicate these directly to the prover – without subsequent internal computation. This kind of protocol was introduced independently by L. Babai, who called it an *Arthur-Merlin game* because the prover plays the role of the wizard Merlin, and the verifier the role of King Arthur.

Example. The method used in Topic 18 to demonstrate that $\overline{GI} \in \mathsf{BP}\cdot\mathsf{NP}$ can be recast as an IP-protocol with "public coins" as follows:

Prover	communication	*Verifier*
		Randomly guess a hash function $h \in H$.
	$\longleftarrow h \longleftarrow$	
Determine a $y \in Y$ with $h(y) = 0$. Let b be a "proof" of "$y \in Y$".		
	$\longrightarrow y, b \longrightarrow$	
		Accept if b is correct and $h(y) = 0$.

For a discussion of the terminology and probability approximations in this example, see the description given in Topic 18. In fact, it is the case that BP·NP = IP(2).

* * * * *

Now we come to another interesting concept, also introduced by Goldwasser, Micali and Rackoff, namely *zero-knowledge*. This means that an IP-proof can be carried out in such a way that the verifier does not obtain any information about the proof itself, but is nevertheless convinced of the *existence* of such a proof, since the IP-protocol is still correct.

The most famous example of this was given in a paper by O. Goldreich, S. Micali, A. Wigderson and is the graph isomorphism problem, *GI*. In order to convince the verifier that two graphs are isomorphic, the simplest thing the prover could do would be to give the verifier an isomorphism (coded in polynomially many bits), which the verifier could then easily check. But then the whole secret would be revealed; the verifier could use this information to tell a third party, etc. In certain contexts – cryptologists rack their brains over such contexts – it may well be that it is not desirable that the proof be revealed, but that the verifier must, nevertheless, be convinced that the prover knows a proof (a graph isomorphism, in our example). A "zero-knowledge proof of knowledge" is actually able to satisfy these apparently paradoxical requirements.

Consider the following protocol for *GI*. Contrary to our previous example, in this protocol it is the prover who begins, and the prover also uses randomness.

Prover	communication	*Verifier*
Randomly guess $i \in \{1,2\}$ and a permutation π of $\{1,\ldots,n\}$, where n is the number of nodes in the graphs G_1 and G_2. Compute the graph $H = \pi(G_i)$.		
	$\longrightarrow H \longrightarrow$	
		Randomly select a $j \in \{1,2\}$.
	$\longleftarrow j \longleftarrow$	
Determine σ so that $\sigma(G_j) = H$.		
	$\longrightarrow \sigma \longrightarrow$	
		Accept if $\sigma(G_j) = H$.

Exercise 20.8. Show that this is an IP-protocol for *GI*. ◁

This protocol is unusual, however, in that it does not reveal anything about the isomorphism (if one exists) between the graphs G_1 and G_2. The protocol fulfills our definition of zero-knowledge: The information that is transmitted on the communication channel (in this case H, j, and σ) contains (statistically) no new information for the verifier. The verifier would be able with his computational resources to generate exactly the same probability distribution for the triples (H, j, σ) as would occur in a typical realization of the protocol. Therefore, the verifier can learn ***absolutely nothing*** new by viewing the communication log.

Definition 20.2. *(Goldwasser, Micali, Rackoff) Suppose $A \in$ IP via a prover-verifier pair (P, V). Then this protocol is a* zero-knowledge *protocol if there is a probabilistic Turing machine M such that M on any input x runs in polynomial time and if $x \in A$, then M outputs a tuple $(y_1, \ldots, y_k)$ so that the distribution of such tuples is exactly the distribution that can be observed on the communication channel of P and V on input x.*[3]

Exercise 20.9.° Show that the protocol given above for *GI* is a zero-knowledge protocol. ◁

Exercise 20.10. Some authors have criticized that since the prover in the definition of IP has unbounded resources, these types of IP-proofs – of which the zero-knowledge ones are most interesting – are not practically implementable.

But let's modify the scenario slightly: Now the prover, like the verifier, will also be a probabilistic, polynomial time-bounded Turing machine, but at

[3] More precisely, what we have defined here is *perfect zero-knowledge with fixed verifier*, in contrast to other definitions of zero-knowledge that exist in the literature. Under weaker definitions, one can show that *all* NP-languages have zero-knowledge IP-proofs, but this does not appear to be the case for our definition. For more on this see the article by Brassard.

the start of the protocol, the prover has some additional information, namely, the "proof" is written on its work tape. (In our example, this would be an isomorphism between the graphs G_1 and G_2, if one exists.) Show that the protocol described above can be used in this situation so that the prover can (in polynomial time) convince the verifier of the existence of an isomorphism without revealing the isomorphism. That is, zero-knowledge proofs are still possible with such modifications to the model. ◁

References

Zero-knowledge proofs are an important topic in cryptology; they can be used, for example, to provide secure identification or authorization in the presence of eavesdropping. See

- A. Fiat, A. Shamir: How to prove yourself: practical solutions to identification and signature problems. *CRYPTO* 86. Lecture Notes in Computer Science 263, Springer, 1987, 186–194.

Surveys of interactive proofs systems and zero-knowledge can be found in

- J.L. Balcázar, J. Diaz, J. Gabarró: *Structural Complexity II*, Springer, 1990, Chapter 11.
- D.P. Bovet, P. Crescenzi: *Introduction to the Theory of Complexity*, Prentice-Hall, 1994, Chapter 10.
- J. Feigenbaum: Overview of interactive proof systems and zero knowledge, Chapter 8 in G.J. Simmons, ed., *Contemporary Cryptography, The Science of Information Integrity*. IEEE, 1992.
- O. Goldreich: Randomness, interactive proofs, and zero-knowledge. in R. Herken, ed., *The Universal Turing Machine: A Half-Century Survey*, Oxford University Press 1988, 377–406.
- S. Goldwasser: Interactive proof systems, in J. Hartmanis, ed., *Computational Complexity Theory*, Proceedings of the Symposium in Applied Mathematics, Vol. 38, AMS, 1989, 108–128.
- J. Köbler, U. Schöning, J. Torán: *The Graph Isomorphism Problem: Its Structural Complexity*, Birkhäuser, 1993, Chapter 2.
- C. Papadimitriou: *Computational Complexity*, Addison-Wesley, 1994, Section 19.2.

Primary sources used in writing this chapter include

- Babai: Trading group theory for randomness, *Proceedings of the 17th Symposium on Theory of Computing*, ACM, 1985, 421–429.

- G. Brassard: Sorting out zero knowledge. *Advances in Cryptology*, 1989, Lecture Notes in Computer Science 434, Springer, 1989.
- O. Goldreich, S. Micali, M. Sipser: Interactive proof systems: provers that never fail and random selection. *Proceedings of the Symposium on Foundations of Computer Science*, IEEE, 1987, 449–461.
- O. Goldreich, S. Micali, A. Wigderson: Proofs that yield nothing but their validity or all languages in NP have zero-knowledge proof systems. *Journal of the ACM* 38 (1991) 691–729.
- S. Goldwasser, S. Micali, C. Rackoff: The knowledge complexity of interactive proof systems. *SIAM Journal on Computing* 18 (1989), 186–208.
- S. Goldwasser, M. Sipser: Private coins versus public coins in interactive proof systems, *Proceedings of the 18th Symposium on Theory of Computing*, ACM, 1986, 59–68.
- S. Micali, ed., *Randomness and Computation*, Vol. 5 of *Advances in Computing Research*, JAI Press, 1989.

21. IP = PSPACE

> We present the surprising result of A. Shamir that the classes IP and PSPACE are the same.

For a long time it was unclear how encompassing the class IP really is. The conjecture was that this class represented only a "small" generalization of the class NP (something like BP·NP, cf. Topic 18). It was not even clear that the class coNP was contained in IP. In fact, there were oracle results that spoke against this (cf. Topic 22).

Triggered by the observation of N. Nisan that by means of a certain arithmetization technique and the use of Toda's results (cf. Topic 19), one could show that PH $\subseteq$ IP (which implies, of course, coNP $\subseteq$ IP as well), there ensued a race toward the potential goal of IP = PSPACE. (Remember that in Topic 20 we saw that IP $\subseteq$ PSPACE.) This race took place by e-mail in December, 1989, among certain "insiders" (see the article by L. Babai). This race was eventually won by A. Shamir. We want to work through the proof of this result in this chapter.

The strategy is to give an interactive proof protocol for QBF, a PSPACE-complete problem, thus proving that $QBF \in$ IP. From this it follows that PSPACE $\subseteq$ IP, and, therefore, that IP = PSPACE. The language QBF consists of all valid quantified boolean formulas with no free variables. Quantification is over *boolean* variables ($\{0,1\}$ or {FALSE, TRUE}).

Example. The following formula is in QBF:

$$\forall x\, \forall y\, \big(x \lor \neg y \lor \exists z\, ((x \land z) \lor (y \land z))\big) .$$

It will be important in what follows that we only allow formulas in which the negations are only applied to variables. Let $QBF' \subseteq QBF$ be the set of all such formulas that have no free variables and are valid.

Exercise 21.1. Show that $QBF \leq^{\mathrm{P}}_{\mathrm{m}} QBF'$, so it is sufficient to prove that $QBF' \in$ IP . ◁

The goal of the desired interactive proof protocol is to get the prover to convince the verifier that the input formula F is valid; and if F is not valid, then the verifier should reject with high probability.

The trick is to interpret the formulas *arithmetically*. We do this in the following way: We assume that the variables can take on integer values. An AND-operation will be interpreted as multiplication ($*$), and an OR-operation as addition ($+$). If the variable x_i is negated, we interpret this as $1 - x_i$.

It remains to show how the quantification can be arithmetized. For a formula of the form $\forall x$, every free occurrence of x in F is replaced once with 0 and once with 1, and each of the resulting formulas is then arithmetized. Let $a_0, a_1 \in \mathbb{Z}$ be the resulting values. The value of $\forall x F$ is then $a_0 * a_1$. For $\exists x F$ we use $a_0 + a_1$ instead. Let *bool*(F) denote the boolean value of a formula F and let *arith*(F) denote its arithmetic value.

Example. We can compute the value of the formula in the previous example as follows:

$$\begin{aligned}
&\forall x \forall y \left(x \vee \neg y \vee \exists z\left((x \wedge z) \vee (y \wedge z)\right)\right)\\
&\equiv \prod_{x=0,1}\prod_{y=0,1}\left(x + (1-y) + \sum_{z=0,1}((x*z)+(y*z))\right)\\
&= \prod_{x=0,1}\prod_{y=0,1}(x + (1-y) + [(x*0)+(y*0)) + ((x*1)+(y*1)])\\
&= \prod_{x=0,1}\left(x + (1-0) + [x+0]\right) * \left(x + (1-1) + [x+1]\right)\\
&= \prod_{x=0,1}(2x+1)*(2x+1) = (1*1)*(3*3) = 9\,.
\end{aligned}$$

Exercise 21.2. Show that

$$\begin{aligned}
bool(F) = \text{TRUE} &\implies arith(F) > 0\,,\\
bool(F) = \text{FALSE} &\implies arith(F) = 0\,.
\end{aligned}$$

Hint: Use structural induction on the formula F. ◁

Instead of convincing the verifier that the boolean value of a formula is TRUE, the prover will instead first communicate to the verifier a value $a \in \mathbb{Z}$ and then try to convince the verifier that the arithmetic value is exactly a. It is precisely this more difficult task, which demands more information from the prover, that makes a correct interactive protocol for QBF' possible.

Now we come to our first technical problem: The arithmetic value a is supposed to be communicated. The prover, with unbounded resources, can clearly compute this number from the formula F, a task that (by the previous exercise) is at least as difficult as QBF. But the value of a could be so large that the binary representation of a doesn't have polynomial length!

Exercise 21.3. Show that for the following formula

$$F = \forall x_1 \ldots \forall x_m \, \exists y \, \exists z \, (y \vee z) ,$$

$arith(F) = 4^{2^m}$. ◁

Exercise 21.4. Show that if the length of a formula F (as a string) is n, then $arith(F) \leq 2^{2^n}$. ◁

So we must find a way to reduce the arithmetic value of the formulas. We can do this by computing modulo some number k of size $2^{O(n)}$. Then we can represent $a \bmod k$ using only $O(n)$ bits. But we must make sure that the properties "$a > 0$" for valid formulas and "$a = 0$" for invalid formulas continue to hold when this modular arithmetic is used.

It is the case, however, that for all a with $0 < a < 2^{2^n}$, there is a prime number k in the interval $[2^n, 2^{3n}]$ such that $a \not\equiv 0 \pmod{k}$.

Exercise 21.5.° Show this. You may use without proof the fact that for every m there are at least $\sqrt{m}$ prime numbers $\leq m$, i.e. $\pi(m) \geq \sqrt{m}$.

Hint: Chinese Remainder Theorem. ◁

In Topic 9 we gave lower bounds for $\pi(n)$, but these were good only for *infinitely many n*. The Prime Number Theorem actually says more, namely that $\pi(n) \sim n/\ln n$. But for the exercise above, the following weaker version would suffice:

Exercise 21.6.° Show that $\pi(n) \geq \sqrt{n}$. ◁

Our desired protocol for $QBF' \in$ IP begins with the following information being communicated from the prover to the verifier in the first round:

Prover	Communication	Verifier
Compute $n = \|F\|$, compute $a = arith(F)$ and determine a prime number $k \in [2^n, 2^{3n}]$ (if possible) with $a \not\equiv 0 \pmod{k}$. Let $\hat{a} = a \bmod k$. Find a "proof" b for the primality of k.		
	$\rightarrow \hat{a}, k, b \rightarrow$	
		Verify that $\hat{a} > 0$, that $k \in [2^n, 2^{3n}]$, and that b is a correct proof that k is a prime.
	⋮	

In the remainder of the protocol, the prover has the task of convincing the verifier that the arithmetic value of F (modulo k) really is $\hat{a}$.

At this point it is not yet clear why the prover must convince the verifier that k is a prime number, since even if k is composite, we can conclude from

$\hat{a} > 0$ that $a > 0$. So far, the only place primality has played any role has been in the context of the Chinese Remainder Theorem above. But in what follows it will be important for the verifier to know that $\{0, \ldots, k-1\} = \mathrm{GF}(k)$ is a field. Otherwise, the prover would be able to "cheat," as we will soon see.

Nor have we discussed what b, the proof of primality, is like. It is in fact possible to certify the primality of a number via a polynomially long (non-interactive) proof, that is, *PRIMES* $\in$ NP. This fact was originally due to V. Pratt, but we will not pursue the proof further here. (See the references at the end of the chapter for more information.)

Another possibility is to have the verifier choose a prime number (from a somewhat larger interval) *at random* in the first round. (Methods for selecting a random prime can be found in the book by Cormen, Leiserson, and Rivest.) If the verifier selects such a prime p at random, then with high probability, $a \not\equiv 0 \pmod{p}$.

Exercise 21.7.° In this alternative, how large must the interval from which the prime number k is chosen be in order that for every $a \in [0, 2^{2^n}]$, the probability is at least $1 - 2^{-n}$ that $a \not\equiv 0 \pmod{k}$? ◁

* * * * *

Now we come to the heart of the protocol, verifying that $arith(F) \bmod k = \hat{a}$, where F is (for the moment) the input formula. This will require multiple rounds. Each round will be associated with some claim of the form form "$arith(F) \equiv \hat{a} \bmod k$," where initially F is the input formula and $\hat{a}$ is the value communicated by the verifier in the first round. In subsequent rounds, F will be some (shorter) formula that occurs as a subformula or instantiation of a formula $\hat{F}$ from a previous round, and $\hat{a}$ will be the value that the prover claimed was $arith(\hat{F}) \bmod k$.

If, for example, F has the form $F = (F_1 \wedge F_2)$, then in the next round the prover must give two numbers a_1 and a_2 along with proofs that a_1 is the arithmetic value of F_1 (modulo k) and that a_2 is the arithmetic value of F_2 (modulo k). (The verifier will check to be sure that $a_0 * a_1 \equiv \hat{a} \bmod k$.) The procedure for $F = (F_1 \vee F_2)$ is analogous, except that the verifier will check that $\hat{a} \equiv a_1 + a_2 \pmod{k}$.

It becomes more interesting when F has the form $F = \forall x\, G$. The variable x occurs freely in G, so the arithmetic value of G is not a number but a function. In fact, it is a polynomial, since the only operations are $+$, $-$, and $*$. The prover will now be required to tell the verifier the coefficients of this polynomial, which we will call p_G, since this task is too difficult for the verifier. The verifier then checks that $p_G(0) * p_G(1) \equiv \hat{a} \pmod{k}$, selects a random number $z \in \{0, \ldots, k-1\} = \mathrm{GF}(k)$, and communicates this number z to the prover. The prover is now expected to provide a proof that the arithmetic value of G (with the number z substituted for the variable x) is precisely

$p_G(z)$. In the case of a formula of the form $F = \exists x\, G$ everything proceeds analogously, except that the verifier checks that $p_G(0) + p_G(1) \equiv \hat{a} \pmod{k}$.

Example. If $F = \forall x \forall y \left(x \vee \neg y \vee \exists z\left((x \wedge z) \vee (y \wedge z)\right)\right)$, as in our previous examples, then

$$\begin{aligned} p_G(x) &= \prod_{y=0,1} \left(x + (1-y) + \sum_{z=0,1} ((x * z) + (y * z)) \right) \\ &= (2x+1) * (2x+1) = 4x^2 + 4x + 1 \; . \end{aligned}$$

Note that this gives more information than merely giving the values $p_G(0) = 1$ and $p_G(1) = 9$.

So at this point the protocol is doing the following: In order to prove that the value of F is $\hat{a}$, the prover must give the verifier the polynomial p_G. Now the task is to verify that the polynomial p_G is correct. We will see below that these polynomials have very low degree (in comparison to the size of the underlying field GF(k)). For this reason, on substitution of a random value, it is very likely that if the prover tried to cheat by giving an incorrect polynomial (which for the moment will not be detected by the verifier) then in the next round the prover will be forced to once again give an incorrect polynomial – if he ever hopes to cause the the verifier to accept – but now for a smaller formula $G(z)$.[1] In the end, the prover's deception will (with very high probability) be found out.

Exercise 21.8. Let $d < k$) be the degree of the polynomials p and p'. Suppose the prover tries (or is forced to try because of previous rounds) to show that p' is the polynomial associated with $G(z)$ when in fact it is really $p \neq p'$. What is the probability that given a random choice of z (as described above), $p(z) \neq p'(z)$? ◁

At the end of the protocol we arrive at the "innermost" parts of F, the variables, which in the previous rounds have been replaced by random numbers. Now the verifier need only check that these random numbers agree with the arithmetic value.

This concludes a description of the protocol by which the prover can convince the verifier that the arithmetic value of a formula is exactly some supposed value. Some comments about its correctness have already been made. What is still missing is a rigorous approximation for the probability of correctness and an argument that the degree of the polynomials is small. As we saw in the previous exercise, the degree of the polynomial plays a role in the probability arguments. Furthermore, the prover must communicate the polynomials. The coefficients themselves come from GF(n) and so require only $O(n)$ bits since $k \leq 2^{3n}$, so what we need is a polynomial bound on the

[1] Technically, $G(z)$ is no longer a formula, since an integer has been substituted for one of the variables.

number of coefficients. In order for this to be possible, the degree should be at most polynomial in n.

Without taking further precautions, the degree of the polynomial p_G could be exponentially large. It is the universal quantifiers that have the possibility of drastically increasing the degree. If, for example, G has the form $\forall y_1 \ldots \forall y_m H(x, y_1, \ldots, y_m)$ and H is a quantifier-free formula that has (due to nested ANDs and ORs) degree c with respect to x, then the polynomial p_G has degree $c2^m$. In order to maintain a low degree for the polynomials associated with a subformula G of F (with some variables already instantiated with random numbers), it is important that (already in F) the number of universal quantifiers between an occurrence of a variable and the quantifier that binds it be small. In what follows, we will only allow one such intervening universal quantifier.

Definition 21.1. *A quantified boolean formula without free variables is said to be* simple *if for every variable that occurs, the number of universal quantifiers that lie between any occurrence of the variable and its binding quantifier is at most 1.*

We denote by QBF″ the set of simple formulas in QBF′.

Exercise 21.9. Show that the degree of any polynomial that comes from a simple formula F of length n is at most $2n$. ◁

Exercise 21.10.◇ Show that *QBF* (or *QBF′*) is polynomial-time reducible to *QBF″*. Therefore, it suffices for our interactive protocol to consider only simple formulas.

Hint: For every occurrence of the situation $\ldots Qx \ldots \forall y \ldots x \ldots$, introduce a new variable (to be a place holder for x). ◁

For the correctness of "*QBF″* $\in$ IP," we still need to give a bound on the probability of error in the protocol. If the input formula F is valid, then the prover can satisfy all of the verifier's demands and produce the correct arithmetic value and all the required polynomials. So in this case, the verifier will accept with probability 1.

If, on the other hand, F is not valid, then there is only a very small chance that the verifier incorrectly accepts. This can only happen if in some round the verifier randomly chooses a number z such that the incorrect polynomial previously given by the prover and the correct polynomial p_G have the same value on z. By the earlier exercises, in any given round this can only happen with probability at most $2n/2^n$. Since there are at most n rounds, we get the following approximation for the probability that the prover can prosper by cheating:

$$Pr[\text{error}] \le 2n^2/2^n \to 0 \quad (n \to \infty) .$$

So the definition of IP is satisfied. It follows that IP = PSPACE , as was to be shown. □

Exercise 21.11. Use $Pr[\text{error}] = 1 - Pr[\text{no error}]$ to get a better approximation. ◁

Finally, we note that in this protocol the numbers randomly chosen by the verifier are given directly to the prover. So this protocol is, in fact, of "Arthur-Merlin" type (cf. Topic 20).

References

The tale of the e-mail race toward IP = PSPACE is told in

- Babai: E-mail and the unexpected power of interaction, *Proceedings of the 5th Structure in Complexity Theory Conference*, IEEE, 1990, 30–44.

The original proof appeared in

- A. Shamir: IP=PSPACE, *Journal of the ACM* 39 (1992) 869–877.

Proofs can also be found in the following books:

- C. Papadimitriou: *Computational Complexity*, Addison-Wesley, 1994.
- D.P Bovet, P. Crescenzi: *Introduction to the Theory of Complexity*, Prentice-Hall, 1988.
- C. Lund: *The Power of Interaction*, MIT Press, 1992.

The fact that *PRIMES* $\in$ NP is from

- V. Pratt: Every prime has a succinct certificate, *SIAM Journal of Computing* (1975), 214–220.

See also

- D. Knuth: *The Art of Computer Programming, Vol. 2: Semi-Numerical Algorithms*, Addison-Wesley, 1981, page 395, Exercise 17.
- E. Kranakis: *Primality and Cryptography*, John Wiley & Sons, 1986, Section 2.6.

For an explanation of how to select prime numbers at random see

- T.H. Cormen, C.E. Leiserson, R.L. Rivest: *Introduction to Algorithms*, MIT Press, McGraw-Hill, 1990, Chapter 33.

22. P $\neq$ NP with probability 1

There are "worlds" in which $\mathsf{P} = \mathsf{NP}$ and others in which $\mathsf{P} \neq \mathsf{NP}$. Furthermore, if a "world" is chosen at random, the probability is 1 that it will be a world in which $\mathsf{P} \neq \mathsf{NP}$.

If one is not familiar with the material that we are about to present, then one would probably assume without further thought that if one could show that $\mathsf{P} \neq \mathsf{NP}$, then from this fact (and a potential proof of this fact), it would immediately follow that for any oracle $\mathsf{P}^A \neq \mathsf{NP}^A$, since although the problem is "shifted" by the oracle, its fundamental structure seems to remain the same. Similarly, if we assumed the (unlikely) case that $\mathsf{P} = \mathsf{NP}$, again we would expect that by a similar argument one could show that that $\mathsf{P}^A = \mathsf{NP}^A$ for all oracles.

Such a "relativization principle" does seem to hold in recursion theory. Every known theorem can be "relativized" by the addition of an oracle mechanism and is in fact still true with any choice of oracle. But in complexity theory things are different: T. Baker, J. Gill and R. Solovay showed that there are languages A and B such that

$$\mathsf{P}^A \neq \mathsf{NP}^A \quad \text{and} \quad \mathsf{P}^B = \mathsf{NP}^B .$$

Exercise 22.1. Show that any PSPACE-complete language can be used for B. ◁

Now we want to show that for "almost all" choices of oracle, $\mathsf{P} \neq \mathsf{NP}$. More precisely, what we mean is this: If we generate the oracle language A according to a random procedure in which for every string $x \in \{0,1\}^*$ (independently of all other strings) is equally likely to be in or out of A (i.e., $\forall x Pr[x \in A] = 1/2$) then

$$Pr[\,\mathsf{P}^A = \mathsf{NP}^A\,] = 0 \text{ , i.e., } Pr[\,\mathsf{P}^A \neq \mathsf{NP}^A\,] = 1.$$

From this, of course, it follows that there *exists* an oracle, relative to which the classes P and NP are different.

This result seems especially attractive: On a scale from 0 to 1, the needle points all the way to the right. Could this be an indication of how the unrelativized question is answered, i.e., that $\mathsf{P} \neq \mathsf{NP}$, unrelativized? This way of thinking, namely that if a statement holds with probability 1 relative to a random oracle then one can conclude (or better conjecture) that the unrelativized statement also holds, is referred to as the ***Random Oracle Hypothesis.*** It can be shown that in statements of this type (i.e., comparisons of complexity classes) the probability will always be either 0 or 1 (Kolmogorov's 0-1 Law). So the "needle" can only point all the way to the left or right of the scale. This is very suggestive. Nevertheless, the Random Oracle Hypothesis has been refuted by a number of counterexamples.

Our goal is to show that for a random A, $Pr[\mathsf{P}^A = \mathsf{NP}^A] = 0$. Let $M_1, M_2, \ldots$ be a listing of all polynomial time-bounded, deterministic oracle Turing machine. That is, $\mathsf{P}^A = \{L(M_i^A) \mid i \geq 1\}$. Momentarily we will define an oracle dependent language $L(A)$. It will be easy to see that $L(A) \in \mathsf{NP}^A$, regardless of the oracle A. Thus, the only issue will be whether or not $L(A) \in \mathsf{P}^A$. We can approximate as follows:

$$\begin{aligned} Pr[\mathsf{P}^A = \mathsf{NP}^A] &\leq Pr[L(A) \in \mathsf{P}^A] \\ &= Pr[\exists i\,(L(M_i^A) = L(A))] \\ &\leq \sum_i Pr[L(M_i^A) = L(A)] \\ &= \sum_i Pr[\forall x\,(x \in L(M_i^A) \,\square\, L(A))]\,. \end{aligned}$$

where $A \,\square\, B = \{x \mid x \in A \Leftrightarrow x \in B\}$, i.e., $A \,\square\, B = \overline{A \triangle B}$.

First let's define the language $L(A)$. For this we imagine that the elements of $\{0,1\}^*$ are arranged in lexicographical order. Whether x (with $|x| = n$) is in $L(A)$ or not, will be determined by the $n2^n$ strings that follow x in lexicographical order.

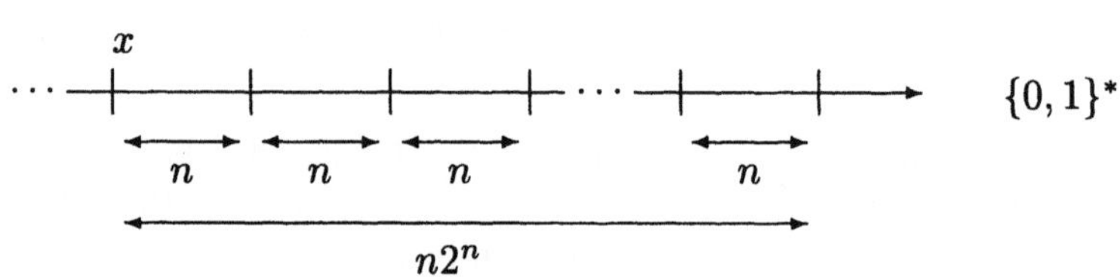

These strings are divided into 2^n blocks of n strings each. x is in $L(A)$ if and only if there is at least one such block of n strings all of which are in A.

Exercise 22.2. Given a random oracle A, what is the probability that a string x with $|x| = n$ is in $L(A)$? To what value does this probability converge as n becomes large? ◁

Exercise 22.3. Show that for *any* oracle A, $L(A) \in \mathsf{NP}^A$. ◁

For every machine M_i, let $x_1 < x_2 < x_3 < \cdots$ be a sequence of "widely separated" strings. For example, if we choose $n_{j+1} = |x_{j+1}| > |x_j|^2 = n_j^2$, then we are guaranteed that the regions of $n_j 2^{n_j}$ strings that determine the membership of each x_j in A are all disjoint and, therefore, that the events "$x_j \in L(A)$" $(j = 1, 2, 3, \ldots)$ are completely independent.

The events $x_j \in L(M_i^A)$ $(i, j = 1, 2, 3, \ldots)$, however, are not completely independent, in particular because the machines M_i can also make very short oracle queries. But as we will see shortly, we do get "sufficient independence" if we choose the x_i's to be so widely separated that $n_{j+1} > 2^{n_j}$. In this way we can ensure that (for large j) machine M_i on input x_j cannot query strings of length n_{j+1}.

Now we can continue the approximation begun above.

$$\begin{aligned}
&Pr[\mathsf{P}^A = \mathsf{NP}^A] \\
&\leq \sum_i Pr[\forall x\,(x \in L(M_i^A) \,\square\, L(A))] \\
&\leq \sum_i Pr[\forall j\,(x_j \in L(M_i^A) \,\square\, L(A))] \\
&= \sum_i \prod_j Pr[x_j \in L(M_i^A) \,\square\, L(A) \mid x_k \in L(M_i^A) \,\square\, L(A), k < j]\,.
\end{aligned}$$

The next step is to prove an upper bound on the probability of $x_j \in L(M_i^A) \,\square\, L(A)$, (or, equivalently, a lower bound for the probability of a "mistake": $x_j \in L(A) \triangle L(M_i^A)$) under the condition that

$$x_k \in L(M_i^A) \,\square\, L(A) \text{ for all } k < j\,.$$

We will refer to this condition as C, and in the probability considerations below, we will always assume condition C, which has the effect of shrinking the probability space of random oracles that we are considering. Essentially, we consider the oracle A to be "fixed" on all strings that are responsible for condition C, all of which will be much shorter than x_j.

We can now sketch a partitioning of the probability space as in the diagram below:

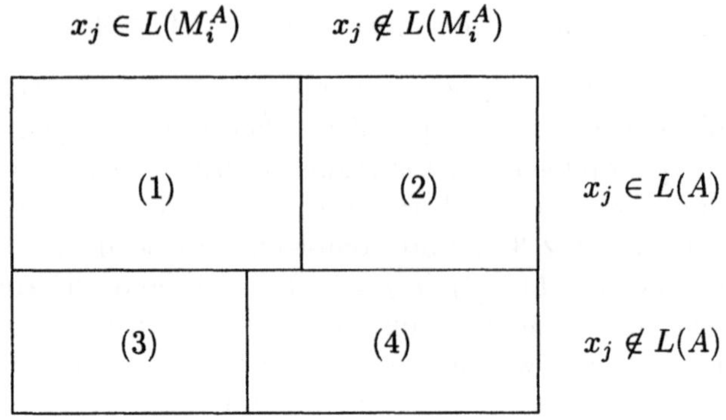

By Exercise 22.2 we have

$$\begin{aligned}(1) + (2) = Pr[x_j \in L(A) \mid C] &= Pr[x_j \in L(A)] > 0.6 , \\ (3) + (4) = Pr[x_j \notin L(A) \mid C] &= Pr[x_j \notin L(A)] > 0.3 .\end{aligned}$$

Now we approximate the conditional probability:

$$\begin{aligned}\frac{(2)}{(2)+(4)} &= Pr[x_j \in L(A) \mid x_j \notin L(M_i^A), C] \\ &= Pr[x_j \in L(A) \mid x_j \notin L(M_i^A)] .\end{aligned}$$

The important observation here, is that in the course of its computation on input x_j, the machine M_i can only query polynomially (in $m = |x_j|$) many strings of the oracle. Let p_i be a polynomial that bounds the number of queries. For the purposes of our approximation, we consider these at most $p_i(m)$ oracle strings to be fixed. These strings can lie in at most $p_i(m)$ different blocks, so there are at at least $2^m - p_i(m)$ blocks that are available for our random experiment. For large m, $p_i(m) \le 2^m/2$, so just as in Exercise 22.2 we can approximate as follows:

$$\begin{aligned}Pr[x_j \in L(A) \mid x_j \notin L(M_i^A)] &\ge 1 - (1 - 1/2^m)^{2^m - p_i(m)} \\ &\ge 1 - (1 - 1/2^m)^{2^m/2} \\ &\ge 1/3 .\end{aligned}$$

since $(1 - 1/2^m)^{2^m/2}$ converges to $\sqrt{1/e} = 0.606\ldots$.

Now we want to show that the probability of error, (2) + (3), is greater than 0. For this we consider two cases, depending on the probability of (3).

Case 1. (3) ≥ 0.1.

Then the value of (2) + (3) is at least 0.1.

Case 2. (3) < 0.1.

In this case, since (3) + (4) > 0.3, we have (4) > 0.2. And since $\frac{(2)}{(2)+(4)} >$ 1/3 it follows that (2) > 0.1.

So in either case we have shown that $Pr[x_j \in L(A) \,\square\, L(M_i^A)] < 0.9$ Putting everything together we see that

$$Pr[\mathsf{P}^A = \mathsf{NP}^A] \leq \sum_i \prod_j 0.9 = \sum_i 0 = 0\,,$$

and so we have proven that $Pr[\mathsf{P}^A = \mathsf{NP}^A] = 0$ or $Pr[\mathsf{P}^A \neq \mathsf{NP}^A] = 1$ □

Exercise 22.4.$^\circ$ Show that $Pr[\mathsf{NP}^A \neq \mathsf{coNP}^A] = 1$. ◁

References

For oracles separating P from NP, see

- T. Baker, J. Gill, R. Solovay: Relativizations of the P=?NP question, *SIAM Journal on Computing* 4 (1975), 431–442.
- C.H. Bennett, J. Gill: Relative to a random oracle A, $\mathrm{P}^A \neq \mathrm{NP}^A \neq \mathrm{coNP}^A$ with probability 1, *SIAM Journal on Computing* 10 (1981), 96–113.

For discussion of the random oracle hypothesis, see

- R. Chang, B. Chor, O. Goldreich, *et al*: The random oracle hypothesis is false, *Journal of Computer and System Sciences* 49 (1994), 24–39.
- S. Kurtz: On the random oracle hypothesis, *Information and Control* 57 (1983), 40–47.

23. Superconcentrators and the Marriage Theorem

We want to study graphs with special, extreme connectivity properties, prove that they exist, and approximate their size. In the next topic, the existence of these graphs will be used to obtain certain lower bounds.

Definition 23.1. *An* n-superconcentrator *is a directed, acyclic graph with* n *input nodes and* n *exit nodes such that for every choice of* k *input nodes and* k *output nodes* $(1 \leq k \leq n)$ *there exist node-disjoint paths through the graph that connect the* k *input nodes with the* k *output nodes (in any order).*

The following sketch clarifies this for $n = 5$ and a specific choice of 3 input nodes and 3 output nodes.

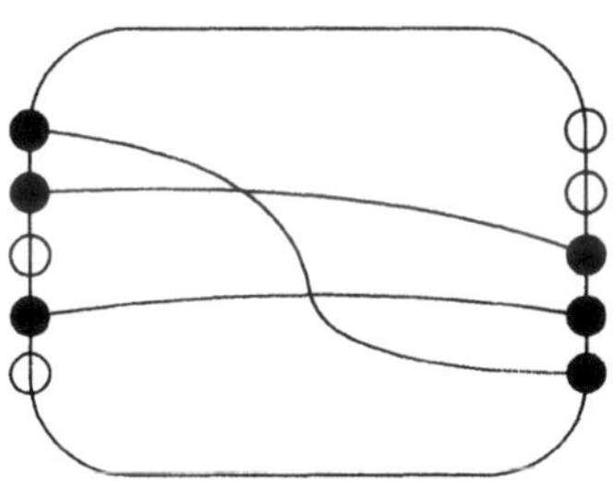

It is trivial that there are n-superconcentrators with $O(n^2)$ edges: the bipartite graph with n input nodes, n output nodes and an edge connecting each input node with each output node is an example.

Exercise 23.1.$^\diamond$ It is also relatively easy to build n-superconcentrators with $O(n \log n)$ edges using a recursive divide-and-conquer algorithm. Do it. $\triangleleft$

It was suspected that this bound is optimal (see, for example, Problem 12.37 in the book by Aho, Hopcroft, and Ullman). Interestingly, it is possible to construct these graphs with only *linear* size (where the size is the number of edges).

Theorem 23.2. *There is a constant* c *such that for every* n *there is an* n-*superconcentrator with* cn *edges.*

Proof. The remainder of this topic will present one possible construction. As in Exercise 23.1, the construction will be recursive. But instead of building an n-superconcentrator out of *two* smaller superconcentrators, this time we will use only *one* αn-superconcentrator (for some $\alpha < 1$) in the recursive step.

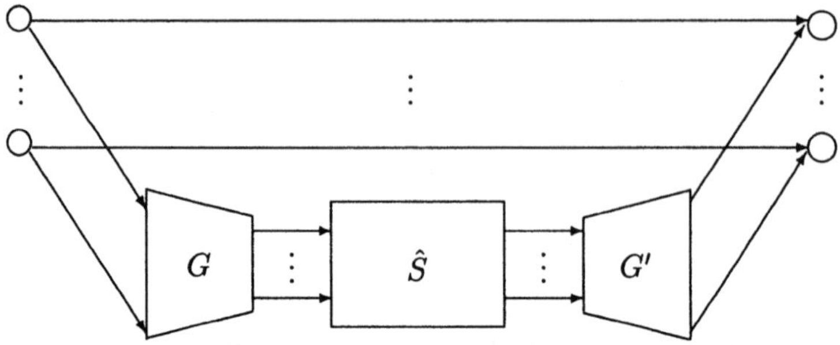

The diagram above indicates the construction. First, each of the n input nodes is connected directly to its corresponding output node. In addition, there is a "detour" through the graph G, which has $n = 6m$ inputs, $4m$ outputs, and certain properties which we will describe below. The $4m$ output nodes of G are connected as inputs to the $4m$-superconcentrator $\hat{S}$, the outputs of which are connected to G', which is identical to G except that the direction of the edges is reversed. (We ignore here and below the possibility that $4m$ may not be an integer. For our asymptotic approximations this will not play a role.) The focus of our attention will be on the graph G. It will be possible to construct such a graph with linear size.

Exercise 23.2. Assume that G has linear size and that the construction is otherwise correct. Show that the size of the resulting n-superconcentrator is cn for an appropriate constant c. ◁

In what follows, we will always assume that $n = 6m$. The desired graph G will have the property that any set of $k \leq n/2 = 3m$ input nodes can be connected with node-disjoint paths to some set of k output nodes. The graph G' has the dual property that for any choice of $k \leq n/2 = 3m$ outputs, there are always k input nodes that can be connected to them by node-disjoint paths.

Exercise 23.3.$^\diamond$ Assuming these properties of the graphs G and G', show that the construction is correct.

Hint: How many inputs of the superconcentrator can be connected directly to output nodes without going through the graphs G, $\hat{S}$, and G'? ◁

The graph G will be a ***bipartite graph***, that is, the nodes fall into two sets: $n = 6m$ input nodes and $4m$ output nodes, and the edges connect a node from each set. We must determine how to arrange (linearly many) edges to get the desired property.

For a given bipartite graph with edge set E, a subset $M \subseteq E$ is called a *matching*, if M consists of edges that are pairwise not connected. We are interested in the maximal size of matchings. Before proceeding with the construction of G, we want to consider maximal matchings in isolation.

Example.

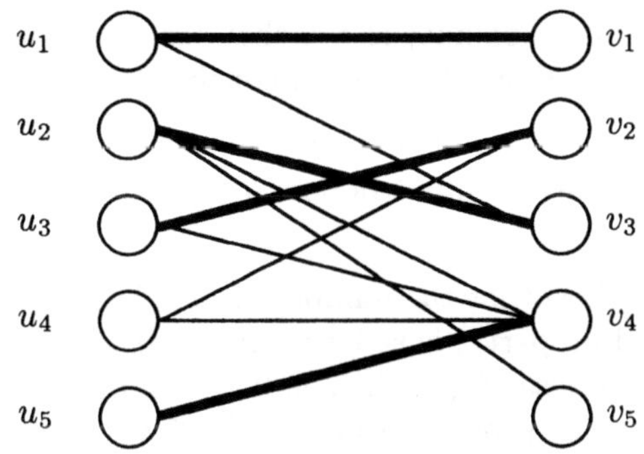

The thick lines indicate a matching M with $|M| = 4$. A matching with 5 edges is not possible since u_3, u_4, u_5 are only connected with nodes v_2, and v_4. Therefore, in any matching, one of the nodes u_3, u_4, and u_5 must be omitted.

Guided by this example, we arrive at the following theorem:

Theorem 23.3. *Let G be a bipartite graph with n input nodes. Let S be a subset of the input nodes with $|S| \leq n$. Then there is a matching starting with S (and connecting the nodes in S to some $|S|$ exit nodes) if and only if for every subset S' of S, $|S'| \leq |N(S')|$, where $N(S')$ is the set of nodes connected to the nodes in S' (i.e., the set of potential "partners" for the nodes in S).*

Exercise 23.4.° Prove Theorem 23.3. ◁

Theorem 23.3 is called the *Marriage Theorem* after the following interpretation. The input nodes are the women, the exit nodes the men (or vice versa), and every edge means that the corresponding pair are "friendly," so that a marriage is not excluded. A maximally-sized matching is then a matching up of the marriage partners that, at least seen globally, leads to the largest amount of satisfaction. Theorem 23.3 says exactly when this is possible.

Now we return to the construction of the graph G. From the perspective of matchings, G should have the property that every subset of $n/2 = 3m$ input nodes can be matched to some $n/2 = 3m$ exit nodes. The theorem says that is the case if and only if for every subset S of input nodes with $|S| \leq 3m$, $|S| \leq |N(S)|$.

We "construct" G probabilistically as follows: We reserve for each input node 6 out-going edges, and correspondingly for each exit node 9 in-coming edges. Altogether this is $6 \cdot 6m = 9 \cdot 4m = 36m$ edges that we may place in G. We will choose the edges randomly under the uniform distribution in the following sense: first we choose for the first edge leaving node 1 a partner position on the exit side, for example the 7th edge entering node 13. So for the first choice we have $36m$ possibilities. For the next choice, $36m - 1$, etc. We will show that the probability is > 0 that the resulting graph has the desired matching property. From this we can conclude that such a graph must *exist.*

Exercise 23.5. How large is the sample space, that is, how many ways are there to connect the $6m$ input nodes to the $4m$ output nodes in the manner just described? ◁

We want to show that the number of "bad" graphs (graphs which *do not* have the desired property) is strictly smaller than the number determined in the preceding exercise. A graph G is bad if and only if there is a k-element subset of S with the property that $|N(S)| \leq k - 1$, where $k \leq n/2 = 3m$.

First we note that this can only happen if $k \geq 3$.

Exercise 23.6. Why? ◁

So assume $k \geq 3$. If G is bad, then there is an integer k and sets S and T such that $|S| = |T| = k$ and $N(S) \subsetneq T$. The calculations below work out somewhat better, however, if we also count situations where $N(S) = T$, even though this does not imply that the graph G is bad. For each k there are $\binom{6m}{k}$ choices for S and $\binom{4m}{k}$ choices for T. For a fixed pair S and T with $|S| = |T| = k$, there are at most $9k^{\underline{6k}}(36m - 6k)!$ many ways to choose the edge relations for G such that $N(S) \subseteq T$ (for each of the $6k$ edges leaving S, choose one of the $9k$ edges entering T, then choose the remaining $36m - 6k$ edges arbitrarily). We are using here the notation for "falling powers," $a^{\underline{b}} = a(a-1)(a-2)\cdots(a-b+1)$. So, for example, $\binom{a}{b} = a^{\underline{b}}/b!$.

Thus to prove the existence of a graph G (and therefore also of G') that is not bad, it is sufficient to show that

$$\sum_{k=3}^{3m} \binom{6m}{k}\binom{4m}{k} 9k^{\underline{6k}}(36m - 6k)! \;<\; (36m)!\,.$$

So it is sufficient to show that

$$\sum_{k=3}^{3m} \frac{\binom{6m}{k}\binom{4m}{k}\binom{9k}{6k}}{\binom{36m}{6k}} < 1\,.$$

To prove this inequality we will use

$$\binom{36m}{6k} \geq \binom{6m}{k}\binom{4m}{k}\binom{26m}{4k}\,.$$

Exercise 23.7. Prove this formula. ◁

Using this we see that it suffices to show that

$$\sum_{k=3}^{3m} \frac{\binom{9k}{6k}}{\binom{26m}{4k}} < 1$$

for large n.

Exercise 23.8.$^\diamond$ Let L_k denote the term $\binom{9k}{6k}/\binom{26m}{4k}$ and analyze the behavior of L_{k+1}/L_k to conclude that L_k – as a function of k with fixed m – is a convex function. Thus the largest summand L_k in the sum above is either the first term ($k = 3$) or the last term ($k = 3m$), as in the following sketch:

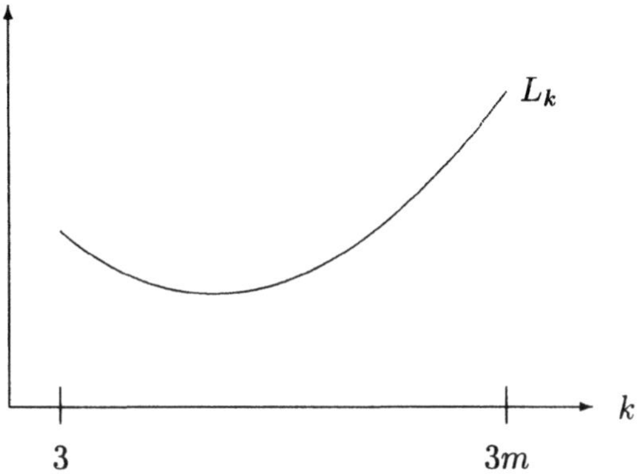

◁

Finally, we show that it is sufficient to show that $3mL_3$ and $3mL_{3m}$ are both smaller than 1. (Note that $3m$ is an upper bound on the number of summands in the sum.)

Exercise 23.9.$^\diamond$ Carry this out to complete the proof. ◁

With that we have proven the existence of superconcentrators of *linear* size and with a *constant* bound on the degree of each node. □

References

- Aho, Hopcroft, Ullman: *The Design and Analysis of Computer Algorithms*, Addison-Wesley, 1975.
- N. Pippenger: Superconcentrators, *SIAM Journal on Computing* 6 (1977), 298–304.
- F.R.K. Chung: Constructing random-like graphs, *Proceedings of Symposium in Applied Mathematics* Vol. 44, American Mathematics Society, 1991, 21–55.
- S.N. Bhatt: *On concentration and connection networks*, MIT/LCS Technical Report 196, 1981.

One can read about additional explicit constructions and application of superconcentrators in the contributed chapter by N. Pippenger in

- J. van Leeuwen, ed.: *Handbook of Theoretical Computer Science*, Elsevier, MIT Press, 1990, 805–833.

24. The Pebble Game

The Pebble game is a model for successive execution of a computation with the use of an auxiliary storage devise. The game can be used to study trade-off effects between the memory use and running time for a particular computation. We will show a lower bound originally proved by Paul, Tarjan, and Celoni (1977) which says that certain graphs, based on superconcentrators, require many pebbles.

The Pebble game is a one-player game on a fixed *directed, acyclic* graph. In the course of the game pebbles are placed on or removed from nodes in the graph according to the following rules:

1. A pebble may be placed on an input node (a node with no predecessors) at any time.
2. If all predecessors of a node u are marked with pebbles, then a pebble may be placed on node u
3. A pebble may be removed from a node at any time.

Note that rule 2 subsumes rule 1, but it is nevertheless useful to distinguish the two cases.

A *move* in this game consists of the placing or removing of one of the pebbles in accordance with one of the three rules. The goal of the game is to place a pebble on some previously distinguished node v (usually an output node) while minimizing the number of pebbles used, by which we mean minimizing the maximum number of pebbles that at any point in the game are simultaneously on the nodes of the graph, i.e., pebbles that have been removed from the graph can be "reused."

A *strategy* for the game is a sequence of legal moves that ends in pebbling the distinguished node v.

Example. The following graph

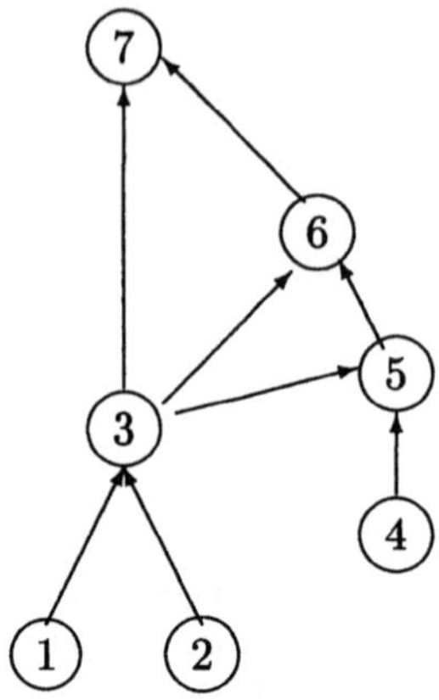

can be pebbled by placing pebbles on nodes 1 through 7 in order without removing any pebbles. This takes only 7 moves but uses 7 pebbles. Another strategy is represented in the following table:

place pebble on node	1	2	3			4	5		6		7
remove pebble from node				1	2			4		5	
number of pebbles on the graph	1	2	3	2	1	2	3	2	3	2	3
time	1	2	3	4	5	6	7	8	9	10	11

This strategy requires 11 moves but only 3 pebbles.

The pebble game is a model for the computation of some result v from given input data. Consider the following machine model:

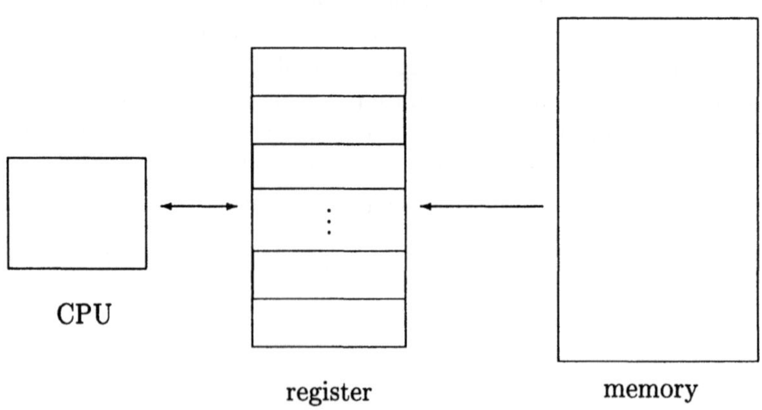

In this model, the use of a register (either to retrieve a value from memory or to store an intermediate result) corresponds to the placing of a pebble in the pebble game. Rule 1 says that at any time a value may be loaded into a register from memory. Rule 2 says that whenever all of the required intermediate results for some operation are located in registers, then the operation can be carried out and the result stored in another register. Finally, Rule 3 says that at any time a register may be "cleared."

The graph in the game indicates the dependency structure of the operations to be performed. Such graphs arise, for example, in the design of compilers. The use of as few pebbles as possible corresponds to the use of as few registers as possible. With the help of the pebble game, certain time-space trade-offs can be studied. As in the example above, often one has the situation that it is possible to perform a pebbling task in relatively few moves (in a short amount of time) but at the cost of using a large number of pebbles (large memory use). On the other hand, there may be another strategy that uses far fewer pebbles but requires more time, since some of the pebbles that are removed must later be "recalculated." If a pebbling task cannot be simultaneously solved with minimal space (pebbles) and time (moves), then we say that the task exhibits a ***time-space trade-off***.

We want to investigate how many pebbles are in general required to pebble graphs with n nodes. We must restrict ourselves to families of graphs with restricted in-degree. Otherwise, the number of pebbles will depend directly on the in-degree of the graph.

For example, consider the family of pyramid graphs:

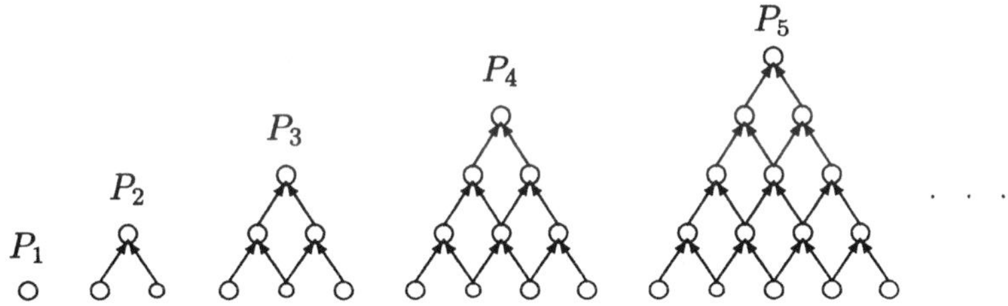

The pyramid graph P_k has $\sum_{i=1}^{k} i = k(k+1)/2 = \Theta(k^2)$ nodes and $k^2 - k = \Theta(k^2)$ edges.

Exercise 24.1. Show that it is possible to pebble the pyramid P_k with $k+1$ pebbles. Note that this is $O(\sqrt{n})$ pebbles with respect to the number of edges, n, in the graph. ◁

Exercise 24.2.$^\diamond$ Show that every pebbling strategy for P_k $(k > 1)$ must use at least $k+1$ pebbles. (Again, this is $\Omega(\sqrt{n})$ pebbles expressed in terms of the number of edges, n, in the graph.) ◁

* * * * *

Now we want to investigate how many pebbles are required for an arbitrary graph with restricted in-degree. We can restrict our attention to graphs of in-degree 2, since every graph with n edges and bounded in-degree $d > 2$ that can be pebbled with $p(n)$ pebbles can be transformed into a graph with at most $2n$ edges and in-degree 2 that can also be pebbled with $p(n)$ pebbles.

Exercise 24.3. Why? ◁

We will need the following lemma:

Lemma 24.1. *Every directed, acyclic graph with n edges and in-degree 2 can be partitioned into two subgraphs G_1 and G_2 so that G_1 contains between $n/2$ and $n/2 + 2$ edges and all edges between the two graphs go from G_1 to G_2 (and none in the other direction).*

We will let A denote this set of edges.

Sketch:

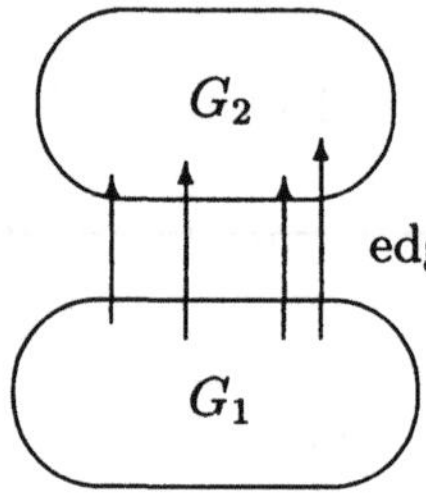

Exercise 24.4. Prove Lemma 24.1. ◁

Now we want to show that every graph with in-degree 2 can be pebbled with $O(n/\log n)$ pebbles. For this we will analyze the following recursive pebbling strategy:

1. If the graph G is small enough (fewer than n_0 edges), then pebble the distinguished node directly. Else continue according to 2, 3, or 4.
2. If the distinguished node v is in graph G_1, then apply the recursive procedure to graph G_1, since pebbling nodes in G_2 cannot be useful.
3. If the distinguished node v is in G_2 and A is *small* ($|A| \le 2n/\log n$), then recursively pebble every predecessor node to A by applying the recursive strategy in G_1. Leave all of these pebbles in place, but remove all other pebbles in G_1 that were used along the way. This will allow us to pebble any input nodes of G_2, so now start a recursive strategy for pebbling v in G_2.
4. If the distinguished node v is in G_2 and A is *big*, (i.e., $|A| > 2n/\log n$), then start a recursive pebbling strategy for v in G_2, but every time this strategy requires placing a pebble on an input node of G_2 that has predecessors in G_1, use the recursive strategy to pebble these nodes in G_1 first, then continue.

For the various cases we get the following recursion relations, where $P(n)$ is the maximal number of pebbles required to pebble a graph with n edges:

1. $P(n) = O(1)$ for $n \leq n_0$.
2. $P(n) \leq P(n/2+2)$.
3. $P(n) \leq 2n/\log n + P(n/2+2)$.
4. $P(n) \leq P(n/2 - 2n/\log n) + P(n/2+2) + 1$.

We need a solution to this recursion. Let's try $P(n) \leq cn/\log n$ for a suitably large constant c.

Exercise 24.5. Confirm that $cn/\log n$ is a solution for cases 1 and 2. ◁

Exercise 24.6.$^\diamond$ Confirm that $cn/\log n$ is a solution for case 3. ◁

Exercise 24.7.$^\diamond$ Confirm that $cn/\log n$ is a solution for case 4.

Hint: Use the equality $\frac{1}{x-a} = \frac{1}{x} + \frac{a}{x(x-a)}$. ◁

With the aid of this result, it is easy to demonstrate the following inclusion relationship between two complexity classes:

$$\mathsf{DTIME}(t(n)) \subseteq \mathsf{DSPACE}(t(n)/\log t(n)) \ .$$

Exercise 24.8. Show that there must be context sensitive languages that cannot be be accepted in linear time.

Hint: The class of context sensitive languages is precisely $\mathsf{NSPACE}(n)$. ◁

* * * * *

Next we want to show that the $O(n/\log n)$ bound on the number of pebbles needed to pebble graphs with n nodes is optimal. This means, we must construct a family of graphs $(G_n)_{n\in I}$, $|I| = \infty$, such that for every constant $c > 0$ and every $n \in I$, at least $c \cdot |G_n|/\log|G_n|$ pebbles are required to pebble the graph G_n. (Note: this implies that the inclusion $\mathsf{DTIME}(t(n)) \subseteq \mathsf{DSPACE}(t(n)/\log t(n))$ cannot be improved.)

The superconcentrators from Topic 23 will prove very useful in obtaining this result. The following lemma demonstrates an important property of superconcentrators with respect to pebbling.

Lemma 24.2. *If j pebbles are placed on any j nodes of an n-superconcentrator $(0 \leq j < n)$ and A is a subset of at least $j+1$ output nodes, then there are at least $n-j$ inputs that are connected to A along pebble-free paths.*

Exercise 24.9.$^\diamond$ Prove Lemma 24.2. ◁

For every n let $C_1(n)$ and $C_2(n)$ be two copies of a 2^n-superconcentrator. By the results in Topic 23 there is a constant d with $|C_i(n)| \leq d2^n$. We construct the family of graphs $\{G_n \mid n \geq 8\}$ recursively beginning with G_8, which is chosen to be a $2^8 = 256$-superconcentrator. G_{n+1} is defined as follows:

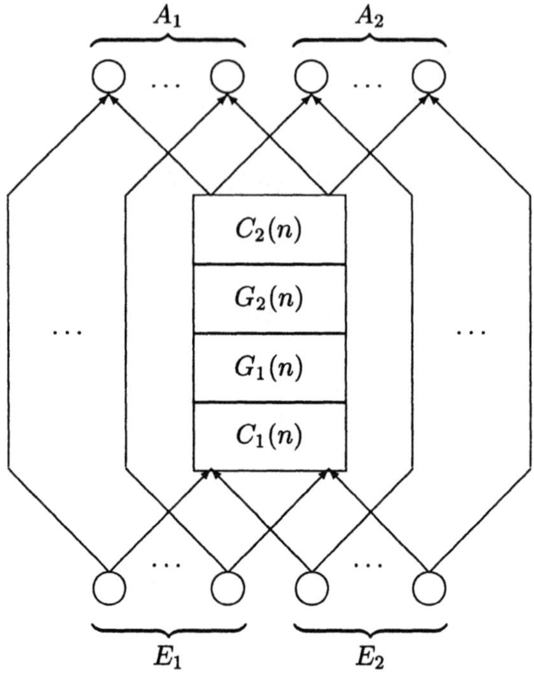

G_{n+1} has 2^{n+1} inputs and outputs, divided into the sets E_1, E_2 and A_1, A_2, each of which has size 2^n. Each input is connected directly to its corresponding output and is also routed through two copies of G_n surrounded by two superconcentrators of the appropriate size, which in a certain sense "decouple" the inputs and outputs. The outputs of $C_1(n)$ are identified with the inputs of $G_1(n)$, similarly for $G_1(n)$ and $G_2(n)$, and $G_2(n)$ and $C_2(n)$. (In his lecture at ICALP 82, Pippenger referred to these graphs as "super-duper-concentrators.")

Exercise 24.10. Show that the size of the graph G_n is asymptotically $\Theta(n2^n)$. So it is sufficient in what follows to show that there is some c such that at least $c2^n$ pebbles are required to pebble G_n. ◁

Exercise 24.11. Show that a $C(n)$ (a 2^n-superconcentrator) and a $G(n)$ together still form a 2^n-superconcentrator. ◁

The clever part of the following proof – which, as one expects, will be done by induction – is to formulate an induction hypothesis that is strong enough to be useful for the inductive step. It is not sufficient to merely assume that $c2^n$ pebbles are required to pebble G_n – although this is what matters in the end – rather, we must also pack into the inductive hypothesis (and therefore also prove in our inductive step) some additional properties of the potential pebbling strategies on G_n.

So what is this hypothesis?

Theorem 24.3. *Let* $\alpha(n) = 2^n/256 = 2^{n-8}$. *In order to pebble at least* $14\alpha(n)$ *outputs of* G_n $(n \geq 8)$ *in any order, beginning with an initial configuration in which at most* $3\alpha(n)$ *nodes are pebbled, there must be an interval of time during which at least* $\alpha(n)$ *nodes remain pebbled and during which time at least* $34\alpha(n)$ *inputs must be pebbled.*

We note the outputs can be pebbled in any order, and that the pebbles are not required to remain on the output nodes, so that the output nodes do not have to be pebbled simultaneously.

Proof. The proof is by induction on n.

Exercise 24.12.$^\diamond$ Verify the base case of the induction, that is, show that the hypothesis holds for G_8.

Hint: Use Lemma 24.2. ◁

Inductive step: Assume that the hypothesis holds for G_n; we must show that it holds for G_{n+1}. Consider an initial configuration on G_{n+1} with at most $3\alpha(n+1) = 6\alpha(n)$ pebbled nodes and assume that in the course of the moves $1, \ldots, t$ at least $14\alpha(n+1) = 28\alpha(n)$ outputs are pebbled. We will refer to this time period as the time interval $[0, t]$. We must show that within the interval $[0, t]$ there is a time interval during which there are always at least $\alpha(n+1) = 2\alpha(n)$ pebbles on the graph and during which at least $34\alpha(n+1) = 68\alpha(n)$ outputs are pebbled.

We distinguish four cases. In case 1–3 we assume that the pebble strategy proceeds somehow "unevenly." In these three cases, we are able to carry out our proof without using the inductive hypothesis, which is only needed in case 4.

Case 1. There is a time interval $[t_1, t_2] \subseteq [0, t]$, during which there are always $3\alpha(n)$ pebbles on the graph and during which at least $7\alpha(n)$ inputs of $G_1(n)$ are pebbled.

Let t_0 be the last time before t_1 at which not more than $6\alpha(n)$ pebbles were on the graph. We apply Lemma 24.2 at time t_0 to the following two subgraphs of G_{n+1}.

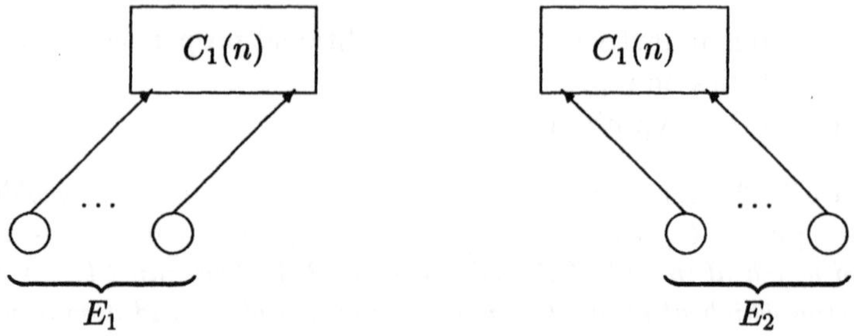

So there is a time t_0 at which there are at least $2^n - 6\alpha(n) = 250\alpha(n)$ pebble-free paths from E_1 to the $7\alpha(n)$ inputs of $G_1(n)$ (= outputs of $C_1(n)$) that are pebbled during the interval $[t_1, t_2]$. The same bound holds for pebble-free paths starting from E_2. So altogether there are $500\alpha(n)$ pebble-free paths and, therefore, that many inputs that remain to be pebbled during the time interval $[t_0, t_2]$. Similarly, during this interval there must be at least $3\alpha(n) - 1 \geq 2\alpha(n)$ pebbles on the graph. This establishes the claim for the interval $[t_0, t_2]$.

Case 2. There is a time interval $[t_1, t_2] \subseteq [0, t]$, during which there are always at least $3\alpha(n)$ pebbles on the graph and during which at least $7\alpha(n)$ inputs of $G_2(n)$ are pebbled.

The proof in this case is analogous to the one given for case 1, but in this case, we apply Lemma 24.2 to the following two subgraphs of G_{n+1}. Note that each of these graphs is a 2^n-superconcentrator (see Exercise 24.11), so the lemma applies.

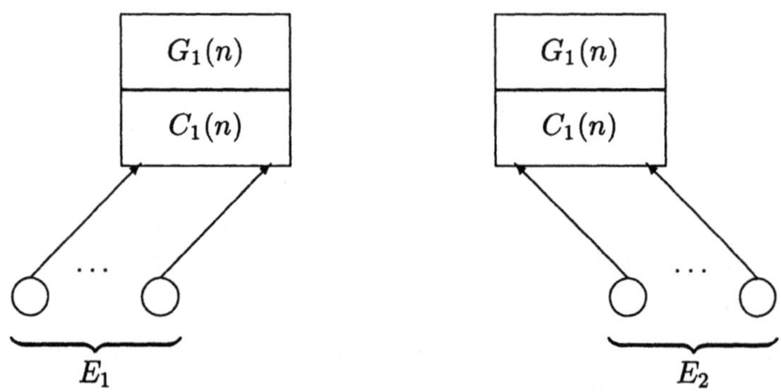

Case 3. There is a time interval $[t_1, t_2] \subseteq [0, t]$, during which there are always $3\alpha(n)$ pebbles on the graph and during which $14\alpha(n)$ outputs of G_{n+1} are pebbled.

During $[t_1, t_2]$ we can assume without loss of generality that at least $7\alpha(n)$ outputs of A_1 are pebbled. Once again the claim can be established by a proof that is analogous to the one used in case 1, this time applying Lemma 24.2

to the two subgraphs of G_{n+1} depicted below, each of which is again a 2^n-superconcentrator (see Exercise 24.11).

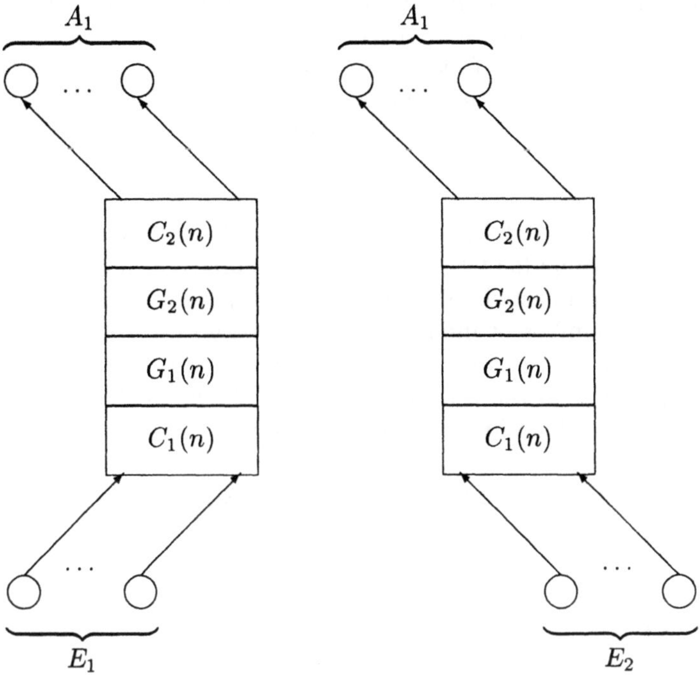

Case 4. None of the cases 1–3 is applicable.

Since we are not in case 3, there must be a time $t_1 \in [0, t]$ such that fewer than $14\alpha(n)$ outputs of G_{n+1} are pebbled during the time interval $[0, t_1]$ and at time t_1 fewer than $3\alpha(n)$ pebbles are on the graph. This means that during the time interval $[t_1, t]$, at least $28\alpha(n) - 14\alpha(n) = 14\alpha(n)$ outputs of G_{n+1} are pebbled. Without loss of generality we may assume that $7\alpha(n)$ of these are in A_1. By Lemma 24.2 (applied to $C_2(n)$), at time t_1 there are at least $2^n - 3\alpha(n) = 253\alpha(n)$ pebble-free paths between these $7\alpha(n)$ outputs of A_1 and the outputs $G_2(n)$. Thus during the time interval $[t_1, t]$, at least $253\alpha(n) \geq 14\alpha(n)$ outputs of $G_2(n)$ must be pebbled.

By the inductive hypothesis, there is a time interval $[t_2, t_3] \subseteq [t_1, t]$, during which at least $34\alpha(n)$ inputs of $G_2(n)$ (= outputs of $G_1(n)$) are pebbled and during which there are always at least $\alpha(n)$ pebbles on graph $G_2(n)$.

Since we are not in case 2, there must be a time $t_4 \in [t_2, t_3]$ so that within the interval $[t_2, t_4]$ fewer than $7\alpha(n)$ inputs of $G_2(n)$ are pebbled and at time t_4, fewer than $3\alpha(n)$ pebbles are on the graph. So during $[t_4, t_3]$ at least $34\alpha(n) - 7\alpha(n) = 27\alpha(n)$ inputs of $G_2(n)$ (= outputs of $G_1(n)$) must be pebbled, beginning from a configuration with at most $3\alpha(n)$ pebbled nodes at time t_4.

By the inductive hypothesis, there is a time interval $[t_5, t_6] \subseteq [t_4, t_3]$, during which at least $34\alpha(n)$ inputs of $G_1(n)$ (= outputs of $C_1(n)$) are pebbled and during which there are always at least $\alpha(n)$ pebbles on graph $G_1(n)$.

Since we are not in case 1, there must be a time $t_7 \in [t_5, t_6]$ such that during the interval $[t_5, t_7]$, fewer than $7\alpha(n)$ inputs of $G_1(n)$ are pebbled, and at time t_7, fewer than $3\alpha(n)$ pebbles are on the graph. So during $[t_7, t_6]$ at least $34\alpha(n) - 7\alpha(n) = 27\alpha(n)$ inputs of $G_1(n)$ (= outputs $C_1(n)$) must be pebbled beginning from a configuration with at most $3\alpha(n)$ pebbled node at t_7.

By Lemma 24.2, it follows that at time t_7 there must be at least $2^n - 3\alpha(n) = 253\alpha(n)$ inputs of E_1, and, correspondingly, at least $253\alpha(n)$ inputs of E_2, that are connected to these $27\alpha(n)$ outputs of $C_1(n)$ by pebble-free paths. So this number of inputs must be pebbled during the time interval $[t_7, t_6]$. Also, during this interval, there are at least $\alpha(n)$ pebbles on each of $G_1(n)$ and $G_2(n)$, so there must be at least $2\alpha(n)$ pebbles on G_{n+1}. This demonstrates the claim for the interval $[t_7, t_6]$. □

Exercise 24.13. Show that it follows from Theorem 24.3 that the $O(n/\log n)$-bound is optimal. ◁

References

For the upper bound on the number of pebbles required see

- J. Hopcroft, W.J. Paul, L. Valiant: On time versus space, *Journal of the ACM* 24 (1977), 332–337.
- K. Wagner, G. Wechsung: *Computational Complexity*, VEB Deutscher Verlag der Wissenschaften, 1986.

For the lower bound see

- W.J. Paul, R.E. Tarjan, J.R. Celoni: Space bounds for a game on graphs, *Mathematical Systems Theory* 10 (1977), 239–251.

25. Average-Case Complexity

In Topic 8, we noticed that the expected running time of an algorithm depends upon the underlying distribution of the instances and may in general be different from the worst-case running time. Now we want to look more carefully at the notions of being easy or hard *on average*. As it turns out, equating easy on average with polynomially-bounded expected running time has serious drawbacks. But in 1984, L. Levin proposed an alternate definition and demonstrated its robustness, thereby initiating the study of average-case complexity.

Many NP-hard problems are of practical importance, but since there is no known polynomial-time algorithm for any of these problems, other types of solutions have been considered: approximation algorithms, probabilistic algorithms, algorithms that work efficiently on an important restricted set of inputs, etc. Another such alternative is to require that the problem only be efficiently solvable *on average* rather than in the worst case, which for some NP-complete problems may be very rare. Indeed, reductions to NP-complete languages typically reduce instances of an NP-problem to instances of the NP-complete problem that are not very "typical." The natural question, of course, is which NP-problems are easy on average and which are hard.

But before we can hope to answer these questions, we need to say what is meant by easy and hard on average. Presumably, this will involve three components: a class of distributions that we allow (the results of Topic 8 indicate that some restriction must be made), a definition of easy on average, and a notion of reduction between (distributional) problems that can be used to define hardness on average. We will restrict our attention to decision problems, although similar things can be done for search problems as well.

For any strings x and y (over some ordered alphabet Σ), let $x < y$ denote that x occurs before y in the standard lexicographical order, and let $x - 1$ be the predecessor of x in this order ($\lambda - 1 = \lambda$). We introduce the following definitions for distributions and density functions over Σ^*:

Definition 25.1. *A (probability)* distribution $\mu = (\mu', \mu^*)$ *can be described by giving either*

- *a (probability)* distribution function μ^*, *i.e., a function* $\mu^* : \Sigma^* \to [0,1]$ *that*

   - *is non-decreasing:* $x < y \Longrightarrow \mu^*(x) \leq \mu^*(y)$, *and*
   - *converges to 1:* $\lim_{x\to\infty}\mu^*(x) = 1$;
- *or a (probability)* density function μ', *i.e., a function* $\mu' : \Sigma^* \to [0,1]$ *such that*

$$\sum_{x\in\Sigma^*} \mu'(x) = 1 .$$

For any distribution μ *or distribution function* μ^*, *the associated density function is*

$$\mu'(x) = \begin{cases} \mu^*(\lambda) & \text{if } x = \lambda, \\ \mu^*(x) - \mu^*(x-1) & \text{otherwise;} \end{cases}$$

and for any distribution μ *or density function* μ', *the associated distribution function is*

$$\mu^*(x) = \sum_{y\leq x} \mu'(y).$$

A *distributional problem* is a pair (A, μ) where A is a decision problem (a language) and μ is a distribution. For technical reasons we will assume that $\mu'(\lambda) = \mu^*(\lambda) = 0$. It seems natural that we should at least allow distributions that can be computed in polynomial time. This leads to the following definition:

Definition 25.2 (P-computable distribution). *A distribution function* μ *is* P-computable *if there is a deterministic algorithm running in polynomial time that on input* x *outputs the binary expansion of* $\mu^*(x)$.

Note that if a distribution function μ^* is P-computable, then μ' is also P-computable, but that the converse may not be true, since to compute a distribution from a density function requires an exponentially large sum.

Exercise 25.1.$^\circ$ Show that if every P-computable density function μ' induces a P-computable distribution function μ^*, then P = NP.

Hint: It easy to check if a polynomial-time nondeterministic machine accepts along a fixed path, but probably hard to tell if there *exists* a path along which it accepts. Design a distributional problem where μ' and μ^* reflect this difference. ◁

Nevertheless, it is usually more convenient to express things in terms of the density function, and we will write μ instead of μ' from now on. Note, however, that for P-computability, we always mean P-computability of μ^*, not of μ'.

If μ is P-computable, then $|\mu^*(x)|$ is polynomially bounded. This implies that it is not possible to place too much weight on the short strings, i.e., there is a polynomial p such that for large n the combined weight of all strings of length n is at least $1/p(n)$. Of course, the definition of P-computable distribution also rules out the universal probability distribution of Topic 8. Later we will discuss a potentially larger class of distributions as well.

We are particularly interested in distributional versions of NP problems.

Definition 25.3 (DistNP). *A distributional problem* (A, μ) *belongs to the class* DistNP *if* $A \in$ NP *and* μ *is a* P*-computable distribution. Another notation for this class is* (NP, P*-computable*).

Typically, a distribution for such a DistNP problem is defined in terms of a density function, which is usually designed to model a random experiment of the following general type: First pick a *size* (length of string, an integer, number of nodes in graph, etc.) for the instance, then randomly select an instance of the given size according to some probabilistic experiment. Unless we specify some other distribution, we will assume that the selection of a size is done in such a way that the probability of selecting size m is roughly proportional to $1/m^2$. This is an easy and natural choice, since $\sum_m 1/m$ diverges and $\sum_m 1/m^2$ converges. Of course, technically, we must scale the probability by $1/c$, where $c = \sum_m 1/m^2$, to get a probability distribution, but often in the literature this scaling is omitted, and one simply works with probability distributions that converge to something other than 1.

Exercise 25.2. An alternative to scaling $\mu(m) = 1/m^2$ is to modify μ slightly so that the sum is 1. Show that $\displaystyle\sum_{m\geq 1} \frac{1}{m(m+1)} = \sum_{m\geq 1} \frac{1}{\overline{m^2}} = 1.$ ◁

For ease of notation we will adopt the convention of writing $1/m^2$ for this density function instead of $1/\overline{m^2}$.

Examples. Each of the following DistNP-problems is defined by giving the form of an instance, the question, and a description of the distribution in terms of a random experiment. For the first example we include an expression for the density function as well.

- *D-HALT*
  - *Instance:* A Turing machine (encoding) M, a string x and an integer k written in unary.
  - *Question:* Does $M(x)$ halt within k steps?
  - *Distribution:* Randomly pick sizes m, n, and k. Randomly choose a string M of length m, and a string x of length n. So the probability density function is

$$\mu(M, x, 1^k) = \frac{1}{|M|^2 \cdot 2^{|M|}} \cdot \frac{1}{|x|^2 \cdot 2^{|x|}} \cdot \frac{1}{k^2}.$$

- *D-3COL*
  - *Instance:* A graph G.
  - *Question:* Is there a 3-coloring of the graph G? (A 3-coloring is an assignment of one of three colors to each of the nodes in the graph in such a way that no pair of adjacent nodes is assigned the same color.)
  - *Distribution:* Randomly pick a size n. Randomly choose a graph with vertices $0, 1, \ldots, n$ by selecting each possible edge independently with probability $1/2$.

- *D-HAM*
  - *Instance:* A graph G.
  - *Question:* Is there a Hamiltonian circuit in G?
  - *Distribution:* Randomly pick a size n. Randomly choose a graph with vertices $0, 1, \ldots, n$ by selecting each possible edge independently with probability $1/2$.

Thus far, the definitions have all been completely natural. Unfortunately, the naive definition for easy on average has serious drawbacks. The obvious definition would be the following: A is easy on average if there is a deterministic algorithm for deciding membership in A with polynomially-bounded expected running time, i.e., the running time $t_A(x)$ should satisfy

$$\sum_{|x|=n} \mu_n(x) \cdot t_A(x) < cn^k ,$$

for some integer constants c and k. Here $\mu_n(x)$ denotes the conditional probability

$$\mu_n(x) = \mu(x \mid x \in \Sigma^n) = \begin{cases} \mu(x)/\mu(|x| = n) & \text{if } |x| = n, \\ 0 & \text{otherwise.} \end{cases}$$

Unfortunately, this definition has serious drawbacks.

Exercise 25.3. Find a function $f : \Sigma^* \to \mathbb{R}$ such that f has a polynomially-bounded expected value, but f^2 does not.[1]

Hint: Let f be exponential (linear exponent) on a small set of inputs of each length. Then f^2 will be exponential with a quadratic exponent on those same inputs. ◁

This implies that a theory of average-case based on polynomially-bounded expected running time would have several significant drawbacks. Such a definition would be machine dependent, since there is a polynomial loss of efficiency when converting between some models of polynomial time computation that we normally regard as equivalent. Thus whether or not a distributional problem is easy on average might depend on the underlying model of computation. Worse still, even for a fixed model of computation, the class of problems that are easy on average would not be closed under operations like composition. This would mean that an algorithm that is easy on average could not necessarily be used as a sub-routine in another algorithm that is easy on average (neglecting the time spent on the sub-routine calls). Using the naive definition of easy on average, this sort of composition of two algorithms that are easy on average might result in an algorithm that is not easy on average.

Levin's solution to these problems is the following definition:

[1] Throughout this topic, we will use the notation f^r or $f^r(x)$ to denote $[f(x)]^r$ and not the r-fold composition of f with itself.

Definition 25.4 (Polynomial on μ-average). *A function f is* polynomial on μ-average *if there is a constant $\varepsilon > 0$ such that*

$$\sum_{x \neq \lambda} \mu(x) \cdot \frac{f^{\varepsilon}(x)}{|x|} < \infty ,$$

that is, the function $f^{\varepsilon}(x)$ is linear on μ-average.

Definition 25.5 (AP). *A distributional problem (A, μ) is in the class* AP *(average polynomial time) if there is an algorithm for A with running time that is polynomial on μ-average.*

Exercise 25.4. Show that if f and g are polynomial on μ-average, then so are $\max(f, g)$, f^k, $f + g$, and $f \cdot g$. ◁

Exercise 25.5.$^{\diamond}$ Show that if the expected value of f is polynomially bounded with respect to some distribution μ, then f is polynomial on μ-average.

Hint: Use the fact that $a < 1 + a^{\delta}$ for all $\delta \geq 1$. ◁

Thus AP has some of the nice closure properties that we expect of a robust complexity class.

Even though the 3-colorability problem is NP-complete, its distributional version, at least with the distribution we have presented, is in AP:

Theorem 25.6. *The distributional version of the 3-colorability problem, D-3COL, is in* AP. □

Exercise 25.6.$^{\diamond}$ Prove Theorem 25.6.

Hint: If a graph G has a copy of K_4, the complete graph with four vertices and six edges, as a subgraph, then G cannot be 3-colored. ◁

Now we want to know if there are any DistNP problems that are hard on average. For this we want to define a reducibility $\leq_r$ between two distributional problems with the following properties:

- *Closure:* If $(A, \mu) \leq_r (B, \nu)$ and (B, ν) is in AP, then (A, μ) is as well.
- *Transitivity:* $\leq_r$ is transitive.

If H is hard for DistNP under a reducibility with these properties, then

$$H \in \mathsf{AP} \iff \mathsf{AP} = \mathsf{DistNP} .$$

It has been shown that if AP = DistNP, then NEXP = EXP, which is considered unlikely.

Once again, the simplest thing to try does not have the desired properties. Polynomial-time many-one reductions may map very likely instances of (A, μ)

(on which an AP-algorithm must run quickly) to very unlikely instances of (B, ν) (on which an AP-algorithm may run very slowly); this would violate the closure property. Thus we must design a reducibility that respects the distributions in some way.

Definition 25.7 (Domination). *Let μ and ν be distributions. Then $\mu \preceq \nu$ (read μ is dominated by ν) if there is a polynomial p such that $\mu(x) \leq p(|x|)\nu(x)$.*

Let (A, μ) and (B, ν) be distributional problems and let $f : A \leq_m^P B$. Then μ is dominated by ν with respect to f, *written $\mu \preceq_f \nu$, if there is a distribution μ_1 for A such that $\mu \preceq \mu_1$ and $\nu(y) = \nu(\text{range}(f)) \cdot \sum_{f(x)=y} \mu_1(x)$.*

Definition 25.8 (Polynomial-time reduction). (A, μ) *is polynomial-time (many-one) reducible to (B, ν) if $A \leq_m^P B$ via a function f such that $\mu \preceq_f \nu$. We will denote this by $f : (A, \mu) \leq_m^P (B, \nu)$.* □

Lemma 25.9. *The reducibility $\leq_m^P$ is transitive; and if $(A, \mu) \leq_m^P (B, \nu)$ and $(B, \nu) \in$ AP, then $(A, \mu) \in$ AP.*

Exercise 25.7. Prove that $\leq_m^P$ is transitive on distributional problems. ◁

Exercise 25.8.[◇] Show that AP is closed under $\leq_m^P$. ◁

Now we can give an example of a distributional version of an NP-complete problem that is DistNP-hard. The problem we will choose is *D-HALT*, the distributional halting problem. Although it is relatively straightforward to show that the usual bounded halting problem is complete for NP, that proof does not carry over directly to the distributional setting. In fact, it is not immediately clear that there are *any* DistNP-complete problems. Certainly there is a many-one reduction from any NP decision problem to the halting problem, but this reduction may not respect the distributions. In particular, we need to show that *D-HALT*, which has a *fixed* distribution, is hard for all NP problems with *any* P-computable distribution. To achieve this, we will need to modify the reduction on instances of the decision problem for the sake of respecting the distributions.

Theorem 25.10. *D-HALT is $\leq_m^P$-complete for* DistNP.

Proof. For any NP-problem A there is a nondeterministic machine N_A that decides membership in A in time $p(n)$ for some polynomial p. We have already noted, however, that the reduction

$$x \mapsto (N_A, x, 1^{p(|x|)})$$

may not respect the distributions involved. Instead we will use a reduction of the form

$$x \mapsto (N_{A,\mu}, \text{code}_\mu(x), 1^{|x|^{O(1)}}) ,$$

where $N_{A,\mu}$ is a machine that depends only on N_A and μ (but not on x) and $\text{code}_\mu(x)$ is an encoding of x.

The success of the proof depends upon finding an encoding satisfying the following lemma:

Lemma 25.11. *Let μ be a* P*-computable distribution. Then there is an encoding function* code_μ *satisfying the following properties:*

- Compression. *For every x,*

$$|\text{code}_\mu(x)| \leq 1 + \min(|x|, \log_2 \frac{1}{\mu(x)}) .$$

- Efficiency. *The function* code_μ *can be computed in polynomial time.*
- Uniqueness. *The function* code_μ *is one-to-one, i.e., if* $\text{code}_\mu(x) = \text{code}_\mu(y)$*, then $x = y$.* □

Exercise 25.9.$^\diamond$ Prove Lemma 25.11.

Hint: Distinguish two cases. The case when $\mu(x) \leq 2^{-|x|}$ is easy. In the other case, recall that $\mu(x) = \mu^*(x) - \mu^*(x-1)$, and define $\text{code}_\mu(x)$ based upon a comparison of the binary representations of $\mu^*(x)$ and $\mu^*(x-1)$. ◁

The reduction is now defined by

$$f : x \mapsto (N_{A,\mu}, \text{code}_\mu(x), 1^{q(|x|)}) ,$$

where $q(|x|)$ is a polynomial that bounds the sum $|x|$, the time required to compute $\text{code}_\mu(x)$, and the time required to run N_A on input x; and $N_{A,\mu}$ is a nondeterministic machine implementing the following algorithm:

> **INPUT** y;
> **GUESS** x such that $\text{code}_\mu(x) = y$;
> **IF** $N_A(x)$ accepts **THEN ACCEPT**
>   **ELSE REJECT;**
> **END.**

This nondeterministic algorithm runs in time $q(|x|)$ on input $y = \text{code}_\mu(x)$, so f is a polynomial-time computable many-one reduction on instances. All that remains is to show that $\mu \preceq_f \nu$, where ν is the distribution of *D-HALT*.

Exercise 25.10.$^\diamond$ Show that $\mu \preceq_f \nu$. ◁

Distributional versions of several other NP-complete problems have also been shown to be $\leq^{\mathrm{P}}_{\mathrm{m}}$-complete for DistNP, including a tiling problem, the Post correspondence problem, word problems for Thue systems and finitely presented groups, and satisfiability.

* * * * *

So what distinguishes distributional versions of NP-complete problems that are hard for DistNP from those that are not? Y. Gurevich provided a partial answer to this question when he observed that, under a plausible complexity theoretic assumption, in many cases the distribution of a distributional problem already determines that the problem cannot be DistNP-complete, regardless of the question. This property of distributions that makes distributional problems unlikely to be DistNP-complete is *flatness.*

Definition 25.12 (Flat distribution). *A probability density function is* flat *if there is an $\varepsilon > 0$ such that for all $x \in \Sigma^*$, $\mu(x) \leq 2^{-|x|^\varepsilon}$. A distribution function is flat if its associated density function is flat.*

So a distribution is flat if no long strings are weighted too heavily – none of them juts out from the others.

Exercise 25.11. Show that the distribution of *D-HAM* is flat. ◁

Exercise 25.12. Show that the distribution of *D-HALT* is not flat. ◁

Theorem 25.13. *No* DistNP *problem with a flat distribution is $\leq^{\mathrm{P}}_{\mathrm{m}}$-complete for* DistNP, *unless* NEXP = EXP.

Proof. Suppose $(H, \nu) \in$ DistNP, ν is flat, and (H, ν) is $\leq^{\mathrm{P}}_{\mathrm{m}}$-complete for DistNP. Since $H \in$ NP, $H \in$ EXP. Let A be an arbitrary decision problem in NEXP. Then there is a polynomial p such that $A \in \mathrm{NTIME}(2^{p(n)})$. We want to define a distributional problem $(A_0, \mu) \in$ DistNP that is related to A. For this let $x' = x01^{2^{p(|x|)}-(|x|+1)}$, define $A_0 = \{x' \mid x \in A\}$, and let μ be defined by

$$\mu(z) = \begin{cases} |x|^{-2}2^{-|x|} & \text{if } z = x' \text{ for some } x, \\ 0 & \text{otherwise.} \end{cases}$$

Exercise 25.13. Show that $A_0 \in$ NP. ◁

Since $A_0 \in$ NP, $(A_0, \mu) \in$ DistNP; and since $(H, \nu))$ is complete for DistNP, there is a reduction $f : (A_0, \mu) \leq^{\mathrm{P}}_{\mathrm{m}} (H, \nu)$. This implies that there is a distribution μ_1 and a polynomial q such that

- $f(x')$ can be computed in $2^{O(q(|x|))}$ time.
- $x \in A$ if and only if $f(x') \in H$,
- $\mu(x') \leq q(|x'|)\mu_1(x')$, and
- $\nu(f(x')) = \nu(\mathrm{range}(f)) \sum_{f(z)=f(x')} \mu_1(z)$.

Now we put these pieces together. First, for notational ease, we will assume that $\nu(\mathrm{range}(f)) = 1$. The argument below can be easily modified if $\nu(\mathrm{range}(f)) = c$ for some constant $c < 1$.

$$\mu(x') \leq q(|x'|)\mu_1(x') \leq q(|x'|) \sum_{f(z)=f(x')} \mu_1(z) \leq q(|x'|)\nu(f(x')) ,$$

so

$$\nu(f(x')) > \frac{\mu(x')}{q(|x'|)} = \frac{|x|^{-2} \cdot 2^{-|x|}}{q(|x'|)} > \frac{1}{2^{|x|} \cdot |x|^2 \cdot q(2^{p(|x|)})} > 2^{-r(|x|)} ,$$

for some polynomial r. But since ν is flat, there is an $\varepsilon > 0$ such that $\nu(f(x')) \leq 2^{-|f(x')|^\varepsilon}$. From this it follows that

$$|f(x')|^\varepsilon \leq -\log(\nu(f(x'))) < r(|x|) ,$$

so $|f(x')|$ is polynomial in $|x|$. Thus $A \in \mathsf{EXP}$: $x \in A$ if and only if $f(x') \in H$, and we can compute $f(x')$ in $2^{O(q(|x|))}$ time, and then determine whether $f(x') \in H$ in $2^{poly(|f(x')|} = 2^{poly(|x|)})$ time.

* * * * *

The theory of average-case complexity has been extended in several ways from the results presented here. One generalization of the theory considers other, less-restrictive reductions between distributional problems. It is fairly straightforward, for example, to generalize polynomial-time many-one reducibility to polynomial-on-average many-one reducibility. All the results presented here remain true in that setting as well. Similarly one can consider other types of reducibilities, such as truth-table or Turing reducibility. Finally, one can define a notion of randomized reduction. Roughly, a randomized reduction from (A, μ) to (B, ν) is given by a probabilistic oracle Turing machine that on input x with oracle B and random bits r runs in time polynomial on $\mu \cdot \mu_0$-average (where μ_0 is the distribution on the random bits r), correctly decides $x \in A$ with probability at least $2/3$, and asks queries in a manner that respects the distributions (so that the reduction may not query oracle instances of low weight too often). The random reduction is many-one or truth-table if the Turing machine behaves in one of these more restrictive ways. There are randomized many-one complete problems for DistNP that have flat distributions.

A second generalization considers a larger class of distributions:

Definition 25.14 (P-samplable distribution). *A distribution μ is called* P*-samplable if there is a randomized algorithm that takes no input (but flips coins) and eventually outputs a string x (if it halts) in such a way that*

- *the probability that the algorithm outputs x is $\mu'(x)$, and*
- *the running time is polynomially bounded in $|x|$.*

Exercise 25.14. Show that all P-computable distributions are P-samplable. ◁

If certain cryptographic one-way functions exist (polynomial-time computable functions that are hard to invert on most instances) then there are P-samplable distributions that are not P-computable.

It can be shown that a version of the bounded halting problem with another so-called *universal distribution* (not to be confused with the universal probability distribution of Topic 8) is $\leq_m^P$-complete for (NP, P-samplable). (Roughly, the universal distribution in this case amounts to randomly selecting a P-samplable distribution from an enumeration, and then sampling according to that distribution.) Furthermore, in the setting of NP-search problems – where a solution must not only give the answer to an NP-predicate but also provide a witness, and reductions must also preserve witnesses – Impagliazzo and Levin have shown that every distributional problem that is complete for (NP-search, P-computable) under randomized many-one reductions is also complete for (NP-search, P-samplable) under randomized many-one reductions. This is a pleasing result, since most natural problems have P-computable distributions, and it says that in some sense, there is no better way to find hard instances of a problem like *SAT* than to pick an instance uniformly at random. A similar result holds for decision problems under randomized truth-table reductions.

References

Below are a number of articles that were used in preparing this topic. Those interested in learning more about average-case complexity are encouraged to consult the bibliographies of these papers for additional references.

- O. Goldreich: Notes on Levin's theory of average-case complexity, available at http://theory.lcs.mit.edu/õded/surveys.html, 1997.
- Y. Gurevich: Average-case completeness, *Journal of Computer and System Sciences* 42 (1991), 346–398.
- R. Impagliazzo: A personal view of average-case complexity, *Proceedings of the 10th annual Conference on Structure in Complexity Theory*, IEEE, 1995, 137–147.
- R. Impagliazzo, L. Levin: No better ways to generate hard NP instances than picking uniformly at random, *Proceedings of the 31st Symposium on Foundations of Computer Science*, IEEE, 1990, 812–821.
- L. Levin: Average case complete problems, *SIAM Journal on Computing* 15 (1986), 285–286.
- J. Wang: Average-case computational complexity theory, Chapter 12 in *Complexity Theory Retrospective II*, Springer, 1997.

26. Quantum Search Algorithms

Widespread interest in quantum computation was sparked by an algorithm of P. Shor for factoring integers on a quantum computer. We investigate here a more recent quantum algorithm of L. Grover for searching a database. This algorithm demonstrates a proven speed-up against the best possible classical algorithm for the same task.

Up to this point, all of the computing devices and all of the complexity classes we have considered have been based on *classical* physics. In the early 1980's, however, P. Benioff proposed a model of computation based on *quantum mechanics.* The model of quantum computation was subsequently formalized, primarily due to the work of D. Deutsch. Widespread interest in quantum computation was sparked in 1994, when P. Shor gave a feasible quantum algorithm for factoring integers, a problem that has no known feasible classical algorithm, a fact which underlies many encryption schemes. Thus Shor's algorithm showed that quantum machines are able – at least in theory – to perform an interesting and important task that classical (probabilistic) machines – perhaps – cannot. There remain, of course, difficulties in implementing such an algorithm on a physical device.

We want to consider here L. Grover's quantum mechanical algorithm for searching a database. This algorithm has the advantages of being somewhat simpler to describe and analyze than Shor's algorithm, since it does not make use of as much number theory, and of demonstrating something that can *provably* be done more efficiently on a quantum machine than on a classical machine.

The database search problem in this context is defined as follows. Suppose we have an *unsorted* data set with $N = 2^n$ entries, exactly one of which matches our selection criteria. For example, the data set could be a phone book from which we want to retrieve the name of a person with a particular phone number. (Note that the usual sorting of a phone book does not assist us in this query.) We will assume that we have a means (either by using an oracle or an easily-computed function) of telling when we have located the proper element in the data set, but we have no information about where in the set this element is located.

Classically, of course, there is nothing we can do but look at each entry in the data set until we happen to find the correct one.

Exercise 26.1. What is the expected number of queries to the data set required by such an algorithm? ◁

Even randomization doesn't help us here:

Exercise 26.2. If a (randomized) algorithm queries m elements from the data set, what is the probability that it will find the target element? ◁

Thus a classical (probabilistic) algorithm must query the data set in at least $N/2 = 2^n/2$ steps to have a probability of success that is greater than $1/2$. Grover's quantum algorithm reduces this number to $O(\sqrt{N})$, demonstrating a quadratic speed-up versus any classical algorithm.

* * * * *

Before defining what we mean by quantum computation, let's return for a moment to classical probabilistic computation. A classical probabilistic computation gives rise to a computation tree. Each node in the tree is labeled with a configuration (instantaneous description of tape contents, head location(s) and internal state) of the Turing machine. Edges in the tree are labeled with real numbers in the interval $[0, 1]$, which correspond to the probability of a transition from the parent configuration to the child configuration. Each level of the tree represents one time step, so the depth of the tree represents the running time of the machine.

Probabilities can be assigned to a node by multiplying the probabilities along the path from the root to that node. The probability of the computation being in configuration c at time t is the sum of the probabilities assigned to each node at level t that has been assigned configuration c.

In order for such a tree to represent a probabilistic computation, it must meet two constraints:

- *Locality.* The probability assigned to the edge from one node to another must correspond to the action of one step of a probabilistic Turing machine, so in particular,
  1. the probability is non-zero only if the underlying nondeterministic Turing machine could actually make such a transition (thus, for example, the only tape cells that can change are the ones that were under a head in the parent configuration), and
  2. the probability depends only on the part of the configuration that determines the action of the machine, and not on the rest of the configuration or its location in the tree.
- *Classical probability.* The sum of all probabilities on any level must be 1.

Exercise 26.3. Show that if the sum of the probabilities on the edges leaving any node equals 1, then the classical probability constraint is satisfied. ◁

For the purposes of complexity considerations, it is usually sufficient to consider probabilities from the set $\{0, \frac{1}{2}, 1\}$.

The computation tree can be represented by a $k \times k$ matrix M, where k is the number of possible configurations and M_{ab}, the entry at location (a, b), is the probability of going from configuration a to configuration b in one step. M^s then represents the transitions that occur in s steps. The probability that a machine accepts on input x after s steps is

$$\sum_{c \in \Gamma_{acc}} \Pr[\text{configuration } c \text{ at step } s \mid \text{configuration } c_0 \text{ at step } 0] ,$$

where Γ_{acc} is the set of all accepting configurations and c_0 is the initial configuration corresponding to an input x.

In a quantum computation, instead of assigning real-valued probabilities to the edges, we assign complex-valued ***probability amplitudes*** (with norm at most 1). The amplitude of a node in the computation tree is again the product of the amplitudes along the path to that node, and the amplitude associated with being in configuration c at step t is the sum of the amplitudes of all nodes at level t labeled with c. Probability amplitudes correspond to probabilities in the following way: The probability is the squared absolute value of the amplitude.

As before, our labeling of the tree must satisfy two constraints:

- *Locality.* This condition is the same as before: the labeling of the tree must correspond to the action of a Turing Machine.
- *Quantum probability.* If one represents the quantum computation by a matrix M, then M must be *unitary*, which means that its inverse is equal to its conjugate transpose.

This quantum probability condition implies that the sum of the ***probabilities*** on any level will be 1 ($\sum |\alpha_c|^2 = 1$). This time, however, it is *not* sufficient to merely require that the sum of the squares of the amplitudes leaving any node be 1. This is due to the effects of *interference* (canceling) among the configurations.

Exercise 26.4. Give an example of a labeled tree where the sum of the probabilities leaving each node is 1, but the sum of the probabilities at some level is not.

Hint: Two levels suffice. ◁

Exercise 26.5. Show that if all of the entries in M are real numbers in $[-1, 1]$, then M is unitary if and only if it is *orthonormal*, that is, the dot product of any two distinct rows or columns is always 0, and the dot product of a row or column with itself is 1.

Hint: Some notation and definitions are perhaps in order here: If M is a matrix, we denote the entry in the ith row and jth column by M_{ij}. The transpose of M is denoted by M^t and defined by $M^t_{ij} = M_{ji}$. In the conjugate transpose M^*, M^*_{ij} is the complex conjugate of M_{ji}. So if the entries are all real, then the transpose and conjugate transpose are the same matrix. The inverse of a matrix M is denoted by M^{-1} and is a matrix such that $M \cdot M^{-1} = M^{-1} \cdot M = I$, where I is the identity matrix, which consists of 1's down the major diagonal and 0's elsewhere. To have an inverse, a matrix must be square, but not all square matrices have inverses. ◁

Note that a unitary matrix M has an inverse, which means that, unlike classical computation, quantum computation is necessarily *reversible*.

For many purposes, it is not necessary to use a particularly rich set of complex numbers; usually rationals and square roots of rationals are more than sufficient. In fact, for the definitions of BQP and NQP, defined below, the set $\{0, \pm 3/5, \pm 4/5, \pm 1\}$ is sufficient for the local transformation amplitudes.

Although the definitions and mental images for probabilistic computation and quantum computation are in many ways similar, there are important and powerful differences. Unlike a probabilistic machine, which we think of as being in one of a set of configurations (with certain probabilities), we consider a quantum machine to be in a *superposition* of configurations. This is something like saying that a quantum machine is simultaneously and to varying degrees in several configurations at once. Upon *observation* of a quantum mechanical device, the superposition collapses to a single configuration. The probability with which each configuration is observed is determined by its amplitude in the superposition.

We denote a configuration (also called a *quantum state*) by $|c\rangle$, and a superposition of such states by

$$|\varphi\rangle = \sum_{c \in \Gamma} \alpha_c |c\rangle \ ,$$

where α_c is the amplitude of $|c\rangle$. Algebraically, the states $|c\rangle$, for all configurations c, form an orthonormal basis in a Hilbert space. Since the basis states $|c\rangle$ are mutually orthonormal, the amplitude α_c of $|c\rangle$ in a superposition $|\varphi\rangle$ is the inner product of $|c\rangle$ with $|\varphi\rangle$, denoted by $\langle c \mid \varphi\rangle$.

If α is the amplitude of $|c\rangle$ in a superposition $|\phi\rangle$, then $|\alpha|^2$ is the probability of observing c when the machine is in superposition $|\phi\rangle$. The probability of accepting is defined as for the probabilistic computation: it is the probability of observing an accepting state at a certain time t.

The important added wrinkle (which provides the added power) in quantum computation is the fact that probability amplitudes can *cancel* (see Exercise 26.4). For example, there may be two paths in the computation tree that both lead to the same configuration c, but one may have probability amplitude α and the other $-\alpha$. So, for example, after some number of steps the superposition may have the form

$$\alpha|c\rangle - \alpha|c\rangle + \sum_{c' \neq c} \alpha_{c'}|c'\rangle \ .$$

In this case, the ***probability*** of being in state $|c\rangle$ is 0. The heart of most quantum algorithms consists in using superposition to "try out" a number of possibilities and using cancellation to reduce the probability of "bad" possibilities while increasing the probability of "good" possibilities.

The classes NQP and BQP can be defined analogously to the classes NP and BPP by replacing the probabilistic machine with a quantum machine:

Definition 26.1. *A language L is in* NQP *if and only if there is a quantum Turing machine Q and a polynomial p such that*

$$x \in L \iff Pr[Q \text{ accepts } x \text{ in } p(|x|) \text{ steps}] \neq 0 \, .$$

A language L is in BQP *if and only if there is a quantum Turing machine Q and a polynomial p such that*

$$x \in L \iff Pr[Q \text{ accepts } x \text{ in } p(|x|) \text{ steps}] > 3/4 \, ,$$
$$x \notin L \iff Pr[Q \text{ accepts } x \text{ in } p(|x|) \text{ steps}] < 1/4 \, .$$

It is not known if BQP is equal to some classical complexity class. It contains BPP, but results of Fortnow and Rogers have led them to "conjecture that BQP contains *no* interesting complexity classes outside BPP." Even if this conjecture holds, BQP-type algorithms will remain interesting, since they can provide a significant increase in speed for some problems (like searching, as we will see shortly) and at least have the potential to solve interesting problems that are probably neither NP-complete nor in P, like Graph Isomorphism (see Topic 18).

NQP, on the other hand, has been exactly characterized in terms of classical counting classes: NQP = $\text{coC}_=\text{P}$, where $\text{C}_=\text{P}$ is the class of languages where acceptance is defined by a nondeterministic machine that has an equal number of accepting and rejecting computations.

* * * * *

So how does one use quantum computation to speed up a search? First we give a formal definition to the search problem. Let $f(i)$ be a function that tells if the ith item in the data set is the item we seek, i.e., there is exactly one *target* $t \in [0, N)$ such that $f(t) = 1$, otherwise, $f(i) = 0$. We would like to design a quantum algorithm that after a certain number of steps with high probability (greater than 1/2 in any case) will be in a configuration that identifies t. That is, imagine that for each $i \in [0, N)$ there is a configuration $|c_i\rangle$ that represents that the item sought is item number i of $N = 2^n$. Then we want the probability of $|c_t\rangle$ to be high at the time we observe our computation. For concreteness, let c_i be the configuration that has i written (as a string of length n) on its work tape and is otherwise uninteresting (the head is at the left of each tape, all other tapes are empty, the internal state is some fixed state σ, etc.).

The quantum algorithm has two main components. The first is used to generate all possible keys (in superposition) and the second is used to separate the value t for which $f(t) = 1$ from the others and amplify its amplitude.

We begin with the first component. Suppose for a moment that we were designing a probabilistic machine instead of a quantum machine. Then we might choose to flip a coin n times and use the outcome of the coin to set the bits of the string on our work tape. More precisely, for each bit in succession, with probability $1/2$ we leave the bit as it is (initially a 0) and with probability $1/2$ we change it to a 1. Now we want to do a similar thing with our quantum machine. If we focus on a single bit, then we are looking for a unitary transformation

$$|0\rangle \mapsto a|0\rangle + b|1\rangle$$

$$|1\rangle \mapsto c|0\rangle + d|1\rangle$$

(i.e., a unitary matrix $M = \begin{bmatrix} a & b \\ c & d \end{bmatrix}$) such that $|a|^2 = |b|^2 = 1/2$.

Exercise 26.6. Find such a matrix.

Hint: It suffices to use real values. ◁

Let W be the matrix (transformation) that is the composition of M applied to each of the n bits in succession. (As a matrix, W is roughly block-diagonal, with copies of M located at appropriate positions near the diagonal, 1's elsewhere on the diagonal and 0's filling the rest of the matrix.)

Exercise 26.7. What superposition results from applying W to $|c_0\rangle$? ◁

Exercise 26.8. What superposition results from applying W to $|c_i\rangle$? ◁

The transformation W is known as the Walsh-Hadamard transformation, and it (or a related operation known as the Fourier transformation) is a component of many quantum algorithms.

Now that we have in some sense generated all the possible keys, we need to do something to distinguish the target t. This is the second component of the algorithm. For this we will simply flip the sign of the amplitude of the target t. Note that any diagonal matrix with 1's and -1's along the diagonal is unitary, so that this kind of sign flipping (on any set of states) can be done, provided we know where to place the 1's and -1's. For this we need to know $f(i)$, which we can assume is determined by an oracle call or some simple, deterministic algorithm. It is known that deterministic computation can be done reversibly, and this fact has been used to show that deterministic computation can be simulated on a quantum machine. Let F denote the transformation that determines $f(i)$ and flips the sign of the amplitude if $f(i) = 1$.

Finally, these two components are combined to form what Grover refers to as the *diffusion transformation* D. The purpose of D is to amplify the amplitude of the state corresponding to the target. Let $\hat{F}$ be the transformation that flips the sign of all the states except $|c_0\rangle$, that is,

$$\hat{F}_{ij} = \begin{cases} 0 & \text{if } i \neq j, \\ 1 & \text{if } i = j = 0, \\ -1 & \text{if } i = j \neq 0. \end{cases}$$

The diffusion transformation is $D = W\hat{F}W$.

Exercise 26.9. Compute D_{ij} for arbitrary i and j. ◁

The transformations F and D form the heart of the algorithm, and W is used once at the beginning as a sort of initialization. With this background laid, the description of the algorithm is relatively short:

1. Initialize by applying W to the initial state $|c_0\rangle$.
2. Repeat the following $O(\sqrt{N})$ times. (We will determine the constant in the O-notation as part of the analysis. It will turn out to be important to do this the correct number of times.)
   a) Apply F. (Flip the amplitude on the target.)
   b) Apply D. (Diffusion)
3. Observe the state of the quantum machine. The probability of $|c_t\rangle$ will be at least $1/2$.

Now we need to show that the algorithm behaves as claimed. In particular, we need to understand what the diffusion transformation is doing. The diffusion transformation can be interpreted as an *inversion about the average* in the following sense: Suppose the quantum machine is in the superposition

$$|\varphi\rangle = \sum_{i \in [0,N)} \alpha_i |c_i\rangle .$$

Let $\alpha = \frac{1}{N} \sum_i \alpha_i$ be the average amplitude over all the states. Then the result of applying D to $|\varphi\rangle$ is to increase (or decrease) each amplitude so that after the operation it is as much above (or below) the average as it was below (or above) the average prior to the operation. That is,

$$\sum \alpha_i |c_i\rangle \mapsto \sum \beta_i |c_i\rangle ,$$

where $\beta_i = \alpha + (\alpha - \alpha_i) = 2\alpha - \alpha_i$.

Lemma 26.2. *The diffusion transformation D is unitary. Furthermore, it performs an inversion about the average as described above.*

Proof. For the proof it is useful to have another representation for D. Let P be the projection matrix $P_{ij} = 1/N$. Then $D = -I + 2P$ (see Exercise 26.9).

Exercise 26.10. Show that D is unitary.

Hint: First show that $P^2 = P$. ◁

Exercise 26.11. Show that D performs an inversion about the average.

Hint: Let x be a vector, what does Px compute? ◁

□

Now we introduce some notation for the superpositions that occur in this computation. Let

$$|\Psi(k,l)\rangle = k|c_t\rangle + \sum_{i \neq t} l|c_i\rangle \,.$$

We want to express the effects of Grover's algorithm using this notation. By Exercise 26.7, step 1 (the initialization) of the algorithm amounts to

$$W : |c_0\rangle \mapsto |\Psi(\tfrac{1}{\sqrt{N}}, \tfrac{1}{\sqrt{N}})\rangle \,.$$

And by Lemma 26.2, each iteration of step 2 is

$$|\Psi(k,l)\rangle \overset{F}{\mapsto} |\Psi(-k,l)\rangle \overset{D}{\mapsto} |\Psi(\tfrac{N-2}{N}k + \tfrac{2(N-1)}{N}l, \tfrac{N-2}{N}l - \tfrac{2}{N}k)\rangle \,.$$

Note that after one iteration, k_1 is still very nearly $1/\sqrt{N}$ (since the average amplitude prior to applying D was very nearly $1/\sqrt{N}$), but l_1 is approximately $3/\sqrt{N}$. The hope is that each iteration increases k by $\Omega(1/\sqrt{N})$, so that after $O(\sqrt{N})$ iterations, $k = \Omega(\sqrt{N} \cdot \frac{1}{\sqrt{N}}) \geq \frac{1}{\sqrt{2}}$.

Let $\Psi_j = |\Psi(k_j, l_j)\rangle$ denote the superposition after j iterations. In the paper where Grover originally presented his algorithm, he proved that there was a number of iterations $j \leq \sqrt{2N}$ such that $k_j^2 \geq 1/2$. His proof followed from a sequence of lemmas about the transformation D, culminating in the following lemma:

Lemma 26.3. *If* $0 < k_j < \frac{1}{\sqrt{2}}$ *and* $l_j > 0$, *then* $\Delta k = k_{j+1} - k_j > \frac{1}{2\sqrt{N}}$, *and* $l_{j+1} > 0$.

The problem with this argument, however, is that Lemma 26.3 only provides a lower bound on Δk. Thus while we know there is an iteration $m \leq \sqrt{2N}$ after which $k_m^2 \geq 1/2$, we don't know what m is. In fact, after exactly $\sqrt{2N}$ iterations the probability is less than 9.5% that we will observe the target. From there it continues to decrease to a negligible probability before it eventually increases again. Thus it is important to know m explicitly.

In order to know precisely when to make our observation, we need a tighter analysis. This was provided in a paper by Boyer, Høyer and Tapp, where explicit formulas are given for k_j and l_j. Using standard techniques (and some patience), the recurrence for k and l can be solved, giving explicit formulas for k_j and l_j.

Lemma 26.4. *Let k_j and l_j be defined as above, then*

$$k_j = \sin((2j+1)\theta) ,$$
$$l_j = \frac{1}{\sqrt{N-1}} \cos((2j+1)\theta) ;$$

where θ is chosen so that $\sin^2(\theta) = 1/N$.

Exercise 26.12.$^\diamond$ Prove Lemma 26.4.

Hint: Although it is a bit arduous to solve the recurrence relations to get the explicit formulas of the lemma, it is straightforward to prove by induction that the formulas are indeed correct. Readers who have forgotten the trigonometric identities may need to refer to an undergraduate calculus text. ◁

From this it follows that $k_m = 1$ when $(2m+1)\theta = \pi/2$, i.e., when $m = (\pi - 2\theta)/4\theta$. Of course this is probably not an integer, but the probability should be almost 1 if we perform approximately this many iterations. Since for small θ, $\sin(\theta) \approx \theta$, the number of iterations needed is approximately

$$(\pi - 2\theta)/4\theta \approx \pi/4\theta \approx \frac{\pi}{4}\sqrt{N} .$$

In fact, after we have generalized the problem slightly, we will prove the following lemma:

Lemma 26.5. *After $\lfloor \frac{\pi\sqrt{N}}{4} \rfloor$ iterations of Grover's algorithm, the probability of failure is less than $1/N$. After $\lfloor \frac{\pi\sqrt{N}}{8} \rfloor$ iterations of Grover's algorithm, the probability of failure is at most $1/2$.*

However, if we iterate twice as many times (about $\frac{\pi\sqrt{N}}{2}$ iterations), the probability of success is negligible!

* * * * *

Before proving Lemma 26.5, we want to generalize the algorithm to handle more than one target. Suppose there is a set of targets T such that

$$f(i) = \begin{cases} 1 & t \in T, \\ 0 & t \notin T. \end{cases}$$

Grover's algorithm (or at least his analysis) dealt only with the case that $|T| = 1$.

What happens if we apply the same algorithm when $|T| > 1$? Define

$$|\Phi(k,l)\rangle = \sum_{i \in T} k|c_i\rangle + \sum_{i \notin T} l|c_i\rangle .$$

Then each iteration of Grover's algorithm has the effect

$$|\Phi(k,l)\rangle \mapsto |\Phi(\tfrac{N-2|T|}{N}k + \tfrac{2(N-|T|)}{N}l, \tfrac{N-2|T|}{N}l + \tfrac{2|T|}{N}k)\rangle .$$

Once again, this recurrence can be solved, this time yielding

$$k_j = \frac{\sin((2j+1)\theta)}{\sqrt{|T|}} ,$$
$$l_j = \frac{\cos((2j+1)\theta)}{\sqrt{N-|T|}} ;$$

where $\sin^2(\theta) = |T|/N$.

The probability of success is greatest when l is smallest, and $l_{\hat{m}} = 0$ if $\hat{m} = (\pi - 2\theta)/4\theta$, but that may not be an integer. Let $m = \lfloor \pi/4\theta \rfloor$ instead. Note that $|m - \hat{m}| \le 1/2$. So $|(2m+1)\theta - (2\hat{m}+1)\theta| \le \theta$. But, by the definition of $\hat{m}$, $(2\hat{m}+1)\theta = \pi/2$, so $|\cos((2m+1)\theta)| \le |\sin(\theta)|$. Thus the probability of failure after m iterations is

$$(N - |T|)l_m^2 = \cos^2((2m+1)\theta) \le \sin^2(\theta) = |T|/N .$$

Since $\theta \ge \sin(\theta) = \sqrt{|T|/N}$, $m \le \frac{\pi}{4\theta} \le \frac{\pi}{4}\sqrt{\frac{N}{|T|}}$, the algorithm requires $O(\sqrt{N/|T|})$ iterations. The expected running time until a target is found can be improved slightly by running the algorithm for fewer iterations (at a cost of a lower probability of success) and repeating the entire algorithm if unsuccessful. This is because the sine function is quite flat near its extreme values, so that the last iterations do less to increase the probability than the earlier ones.

The case where $|T| = N/4$ is particularly interesting. In this case, $\sin^2\theta = 1/4$, so $\theta = \pi/6$, and

$$l_1 = \frac{t}{N - |T|} \cos(3\theta) = 0 .$$

This means that the probability of success is 1 after just one iteration. It should be mentioned, that this really involves *two* queries to the data set, one to determine if there is a phase shift (sign flip) and one as part of the "uncomputation" which makes this reversible.

Exercise 26.13. What is the expected number of queries required by the naive classical probabilistic algorithm when $|T| = N/4$? ◁

Exercise 26.14. What is the worst case for a classical algorithm? (Imagine that an adversary is determining the outcome of your coin tosses.) ◁

Thus the quantum algorithm uses only half of the number of queries expected for a classical probabilistic algorithm, and exponentially fewer (in n) than a classical algorithm uses in the worst case.

* * * * *

There have been other generalizations of Grover's algorithm, a few of which we summarize briefly here. The first two generalizations deal with the case when $|T|$ is unknown. Suppose first that we want to locate one of the targets $t \in T$, but we don't know how many targets there are. If we use $\frac{\pi}{4}\sqrt{N}$ iterations, we will almost certainly find the target t if it is unique. But if $|T| = 4$, then the probability of success after this many iterations is nearly 0. Boyer, Høyer, and Tapp give an algorithm with expected running time $O(\sqrt{N})$ for finding a target in this case as well. The main idea is to randomly select m, the number of iterations (from some set M, where initially $M = \{1\}$), and then to run Grover's algorithm for that many iterations. If this is not successful, it is done again, but with a larger set M.

Brassard, Høyer, and Tapp also consider the problem of approximating $|T|$, rather than finding an element of T. In their recent paper they give an algorithm that demonstrates a trade-off between the accuracy of the approximation and the running time of the algorithm. Furthermore, they show that their algorithm is in some sense optimal. This paper also considers the problem of *amplitude amplification*, the key ingredient in Grover's algorithm, in a more general setting. This allows them to demonstrate a speed-up between quantum and classical search algorithms even in the case where better than brute force methods exist classically.

All of the algorithms above begin from a superposition with only one non-zero amplitude. Another way to generalize the problem is to consider other possible initial superpositions, such as might occur if quantum searching were used as a subroutine in a more complicated quantum algorithm. Results of Biham, Biham, Biron, Grassl, and Lidar show that the optimal time for observation can be determined in this situation as well and that it depends only on the means and variances of the initial amplitudes on T and $\overline{T}$.

Finally, we make two comments on Grover's algorithm. One might ask if there are even better quantum search algorithms which require, say, $O(\log N)$ queries to the database. But this is not possible. Grover's algorithm is optimal in the sense that any quantum algorithm for searching must make at least $\Omega(\sqrt{N})$ queries to the database. Also, the reader may have noticed that we have assumed throughout that N is a power of 2. This assumption simplifies the arguments and notation somewhat, but it is not an essential restriction. It can be avoided by replacing the Walsh-Hadamard transformation by any transformation in a large class of transformations, of which the Walsh-Hadamard transformation is the simplest when N is a power of 2.

References

Foundational work in the theory of quantum computation can be found in

- P. Benioff: The computer as a physical system: A microscopic quantum mechanical Hamiltonian model of computers as represented by Turing machines, *Journal of Statistical Physics* 22 (1980), 563–591.
- E. Bernstein, U. Vazirani: Quantum Complexity Theory, *Proceedings of the 25th Annual Symposium on Theory of Computing*, ACM, 1993, 11–20.
- D. Deutsch: Quantum Theory, the Church-Turing principle and the universal quantum computer, *Proceedings of the Royal Society London Series A* 400 (1985), 96–117.
- R.P. Feynman: Simulating physics with computers, *International Journal of Theoretical Physics* 21:6/7 (1981/82), 467–488.

Prior to the results of Shor and Grover, there were already indications that quantum computation is more powerful than classical computation (on somewhat contrived problems).

- D. Deutsch, R. Jozsa: Rapid solutions of problems by quantum computation, *Proceedings of the Royal Society of London*, 1992, 553–558.
- D. Simon: On the power of Quantum Computation, *SIAM Journal on Computing*, 26:5 (1997), 1474–1483.

Many papers on Grover's algorithm and its generalizations (as well as a number of other topics related to quantum computation) are available as LANL preprints at http://xxx.lanl.gov. The site is easily searchable, so we include here only those papers that were most instrumental in preparing this topic.

- E. Biham, O. Biham, D. Biron, M. Grassl, D. Lidar: Exact solution of Grover's quantum search algorithm for arbitrary initial amplitude distribution, LANL preprint quant-ph/9807027.
- M. Boyer, G. Brassard, P. Høyer, A. Tapp: Tight bounds on quantum searching, *Proceedings of 4th Workshop on Physics and Computation*, 1996, 36–43. Final version to appear in *Fortschritte der Physik*. Also LANL preprint quant-ph/9605034.
- G. Brassard, P. Høyer, A. Tapp: Quantum Counting, LANL preprint quant-ph/9805082.
- L. Grover: A fast quantum mechanical algorithm for database search, *Proceedings of the 28th Annual Symposium on Theory of Computing*, ACM, 1996, 212. Also LANL preprint quant-ph/9605043.
- L. Grover: A framework for quantum mechanical algorithms, *Proceedings of the 30th Annual Symposium on Theory of Computing*, ACM, 1998. Also LANL preprint quant-ph/9711043.

Shor's algorithm originally appeared in

- P. Shor: Algorithms for quantum computation: Discrete log and factoring, *Proceedings of the 35th Symposium on Foundations of Computer Science*, IEEE, 1994, 124–134.

but see also

- A. Ekert, R. Jozsa: Quantum computation and Shor's factoring algorithm, *Reviews of Modern Physics* 68 (1996), 733–753.
- P. Shor: Polynomial-time algorithms for prime factorization and discrete logarithms on a quantum computer, *SIAM Journal on Computing* 26:5 (1997), 1484–1509. Also LANL preprint quant-ph/9508027.

For information on the relationship between quantum complexity classes and classical complexity classes, see

- L. Adleman, J. Demarrais, M-D.A. Huang: Quantum computability, *SIAM Journal on Computing* 26:5 (1997), 1524–1540.
- C. Bennett, E. Bernstein, G. Brassard, U. Vazirani: Strengths and weaknesses of quantum computing, *SIAM Journal on Computing* 26:5 (1997), 1510–1523.
- S. Fenner, F. Green, S. Homer, R. Pruim: Quantum NP is hard for PH, to appear in *Proceedings of the 6th Italian Conference on Theoretical Computer Science*, 1998.
- L. Fortnow, J. Rogers: Complexity limitations on quantum computation, *Proceedings of the 13th IEEE Conference on Computational Complexity*, IEEE, 1998, 202–209.
- J. Watrous: Relationships between quantum and classical space-bounded complexity classes, *Proceedings of the 13th IEEE Conference on Computational Complexity*, IEEE, 1998, 210–227.

For a survey of results in quantum computational complexity from a somewhat different perspective see

- A. Berthiaume: Quantum Computation, chapter 2 in *Complexity Retrospective II*, Springer, 1997.

Solutions

1.1. For every decidable language A and any (arbitrary) language B, $A \leq_T B$.

1.2. The halting problem $H = \{(x, y) \mid y \in W_x\}$ is m- (and therefore also T-) complete for the class of computably enumerable languages. For if A is computably enumerable then there is an i such that $A = W_i$. The map $y \mapsto (i, y)$ is an m-reduction from A to H.

Now let A be a language which is T-equivalent to the halting problem and suppose there is a language B which is computably enumerable and T-incomparable to A. Since B is computably enumerable, $B \leq_T H$ and since $H \leq_T A$, it follows that $B \leq_T A$. Contradiction.

1.3. If there are two Turing incomparable, computably enumerable languages, then neither one can be computable (exercise 1.1). But by the claim one would have to be computable if the incomparability could be demonstrated effectively.

1.4. It is sufficient to show that if A is computably enumerable and h is computable, then $h^{-1}(A)$ is computably enumerable.

The following procedure enumerates $h^{-1}(A)$:

> **FOR** all pairs of integers (i, j) **DO**
>
>   **IF** $h(i) = j$-th element enumerated into A **THEN OUTPUT** i;
>
>   **END**
>
> **END**

This can be shown even more simply, but this method shows $\overline{B}$ is many-one reducible to A via $g \circ f$. Since A is computably enumerable it follows that $\overline{B}$ is computably enumerable.

1.5. The element with highest priority, $(0, x) \in L_A$, reaches its final location at the very beginning.

The element with the second highest priority, $(0, x) \in L_B$, can be removed from of L_A and "slid over" at most one time. So there are at most two "incarnations" for this element.

The element with the third highest priority, $(1, x) \in L_A$, has at most three possible "incarnations."

In general the number of incarnations satisfies the recursive formula: $f(n) = 1+f(n-1)+f(n-3)+f(n-5)+\cdots+f(a)$, where a is 0 or 1, and $f(0)$ is defined to be 1. This results in the Fibonacci sequence $1, 1, 2, 3, 5, 8, 13, 21, \ldots$ since

$$\begin{aligned} f(n) &= f(n-1) + f(n-2) \\ &= f(n-1) + f(n-3) + f(n-4) \\ &= f(n-1) + f(n-3) + f(n-5) + f(n-6) \\ &= f(n-1) + f(n-3) + f(n-5) + f(n-7) + f(n-8) \\ &\vdots \end{aligned}$$

2.1. The numbers a and b must be relatively prime.

2.2. The given system of equations has a solution if and only if

$$\sum_{i=1}^{k}(f_i(x_1,\ldots,x_n))^2 = 0$$

has a solution.

2.3. This problem can be reduced to the solution of the equation

$$\prod_{i=1}^{k} f_i(x_1,\ldots,x_n) = 0 .$$

2.4. $f(x_1, x_2, \ldots, x_n) = 0$ has a solution if and only if one of the 2^n equations

$$\begin{aligned} f(x_1,x_2,\ldots,x_n) &= 0 \\ f(-x_1,x_2,\ldots,x_n) &= 0 \\ f(x_1,-x_2,\ldots,x_n) &= 0 \\ &\vdots \\ f(-x_1,-x_2,\ldots,-x_n) &= 0 \end{aligned}$$

has a solution in $\mathbb{N}$. This demonstrates the existence of a Turing reduction between the two problems.

With the help of the previous exercise, this disjunction can be converted into a single equation. That gives a many-one reduction.

2.5. Every natural number x can be written as $x = u^2 + v^2 + w^2 + z^2$ with $u, v, w, z \in \mathbb{Z}$. So $f(x_1, \ldots, x_n) = 0$ has solutions in the natural numbers if and only if

$$f(u_1^2 + v_1^2 + w_1^2 + z_1^2, \ldots, u_n^2 + v_n^2 + w_n^2 + z_n^2) = 0$$

has integer solutions.

2.6. The register R_j can be set to zero by:

a : IF $R_j = 0$ GOTO d
b : DEC R_j
c : GOTO a
d :

The instruction $R_m := R_j$ can be simulated by:

a : "$R_n := 0$"
b : "$R_p := 0$"
c : IF $R_j = 0$ GOTO h
d : DEC R_j
e : INC R_n
f : INC R_p
g : GOTO c
h : IF $R_p = 0$ GOTO l
i : DEC R_p
j : INC R_j
k : GOTO h
l :

2.7. If the register R_j has the value 0, that is, W_j has a 0 in the appropriate place in the sequence-number coding (where N_i has a 1), then there will be a 1 in the corresponding bit of $B \cdot T - 2 \cdot W_j$ at the next step. So N_{i+1} cannot have a 1 there but rather must have a 0. Because of the previous equation, $B \cdot N_i \leq^* N_l + N_{i+1}$, N_l must have a 1 there, so the next instruction to be executed will be instruction l, as desired.

If the register R_j contains a value > 1, then $B \cdot T - 2 \cdot W_j$ has a 0 in the bit corresponding to the next step. (This explains the factor of 2 – to avoid changing the value of the bit at the current time step. This is also why we needed the condition $B < 2 \cdot S$.) So N_{i+1} must have a 1 and N_l a 0 at that position. Thus, the next instruction to be executed will be instruction $i + 1$, as desired.

2.8. The exercise follows immediately from the hint and the observation that $\binom{0}{0} = \binom{1}{0} = \binom{1}{1} = 1$ and $\binom{0}{1} = 0$.

The hint can be proven as follows: $\binom{y}{x}$ is the coefficient on the term T^x in the expression $(1+T)^x$. Mod 2, these coefficients can be computed as follows:

$$\begin{aligned}(1+T)^y \equiv (1+T)^{y_n \ldots y_0} &\equiv \prod_{i=0}^{n} (1+T)^{2^i \cdot y_i} \\ &\equiv \prod_{i=0}^{n} (1+T^{2^i})^{y_i} \equiv \prod_{i=0}^{n} \left(\sum_{j=0}^{y_i} \binom{y_i}{j} T^{2^i \cdot j} \right) .\end{aligned}$$

In the product on the right side there is exactly one choice of terms which when multiplied together give a term T^x. This term is obtained by setting $j = y_i$ in each sum. Thus, we get $\binom{y}{x} \equiv \prod_{i=0}^{n} \binom{y_i}{x_i} \pmod 2$, which is what we wanted to prove.

Note: the computation above would be correct modulo any prime number p. (Use p^i instead of 2^i.)

2.9. We reduce $\overline{\mathsf{Dioph}(\mathbb{N})}$ to the problem in question. $f \in \overline{\mathsf{Dioph}(\mathbb{N})}$ if and only if $f^2 \in \overline{\mathsf{Dioph}(\mathbb{N})}$. The polynomial f^2 has only non-negative values. The polynomial f^2 can be written as $f^2 = g - h$, where g has all the terms of f^2 with positive coefficients and h has all the terms with negative coefficients (once more negated). The polynomials g and h then have only positive coefficients. Furthermore, since $f^2 \geq 0$, we have $g \geq h$. So we get:

$$\begin{aligned} f \in \overline{\mathsf{Dioph}(\mathbb{N})} &\Longleftrightarrow f^2 \in \overline{\mathsf{Dioph}(\mathbb{N})} \\ &\Longleftrightarrow \forall x\ h(x) < g(x) \\ &\Longleftrightarrow \forall x\ h(x) + 1 \leq g(x)\ . \end{aligned}$$

The map $f \mapsto (h+1, g)$ yields the desired reduction.

2.10. We imagine the polynomial f as a tree structure. The leaves of the tree are labeled with the variables $x_1, \ldots, x_n$ and the coefficients, and the internal nodes of the tree are labeled with the operations $+$ and $*$. The root of the tree represents the function f.

Every internal node is now assigned a new variable $y_0, \ldots, y_k$, y_0 being assigned to the root. Then $f = 0$ is equivalent to requiring that $y_0 = 0$ and that for each branching of the form

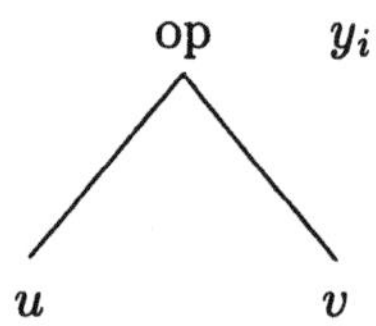

$y_i = u \text{ op } v$ (i.e., $y_i - (u \text{ op } v) = 0$), where op $\in \{+, *\}$ and u and v may be new variables $(y_0, \ldots, y_k)$, original variables $(x_1, \ldots, x_n)$, or coefficients.

None of the Diophantine equations f_i has a total degree greater than two. Therefore, the Diophantine equation that is equivalent to the conjunction of all of these equations (namely, $\sum f_i^2 = 0$) has total degree at most four.

3.1. Assignment statements have loop-depth 0. If R is a LOOP-program of the form $P; Q$ where P and Q have loop-depth p and q, respectively, then R has loop-depth $\max(p, q)$. If R is a program of the form `LOOP` X `DO` P `END` and P has loop-depth p, then R has loop-depth $p + 1$.

3.2. The following program simulates subtraction ($\dot{-}$):

$Y := 0$; $Z := 0$;
LOOP X DO $Y := Z$; $Z := Z + 1$ END;
$X := Y$

3.3. The following program simulates "IF $X = 0$ THEN P END":

$Y := 0$; $Y := Y + 1$;
LOOP X DO $Y := 0$ END;
LOOP Y DO P END

3.4. In the following, instructions that appear in quotation marks indicate suitable LOOP(1)-programs, which exist by the previous exercises.

"$Z := X \dot{-} k$"; $Y := 1$;
LOOP Z DO $Y := 0$ END;
"$W := X \dot{-} m$"; $(m = k - 1)$
$U := 0$;
LOOP W DO $U := 1$ END;
LOOP U DO $Y := Y + 1$ END;
"$Y := Y \dot{-} 1$";
LOOP Y DO P END

3.5. Let the input register of A_n be S and the output register T.

$A := 1$; $X := n$;
LOOP S DO D_n END;
$T := 1$;
LOOP A DO $T := 0$ END

D_n must be a LOOP(1)-program so that A_n will be a LOOP(2)-program.

3.6. The following program simulates w:

$Y := X_1$;
LOOP X_2 DO $Y := 0$ END

3.7. A LOOP(1)-program for x MOD k:

$Z_1 := 0$;
$Z_2 := 1$;
$\vdots$
$Z_k := k - 1$;
LOOP X DO
  $Z_{k+1} := Z_1$;
  $Z_1 := Z_2$;
  $Z_2 := Z_3$;
  $\vdots$
  $Z_k := Z_{k+1}$;
END;
$Y := X_1$

A LOOP(1)-program for x DIV k:

$Z_1 := 0$;
$Z_2 := 0$;
$\vdots$
$Z_k := 0$;
LOOP X DO
  $Z_{k+1} := Z_k$;
  $Z_k := Z_{k-1}$;
  $\vdots$
  $Z_2 := Z_1 + 1$;
  $Z_1 := Z_{k+1}$;
END;
$Y := X_1$

3.8. A LOOP(0)-program can only consist of a sequence of instructions of the form $X := 0$, $X := Y$ and $X := X + 1$. From this it is clear that only the given functions can be computed.

3.9. $w(f, x) + w(g, w(1, x))$

3.10. $k_1 + \cdots + k_{(x \text{ MOD } t)} = w(k_1, (x \text{ MOD } t) \dot{-} 1) + w(k_2, (x \text{ MOD } t) \dot{-} 2) + \cdots + w(k_{t-1}, (x \text{ MOD } t) \dot{-} [t-1])$

3.11. For each index position $i \in \{1, \ldots, n\}$ one has $M + K$ many different equivalence classes, so altogether there are $(M + K)^n$.

3.12. *Case 6:* Let $\hat{M} = \max(M_1, M_2) + K_2$ and $\hat{K} = K_1 \cdot K_2$. Let $i \in \{1, \ldots, n\}$ be arbitrary. It suffices to show that $w(f(\boldsymbol{x}), g(\boldsymbol{x}))$ and $w(f(\boldsymbol{x}'), g(\boldsymbol{x}'))$ differ by a constant γ (independent of $\boldsymbol{x}$), where $\boldsymbol{x} = (x_1, \ldots, x_n)$ and

$$x' = (x_1, \ldots, x_{i-1}, x_i + \hat{K}, x_{i+1}, \ldots, x_n) ,$$

and each $x_i > \hat{M}$. By the inductive hypothesis, there are constants β_i and β_i' such that

$$f_1(x') - f_1(x) = K_2 \cdot (K_1 \cdot \beta_i) = \hat{K} \cdot \beta_i$$

and

$$f_2(x') - f_2(x) = K_1 \cdot (K_2 \cdot \beta_i') = \hat{K} \cdot \beta_i' .$$

If $\beta_i' > 0$, then by the choice of $\hat{M}$ (and because $x_i > \hat{M}$), $f_2(x)$ and $f_2(x')$ are both strictly greater than 0. Thus, the value of the function w is 0 at both places. So in this case, $\gamma = 0$. If $\beta_i' = 0$ and $f_2(x) > 0$, then we also have $\gamma = 0$. In the case that $\beta_i' = 0$ and $f_2(x) = 0$, the value of w is given by f_1, so $\gamma = K_1 K_2 \beta_i = \hat{K}\beta_i$.

Case 7: Let $\hat{M} = M$ and $\hat{K} = k \cdot K$. Let $i \in \{1, \ldots, n\}$ be arbitrary. It is sufficient to show that $f(x)$ DIV k and $f(x')$ DIV k differ by a constant γ (independent of x), where $x = (x_1, \ldots, x_n)$ and

$$x' = (x_1, \ldots, x_{i-1}, x_i + \hat{K}, x_{i+1}, \ldots, x_n) ,$$

and $x_i > \hat{M}$. By the inductive hypothesis, there are constants β_i and β_i' such that $f(x') - f(x) = k \cdot K \cdot \beta_i = \hat{K}\beta_i$. So we have

$$f(x') \text{ DIV } k - f(x) \text{ DIV } k = K\beta_i = \hat{K}\frac{\beta_i}{k} .$$

3.13. By Lemma 3.4, the value of $f(x)$ for $x \in \mathbb{N}^n$ can be determined in the following manner: First, one repeatedly reduces each component x_i of x (provided $x_i > M$) by K until one gets two points $x_i^{(0)}$ and $x_i^{(1)}$ that lie in the interval $(M, M + 2K]$ as sketched in the diagram below.

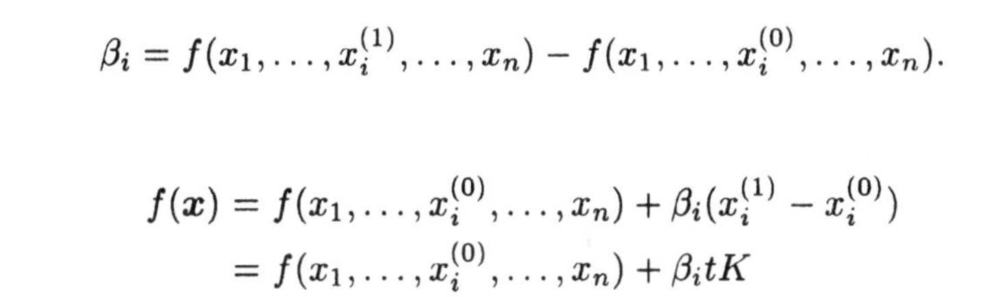

Clearly, $x_i^{(0)} = M + (x_i \text{ MOD } K)$, $x_i^{(1)} = x_i^{(0)} + K$, and $x_i = x_i^{(0)} + tK$ for an appropriately chosen integer constant $t \geq 0$. Now let

$$\beta_i = f(x_1, \ldots, x_i^{(1)}, \ldots, x_n) - f(x_1, \ldots, x_i^{(0)}, \ldots, x_n).$$

Then

$$\begin{aligned} f(x) &= f(x_1, \ldots, x_i^{(0)}, \ldots, x_n) + \beta_i(x_i^{(1)} - x_i^{(0)}) \\ &= f(x_1, \ldots, x_i^{(0)}, \ldots, x_n) + \beta_i tK \end{aligned}$$

By reducing each component x_i in this manner, we arrive at an f-value for a point in Q. Thus, if the two functions are different, they must differ on a point in Q.

3.14. Let $M = \max(M_1, M_2)$ and $K = K_1 \cdot K_2$. The equivalence relation $\overset{M,K}{\equiv}$ refines both $\overset{M_1,K_1}{\equiv}$ and $\overset{M_2,K_2}{\equiv}$. This means that the two given functions f_1 and f_2 agree if and only if all multi-linear functions on the common equivalence classes agree. As in the previous exercise, these functions are completely characterized by their values on points $\boldsymbol{x}$ with $x_i < M + 2K$.

3.15. Logical NOR can be used to simulate the boolean functions AND, OR, and NOT:

$$\begin{aligned} \text{NOT}(x) &= \text{NOR}(x, x) \\ \text{AND}(x, y) &= \text{NOR}(\text{NOT}(x), \text{NOT}(y)) \\ &= \text{NOR}(\text{NOR}(x, x), \text{NOR}(y, y)) \\ \text{OR}(x, y) &= \text{NOR}(\text{NOR}(x, y), \text{NOR}(x, y)) \end{aligned}$$

So it is sufficient to give a LOOP(1)-program for NOR:

```
Y := 1;
LOOP X1 DO Y := 0 END;
LOOP X2 DO Y := 0 END
```

3.16. We can simulate n input variables $X_1, \ldots, X_n$ with a single input variable X by adding the following preamble to our program:

```
X1 := X MOD 2;
X2 := X MOD 3;
X3 := X MOD 5;
  ⋮
Xn := X MOD pn;
```

where p_n is the nth prime number. By the Chinese Remainder Theorem, we know that there is a suitable value for X for any choice of $X_1, \ldots X_n$.

4.1.

```
INPUT x;
k := f(|x|);
p := 0;
FOR y ∈ Σ*, |y| = |x| DO
    [Run M on y];
    IF M accepts THEN
        IF y = x THEN REJECT END;
        p := p + 1;
    END;
END;
IF p = k THEN ACCEPT ELSE REJECT END.
```

Note: The boxed portion of the algorithm is nondeterministic.

If $x \notin A$, then there is a nondeterministic computation of this algorithm that accepts on input x: at each pass through the for loop, if $y \in A$ a path must be chosen that causes M to accept y. In this case, at the end of the loop we will have $p = k$.

If, on the other hand, there is a nondeterministic computation that causes this algorithm to accept x, then since at the end of the loop $p = k$, all of the strings y such that $|y| = |x|$ and $y \in A$ were discovered, and none of them was x, so $x \notin A$.

4.2. Time complexity: $t_f(n) + 2^{O(n)} \cdot t_M(n)$;
Space complexity: $s_f(n) + O(n) + s_M(n)$.

4.3. It is sufficient if the nondeterministic machine computes f in the following sense:

1. Every nondeterministic computation is either "successful" and outputs a numeric value or is "unsuccessful" and outputs nothing.
2. At least one output is successful and, therefore, produces an output.
3. All successful computations produce the same output value, namely $f(n)$.

4.4. One can modify the algorithm given in Solution 4.1 to use g instead of f, to loop over all y interpreted as expressions, and to "verify that $S \stackrel{*}{\Rightarrow} y$" instead of "starting M on y."

4.5.

```
{ Assume k = |T_i^n| }
p := 0;
FOR y ∈ (V ∪ Σ)*, |y| ≤ n DO
    f := FALSE;
    m := 0;
    FOR z ∈ (V ∪ Σ)*, |z| ≤ n DO
        IF [S ⇒^i_G z] THEN
            m := m + 1;
            IF (z ⇒_G y) OR (z = y) THEN f := TRUE END;
        END;
    END;
    IF m < k THEN REJECT END;
    IF f THEN p := p + 1 END;
END;
{ Now p = |T_{i+1}^n| }
```

Note: the boxed portion of the algorithm is nondeterministic.

In the inner loop the counter m is compared against k to check that the nondeterministic choices were made correctly. The computation only continues to the outer loop if this is the case. In this way we can be certain that the number p is correct at the end of the algorithm (in the case that a nondeterministic computation reaches that point without rejecting sooner.)

5.1. L- and NL-machines are off-line Turing machines, which means that their specially designated input tapes can only be used to read the input. For the purposes of this exercise, let a configuration of such a machine be an instantaneous description of the current state, the head position on the (read-only) input tape, the head position on the work tape, and the contents of the work tape. Let Z be the set of all such configurations, and A the alphabet. Then a $c \cdot \log n$ space-bounded Turing machine has at most

$$a = |Z| \cdot (n+2) \cdot (c \cdot \log n) \cdot |A|^{c \cdot \log n} = O(n^k)$$

many different configurations, where k is an appropriate constant. So if the computation runs for more than a steps, some configuration must be repeated. But then the machine must be in an infinite (non-terminating) loop, and, therefore, does not accept.

To see that NL $\subseteq$ P, consider the following procedure for some fixed NL-machine: On input x, systematically generate all configurations that can be reached from the starting configuration until a halting configuration is reached or all reachable configurations have been generated. Since the number of configurations is bounded as above, this can be done in polynomial time.

5.2. Let M_1 and M_2 be two log-reduction machines. On input x, it is not possible to simply let the machines run one after the other, since M_1 may output a string that is polynomially long in the length of x and, therefore, cannot be stored in logarithmic space. Instead we proceed like the ***pipe*** concept in UNIX: We start M_2 as the main process (on an empty tape), but whenever M_2 tries to read an input tape symbol we start M_1 on input x as a sub-process to generate this symbol. (All other output symbols produced by M_1 are immediately erased.) Since M_1 requires only logarithmic space (which can be reused each time the process is run) and polynomial time, the total space devoted to process M_1 is logarithmic and the time for M_1 is polynomial.

5.3. It is clear that $PATH \in$ NL: Nondeterministically guess a path from a to b. This can be done by nondeterministically generating a sequence of n nodes in the graph and checking to see if adjacent pairs in the sequence are adjacent in the graph and if both a and b occur in the sequence. The only space needed is the space to store a pair of nodes and a counter.

Now let A be in NL via a $O(\log n)$ space-bounded machine M. By Exercise 5.2, this machine has at most polynomially many configurations on an input of length n. The desired reduction of A to $PATH$ outputs for any x the graph in which each such configuration is a node, and the there is an edge from c_i to c_j if c_j is a configuration that could follow c_i in the computation on input x. This can be done, for example, by producing for each configuration the finite list of possible successor configurations.

The start node a in the *PATH*-problem is the start configuration of the Turing machine. The end node in the *PATH*-problem is a unique accepting condition. (The machine M can be modified so that there is always one unique halting configuration.) Since each configuration can be written down in $O(\log n)$ bits, this reduction is logarithmically space-bounded.

5.4. A configuration can, in general, have more than one predecessor configuration. If the graph described in the solution to Exercise 5.2 is interpreted as an undirected graph, then it may be possible on some input x that is not in the language to nevertheless reach the halting configuration by traveling some of the edges "backwards," that is, by traveling from a configuration to a possible predecessor rather than to a successor.

5.5. Consider the following algorithm on an input of length n.

Success := **FALSE**;
WHILE NOT Success **DO**
  Choose one of a) and b) with equal probability:
  a) Move the read-only head on the input tape one cell to the right.
    IF the end of the input is reached **THEN** Success := TRUE;
  b) Move the read-only head on the input tape
      back to the first input symbol;
END

The probability of successfully reaching the end of the input on the first attempt is 2^{-n}. Each additional attempt costs at least one step, so the expected value of the time until the algorithm successfully halts is at least 2^n.

5.6. For the following directed graph the same statements are true as were made in the preceding exercise.

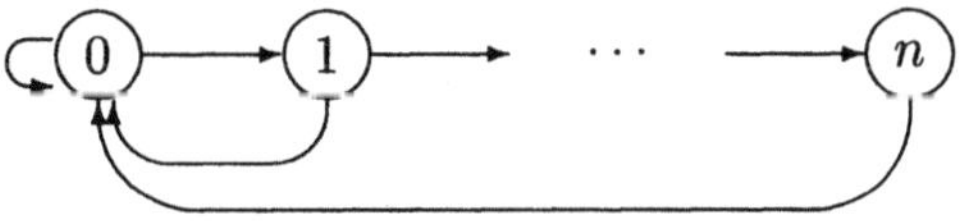

So if we choose $a = 0$ and $b = n$, then the expected length of time to get from a to b is exponential.

5.7. If the edge probabilities are not all the same, then there must be edges with probability greater than $1/2e$ and others with probability less than $1/2e$ (since the sum of all probabilities is 1). Let $p_{\max} > 1/2e$ be the maximal edge probability that occurs in the graph. There must be at least one edge (u, v) with this probability that has an adjacent edge (v, w) with a strictly smaller probability. (Since G is connected, if this were not the case, every edge would have probability $p_{\max}$, but then the sum over all edges would be greater than 1.) All other edges adjacent to (u, v) have probability at most $p_{\max}$. So $P_{(u,v)} = p_{\max}$ must be strictly larger than the weighted sum of the adjacent edges' probabilities, i.e.,

$$P_{(u,v)} > \frac{1}{d(v)} \cdot \sum_{(v,w)\in G} P_{(v,w)} ,$$

as was to be shown.

5.8. Let Y be the following 0-1-valued random variable

$$\begin{cases} 1 & \text{if } X \geq a, \\ 0 & \text{if } X < a. \end{cases}$$

Then $X \geq a \cdot Y$. From this it follows that $E(X) \geq E(a \cdot Y) = a \cdot E(Y) = a \cdot Pr[X \geq a]$.

5.9. On average, we must visit node u $d(u)$ times until v occurs as the successor node. So $E(u,v)$ can be bounded above by $d(u) \cdot E(u,u) = d(u) \cdot 2e/d(u) = 2e$. (This is in general a very crude approximation, since it possible to get from u to v via some other route that does not use the edge (u,v).)

5.10. We proceed by induction on n, the number of nodes in the graph. The statement is clearly true for graphs with only one node. Let G be a connected graph with $n+1$ nodes. There must be a node that can be removed without destroying the connectivity of the graph. In the remaining graph, by the inductive hypothesis, there must be a path of length $2n$. The removed node was attached to this path by at least one edge. By traveling this edge once in each direction, we obtain a path of length at most $2n+2$ that includes this node as well.

5.11. Let X be the number of steps in a random walk from a to b. By Markov inequality (letting $a = 2E(X)$) we get $Pr[X > 8en] \leq Pr[X \geq 2E(X)] \leq E(X)/(2E(X)) = 1/2$.

5.12. For each of the n nodes we must determine a first, second, etc. up to dth adjacent node. Each time we have (roughly) n possibilities. So for each node we have no more than n^d possibilities, and altogether there are no more than $(n^d)^n = n^{dn}$ possible ways to specify such a graph.

6.1.

x_1	x_2	x_3	
0	0	0	0
0	0	1	0
0	1	0	0
0	1	1	0
1	0	0	0
1	0	1	0
1	1	0	0
1	1	1	0

Unsatisfiable!

6.2. Correctness: The last clause ($\emptyset$) in a resolution proof is clearly unsatisfiable. Now we work inductively from back to front and show that the set of input clauses to a resolution proof is unsatisfiable. Let K_1, K_2 be two resolvable clauses with resolvent $K_3 = K_1 \cup K_2 - \{x_i, \overline{x_i}\}$ that occurs in portion of the proof already considered (at which time it represented an input clause). Suppose that the set of input clauses to the resolution proof, now augmented by clauses K_1 and K_2 is satisfiable via an assignment α. Then, in particular, α must satisfy K_1 and K_2. The variable x_i, on which the resolution occurred, is true in one of these clauses, its negation in the other false (or vice versa). Thus in one of the clauses, a different literal must be true under α. This literal remains in the resolvent K_3, so K_3 is also true under α. But this contradicts the inductive hypothesis.

Completeness: For an unsatisfiable set of clauses with one variable there is an obvious resolution proof. Now assume completeness for sets of clauses containing up to n variables. Consider an unsatisfiable set of clauses M with $n+1$ variables.

First put $x_{n+1} = 0$ (all occurrences of x_{n+1} can now be stricken, and for each occurrence of $\overline{x_{n+1}}$ the entire clause in which it occurs can be stricken). This results in another unsatisfiable set of clauses M_0. Analogously form M_1 by putting $x_{n+1} = 1$. By induction there are resolution proofs for M_0 and M_1. Now we reconstruct the original clauses from M – that is, we reintroduce x_{n+1} in M_0 and $\overline{x_{n+1}}$ in M_1 and also in the corresponding resolvents in both resolution proofs. Either one of the resulting resolution proofs still contains the empty clause (now derived from M), in which case we are done, or we have the resolvents $\{x_{n+1}\}$ and $\{\overline{x_{n+1}}\}$, from which we can derive the empty clause in one more resolution step.

6.3. We construct the path from back to front, starting at the empty clause. If we are at a clause K in the path with $\alpha(K) = 0$, then exactly one of the predecessors of this clause is true under α, the other false. We select the one that is false under α and continue the construction from there.

6.4. The existence of a SUPER proof system for refutation is equivalent to the existence of a nondeterministic, polynomial time-bounded algorithm for $\overline{SAT}$, so $\overline{SAT} \in \mathsf{NP}$. Since SAT is NP-complete, $\overline{SAT}$ is coNP-complete. By the closure of NP under polynomial reductions coNP $\subseteq$ NP, so coNP = NP.

In the other direction: If NP = coNP, then $\overline{SAT} \in \mathsf{NP}$, so there is a nondeterministic, polynomial time-bounded Turing machine for $\overline{SAT}$. The "possible next configuration calculus" of this machine is then a SUPER proof system for refutation.

6.5.

Type 1-clauses:

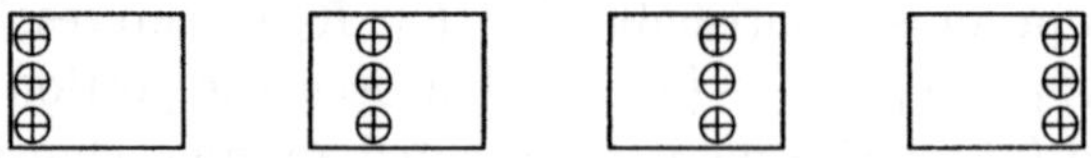

Type 2-clauses:

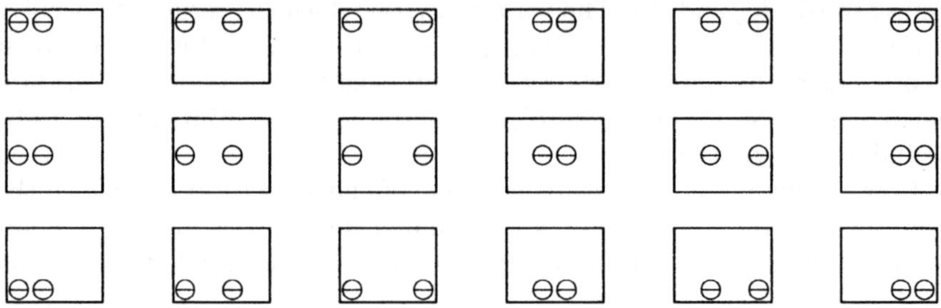

6.6. Empty positions in the diagram below are understood to be 0's.

		1			
					1
			1		
1					
	1				

6.7. $(n+1)!$

6.8. The type 1 clause that has the 0-column of α filled with $\oplus$.

6.9. The same clause as in the preceding exercise.

6.10. A $\ominus$ in the 0-column would cause the clause to be true under α.

6.11. Since α is critical, the diagram for α must have n 1's, each in a different row. Since $n/2$ $\oplus$'s occur in the 0-column, $n/2$ possible rows are ruled out. Since S has already fixed $n/8$ 1's, that rules out (in the worst case) another $n/8$ positions. So at least $n - (n/2 + n/8) = 3n/8$ possibilities remain.

6.12. If there were two $\ominus$'s in one column then at least one would have to be in a position where there is a 0 in α. From this it would follow that the clause is true under α.

6.13. The alteration from 0 to 1 (in the original 0-column) has no effect, since that position of K^S does not contain $\oplus$. The alteration from 1 to 0 (in one of the $3n/8$ 1-positions) has no effect, since that position of K^S (by assumption) does not contain $\ominus$.

6.14. Suppose fewer than $\frac{(3n/8+1)\cdot(n/2)}{n\cdot(n+1)} \cdot t$ clauses are taken care of. Since the position was chosen maximally, in every other position strictly fewer than $\frac{(3n/8+1)\cdot(n/2)}{n\cdot(n+1)} \cdot t$ $\oplus$'s occur. Now we sum over all positions in the clauses and obtain an upper bound on the number of $\oplus$'s in all t clauses together: there are strictly fewer than $(3n/8+1)\cdot(n/2)\cdot t$. This is a contradiction, since we have argued that each of the t clauses that is input to the greedy algorithm has at least $(3n/8+1)\cdot(n/2)$ $\oplus$'s.

7.1. A tautology has a model of every size, so choose something like $F = (P \vee \neg P)$, where P is 0-ary.

7.2. We let F express that there are at least 3 different elements in the universe, but that in any set of 4 elements, two of them are the same:

$$\begin{aligned} F = {} & \exists x \exists y \exists z\, (\neg(x = y) \wedge \neg(x = z) \wedge \neg(y = z)) \\ & \wedge \forall u \forall x \forall y \forall z\, (u = x \vee u = y \vee u = z \vee x = y \vee x = z \vee y = z)\,. \end{aligned}$$

7.3. We describe a recursive procedure that evaluates F using A. L represents a list of variable conditions, which is initially empty.

```
PROCEDURE eval (F, A, L) : BOOLEAN;
VAR b : BOOLEAN;
BEGIN
   IF F = (G ∘ H) THEN { ∘ is a boolean operation }
      RETURN eval(G, A, L) ∘ eval(H, A, L) END;
   IF F = ∃x G THEN
      b := FALSE;
      FOR w := 1 TO |A| DO
         b := b OR eval(G, A, L ∪ {(x, w)})
      END;
      RETURN b;
   END;
   IF F = ∀x G THEN
      b := TRUE;
      FOR w := 1 TO |A| DO
         b := b AND eval(G, A, L ∪ {(x, w)})
      END;
      RETURN b;
   END;
   IF F = P(x_1, ..., x_m) { where (x_i, w_i) ∈ L }
      THEN RETURN The value of the relation corresponding to P
                  on the tuple (w_1, ..., w_m)
   END;
   IF F = (x_i = x_j) THEN RETURN w_i = w_j END;
END
```

The running time of this algorithm is polynomial, the degree of the polynomial depending on the number of quantifiers in F. (Remember F is not part of the input to the algorithm but fixed.)

7.4. An NP-algorithm for a given formula F on input 1^n guesses nondeterministically a structure A appropriate for F. This can be written down using polynomially (in n) many bits; the polynomial depends on F. Then the algorithm tests as in the previous exercise whether A is a model for F. This shows that the problem is in NP.

On input of a binary representation of n everything works just as above, but the running time is increased to $(2^{n'})^k = 2^{kn'}$, with respect to the new logarithmically shorter input length n'.

7.5. An NP-algorithm for a given formula F on input $\mathsf{A} = (M; R)$ – coded as a string – nondeterministically guesses relations R_i on the universe for each P_i in the formula. These can be written down using polynomially many bits. Then the algorithm tests, as in the previous two exercises, whether $\mathsf{A}' = (M; R, R_1, \dots, R_m)$ is a model for F. This shows that the problem is in NP.

7.6.

$$\begin{aligned}\forall \boldsymbol{x}\forall \boldsymbol{y} \Bigg(\bigwedge_{i=1}^{n} \mathrm{Min}(y_i) \to \\ \Big(\bigwedge_{i=2}^{n} \mathrm{Min}(x_i) \wedge \mathrm{Min}(x_1) &\to (E(x_1) \to P_{(z_0,1)}(\boldsymbol{x},\boldsymbol{y}) \\ &\qquad \wedge(\neg E(x_1) \to P_{(z_0,0)}(\boldsymbol{x},\boldsymbol{y})))\Big) \\ \wedge \Big(\bigwedge_{i=2}^{n} \mathrm{Min}(x_i) \wedge \neg\mathrm{Min}(x_1) &\to (E(x_1) \to P_1(\boldsymbol{x},\boldsymbol{y}) \\ &\qquad \wedge(\neg E(x_1) \to P_0(\boldsymbol{x},\boldsymbol{y})))\Big) \\ \wedge \bigvee_{i=2}^{n} \Big(\neg\mathrm{Min}(x_i) &\to P_{\sqcup}(\boldsymbol{x},\boldsymbol{y})\Big)\Bigg)\end{aligned}$$

7.7. $\forall \boldsymbol{x}\forall \boldsymbol{y} \bigwedge_{a \in \Gamma} \bigwedge_{\substack{b \in \Gamma \\ b \neq a}} \neg(P_a(\boldsymbol{x},\boldsymbol{y}) \wedge P_b(\boldsymbol{x},\boldsymbol{y}))$

7.8. $\forall \boldsymbol{x}\forall \boldsymbol{y} \left(\bigwedge_{i=1}^{k}(\mathrm{Min}(x_i) \wedge \mathrm{Max}(y_i)) \to P_{(z_e,\sqcup)}(\boldsymbol{x},\boldsymbol{y})\right)$

7.9.

$$\begin{aligned} F \;=\; & \forall x\, \neg(x < x) \\ & \wedge\, \forall x \forall y\, (x < y \rightarrow \neg(y < x)) \\ & \wedge\, \forall x \forall y \forall z\, ((x < y) \wedge (y < z) \rightarrow (x < z)) \\ & \wedge\, \forall x \forall y\, ((x < y) \vee (y < x) \vee (x = y)) \end{aligned}$$

7.10. Suppose NP_1 is closed under complement and let $L \in \mathsf{NEXP}$. Then the language

$$t(L) = \{1^n \mid \mathit{bin}(n) \in L\}$$

(where $\mathit{bin}(n)$ is the binary representation of n) is in NP. By our assumption, $\overline{t(L)} \in \mathsf{NP}$. From this it follows that $\overline{L} \in \mathsf{NEXP}$.

In the other direction, suppose NEXP is closed under complement, and let $L \in \mathsf{NP}$. Then the language

$$b(L) = \{\mathit{bin}(n) \mid 1^n \in L\}$$

is in NEXP. By assumption, $\overline{b(L)}$ is in NEXP. From this it follows that $\overline{L} \in \mathsf{NP}$. This result originated with

- R.V. Book: Tally languages and complexity classes, *Information and Control* 26 (1974), 186–193.

8.1. Since the Kolmogorov complexity of a string is the length of some program, it is clear that this must be ≥ 0. The length of a program that has a "dummy" input instruction and then proceeds to output x without making any use of the input provides an upper bound for $K(x \mid y)$, i.e., $K(x \mid y) \leq K(x)$. For any string $x \in \{0,1\}^*$, "**OUTPUT** 'x' " is always a possible program that outputs x. This program has length $|x| + c'$ for some constant c'. So $K(x) \leq |x| + c'$.

8.2. The program "**INPUT** v; **OUTPUT** v", where v is a variable, has constant length, so $K(x \mid x) \leq c$ for all x.

8.3. There is a program of fixed length that, by means of a suitable approximation algorithm, on input n produces the first n digits of π. Let c be the length of such a program. Then for all n, $K(\pi_n \mid n) \leq c$.

8.4. In the worst case, the K-values of the 2^n strings of length n are distributed as follows: $K = 0$ once , $K = 1$ twice, $K = 2$ four times, ... $K = n-1$ 2^{n-1} times, and finally $K = n$ for one string. If we add these values and divide by the number of strings (2^n) we get

$$\begin{aligned}
E(K(x)) &\geq \frac{1}{2^n} \cdot \left(n + \sum_{i=0}^{n-1} i2^i\right) \\
&= \frac{n}{2^n} + \sum_{i=0}^{n-1} i2^{i-n} \\
&= \frac{n}{2^n} + \sum_{j=1}^{n} (n-j)2^{-j} \\
&\geq \frac{n}{2^n} + \sum_{j=1}^{n} n2^{-j} - \sum_{k=0}^{\infty} k2^{-k} \\
&= n\left(2^{-n} + \sum_{j=1}^{n} 2^{-j}\right) - \sum_{k=0}^{\infty}\sum_{l=1}^{k} 2^{-k} \\
&= n - \sum_{l=1}^{\infty}\sum_{k=l}^{\infty} 2^{-k} \\
&= n - 2\,.
\end{aligned}$$

The same argument also holds for $E(K(x \mid y))$, where y is arbitrary.

8.5. Suppose $x \mapsto K(x)$ is computable via a program M (which halts on all inputs). We can use M as a sub-routine in the following sequence of programs $P_1, P_2, \ldots$, where P_m is

```
x := λ;
REPEAT
    x := successor of x;
UNTIL M(x) outputs a value ≥ m;
OUTPUT x
```

Notice that the the constant m is a parameter in this program. The length of P_m is $O(1) + \log m$; furthermore, each program m describes some string x_m, namely the lexicographically first string such that $K(x) \geq m$. But since P_m describes x_m, $K(x_m) \leq |P_m| = O(1) + \log m$. For large m, $O(1) + \log m < m$, which is a contradiction, since $K(x_m) \geq m$. Thus the function $x \mapsto K(x)$ cannot be computable.

(This proof resembles the Berry Paradox; see page 7 of the book by Machtey and Young.)

8.6. The argument here is similar to that used in the Exercise 8.4.

$$\sum_{\{x:|x|=n\}} 2^{-2K(x|n)} \leq 2^{-2n} + \sum_{i=0}^{n-1} 2^i 2^{-2i}$$

$$= 2^{-2n} + \sum_{i=0}^{n-1} 2^{-i}$$
$$\leq 2 .$$

8.7. There are at most $1+2+4+\cdots+2^{\log m-k-1} = 2^{\log m-k}-1 = m2^{-k}-1$ programs of length $< \log m - k$. Each one describes at most one string x with $K(x \mid y) < \log m - k$. So there must be at least $m - m2^{-k}+1 = m(1-2^{-k})+1$ strings left over.

8.8. There are only $\binom{n}{3n/4} = \binom{n}{n/4}$ strings of length n with $\frac{3}{4}n$ 1's and $\frac{1}{4}n$ 0's. By Stirling's formula ($n! \sim \sqrt{2\pi n} \cdot (\frac{n}{e})^n$), we get:

$$\binom{n}{n/4} = \frac{n!}{(n/4)! \cdot (3n/4)!}$$
$$\sim \sqrt{\frac{8}{3\pi n}} \cdot \left(\frac{4}{3}\right)^{3n/4} \cdot 4^{n/4}$$
$$= \sqrt{\frac{8}{3\pi n}} \cdot (1.7547...)^n .$$

There is an algorithm of length $O(1) + \log i$ that outputs the ith string of length n with the property that it has $\frac{3}{4}n$ 1's and $\frac{1}{4}n$ 0's. Since $\log i$ is bounded by $\log\left(\sqrt{\frac{8}{3\pi n}} \cdot (1.7547...)^n\right) \leq (0.8112...) \cdot n$, this length is strictly less than n. So such a string cannot be Kolmogorov-random.

The approximation above can also be obtained via the Binomial Theorem:

$$1 = \left(\frac{1}{4} + \frac{3}{4}\right)^n$$
$$= \sum_{i=0}^{n} \binom{n}{i} (1/4)^i (3/4)^{n-i}$$
$$\geq \sum_{i=0}^{n/4} \binom{n}{i} (1/4)^i (3/4)^{n-i}$$
$$= \sum_{i=0}^{n/4} \binom{n}{i} \left(\frac{3/4}{1/4}\right)^{(n/4)-i} (1/4)^{n/4} (3/4)^{3n/4}$$
$$\geq (1/4)^{n/4} (3/4)^{3n/4} \cdot \sum_{i=0}^{n/4} \binom{n}{i} .$$

From this it follows that $\sum_{i=0}^{n/4} \binom{n}{i} \leq 4^{n/4} \cdot (4/3)^{3n/4} = (1.7547...)^n$. In general, it can be shown in the same manner that $\sum_{i=0}^{\lambda n} \binom{n}{i} \leq 2^{n \cdot H(\lambda)}$, where $0 \leq$

$\lambda \leq 1/2$ and $H(\lambda) = -[\lambda \log \lambda + (1-\lambda)\log(1-\lambda)]$ is the entropy function. See

- D. Welsh: *Codes and Cryptography*, Oxford University Press, 1988, p. 39.

8.9. Let $T_A(x)$ be the running time of algorithm A on input x. Then

$$T_A^{\mathrm{wc}}(n) = \max\{T_A(x) \ : \ |x| = n\}$$

is the worst-case complexity of A, and

$$T_A^{\mathrm{av},\mu}(n) = \sum_{\{x:|x|=n\}} \mu(x) T_A(x)$$

is the average-case complexity under the universal distribution μ. We have already seen that $T_A(x_n) = T_A^{\mathrm{wc}}(n)$ and $\mu(x_n) \geq \alpha$ for some constant α. From this it follows that

$$\begin{aligned} T_A^{\mathrm{av},\mu}(n) &= \sum_{\{x:|x|=n\}} \mu(x) T_A(x) \\ &\geq \mu(x_n) T_A(x_n) \\ &= \mu(x_n) T_A^{\mathrm{wc}}(n) \\ &\geq \alpha \cdot T_A^{\mathrm{wc}}(n)\ , \end{aligned}$$

as was to be shown.

9.1. Since $p_i \geq 2$, $n_i \leq \log_2 n$. So $|bin(n_i)| \leq \log\log n$ and the length of the encoding of the finite sequence $n_1, \ldots, n_k$ is $O(k \log\log n) = O(\log\log n)$.

9.2. Suppose we have shown that $p_m \leq m \log^2 m$. Then we can put $n \leq \pi(n) \log^2 \pi(n)$ and solve for $\pi(n)$:

$$\pi(n) \geq \frac{n}{\log^2 \pi(n)} \geq \frac{n}{\log^2 n} \quad \text{since } \pi(n) \leq n\ .$$

9.3.

> **INPUT** $\langle m, k \rangle$;
> Determine the mth prime number. Call it p.
> Compute $n := p * k$ and **OUTPUT** n;

9.4. We can determine the length of w from the initial portion of the coding string (the end of which is marked with a '1'); then we can read w. Since we know how long w is, this is self-terminating.

The length of the coding is given by

$$|\mathrm{code}(w)| = |w| + 2\log|w|.$$

We get the bound on p_m by plugging in:

$$\log n \leq K(bin(n)) \leq \log m + 2\log\log m + \log n - \log p_m ,$$

from which it follows that

$$\log p_m \leq \log m + 2\log\log m$$
$$p_m \leq m \log^2 m .$$

9.5. If we let $\text{code}'(w) = \text{code}(bin(|w|))w$ then the length of an encoding of a string of length n is $n + \log n + 2\log\log n$. This can be iterated further to give an encoding of length $n + \log n + \log\log n + \log\log\log n + \cdots + 2\log^{(m)} n$.

By using code′ instead of code, our approximation is improved to

$$\pi(n) \geq \frac{n}{\log n(\log\log n)^2} .$$

9.6. If n is prime, then it can be described by giving its index in the increasing sequence of prime numbers. This leads to the following contradiction: $K(bin(n)) \leq \log \pi(n) \leq \log n - \Omega(\log\log n)$.

9.7. We get: $2^n \leq K \leq g \cdot (c + 2\log(g+n)) + d$. Since every n-place boolean function can be computed with $O(2^n)$ gates, $\log(g+n) = O(n)$. Plugging in yields: $g \geq 2^n/O(n) = \Omega(2^n/n)$.

9.8. A formula corresponds to a binary tree in which all interior nodes (the gates) have exactly two children. In such a tree it is always the case that the number of interior nodes is 1 less than the number of leaves. So the number of times an input is mentioned is $1 + g$. The postfix code for a formula consists of $1 + g$ inputs, each requiring about $\log(n)$ bits, and g operations, each requiring a constant number of bits. So the length of an encoding of a formula with g gates using postfix notation is bounded above by $O(g) + O(g \log n) = O(g \log n)$. From this it follows as in the previous exercise that $2^n \leq K \leq O(g \log n)$, so $g = \Omega(2^n/\log n)$.

9.9. Every state that appears in one of the crossing sequences occurs at some point in the computation and, therefore, contributes 1 step to the total running time. On the other hand, every state that occurs at some point in the computation must appear once in some crossing sequence.

9.10. If the crossing sequences (at i) are identical, then both computations behave exactly the same in the portions of the computation during which the tape head is left of i. But by our assumption that Turing machines only halt with the tape head at the left end of the tape, they must either both accept or both reject.

9.11. See above.

9.12. We can paste together the portions of the computations (left and right of position i) and we see that the computation remains essentially unchanged.

9.13. Suppose the crossing sequences are identical. Apply the lemma from Exercise 9.12 to show that the crossing sequences (at position i) of $w0^{|w|}w$ and $w0^{|w|}w'$ are also identical. Now apply the lemma from Exercise 9.10 with $x = w0^{i-|w|}$, $y = 0^{2|w|-i}w$ and $z = 0^{2|w|-i}w'$. But $xy \in L$ and $xz \notin L$. This is a contradiction, so the crossing sequences must be different.

9.14.

> **INPUT** $\langle M, m, i, c\rangle$;
> **FOR** w, $|w| = m$ **DO**
> Simulate M on input $w0^{|w|}w$ and
> note the crossing sequence at position i.
> If this crossing sequence is the same as c, then output w;
> **END**

9.15.

$$\begin{aligned}
time_M(x) = \sum_{i=-\infty}^{\infty} |CS_M(x,i)| &\geq \sum_{i=n/3}^{2n/3-1} |CS_M(x,i)| \\
&\geq \sum_{i=n/3}^{2n/3-1} (n/3 - O(\log n)) \\
&\geq n^2/9 - O(n \log n) = \Omega(n^2) .
\end{aligned}$$

10.1. The probability is $\geq (1-\delta)(1-\varepsilon)$.

10.2. Using Exercise 8.8, this number is at most

$$\sum_{i=0}^{\varepsilon 2^n} \binom{2^n}{i} \leq 2^{H(\varepsilon)2^n} ,$$

where H is the entropy function.

10.3. For PAC-learnability it suffices to choose $m \geq \frac{\ln 2}{\varepsilon}(\log|H| + \log(1/\delta))$. Now let $|H| = 2^{p(n)\cdot m^{1-\alpha}}$ and plug in

$$m \geq \frac{\ln 2}{\varepsilon}\Big(p(n)\cdot m^{1-\alpha} + \log(1/\delta)\Big) = \frac{\ln 2 \cdot p(n)}{\varepsilon} \cdot m^{1-\alpha} + \frac{\ln 2 \cdot \log(1/\delta)}{\varepsilon} .$$

From this we get

$$m^{\alpha} \geq \frac{p(n)\ln 2}{\varepsilon} + \frac{\log(1/\delta)\ln 2}{\varepsilon m^{1-\alpha}} .$$

It suffices to choose

$$m^\alpha \geq \frac{p(n)\ln 2}{\varepsilon} + \frac{\log(1/\delta)\ln 2}{\varepsilon} .$$

From this we get

$$m \geq \left(\frac{p(n)\ln 2 + \log(1/\delta)\ln 2}{\varepsilon}\right)^{1/\alpha} .$$

This is polynomial in n, $1/\varepsilon$ and $1/\delta$.

10.4. There are $2n+1$ possibilities for the choice of a literal z_{ij}. So there are at most $(2n+1)^k$ possible monomials (in fact, there are fewer). A $DNF_{n,k}$-formulas consists of an arbitrary subset of these monomials (conjunctively combined). There are $2^{(2n+1)^k}$ such subsets.

10.5. Let the function to be learned be $f = \bigvee_{i=1}^{l} m_i$, where the monomials m_i represent a certain choice of the $\leq (2n+1)^k$ monomials with at most k literals. The hypothesis function h initially includes all possible monomials with at most k literals. In each pass through the loop, the only monomials m removed from h are the monomials such that $m \notin \{m_1, \ldots, m_l\}$. This guarantees consistence with the negative examples. But h is also consistent with respect to the positive examples since we always ensure that $h \geq f$.

11.1. Every n-place boolean function is equivalent to a logic formula, which can be expressed in either disjunctive normal form or conjunctive normal form. These two forms correspond correspond to depth 2 OR-AND and AND-OR circuits. But the size of the formulas generated in this way is exponential in general.

11.2.

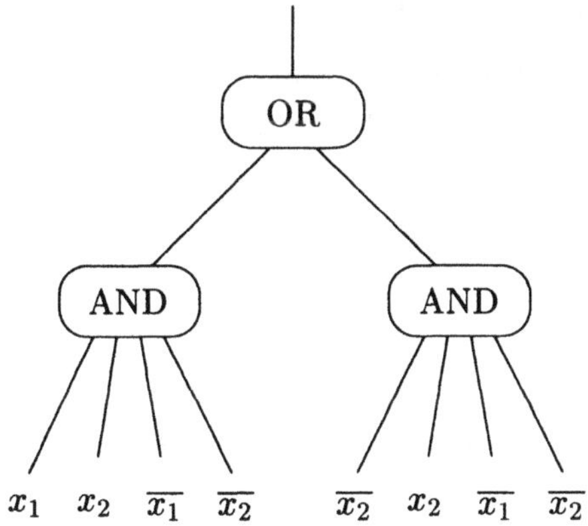

11.3. The fan-in on the first level (at the AND-gates) is d and the fan-in on the second level (at the OR-gates) is c^d.

11.4. Replace all AND-gates with OR-gates (and vice versa) and all x_i input gates with $\overline{x_i}$ (and vice versa). This corresponds to DeMorgan's laws:

$$\overline{x \vee y} = \overline{x} \wedge \overline{y} ,$$
$$\overline{x \wedge y} = \overline{x} \vee \overline{y} .$$

This method works for any function. For parity in particular there is an even simpler method: Since

$$\overline{par(x_1, x_2, \ldots, x_n)} = par(\overline{x_1}, x_2, \ldots, x_n) ,$$

we only need to swap x_1 with $\overline{x_1}$.

11.5. Since

$$par_n(0, x_2, \ldots, x_n) = par_{n-1}(x_2, \ldots, x_n)$$

and

$$par_n(1, x_2, \ldots, x_n) = \overline{par_{n-1}}(x_2, \ldots, x_n) ,$$

these restrictions always result in another parity function or its complement.

11.6. Every AND-gate on level 1 of a depth 2 circuit for par_n must have n inputs. That is, every variable or its complement must be one of the inputs. Suppose this were not the case, i.e., there is some AND-gate that is missing (WLOG) both x_n and $\overline{x_n}$. The inputs are $x_1^{i_1}, x_2^{i_2}, \ldots, x_{n-1}^{i_{n-1}}$ with $i_j \in \{-1, +1\}$. This AND-gate outputs 1 (and therefore the entire circuit outputs 1) if we put $x_j = 1$ exactly when $i_j = 1$ ($j = 1, 2, \ldots, n-1$). Now we can set x_n to be either 0 or 1 without changing the output of the circuit. So the circuit does not correctly compute parity. Contradiction.

Now if each AND-gate in the circuit has n inputs, as we have just shown is necessary, then each of these AND-gates can only capture one row of the truth table for par_n. Since there are 2^{n-1} rows of the truth table with the value 1, there must be 2^{n-1} AND-gates.

11.7. Using XOR-gates with two inputs, we can compute parity with a circuit in the form of a balanced tree:

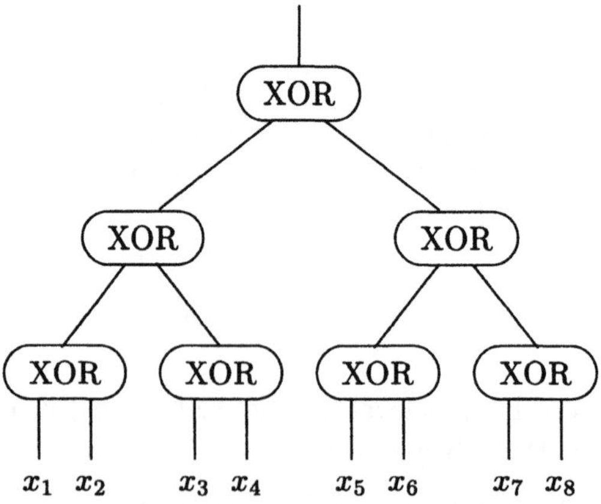

Each XOR-gate can now be replaced by a small circuit of AND- and OR-gates. Note that we need to provide this circuit with both variables and their negations, and that the circuit likewise "outputs" both XOR and $\overline{\text{XOR}}$.

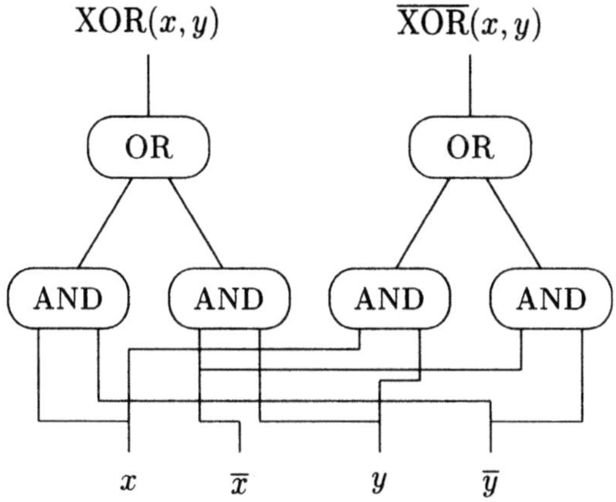

As one can see, the above solution only requires AND- and OR-gates of constant fan-in (namely 2). The boolean functions that can be computed by constant fan-in $O((\log n)^k)$ depth circuits form the class NC^k. So we have just shown that PARITY $\in \mathsf{NC}^1$. In fact, *all* symmetric boolean functions are in the class NC^1.

11.8. Let Y_i be a random variable that is 1 if the ith trail results in success, 0 otherwise. $E(Y_i) = 1 \cdot p + 0 \cdot q = p$. So $E(X) = E(\sum_{i=1}^n Y_i) = \sum_{i=1}^n E(Y_i) = n \cdot p$. Furthermore, $V(X) = E((X - E(X))^2) = E(X^2) - E(X)^2 = E((\sum_{i=1}^n Y_i)^2) - (np)^2 = E(\sum_{i=1}^n \sum_{j=1}^n Y_i Y_j) - (np)^2 = n(n-1)p^2 + np - (np)^2 = n \cdot p \cdot (1-p)$.

11.9. $Pr[\ |X - E(X)| \geq a\ ] = Pr[\ (X - E(X))^2 \geq a^2\ ]$. By Markov's inequality, $Pr[\ (X - E(X))^2 \geq a^2\ ] \leq E((X - E(X))^2)/a^2 = V(X)/a^2$.

11.10. $Pr[X \leq 17] \leq Pr[|X - E(X)| \geq 13] \leq \frac{V(X)}{13^2} = \frac{100 \cdot 0.3 \cdot 0.7}{169} = 0.124...$

11.11.

$$\begin{aligned} Pr[X \geq a] &= \sum_{i=a}^{n} \binom{n}{i} p^i (1-p)^{n-i} \\ &\leq \sum_{i=a}^{n} \binom{n}{i} p^i \\ &\leq p^a \sum_{i=a}^{n} \binom{n}{i} \\ &\leq p^a \cdot 2^n . \end{aligned}$$

In fact, we can show an even better approximation:

$$\begin{aligned}
Pr[X \geq a] &= \sum_{i=a}^{n} \binom{n}{i} p^i (1-p)^{n-i} \\
&= \sum_{i=0}^{n-a} \binom{n}{a+i} p^{a+i} (1-p)^{n-a-i} \\
&\leq \sum_{i=0}^{n-a} \binom{n}{a} \binom{n-a}{i} p^{a+i} (1-p)^{n-a-i} \\
&= \binom{n}{a} p^a \sum_{i=0}^{n-a} \binom{n-a}{i} p^i (1-p)^{n-a-i} \\
&= \binom{n}{a} p^a \\
&\leq n^a p^a \\
&= (np)^a \,.
\end{aligned}$$

Using this approximation, the approximations in Exercises 11.16 and 11.20 can also be improved.

11.12. Suppose there is a family of polynomial-size, depth t circuits for PARITY. If we artificially add a new first level consisting of (AND- or OR-gates) with fan-in 1 (one connected to each variable used in the gate), then we get a depth $t+1$ circuit with constant input fan-in, which contradicts the claim.

11.13. Let X be the random variable that contains the number of variables that remain in S_n^r. Then

$$\begin{aligned}
&Pr[\text{ fewer than } \sqrt{n}/2 \text{ variables remain in } S_n^r] \\
&\quad \leq \; Pr[|X - E(X)| \geq \sqrt{n}/2] \leq \frac{V(X)}{(\sqrt{n}/2)^2} \\
&= O\,(\frac{1}{\sqrt{n}})\,.
\end{aligned}$$

In fact, it is possible to prove much sharper bounds (look for Chernoff bounds, cf. Topic 17).

11.14. We must show that for every n we can find a restricted circuit with exactly n inputs. Let n be fixed. As a starting point, consider the circuit S_{4n^2}. With probability greater than 0, the circuit $S_{4n^2}^r$ still has at least n inputs. Thus there *exists* a restricted circuit with m inputs where $n \leq m \leq 4n^2$. The size of this circuit is $O((4n^2)^k) = O(n^{2k})$. If we now set any $m-n$ of the inputs to 0, then we get the desired circuit which is polynomial in size and has exactly n inputs.

11.15.

$$\begin{aligned}
&Pr[\text{AND-gate not } 0] \\
&\qquad \le Pr[\text{all inputs} \neq 0] \\
&\qquad \le Pr[\text{an arbitrary, fixed input is not } 0]^{4k \ln n} \\
&\qquad \le (3/4)^{4k \ln n} \qquad (\text{for } n \ge 4) \\
&\qquad = n^{4k \ln(3/4)} \\
&\qquad \le n^{-k} \qquad (\text{since } \ln(1-x) \le -x)
\end{aligned}$$

11.16.

$$\begin{aligned}
&Pr[\text{AND-gate depends on more than } a \text{ variables}] \\
&\qquad \le \sum_{i=a}^{4k \ln n} \binom{n}{i} (1/\sqrt{n})^i (1 - 1/\sqrt{n})^{n-i} \\
&\qquad \le (1/\sqrt{n})^a \cdot 2^{4k \ln n} \qquad (\text{Exercise 11.11}) \\
&\qquad = n^{-a/2} \cdot n^{8k} \\
&\qquad = n^{8k-a/2}
\end{aligned}$$

Solving $8k - a/2 = -k$ for a, we obtain the constant $a = 18k$.

11.17.

$$\begin{aligned}
&Pr[\text{the AND-gate is not constant} = 0] \\
&\qquad \le Pr[\text{none of the OR-gates obtains the value } 0] \\
&\qquad \le (Pr[\text{an arbitrary, fixed OR-gate does not get set to } 0])^{d \cdot \ln n} \\
&\qquad \le (1 - 4^{-c})^{d \cdot \ln n} \qquad (\text{for } n \ge 4) \\
&\qquad = n^{d \cdot \ln(1-4^{-c})} \\
&\qquad \le n^{-d \cdot 4^{-c}} \qquad (\text{since } \ln(1-x) \le -x) \\
&\qquad = n^{-k} \qquad (\text{plugging in } d)
\end{aligned}$$

11.18. In this case there are at most $d \cdot \ln n$ such OR-gates, and each one has fan-in at most c. So $|H| \le c \cdot d \cdot \ln n$.

11.19. If there were an OR-gate with a set of variables disjoint from H, then the set of OR-gates that defined H would not be maximal, since this OR-gate with disjoint variables could be added to the set.

11.20. By Exercise 11.18, $|H| \le cd \ln n$. So by Exercise 11.11 we get the approximation:

$$\begin{aligned}
Pr[h > a] &\le 2^{cd \ln n} \cdot (1/\sqrt{n})^a \\
&\le n^{2cd} \cdot n^{-a/2} \\
&= n^{2cd-a/2} .
\end{aligned}$$

Solving $2cd - a/2 = -k$ for a, we get $a = 4cd + 2k$.

12.1. $\mathrm{OR}(x_1, \ldots, x_n) = 1 - \prod_{i=1}^{n}(1 - x_i)$.

12.2. The error probability is $(1/2)^t$. We put $(1/2)^t \le \varepsilon$ and get $t \ge \log(1/\varepsilon)$.

12.3. $\mathrm{AND}(x_1, \ldots, x_n) \approx p(1 - x_1, \ldots, 1 - x_n)$. This corresponds to the DeMorgan law:

$$\mathrm{AND}(x_1, \ldots, x_n) = \mathrm{NOT}(\mathrm{OR}(\mathrm{NOT}(x_1), \ldots, \mathrm{NOT}(x_n))) .$$

12.4. $Pr(|T \cap S_{\log n+2}| > 1) \le Pr(|T \cap S_{\log n+2}| \ge 1) \le \binom{n}{1} \cdot 2^{-(\log n+2)} = 1/4$.

12.5. The probability is $\ge 3/4$ that case 1 does not occur, and in case 2, the probability is $\ge 2/3$ that there is an i with $|T \cap S_i| = 1$. Therefore, we get a probability of at least $(3/4) \cdot (2/3) = 1/2$.

12.6. $O(\log(s/\varepsilon) \cdot \log^d(s))$. As long as $s = s(n)$ is a polynomial, $\varepsilon = 1/4$ (for example) is a constant and the depth d is constant, then this is polylogarithmic in n.

12.7. Suppose there is no choice of random decisions with the property that for at least $0.9 \cdot 2^n$ values of a, $p(a) = f(a)$. That means that for all random decisions which lead to a polynomial p, there are less than $0.9 \cdot 2^n$ values of a with $p(a) = f(a)$. But then the expected value must be less than $0.9 \cdot 2^n$, a contradiction.

12.8. In one direction the function is $x \mapsto 1 - 2x$, in the other $x \mapsto (1-x)/2$.

12.9. The number of 1's in a 0-1 vector is odd if and only if the number if -1 terms in the corresponding $(+1/-1)$-vector is odd. This corresponds to a product $= -1$.

12.10. If the polynomial q contains a term of the form y_i^2, then we can replace that term by 1, since we are only interested in the polynomial for $y_i \in \{-1, 1\}$. Thus exponents greater than 1 are unnecessary.

12.11. Using Stirling's formula we can show that $\binom{2n}{n} \le \frac{2^{2n}}{\sqrt{\pi n}}$ From this it follows that

$$\begin{aligned}
\sum_{i=0}^{(n+\sqrt{n})/2} \binom{n}{i} &= \sum_{i=0}^{n/2} \binom{n}{i} + \sum_{i=(n/2)+1}^{(n/2)+(\sqrt{n}/2)} \binom{n}{i} \\
&\le \frac{1}{2} 2^n + (\sqrt{n}/2) \binom{n}{n/2} \\
&\le \frac{1}{2} 2^n + (\sqrt{n}/2) \frac{2^n}{\sqrt{\pi n/2}} \\
&< 0.9 \cdot 2^n .
\end{aligned}$$

12.12. Since $y_i \in \{-1,+1\}$,

$$\begin{aligned} q(y_1,\ldots,y_n)\cdot\prod_{i\notin T} y_i &= \prod_{i=1}^{n} y_i \cdot \prod_{i\notin T} y_i \\ &= \prod_{i\in T} y_i \cdot \prod_{i\notin T} y_i^2 \\ &= \prod_{i\in T} y_i \,. \end{aligned}$$

12.13. We have already shown an upper bound of $O(\log(s/\varepsilon)\cdot\log^t(s))$ for the degree of an approximating polynomial. Now treat t as a (yet undetermined) function of n. By comparison with the lower bound $\sqrt{n}/2$ (for the degree of an approximating polynomial for PARITY) we see that for certain constants d and e, it must be that $e\log^{dt} n \geq \sqrt{n}$. Solving for t yields $t = \Omega(\frac{\log n}{\log\log n})$.

12.14. Let $G \in \mathrm{AC}^0$ via the constant depth bound t' and the polynomial size-bound p'. If we replace the fictitious G-gates in the reduction circuit with the AC^0 realization of G, we get an AC^0 circuit for F of depth $\leq t\cdot t'$ and size $\leq p(n)\cdot p'(p(n))$.

12.15. The majority function is a special case of threshold function $T_k(x_1,\ldots,x_n)$, where $T_k(x_1,\ldots,x_n) = 1$ exactly if at least k of the x_i's have the value 1. So $maj(x_1,\ldots,x_n) = T_{\lceil n/2\rceil}(x_1,\ldots,x_n)$.

In the other direction, the majority function can also simulate arbitrary threshold functions. Suppose, for example, that $k < n/2$. Then

$$T_k(x_1,\ldots,x_n) = maj_{2(n-k)}(x_1,\ldots,x_n,\underbrace{1,\ldots,1}_{n-2k}) \,.$$

If $k > n/2$, then

$$T_k(x_1,\ldots,x_n) = maj_{2k}(x_1,\ldots,x_n,\underbrace{0,\ldots,0}_{2k-n}).$$

We can also construct the Exact-k functions from the functions T_k. E_k is 1 if and only if exactly k of the x_i's have the value 1.

$$\begin{aligned} E_k(x_1,\ldots,x_n) &= T_k(x_1,\ldots,x_n) \wedge T_{n-k}(\overline{x_1},\ldots,\overline{x_n}) \\ &= T_k(x_1,\ldots,x_n) \wedge \overline{T_{k+1}(x_1,\ldots,x_n)} \,. \end{aligned}$$

Finally, we get the parity function via the following circuit of constant depth. (In the diagram below, assume that n is odd and that $x = (x_1,\ldots,x_n,\overline{x_1},\ldots,\overline{x_n})$.)

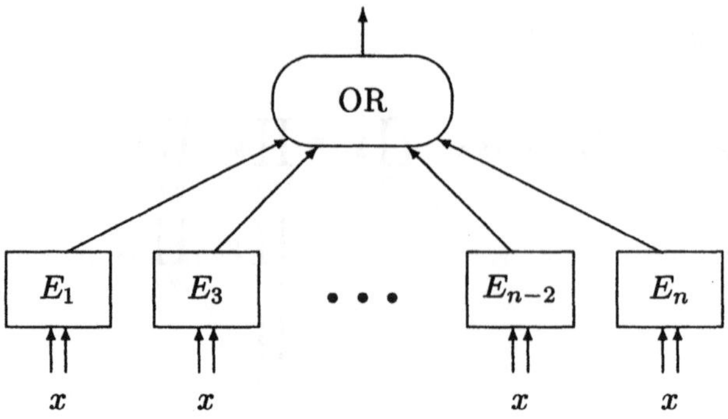

Analogous arguments can be used to show that *all* symmetric functions can be reduced to majority by AC^0-reductions.

12.16. If a_i is a boolean function in the variables $S \subsetneq \{x_1, \ldots, x_n\}$, $|S| < n$, then a_i can be written in (unabbreviated) disjunctive normal form. Then $a_i = 1$ if and only if *exactly one* clause of the disjunction is true. Since at most one clause is true, we can get rid of the disjunction and feed the outputs of the ANDs (weighted with the $w_i's$) directly into the threshold gate.

12.17. In polynomial p the monomials with i variables have coefficients $\beta_1, \ldots, \beta_{\binom{n}{i}}$. So every such monomial in polynomial q has coefficient $\sum_{i=1}^{\binom{n}{i}} \beta_i$.

13.1.

Let $x_1, \ldots, x_n$ be the common variables of F and G. We can give a truth table for H by first giving "simplified" truth tables for F and G that only consider the common variables $x_1, \ldots, x_n$. We place a value of 0 (or 1) in the truth table whenever the values assigned to $x_1, \ldots, x_n$ are already sufficient to determine the truth value of F or G. We place a ? when the value depends on the assignment to the remaining variables.

For formulas F and G, for which $F \rightarrow G$ not every combination of $0, 1, ?$ is possible. For example, the combination $F = ?$ and $G = ?$ is not possible, since this would mean that there exists an assignment (of all variables) that makes F true but G false, contradicting $F \rightarrow G$.

The following table shows all possible combinations of values for F and G along with the correct choice for the formula H. This demonstrates that a formula H exists.

F	H	G
0	0	0
0	0	?
0	0 or 1	1
1	1	1
?	1	1

See also

- G.S. Boolos, R.C. Jeffrey: *Computability and Logic*, Cambridge University Press, 2nd edition, 1980.

13.2. In order to be able to distinguish the encodings of occurrences of distinct variables we need a certain number of bits, and this number increases with the number of variables. With 1 bit we can distinguish at most 2 variables; with 2 bits, at most 4, etc. In order to write down m different variables, we need at least $\Omega(m \log m)$ bits. So in a formula coded with n bits, only $m = O(n/\log n)$ variables can occur.

13.3. Suppose an arbitrary assignment of all variables (x, y, and z variables) in F_n and G_n is given. If this assignment makes F_n true, $x \in A$, since F_n is a Cook formula for "$A \in \mathsf{NP}$." Since G_n is a Cook formula for "$\overline{A} \in \mathsf{NP}$," $G(x,z) = 0$ and $\neg G(x,z) = 1$. So $F_n \to \neg G_n$.

13.4. We must show that $x \in A \Leftrightarrow H_n(x) = 1$. If $x \in A$, then F_n is satisfiable. So there is an assignment to the x,y-variables with $F_n(x,y) = 1$. Since $F_n \to H_n$ $H_n(x) = 1$.

On the other hand, if $x \notin A$, then there is an assignment to the x,z-variables with $G_n(x,z) = 1$. Since $H_n \to \neg G_n$ (equivalently: $G_n \to \neg H_n$), $\neg H_n(x) = 1$, i.e., $H_n(x) = 0$. (In fact, we have $F_n \leftrightarrow \neg G_n$.)

13.5. Choose $A_1 = A$ and $A_2 = \overline{A}$.

13.6. Let $F_n(x,y)$ be the Cook formula for "$A_1 \in \mathsf{NP}$" and let $G_n(x,z)$ the Cook formula for "$A_2 \in \mathsf{NP}$." Since A_1 and A_2 are disjoint, $F_n \to \neg G_n$. If an interpolant of F_n and $\neg G_n$ has polynomial-size circuits (i.e., $\mathrm{int}(F_n, G_n)$ is polynomial in n), then A_1 and A_2 are PC-separable.

13.7. Suppose that the last two statements are false i.e., $\mathsf{NP} = \mathsf{coNP}$ and interpolants can be computed in polynomial time. We will show that $\mathsf{P} = \mathsf{NP}$. Since $\mathsf{NP} = \mathsf{coNP}$, both SAT and $\overline{SAT}$ are NP-complete. For SAT and $\overline{SAT}$ there are corresponding Cook formulas $F_n(x,y)$ and $G_n(x,z)$, and $F_n \to \neg G_n$. In polynomial time (in n) we can compute their interpolant $H_n(x)$, for which $x \in SAT \Leftrightarrow H_n(x) = 1$. From this it follows that $SAT \in \mathsf{P}$, so $\mathsf{P} = \mathsf{NP}$.

13.8. Consider the language

$$A = \{\langle H(x,y), a\rangle \mid H \text{ is a boolean formula and } a \text{ an assignment to the } x\text{-variables such that there is an assignment to the } y\text{-variables that makes } H \text{ true}\} .$$

This language A is in NP and has by hypothesis polynomial-size circuits. This means there is a sequence of circuits $c_1, c_2, \ldots$ of polynomial size such that

$$c_{|\langle H,a\rangle|}(\langle H,a\rangle) = 1 \iff \langle H,a\rangle \in A \iff \exists b\, H(a,b) = 1 .$$

Now let F and G be two formulas of length n with $F \to G$. ($F = F(x,y)$ and $G = G(x,z)$; i.e., x is the set of common variables.) Let c_F be a circuit (family) for A as above but with the first parameter fixed equal to F ($H = F$). Then $c_F(a) = 1 \iff \exists b\, F(a,b) = 1$. We claim that c_F is a circuit for an interpolant of F and G. It is clear that every assignment that satisfies F also makes $c_F = 1$. Now let a be an assignment such that $c_F(a) = 1$. Then there is an assignment b such that $F(a,b) = 1$. Since $F \to G$, it must be the case that for every assignment d, $G(a,d) = 1$. Thus $c_F \to G$.

14.1. Every branching in a branching program of the form

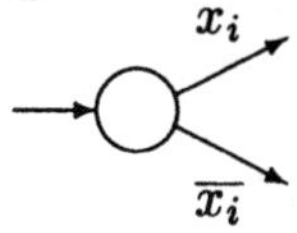

can be locally replaced with the following sub-circuit:

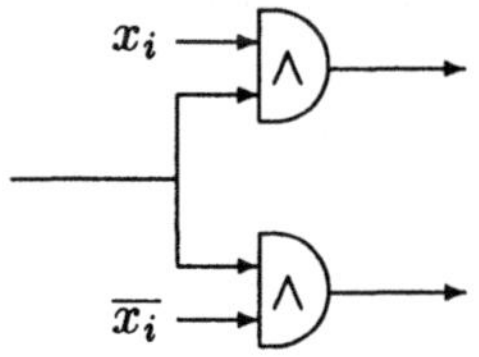

Finally, all connections that lead into an accepting node are joined together in one big OR-gate.

14.2. *BP-INEQ* $\in$ NP: The following describes a nondeterministic Turing machine M for *BP-INEQ*:

INPUT $\langle B, B'\rangle$;
GUESS $x_1, \ldots, x_n \in \{0,1\}$;
IF $B(x_1,\ldots,x_n) \neq B'(x_1,\ldots,x_n)$ **THEN ACCEPT**
  ELSE REJECT
END

BP-INEQ is NP-hard: The goal of this proof is to construct from a predicate logic formula, two branching programs that are inequivalent if and only if the formula is satisfiable. Consider an example: Let $F = (x_1 \vee \neg x_2 \vee x_4) \wedge (x_3 \vee x_2 \vee \neg x_1)$. This formula is satisfiable. From this we must construct a branching formula B_F with $B_F \equiv F$. B_F is made up of subgraphs that represent the individual clauses of F:

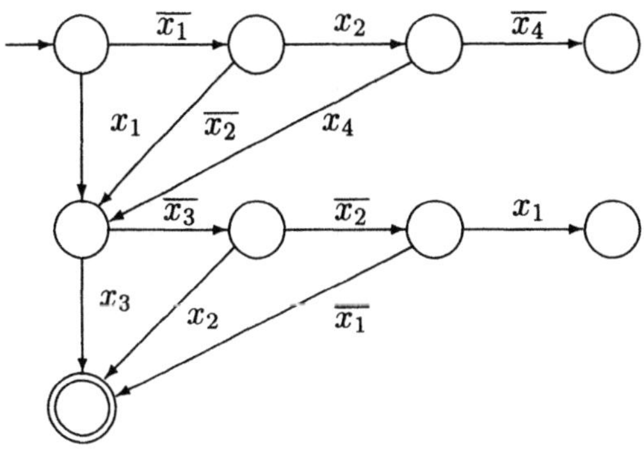

The second branching program will be a program B_U that computes the 0-function.

If $F \in SAT$, then there is an assignment on which B_F computes the value 1. Since B_U computes 0 on every input, these branching programs are inequivalent, i.e. $(B_F, B_U) \in$ *BP-INEQ*. On the other hand, if B_F and B_U are different, then there is an input on which B_F computes the value 1. Since $B_F \equiv F$ this is also a satisfying assignment for F. Altogether we have:

$$F \in SAT \iff (B_F, B_U) \in \textit{BP-INEQ} .$$

It is clear that from any formula in conjunctive normal form one can construct a branching program B_F. If F consists of k clauses, then B_F has at most $4k + 1$ nodes. The size of B_U is a constant for all inputs. For example, B_U could be a branching program that consists of a single rejecting terminal node. So the construction of B_F and B_U from the formula F can be carried out in polynomial time.

Note that the branching program B_F is not, in general, one-time-only and that this is significant for the proof.

14.3. The polynomials in the individual nodes are:

$$\begin{aligned}
p_1 &= 1 \\
p_2 &= x_1 \\
p_3 &= (1 - x_1) + x_1 x_2 + x_1(1 - x_2)x_3 \\
p_4 &= x_1(1 - x_2) \\
p_5 &= (1 - x_1)x_2 + x_1 x_2^2 + x_1(1 - x_2)x_2 x_3 \\
p_6 &= x_1(1 - x_2)(1 - x_3) + (1 - x_1)(1 - x_2) + \\
&\quad x_1 x_2(1 - x_2) + x_1(1 - x_2)^2 x_3 \\
p_B &= p_6
\end{aligned}$$

Truth table:

x_1	x_2	x_3	p_1	p_2	p_3	p_4	p_5	p_6	B
0	0	0	1	0	1	0	0	1	1
0	0	1	1	0	1	0	0	1	1
0	1	0	1	0	1	0	1	0	0
0	1	1	1	0	1	0	1	0	0
1	0	0	1	1	0	1	0	1	1
1	0	1	1	1	1	0	0	1	1
1	1	0	1	1	1	0	1	0	0
1	1	1	1	1	1	0	1	0	0

As one can see, $p_B = B$. Now we prove the claim:

Let $x_1, \ldots, x_n \in \{0,1\}$ and let V_m be the set of all nodes in B that are reachable from v_{start} in exactly m steps. Then for all $v \in V_m$:

$$p_v(x_1, \ldots, x_n) = \begin{cases} 1 & \text{if } v \text{ is reachable on the } m\text{th step} \\ & \text{of } B(x_1, \ldots, x_n), \\ 0 & \text{otherwise.} \end{cases}$$

Base case. $m = 0$: $\quad p_{v_{start}} = 1 \quad \checkmark$

Inductive step. Assume the claim is valid for all nodes that can be reached in $\leq m$ steps.

Let v be a node in B that is reached in step $m+1$ step of the computation and let the nodes $v_1, \ldots, v_l$ be the predecessors of v. Every assignment to $x_1, \ldots, x_n$ determines exactly how the branching program is traversed. v is reached in step $m+1$, then there is *exactly* one node v_i, $1 \leq i \leq l$, which was visited in the m-th step. By the inductive hypothesis, on input $x_1, \ldots, x_n$,

$$\begin{aligned} p_v = \alpha_1 \cdot \underbrace{p_{v_1}}_{=0} + \alpha_2 \cdot \underbrace{p_{v_2}}_{=0} + \ldots + \alpha_{i-1} \cdot \underbrace{p_{v_{i-1}}}_{=0} \\ + \alpha_i \cdot \underbrace{p_{v_i}}_{=1} + \alpha_{i+1} \cdot \underbrace{p_{v_{i+1}}}_{=0} + \ldots + \alpha_n \cdot \underbrace{p_{v_n}}_{=0} = \alpha_i \ . \end{aligned}$$

So the value of p_v is completely determined by α_i. There are two possibilities for the label of the edge (v_i, v):

- $x_j = 0$, in which case $p_v = \alpha_i = 1 - x_j = 1$.
- $x_j = 1$, in which case $p_v = \alpha_i = x_j = 1$.

Since every computation of B halts in some terminal node v_e after finitely many steps, $p_{v_e} = 1$. Finally, p_B is the sum of all polynomials of accepting terminal nodes so

$$p_B(x_1, \ldots, x_n) = B(x_1, \ldots, x_n) \ .$$

14.4. Consider the following counterexample: Here are two branching programs B_2 and B_2' for the function $f(x_1, x_2) = \neg x_1 \vee x_2$:

B_2: $p_{B_2}(x_1, x_2) = 1 - x_1 + x_1 x_2$

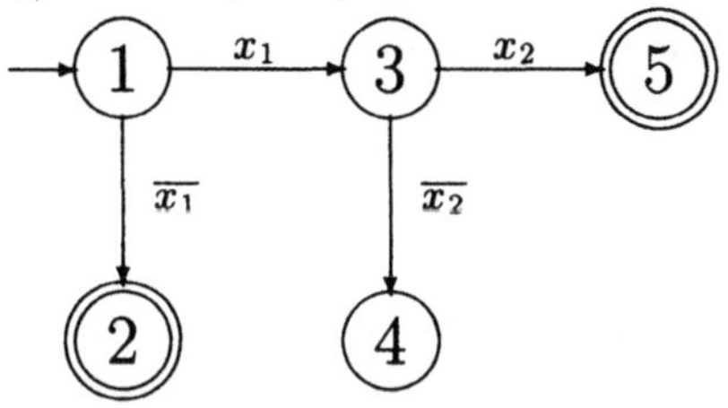

B_2': $p_{B_2'}(x_1, x_2) = 1 - x_1^2 + x_1^2 x_2$

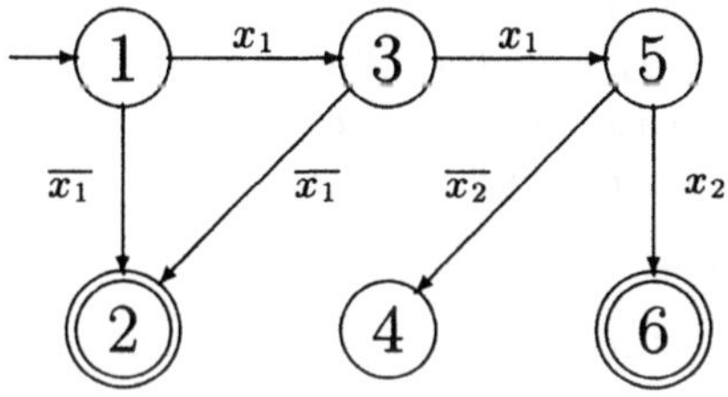

B_2 and B_2' are equivalent, but p_{B_2} and $p_{B_2'}$ are not identical: $p_{B_2}(3,0) \neq p_{B_2'}(3,0)$.

14.5. The proof is by induction on the number of variables, n.

If $n = 1$, then p and q are lines. If they are not identical, then they can only intersect in one point, so they must be different in at least $|S| - 1$ points.

Now suppose $n > 1$. Then

$$\begin{aligned} p(x_1, \ldots, x_n) &= \sum_{i_1=0}^{1} \cdots \sum_{i_n=0}^{1} a_{i_1,\ldots,i_n} \cdot x_1^{i_1} \cdot \ldots \cdot x_n^{i_n} \\ &= \underbrace{x_1^0}_{=1} \cdot \underbrace{\left(\sum_{i_2=0}^{1} \cdots \sum_{i_n=0}^{1} a_{0,i_2,\ldots,i_n} \cdot x_2^{i_2} \cdot \ldots \cdot x_n^{i_n} \right)}_{=: p_0(x_2,\ldots,x_n)} \\ &\quad + x_1^1 \cdot \underbrace{\left(\sum_{i_2=0}^{1} \cdots \sum_{i_n=0}^{1} a_{1,i_2,\ldots,i_n} \cdot x_2^{i_2} \cdot \ldots \cdot x_n^{i_n} \right)}_{=: p_1(x_2,\ldots,x_n)} \\ &= p_0(x_2, \ldots, x_n) + x_1 \cdot p_1(x_2, \ldots, x_n) \,. \end{aligned}$$

Analogously, $q(x_1, \ldots, x_n) = q_0(x_2, \ldots, x_n) + x_1 \cdot q_1(x_2, \ldots, x_n)$.

Since $p \neq q$, either $p_0 \neq q_0$ or $p_1 \neq q_1$. First we handle the case when $p_1 \neq q_1$. By the inductive hypothesis, p_1 and q_1 differ on at least $(|S| - 1)^{n-1}$

points. We will show that for every $(x_2, \ldots, x_n)$ there is at most one choice for x_1 such that p and q are equal on the input $(x_1, x_2, \ldots, x_n)$. Solving the equation

$$p_0(x_2, \ldots, x_n) + x_1 \cdot p_1(x_2, \ldots, x_n) = q_0(x_2, \ldots, x_n) + x_1 \cdot q_1(x_2, \ldots, x_n)$$

for x_1 we get:

$$x_1 = \frac{p_0(x_2, \ldots, x_n) - q_0(x_2, \ldots, x_n)}{q_1(x_2, \ldots, x_n) - p_1(x_2, \ldots, x_n)},$$

which is only a solution if the value is in S. There are at least $|S| - 1$ choices for x_1, which lead to different values of p and q. So altogether there are at least $(|S| - 1) \cdot (|S| - 1)^{n-1} = (|S| - 1)^n$ choices for $(x_1, \ldots, x_n)$ that lead to different values of p and q.

If $p_1 = q_1$, but $p_0 \neq q_0$, then the value of x_1 doesn't matter for the equality of p and q. So in this case there are actually at least $|S|(|S| - 1)^{n-1}$ values for $(x_1, \ldots, x_n)$ that make p and q different.

14.6. Let $S = \{0, 1\}$ in Theorem 14.2.

14.7. The polynomials p_B and $p_{B'}$ from one-time-only branching programs are multi-linear. By Exercise 14.3, they must agree on all values in $\{0, 1\}^n = S^n$. By the previous exercise it follows that $p_B = p_{B'}$.

14.8. B and B' are equivalent, so $p_B = p_{B'}$ for all $x_1, \ldots, x_n \in \{1, \ldots, 2n\}$. Thus $Pr[M(B, B') \text{ rejects}] = 1$

14.9. Let p be the probability that the algorithm accepts. By Theorem 14.2,

$$p \geq \frac{(|S| - 1)^n}{|S|^n} = \frac{(2n - 1)^n}{(2n)^n} = (1 - \frac{1}{2n})^n \geq \frac{1}{2}.$$

More precisely, it can be shown that $\lim_{n \to \infty}(1 - \frac{1}{2n})^n = \sqrt{\frac{1}{e}} = 0.6065\ldots$.

14.10. We will describe a reduction that maps each boolean formula F in conjunctive normal form to two one-time-only branching programs B_1 and B_2, such that F is satisfiable if and only if there is an argument tuple $\boldsymbol{y}$ with $f_{B_1}(\boldsymbol{y}) = 1$ and $f_{B_2}(\boldsymbol{y}) = 0$. Expressed differently: F is unsatisfiable if and only if $f_{B_1}(\boldsymbol{y}) \leq f_{B_2}(\boldsymbol{y})$ for all $\boldsymbol{y}$.

Let F be a CNF-formula with k clauses and in which the n variables $x_1, \ldots, x_n$ occur. The variable set $\boldsymbol{y}$ for each of the branching programs is

$$\begin{matrix} y_{11} & \cdots & y_{1k} \\ y_{21} & \cdots & y_{2k} \\ & \ddots & \\ y_{n1} & \cdots & y_{nk} \end{matrix}$$

The (intended) connection between a satisfying assignment $\boldsymbol{x} = (x_1, \ldots, x_n)$ for F and an assignment $\boldsymbol{y} = (y_{11}, \ldots, y_{nk})$, for which $B_1(\boldsymbol{y}) = 1$ and $B_2(\boldsymbol{y}) = 0$ is the following:

$$x_i = 1 \Rightarrow \begin{cases} y_{ij} = 1 & \text{if } x_i \text{ occurs in clause } j, \\ y_{ij} = 0 & \text{otherwise;} \end{cases}$$

$$x_i = 0 \Rightarrow \begin{cases} y_{ij} = 1 & \text{if } \neg x_i \text{ occurs in clause } j, \\ y_{ij} = 0 & \text{otherwise.} \end{cases}$$

The basic construction of B_1 is indicated in the following sketch:

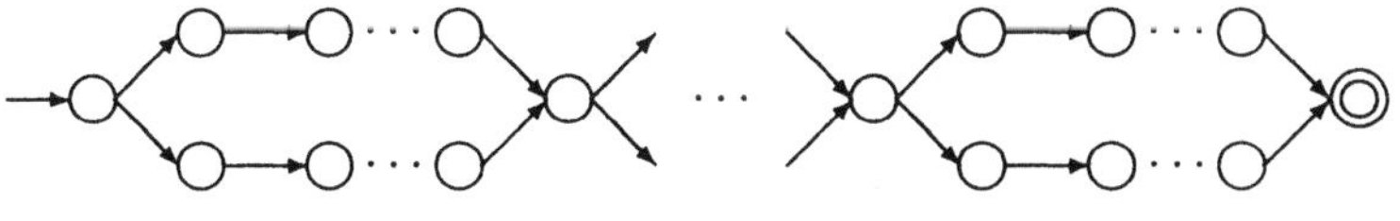

Undrawn edges are to be understood as leading to a rejecting terminal node. For every $i = 1, \ldots, n$, there are two separate paths between the connecting nodes. The k edges on the upper path are labeled with y_{ij} ($j = 1, \ldots, k$) if x_i occurs in clause j, otherwise with $\overline{y_{ij}}$. The labels on the lower path are determined analogously, but with $\neg x_i$ playing the role that x_i played in the upper path.

For example, the formula

$$F = (x_1 \vee \neg x_2) \wedge (x_2) \wedge (\neg x_1 \vee \neg x_2)$$

maps to the following branching program B_1:

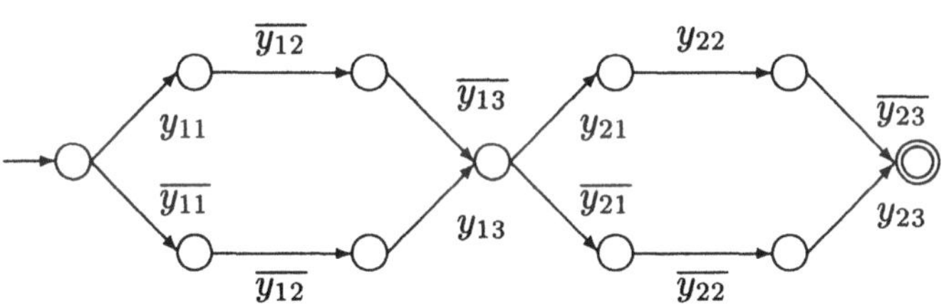

Clearly, there are 2^n paths from the start node to the accepting terminal node. And since the branching program is one-time-only, there are 2^n assignments to y for which $B_1(y) = 1$. These assignments can be assigned to 2^n original assignments for x as described above.

Every satisfying assignment for F corresponds to an assignment to y with the property that, in the arrangement of the y_{ij}'s illustrated above, every column contains a 1. The following branching program B_2 will describe all y-assignments except those that correspond to satisfying assignments to F in this way, that is all assignments for which there is some column with no 1's in it.

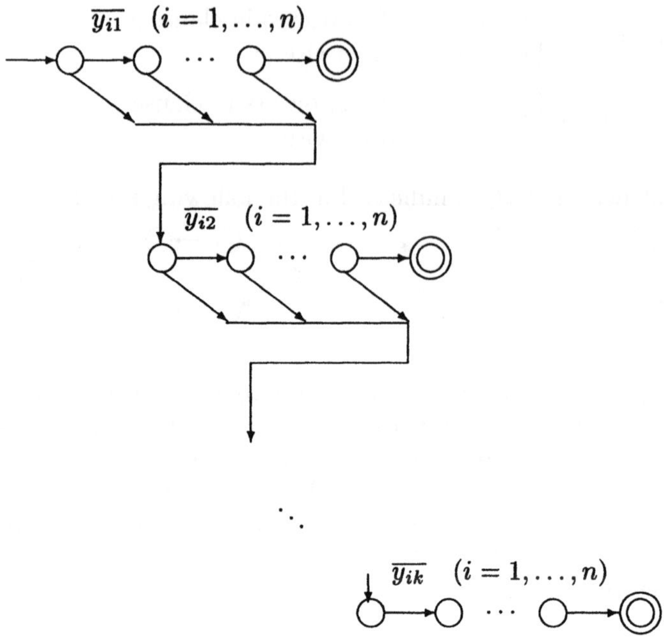

Notice that B_2 only depends on k and n, and not on the inner structure of F itself.

For example, the formula F from above, for which $k = 3$ and $n = 2$, results in the following branching program B_2:

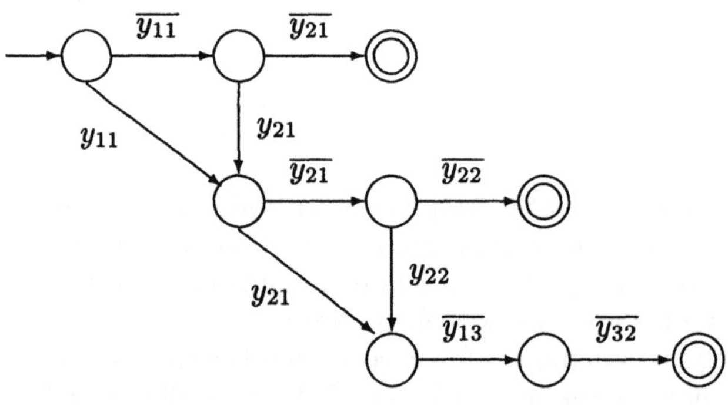

Now F is satisfiable if and only if there is an assignment y with $B_1(y) > B_2(y)$, so the inclusion problem for one-time-only branching programs is coNP-complete.

14.11. This is because f is *critical*, that is, for ever x with $f(x) = 1$ and every x' that differs from x in any bit, $f(x') = 0$. So if some path in the branching program accepts x but does not query every bit, then that path cannot distinguish between x and x', and will incorrectly accept x'. This contradicts the assumption that B correctly computes the function f.

14.12. Suppose $k(\boldsymbol{x}) = k(\boldsymbol{x}')$. Since the polynomials associated with $\boldsymbol{x}$ and $\boldsymbol{x}'$ are different, by the Interpolation Theorem, this difference must show itself in any $n/3$ queries that are answered yes, since each such determines a point on the polynomial. So the $\boldsymbol{x}$-path and the $\boldsymbol{x}'$-path must be different both above and below $k(\boldsymbol{x}) = k(\boldsymbol{x}')$:

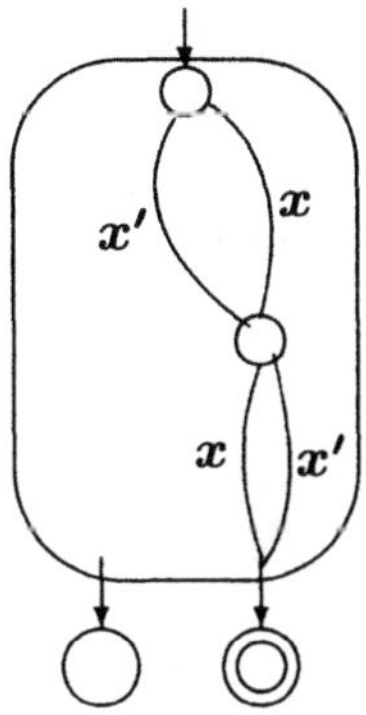

By following the $\boldsymbol{x}$-path above $k(\boldsymbol{x})$ and the $\boldsymbol{x}'$-path below, we get a new accepting path, corresponding to an assignment $\hat{\boldsymbol{x}}$ for which $f(\hat{\boldsymbol{x}}) = 1$. This in turn corresponds to another polynomial in $\mathcal{POL}$. (There can be no conflicting definitions for $\hat{\boldsymbol{x}}$ since B is one-time-only.) But this is impossible, since the polynomials corresponding to $\boldsymbol{x}$ and $\hat{\boldsymbol{x}}$ cannot be equal in $n/2 \geq n/3$ places and different in others.

15.1. If P = NP, then all languages (except for $\emptyset$ and Σ^*) in NP are also NP-complete. In particular, all finite sets are NP-complete. But an infinite language such as *SAT* can not be isomorphic (and, therefore, certainly not P-isomorphic) to a finite language.

15.2. Let x be a boolean formula and let $y = y_1 y_2 \dots y_k$ be an arbitrary string (WLOG over $\{0,1\}^*$). Now let

$$p_{SAT}(x,y) = x \wedge (z \vee \neg z) \wedge u^{y_1} \wedge \cdots \wedge u^{y_k} \ ,$$

where $z, u_1, \dots, u_k$ are new variables that do not occur in x, y^0 means y and y^1 means $\neg y$. It is clear that p_A is polynomial-time computable and that this formula is satisfiable if and only if x is satisfiable. Furthermore, the formula is longer than $|x| + |y|$. Injectivity in argument y is also clear, and from a formula $p_A(x,y)$ as above it is easy to reconstruct y. (This is the reason for the variable z – it allows us to detect where the y part of the formula begins.) So d_A also exists as required.

15.3. Let $A \leq_m^P B$ via f and $B \leq_m^P A$ via g. Now put

$$f'(x) = p_B(f(x), x) \text{ and } g'(x) = p_A(g(x), x) \ .$$

By the properties of p_A and p_B f' and g' are correct polynomial-time computable reductions from A to B and from B to A, respectively. Furthermore,

$|f'(x)| > |f(x)| + |x| \geq |x|$ and $|g'(x)| > |g(x)| + |x| \geq |x|$. The inverse functions for f' and g' are d_B and d_A and are therefore polynomial-time computable.

15.4. Let $A \leq_m^P B$ via the injective function f and $B \leq_m^P A$ via the injective function g. Furthermore, suppose that $|f(x)| > |x|$, $|g(x)| > |x|$, and that the functions f^{-1} and g^{-1} are polynomial-time computable. We need to define a bijective function h that is a reduction from A to B. For the definition of $h(x)$ there are essentially two choices available: $f(x)$ or $g^{-1}(x)$. (Of course, the latter choice only exists if x is in the range of g.)

Sketch:

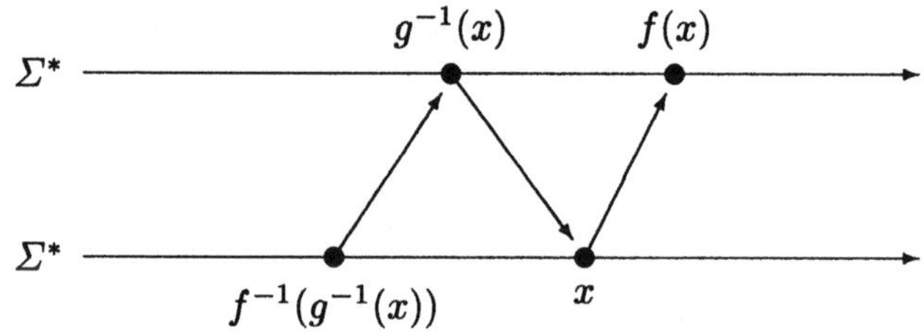

By applying the functions g^{-1} and f^{-1} we can proceed in a zig-zag manner backwards from x until we arrive at a string that is not in the range of g or f, respectively. (In the example above $f^{-1}(g^{-1}(x))$ is no longer in the range of g, so the zig-zag chain ends on the lower line.) Now define

$$h(x) := \begin{cases} f(x), & \text{if the chain starting with } x \text{ ends on the lower line} \\ g^{-1}(x), & \text{if the chain starting with } x \text{ ends on the upper line} \end{cases}$$

Since the functions f and g are length-increasing, no zig-zag chain can be longer than $|x|$, so h can be computed in polynomial time.

Next we must show that h is a bijection. For the proof of injectivity, let x and y be distinct strings such that $h(x) = h(y)$. Since f is injective, this can only happen if $h(x) = f(x)$ and $h(y) = g^{-1}(y)$ (or vice versa). But then x and y are in the same zig-zag chain and the definition of h would either have used f both times or g^{-1} both times. This is a contradiction.

For the proof of surjectivity, let z be an arbitrary string. We must show that z is in the range of h. Consider a zig-zag chain starting at z (in the upper line). If this chain ends in the upper line (including the case that z is not in the range of f), then for $x = g(z)$, $h(x) = g^{-1}(x) = z$. If the chain ends in the lower line, then $x = f^{-1}(z)$ must exist and $h(x) = z$.

The inverse function for h is also bijective and can be defined using a similar case distinction, so it is also polynomial-time computable.

15.5. Let y be the encoding of some satisfiable formula φ_y, and let $l = |y|$. For any x, the formula

$$\psi(x) = \varphi_y \wedge (x \vee \neg x)$$

is also satisfiable. Let $f(x)$ be the encoding of $\psi(x)$ as a string. Then under a reasonable encoding scheme, $|f(x)| \leq |y|+4|x|+k = 4|x|+l+k = 4|x|+C$, for some constants k and C. Thus there are at least 2^m strings of length $4m+C$ in SAT, i.e., for large enough n, there are at least $2^{(n-C)/4} = 2^{-C/4}2^{n/4}$ strings of length at most n in SAT.

15.6. By the previous exercise, SAT contains at least $\varepsilon 2^{\delta n}$ strings of length n for some constants $\delta > 0$ and $\varepsilon > 0$. If SAT were P-isomorphic to a language S, where S contained only $\leq p(n)$ strings of length at most n, then there would be a bijective function f mapping SAT to S. Since f is polynomial-time computable there must be a polynomial q such that $|f(x)| \leq q(|x|)$. From this we get the following contradiction: f maps $2^{\delta n}$ strings injectively into $p(q(n))$ possible range elements.

15.7. $SAT \leq_m^P LeftSAT$ via the reduction $F \mapsto (F, \lambda)$.

$LeftSAT \leq_m^P SAT$ via the reduction $(F, a_1 \dots a_i) \mapsto F(x_1, \dots, x_n) \wedge (a_1 \dots a_i \leq^* x_1 \dots x_n)$, where the formula $(a_1 \dots a_i \leq^* x_1 \dots x_n)$ is defined as follows: Let $E = \{j \in \{1, \dots, i\} \mid a_j = 1\}$ and $N = \{j \in \{1, \dots, i\} \mid a_j = 0\}$. Then

$$(a_1 \dots a_i \leq^* x_1 \dots x_n) = \bigwedge_{j \in E} \left(x_j \vee \bigvee_{l \in N, l<j} x_l \right) .$$

Another way to show that $LeftSAT \leq_m^P SAT$ is simply to observe that $LeftSAT$ is in NP and that SAT is NP-complete.

15.8. Let $b_1 \dots b_i$ be an initial segment of b, which we assume by induction belongs to T. By the construction of U, $b_1 \dots b_i 0$ and $b_1 \dots b_i 1$ are added to U, so the correct initial section of b of length $i+1$ – let's call it b' – is in U.

If (F, b') has the same g-value as some other string in U, then the smaller of the two is stricken, but this cannot be b', since it is the largest element of U for which $(F, b') \in LeftSAT$ and g is a correct reduction. So after the first reduction of U, each string in U has a distinct g-value, and b' is among them. If U contains more than $m = p(q(|F|))$ strings, then U is restricted to the first m of these. But this must include b', since at most m possible values of g are available for elements of $LeftSAT$ (including (F, b')):

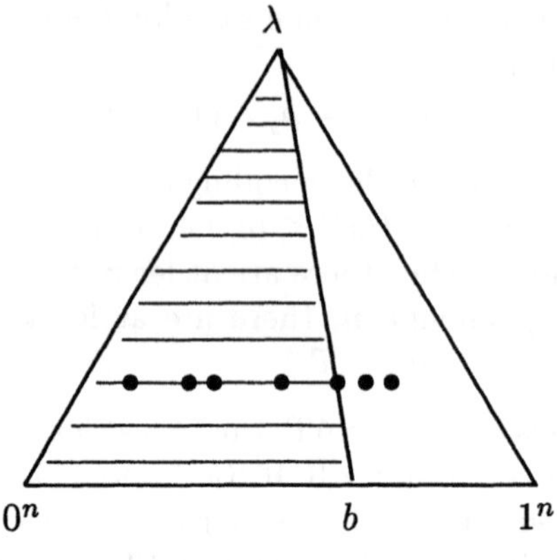

The sketch above shows a possible distribution of the strings in U following the first reduction step.

16.1. Suppose $\Sigma_i^P = \Pi_i^P$. Let $L \in \Sigma_{i+1}^P$. Then there is a language $L' \in \Pi_i^P$ with

$$L = \{x \mid \exists y \, \langle x, y \rangle \in L'\} .$$

By assumption, L' is also in Σ_i^P. Let

$$L' = \{\langle x, y \rangle \mid \exists z_1 \forall z_2 \ldots Q z_i \, \langle x, z_1, \ldots, z_i \rangle \in A\} ,$$

where A is a language in P. Then we have

$$\begin{aligned} L &= \{x \mid \exists y \, \langle x, y \rangle \in L'\} \\ &= \{x \mid \exists y \exists z_1 \forall z_2 \ldots Q z_i \, \langle x, y, z_1, \ldots, z_i \rangle \in A\} \\ &= \{x \mid \exists u \forall z_2 \ldots Q z_i \, [u = \langle y, z_1 \rangle \wedge \langle x, y, z_1, \ldots, z_i \rangle \in A]\} . \end{aligned}$$

The expression in square brackets is a predicate in P, so L in Σ_i^P.

Now suppose that $\Sigma_i^P = \Sigma_{i+1}^P$. We show by induction on k that for all $k \geq 1$, $\Sigma_i^P = \Sigma_{i+k}$. From this it follows that $\mathsf{PH} = \Sigma_i^P$. The base case of the induction is clear. For the induction step let L be a language in Σ_{i+k+1}^P. Then for some language $L' \in \Pi_{i+k}^P$,

$$L = \{x \mid \exists y \, \langle x, y \rangle \in L'\} .$$

By the inductive hypothesis $\overline{L'} \in \Sigma_i^P$, so $L' \in \Pi_i^P$. From this it follows that $L \in \Sigma_{i+1}^P$. By assumption $\Sigma_{i+1}^P = \Sigma_i^P$, so $L \in \Sigma_i^P$.

Finally, suppose $\mathsf{PH} = \Sigma_i^P$. Since $\Pi_i^P \subseteq \mathsf{PH}$ it is immediate that $\Pi_i^P \subseteq \Sigma_i^P$, so $\Pi_i^P = \Sigma_i^P$.

16.2. Choose a language over the one-element alphabet $\{1\}$ that is not in P. This language has polynomial-size circuits (for each n design a circuit that on input 1^n outputs either 1 or 0 according to whether or not $1^n \in L$). Such a language L that is not in P (in fact, not even computable) can be easily defined by diagonalization, for example

$$L = \{1^n \mid \text{the } n\text{-th polynomial-time machine on input } 1^n, \text{ does not accept}\} .$$

16.3. If L has polynomial-size circuits then the corresponding circuits $c_1, c_2, c_3, \ldots$ can be coded in a sparse set:

$$S = \{\langle 1^n, y\rangle \mid y \text{ is an initial segment of } c_n\} .$$

With this language as oracle, we can use polynomially many oracle queries to reconstruct the circuit $c_{|x|}$ and then simulate the circuit on x.

On the other hand, if $L \in \mathsf{P}^S$ for some sparse set S, then the configuration transition of the Turing machine can be suitably coded into a circuit, demonstrating the L has polynomial-size circuits. Details of this can be found in

- U. Schöning: *Complexity and Structure*, Springer, 1986.
- I. Wegener: *The Complexity of Boolean Functions*, Teubner-Wiley, 1987.
- J. Köbler, U. Schöning, J. Torán: *The Graph Isomorphism Problem: Its Structural Complexity*, Birkhäuser, 1993.

16.4. Self-reducibility of *SAT* means that can find a witness (a satisfying assignment) for a formula $F \in SAT$ by recursively testing other formulas for membership in *SAT* in the following manner: To determine the value of a variable x in a satisfying assignment for F temporarily assign it the value 1. This produces a new formula with fewer variables. If this formula is satisfiable, then there is a satisfying assignment for F in which $x = 1$, else we try $x = 0$. By this same recursive procedure we get a satisfying assignment for the modified formula with $x = 1$ or $x = 0$. This combined with $x = 0$ is a satisfying assignment for F.

Now we want to design a circuit that realizes this method. Suppose we are given polynomial-size circuits for *SAT*. We will use the following notation for these circuits:

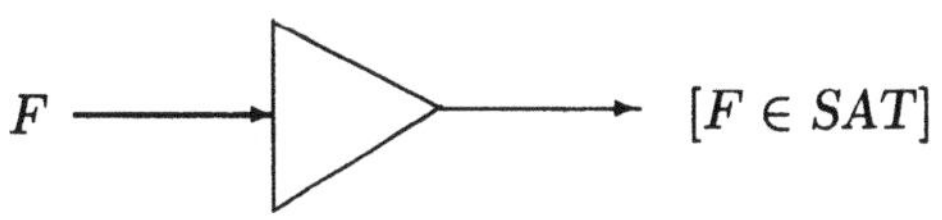

The thick lines indicate a bus of wires. The input to this circuit is the formula F, coded as binary string, and the (single) output is 1 if and only if $F \in SAT$.

We also need another simply-constructed, polynomial-size circuit, which we will denote by

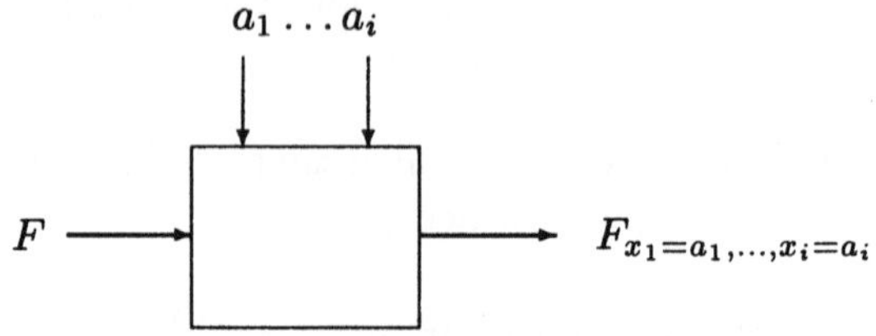

This circuit has $n+i$ inputs and (WLOG) n outputs. The inputs to this circuit are the encoding of F and i additional bits $a_1, \ldots, a_i$. The output is an encoding of the formula that results from substituting the values $a_1, \ldots a_i$ into the formula F for the variables $x_1, \ldots, x_i$. The details of this circuit depend on the encoding used for formulas.

The desired witness circuit is built as follows:

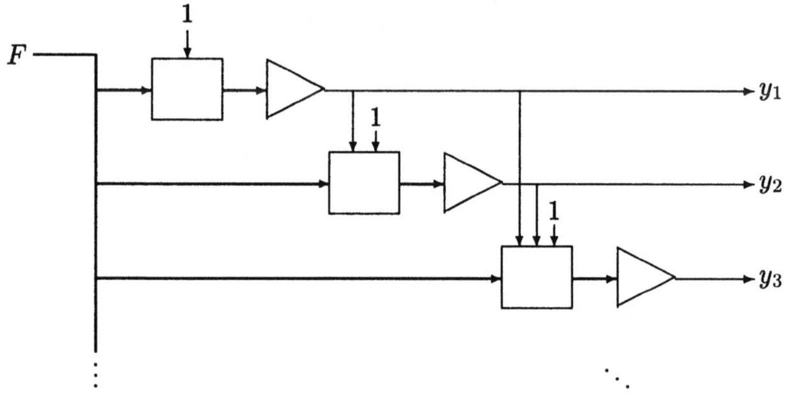

16.5. ($\subseteq$) Let $x \in L$. Then for every y, the formula $f(\langle x, y \rangle)$ is satisfiable. Choose for c the appropriate polynomial-size witness circuit for SAT, which exists by the assumption and the previous exercise. Then c will produce a satisfying assignment for every input $F = f(\langle x, y \rangle) \in SAT$.

($\supseteq$) If $y = c(f(\langle x, y \rangle))$ is a satisfying assignment for $F = f(\langle x, y \rangle)$, then F is satisfiable (regardless of how y came to be).

16.6. It is clear that all languages in BH_i, $i = 1, 2, 3, \ldots$ are contained in BH. For the reverse direction, let L be a language in BH. Then there is a finite expression that represents the application of the intersection, union, and complement operators used to build L. We will show by induction on the structure of this expression that L is in BH_k for some $k \geq 1$. By DeMorgan's laws we can bring all complement operations to the "inside" of the expression, so that we only need to consider intersection and union over NP and coNP languages. All NP and coNP languages are in BH_2. Furthermore, observe that all languages in BH_k with k even can be expressed in the form

$$A = (A_1 - A_2) \cup (A_3 - A_4) \cup \cdots \cup (A_{k-1} - A_k) ,$$

where each A_i is a language in NP. It only remains to show that the intersection of any two such languages A and A' can again be expressed in this form. Now we can apply the distributive law to "multiply out" the expression and use the equivalence

$$(A_i - A_{i+1}) \cap (A'_j - A'_{j+1}) = (A_i \cap A'_j) - (A_{i+1} \cup A'_{j+1})$$

and the fact that NP is closed under intersection and union to see that the result has the desired form. (This result is due to Hausdorff (1928)).

17.1. Let M be a probabilistic algorithm for "$L \in$ RP," and let M' be a probabilistic algorithm for "$\overline{L} \in$ RP." Then the following algorithm has the desired behavior:

INPUT x;
Simulate M on x; let the result be $y \in \{0,1\}$;
Simulate M' on x; let the result be $y' \in \{0,1\}$;
IF $(y = 1)$ **AND** $(y' = 0)$ **THEN ACCEPT**
ELSE IF $(y = 0)$ **AND** $(y' = 1)$ **THEN REJECT**
ELSE OUTPUT "don't know"

In the other direction, from an algorithm of the type given above (with three possible outcomes: accept, reject, or don't know) we can get an RP-algorithm for L (or for $\overline{L}$) by making the following modifications to the algorithm:

- In the first case, to show $L \in$ RP: "don't know" becomes "reject."
- In the second case, to show $L \notin$ RP: "don't know" and "accept" become "reject," and "reject" becomes "accept."

17.2. Let $L \in$ ZPP. Then L can be computed by a polynomial time-bounded probabilistic machine M_0 as in the previous exercise. We use this machine as a sub-program in the following machine M_1:

INPUT x;
REPEAT
  $y :=$ result of simulation of M_0 on x;
UNTIL $y \neq$ "don't know";
IF $y =$ accept **THEN ACCEPT**
  ELSE REJECT END

Let ε be the (least) probability that the machine M_0 gives a definite answer (accept or reject). The expected number of passes through the repeat-until loop of M_1 is then

$$\sum_{i=1}^{\infty} \varepsilon \cdot (1-\varepsilon)^{i-1} \cdot i \;=\; \frac{1}{\varepsilon}\,.$$

So the expected running time is polynomial. In fact, expected running time would still be polynomial even if ε were dependent on n in such a way that $\varepsilon = \varepsilon(n) = \Omega(\frac{1}{n^k})$.

In the other direction, let M be the algorithm with expected polynomial running time $p(n)$.

By Markov's inequality, the probability that the running time is actually more than $2p(n)$ (twice the expected running time) is at most $1/2$ (otherwise the "slow" running times would already force the expected running time to be more than $p(n)$). So if we simulate M for $2p(n)$ steps, we get an algorithm of the type in the preceding exercise, with a probability constant of $1/2$, i.e. our new algorithm answers "don't know" whenever M has not answered with "accept" or "reject" within $2p(n)$ steps.

17.3. The probability that we fail to get acceptance t times (provided the input is in L) is at most $(1-\varepsilon)^t$. If we want $(1-\varepsilon)^t \leq 2^{-n}$, we see that $t \geq \frac{-n}{\log_2(1-\varepsilon)} = \Omega(\frac{n}{\varepsilon})$ is sufficient.

17.4. If we repeat a Bernoulli trial t times independently, where each of the trials has a probability γ of success, and let X be a random variable that counts the number of successes, then the following approximations are valid for $r \geq 0$:

$$Pr[X - t\gamma \geq r] \leq e^{-r^2/(4t\gamma(1-\gamma))} \leq e^{-r^2/t} ,$$

and

$$Pr[t\gamma - X \geq r] \leq e^{-r^2/(4t\gamma(1-\gamma))} \leq e^{-r^2/t} ,$$

since $\gamma(1-\gamma) \leq 1/4$. Derivations of these (or similar) approximations can be found in many places, for example in

- N. Alon, J.H. Spencer: *The Probabilistic Method*, Wiley, 1992, 233ff.
- H. Chernoff: A measure of the asymptotic efficiency for tests of a hypothesis based on the sum of observations, *Annals of Mathematical Statistics* 23 (1952), 493–509.
- Cormen, Leiserson, Rivest: *Introduction to Algorithms*, MIT Press, 1990, 121ff.
- T. Hagerup, C. Rüb: A guided tour of Chernoff bounds, *Information Processing Letters* 33 (1989/90), 305–308.
- E. Kranakis: *Primality and Cryptography*, Wiley-Teubner, 1986, 91ff.
- C. Papadimitriou: *Computational Complexity*, Addison-Wesley, 1994, 258ff.
- E.M. Palmer: *Graphical Evolution*, Wiley, 1985, 133ff.
- P.E. Pfeiffer: *Concepts of Probability Theory*, Dover, 1978, 281ff.

Applying these inequalities in our case yields:

$$\sum_{i=0}^{\alpha t} \binom{t}{i} \cdot \gamma^i \cdot (1-\gamma)^{t-i} = Pr[X - \alpha t \geq \varepsilon t/2] \leq e^{-\varepsilon^2 t/4} \leq 2^{-\Omega(t)} .$$

To get an error probability of 2^{-n}, we must choose $t \geq (c/\varepsilon^2) \cdot n$ where c is a suitable constant.

The approximations in the case $x \notin L$ are similar:

$$\sum_{i=\alpha t}^{t} \binom{t}{i} \cdot \delta^i \cdot (1-\delta)^{t-i} = Pr[\alpha t - X \geq \varepsilon t/2] \leq e^{-\varepsilon^2 t/4} \leq 2^{-\Omega(t)} ,$$

where $\delta = \alpha - \varepsilon/2$.

17.5. Deterministic polynomial time computations (with a fixed input length) can be transformed into polynomial-size circuits. (Details can be found in the book by Köbler, Schöning, and Torán.) If we fix a fortunate choice of the random variable z, then our probabilistic algorithm becomes a deterministic algorithm and we can apply the same principle to construct polynomial-size circuits.

17.6. (For an explanation of self-reducibility, see Topic 16, the book by Köbler, Schöning, and Torán.)

Let M be a BPP-algorithm for SAT, which we are assuming exists. After probability amplification, assume the error rate is at most 2^{-n}. Now to show that $SAT \in$ RP we use the following probabilistic algorithm (the only probabilistic part is the use of M as a sub-routine). The algorithm makes use of an array $a_1, \ldots, a_n$ of bit values.

INPUT $F(x_1, \ldots, x_n)$; (F is a formula in the variables $x_1, \ldots, x_n$)
FOR $i := 1$ **TO** n **DO**
  IF $M(F(a_1, \ldots, a_{i-1}, 1, x_{i+1}, \ldots, x_n)) = 1$ **THEN** $a_i := 1$
  ELSE $a_i := 0$ **END**
END;
IF $F(a_1, \ldots, a_n) = 1$ **THEN ACCEPT**
  ELSE REJECT END

If $F \notin SAT$, then this algorithm will always reject. If $F \in SAT$, then with probability at least $(1-2^{-n})^n \geq 1/2$ a satisfying assignment $a_1 \ldots a_n$ for F is constructed by the algorithm, which causes it to accept. So this algorithm demonstrates that $SAT \in$ RP.

17.7. Let x and y be arbitrary distinct element from $\{0,1\}^r$. Then

$$\begin{aligned} & Pr[h(x) = h(y)] \\ &= \sum_{z \in \{0,1\}^s} Pr[h(x) = z \wedge h(y) = z] \end{aligned}$$

$$\begin{aligned}
&= \sum_{u\in[0,p-1]} \sum_{u'} Pr[(ax+b) \bmod p = u \wedge (ay+b) \bmod p = u'] \\
&\le p \cdot \lceil p/2^s \rceil \cdot \frac{1}{p^2} \\
&\le (p/2^s + 1) \cdot 1/p \\
&= 1/2^s + 1/p \\
&\le 1/2^s + 1/2^r \,.
\end{aligned}$$

Here the last sum runs over all $u' \in [0, p-1]$ with $u' \equiv u \pmod{2^s}$.

17.8. Let $h_1, h_2 \in H$ and $x_1, x_2 \in X$ be chosen uniformly at random We need an upper bound for $Pr[(h_1, h_1(x_1)) = (h_2, h_2(x_2))]$, i.e for $Pr[h_1 = h_2 \wedge h_1(x_1) = h_2(x_2)]$. This is exactly $1/|H|$ multiplied by $Pr[h(x_1) = h(x_2)]$, where $h \in H$ and $x_1, x_2 \in X$ are chosen at random. If $x_1 \neq x_2$, then this probability – by the definition of almost universal – is at most $1/2^s + 1/2^r$. Since $|X| \ge 2^l$, the probability for $x_1 = x_2$ is at most $1/2^l$. So we can give an upper bound of

$$\frac{1}{|H|} \cdot (1/2^s + 1/2^r + 1/2^l) \le (1 + 2/2^{2e}) \cdot \frac{1}{|H| 2^s} \,.$$

17.9. Let X be the set of 0-1 sequences of length k with not more than $k/2$ 1's. Let D be a distribution that is ε-similar to the $(p, 1-p)$ distribution (of length k), and let E be the "correct" $(p, 1-p)$-distribution. We approximate as follows:

$$\begin{aligned}
Pr_D(X) &\le Pr_E(X) + \varepsilon \\
&= \sum_{i=0}^{k/2} \binom{k}{i} p^i (1-p)^{k-i} + \varepsilon \\
&\le 2^{-\Omega(k)} + \varepsilon \,.
\end{aligned}$$

So it must be that $\varepsilon = 2^{-\Omega(k)}$.

17.10. Let X be an arbitrary set of 0-1 strings. Then

$$\begin{aligned}
&|Pr[t(F) \in X] - Pr[H \in X]| \\
&\le |Pr[t(F) \in X] - Pr[t(G) \in X]| + |Pr[t(G) \in X] - Pr[H \in X]| \\
&\le |Pr[t(F) \in X] - Pr[t(G) \in X]| + \delta_2 \\
&\le |Pr[F \in t^{-1}(X)] - Pr[G \in t^{-1}(X)]| + \delta_2 \\
&\le \delta_1 + \delta_2 \,.
\end{aligned}$$

18.1. If for every language $A \in \mathsf{C}$ gilt, the language $\{\langle x, y\rangle \mid x \in A,\ y \in \Sigma^*\} \in \mathsf{C}$, then $\mathsf{C} \subseteq \mathsf{BP}\cdot\mathsf{C}$.

18.2. Let q be an arbitrary polynomial and let A be a language in BP·C. So for some language $B \in \mathsf{C}$ and some constants α and ε,

$$x \in A \Longrightarrow Pr[\,\langle x, y\rangle \in B\,] \geq \alpha + \varepsilon/2\,,$$
$$x \notin A \Longrightarrow Pr[\,\langle x, y\rangle \in B\,] \leq \alpha - \varepsilon/2\,.$$

In order to amplify the probability to reach an error rate of at most $2^{-q(n)}$, we use the well-known technique of replacing B with the language B' described by the following algorithm.

INPUT $\langle x, y_1 \cdots y_t\rangle$;
$s := 0$;
FOR $i := 1$ **TO** t **do**
  IF $\langle x, y_i\rangle \in B$ **THEN** $s := s + 1$ **END**;
END;
IF $s > \alpha t$ **THEN ACCEPT**
  ELSE REJECT END

Here t is a linear function in $q(|x|)$.

What we need is that this algorithm is "of type C," so that $B' \in \mathsf{C}$. Since this program uses B as a sub-program, it is clear that $B' \in \mathsf{P}(B)$, but that characterization is to coarse, since it would not, for example, apply with the class NP in the role of C (unless NP = coNP). If we look more closely, we see that this reduction is actually *positive* (or *monotone*). This means that from $B_1 \subseteq B_2$ it follows that $L(M, B_1) \subseteq L(M, B_2)$. We will use the notation Pos for this type of reduction, so $B' \in \mathsf{Pos}(B)$. P, NP and many other classes are closed under Pos(·).

18.3. Let $A \in$ BP·BP·C. Then there are constants α and ε, and a language $B \in$ BP·C such that

$$x \in A \Longrightarrow Pr[\,\langle x, y\rangle \in B\,] \geq \alpha + \varepsilon/2\,,$$
$$x \notin A \Longrightarrow Pr[\,\langle x, y\rangle \in B\,] \leq \alpha - \varepsilon/2\,.$$

For $B \in$ BP·C we can apply probability amplification, so there is a language $C \in \mathsf{C}$ with

$$\langle x, y\rangle \in B \Longrightarrow Pr[\,\langle x, y, z\rangle \in C\,] \geq 1 - \varepsilon/4\,,$$
$$\langle x, y\rangle \notin B \Longrightarrow Pr[\,\langle x, y, z\rangle \in C\,] \leq \varepsilon/4\,.$$

Putting this together, we get

$$x \in A \Longrightarrow Pr[\,\langle x, y\rangle \in C\,] \geq \alpha + \varepsilon/2 - \varepsilon/4 = \alpha + \varepsilon/4\,,$$
$$x \notin A \Longrightarrow Pr[\,\langle x, y\rangle \in C\,] \leq \alpha - \varepsilon/2 + \varepsilon/4 = \alpha - \varepsilon/4\,.$$

This shows that $A \in$ BP·C with the constants α and $\varepsilon/2$.

18.4. Let L be a language in $\mathsf{Op{\cdot}BP{\cdot}C}$. By the statement of the exercise, there is a language $A \in \mathsf{BP{\cdot}C}$, a polynomial p, and a predicate Q such that

$$x \in L \iff Q(x, A_{\leq p(n)}) ,$$

where $n = |x|$. For the language A, there is a language $B \in \mathsf{C}$ such that for all y with $|y| \leq p(n)$,

$$Pr[\, y \in A \iff \langle y, z\rangle \in B\,] \geq 1 - \delta ,$$

where the probability is over z chosen uniformly at random. Because of probability amplification, we can choose $\delta = 2^{-p(n)-3}$. Now it follows that

$$Pr[\, \forall y, |y| \leq p(n)\ (\langle y, z\rangle B \iff y \in A)\,] \geq 1 - 2^{p(n)+1}2^{-p(n)-3} = 3/4 .$$

From this it follows that

$$Pr[\, x \in L \iff Q(x, B(y)_{\leq p(n)})\,] \geq 3/4 ,$$

where we are using $B(y)$ to denote the set $\{x \mid \langle x, y\rangle \in B\}$. So $L \in \mathsf{BP{\cdot}Op{\cdot}C}$.

18.5. $n!/m$

18.6. $X = \{\, \langle G, \pi\rangle \mid G$ is isomorphic to G_1 or to G_2 and $\pi \in Aut(G)\,\}$.

18.7. Suppose first that the strings y and y' differ in exactly one bit, say in the first bit: $y_1 \neq y_2$. For every bit position $j = 1, \ldots, b$ in the result string,

$$h(y)_j = \bigoplus_{i=1}^{a}(h_{ij} \wedge y_i) = \beta \oplus (h_{1j} \wedge y_1)$$

and

$$h(y')_j = \bigoplus_{i=1}^{a}(h_{ij} \wedge y'_i) = \beta \oplus (h_{1j} \wedge y'_1) ,$$

where $\beta = \bigoplus_{i=2}^{a}(h_{ij} \wedge y_i) = \bigoplus_{i=2}^{a}(h_{ij} \wedge y'_i)$. WLOG, we may assume that $y_1 = 0$ and $y'_1 = 1$. Then $h(y)_j = 0$ and $h(y')_j = m_{1,j}$. So $h(y')_j = 0$ or 1 with probability $1/2$ for each. Since the bits $m_{1,j}$ are chosen independently, $Pr[\, h(y) = z \wedge h(y') = z\,] = 2^{-2b}$.

This argument can easily be generalized to the case where y and y' differ in more than one bit.

18.8. Choose $u_1, \ldots, u_{p(n)}$ randomly. We approximate the probability that then (the rest of) statement (1) does not hold:

$$\begin{aligned} &Pr[\, \exists v\, (u_1 \oplus v \notin E \wedge \cdots \wedge u_{p(n)} \oplus v \notin E)\,] \\ &\leq \sum_v Pr[\, u_1 \oplus v \notin E \wedge \cdots \wedge u_{p(n)} \oplus v \notin E\,] \end{aligned}$$

$$= \sum_v \prod_{i=1}^{p(n)} Pr[\, u_i \oplus v \notin E\,]$$
$$= \sum_v \prod_{i=1}^{p(n)} 2^{-n}$$
$$= \sum_v (2^{-n})^{p(n)}$$
$$= 2^{p(n)} \cdot (2^{-n})^{p(n)}$$
$$= 2^{-(n-1)p(n)} < 1 \,.$$

18.9. Suppose there is a choice of $u_1, \ldots, u_{p(n)}$, such that for every v there is an $i \le p(n)$ with $u_i \oplus v \in \overline{F}$. Partition the set of v's (i.e., $\{0,1\}^{p(n)}$) according to the i's:

$$\{0,1\}^{p(n)} = V_1 \cup \cdots \cup V_{p(n)} \,,$$

where $V_j = \{v \mid u_j \oplus v \in \overline{F}\}$. For at least one j, $|V_j| \ge 2^{p(n)}/p(n)$. From this it follows that $|\overline{F}| \ge 2^{p(n)}/p(n)$ and, therefore, that $|F| \le (1 - 1/p(n))2^{p(n)}$, which is a contradiction to our assumption (for large enough n).

18.10. $\Sigma_2^P = \exists\cdot\mathsf{coNP} \overset{\text{asm.}}{\subseteq} \exists\cdot\mathsf{BP}\cdot\mathsf{NP} \overset{\text{Lm. 18.2}}{\subseteq} \mathsf{BP}\cdot\exists\cdot\mathsf{NP} = \mathsf{BP}\cdot\mathsf{NP} \overset{\text{Th. 18.7}}{\subseteq} \Pi_2^P$.

19.1. P is contained in ⊕P since a P-machine is also a ⊕P-machine.

⊕P is also closed under complementation since every ⊕P-machine can be extended with one "dummy" accepting path, transforming an odd number of accepting paths into an even number of accepting paths and vice versa.

19.2. Let L be a language in FewP as witnessed by a machine M that has at most $p(n)$ accepting computation paths. A computation has length at most $q(n)$, so it can be represented by a string of length $q(n)$. Consider now the following new non-deterministic machine M':

INPUT x;
GUESS $m \in \{1, \ldots, p(|x|)\}$;
GUESS $y_1, \ldots, y_m$, $|y_i| = q(|x|)$ with $y_1 < \cdots < y_m$;
IF all y_i represent accepting computations **THEN ACCEPT**
  ELSE REJECT;
END

If $x \notin L$, then machine M' has 0 (an even number) accepting paths on input x. On the other hand, if $x \in L$, then M has $m > 0$ accepting paths and M' has $\sum_{i=1}^{m} \binom{m}{i} = 2^m - 1$ (an odd number) accepting paths.

19.3. AND-function: $f(\langle F_1, \ldots, F_n \rangle) = F_1' \wedge \cdots \wedge F_n'$. Here F_i' is a version of the formula F_i with the variables renamed in such a way that no variable occurs in more than one formula F_i'.

OR-function: $f(\langle F_1, \ldots, F_n \rangle) = F_1 \vee \cdots \vee F_n$.

A NOT-function is nothing other than a polynomial time many-one reduction to the complement of the language. In the case of SAT, such a function exists if and only if NP = coNP.

19.4. It suffices to show that $SAT \in \mathsf{BP}\cdot\oplus\mathsf{P}$, since $\mathsf{BP}\cdot\oplus\mathsf{P}$ is closed under polynomial time many-one reductions. Let M be a probabilistic algorithm that transforms input formulas F into formulas F' with

$$F \in SAT \Longrightarrow Pr[F' \in \oplus SAT] > \frac{1}{p(|F|)},$$
$$F \notin SAT \Longrightarrow F' \notin \oplus SAT.$$

Now it suffices to show that for any $\varepsilon > 0$ there is a probabilistic algorithm M' that transforms F into F'' with

$$F \in SAT \Longrightarrow Pr[F'' \in \oplus SAT] > 1 - \varepsilon,$$
$$F \notin SAT \Longrightarrow F'' \notin \oplus SAT.$$

For this all that is needed is to let F'' consist of t independent formulas of the form F' (i.e., $F_1', \ldots, F_t'$) combined using the OR-function h for $\oplus SAT$: $F'' = h(F_1', \ldots, F_t')$. We must still determine how large t must be chosen (depending on p and ε). On input $F \in SAT$ the probability of having no "successes" ($F_i' \in \oplus SAT$) in t trials is at most

$$(1 - \frac{1}{p(|F|)})^t = ((1 - \frac{1}{p(|F|)})^{p(|F|)})^{\frac{t}{p(|F|)}} \leq d^{\frac{t}{p(|F|)}},$$

where $d > 1/e$. This probability is supposed to be less than ε. From this we see that $t \geq 1.45 \cdot \log(1/\varepsilon) \cdot p(|F|)$ suffices. (In fact, from this we see that ε can even be a function of the form $2^{-q(n)}$ where q is an arbitrary polynomial.)

19.5. The following language

$$A = \{ F(X,Y) \mid F \text{ is a boolean formula and } X \text{ and } Y \text{ sets of variables occurring in } F \text{ such that for at least one assignment of the } X\text{-variables there is an odd number of assignments of the } Y\text{-variables with } F(X,Y) = 1 \}$$

is clearly complete for $\exists\cdot\oplus\mathsf{P}$. It is sufficient to show that A is probabilistically reducible to $\oplus SAT$. This is achieved by the given probabilistic algorithm which transforms F into F'' if we consider the "halving process" of the algorithm to act only on the X-variables and not the Y-variables. From this we get:

$F(X,Y) \in A \Longrightarrow$ with high probability there are an odd number of X-assignments for which there are an odd number of Y-assignments that make $F'' = 1$

$\Longrightarrow$ with high probability there is an odd number of X, Y-assignments with $F'' = 1$.

$F(X,Y) \notin A \Longrightarrow$ there is no X-assignment for which there is an odd number of Y-assignments that make $F'' = 1$

$\Longrightarrow$ there are an even number of X, Y-assignments with $F'' = 1$.

19.6. If $\oplus\mathsf{P} \subseteq \mathsf{PH}$, then $\oplus SAT \in \mathsf{PH}$. Thus there exists a k such that $\oplus SAT \in \Sigma_k^P$. Since $\oplus SAT$ is complete for $\oplus\mathsf{P}$ and Σ_k^P is closed under many-one reductions, it follows that $\oplus\mathsf{P} \subseteq \Sigma_k^P$. From this we get $\mathsf{PH} \subseteq \mathsf{BP}\cdot\oplus\mathsf{P} \subseteq \mathsf{BP}\cdot\Sigma_k^P \subseteq \forall\cdot\exists\cdot\Sigma_k^P = \forall\cdot\Sigma_k^P = \Pi_{k+1}^P$.

19.7. Since $\mathsf{BP}\cdot\oplus\mathsf{P} = \forall\cdot\exists\cdot\oplus\mathsf{P}$ the following language is complete for $\mathsf{BP}\cdot\oplus\mathsf{P}$:

$\{ F(X,Y,Z) \mid F$ is a boolean formula and X, Y and Z are sets of variables occurring in F such that for every X-assignment there is at least one Y-assignment for which there is an odd number of Z-assignments with $F(X,Y,Z) = 1 \}$

19.8. $a \equiv 0 (\text{mod } b) \Longrightarrow \exists x \in \mathbb{N}\, bx = a \Longrightarrow \exists x \in \mathbb{N}\, b^p x^p = a^p \Longrightarrow a^p \equiv 0 (\text{mod } b^p)$.

On the other hand, $a \equiv 1 (\text{mod } b) \Longrightarrow \exists x \in \mathbb{N}\; bx + 1 = a \Longrightarrow \exists x \in \mathbb{N}\; (bx+1)^p = a^p \Longrightarrow \exists x \in \mathbb{N}\; a^p = \sum_{i=0}^{p} \binom{p}{i} (bx)^i \Longrightarrow \exists x \in \mathbb{N}\; a^p = 1 + b \cdot \left(\sum_{i=1}^{p} \binom{p}{i} b^{i-1} x^i\right) \Longrightarrow a^p \equiv 1 (\text{mod } b)$.

19.9. Every non-deterministic computation tree can be augmented with one additional "dummy" accepting path. The class #P is therefore closed under "+1" (in fact, under addition).

By attaching two non-deterministic computation trees "one after the other" (in the sense that the second computation is only started in the case that the first one ended in an accepting state) we get a non-deterministic computation tree for which the number of accepting paths is precisely the product of the numbers of accepting paths on the original trees. This shows that #P is also closed under multiplication. It is important to note that the (non-deterministic) running times merely add. This means that to compute $\mathsf{acc}_M(x)^{p(|x|)}$ on input x, we can attach $p(|x|)$ copies of M-computations one after another. This results in a running time that increases by a factor of $p(|x|)$, which is still polynomial provided M ran in polynomial time.

20.1. If in some calculus there is polynomially long proof for the statement "$x \in A$," then $A \in \mathsf{NP}$: On input x one can guess a potential, polynomially long proof and verify that it is correct. (For this we need that proofs in our calculus can be verified in polynomial time. This will be the case if, for example, the individual steps in the proof are easily checked for syntactic correctness.)

If A is in NP, then one can define the "configuration transition calculus" corresponding to the NP machine. A t-step proof of $x \in A$ consists of a sequence of legal transitions that result in an accepting configuration.

20.2. Let A be computable by an interactive proof system (in the given sense). Then $A \in \mathsf{NP}$, since on input x one can simulate the computation of the verifier and nondeterministically guess the communication of the prover. $x \in A$ if and only if such a nondeterministic algorithm accepts x.

20.3. Just as in the case of a nondeterministic or alternating Turing machine, the configuration transitions of the prover and verifier can be viewed as a tree structure with the start configuration as the root. Prover branchings are to be understood and evaluated as existential branchings, and verifier branchings (which are used to generate random numbers) as randomized or probabilistic branchings.

Example.

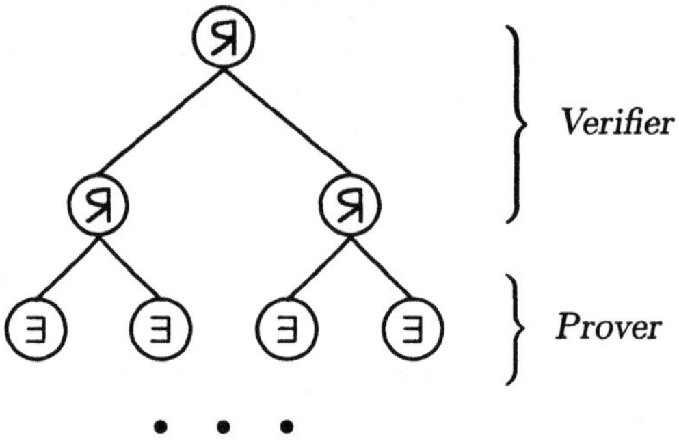

Such a computation tree is evaluated as follows: The accepting and rejecting leaves receive the value 1 or 0, respectively. The value of an existential node is the maximum of values of its children, the value of a probabilistic node is the mean of the values of its children. By the definition of an interactive proof system for the language A, the root must receive a value $\alpha > 2/3$ if $x \in A$ and $\alpha < 1/3$ if $x \notin A$.

The evaluation of such computation tree can be done by a polynomial space-bounded machine (in exponential time) by evaluating the tree using a depth-first, back-tracking algorithm. At no time does this require more space than that required to store one path through the tree. Since the tree has polynomial depth and each node can be stored in polynomial space, this is a PSPACE simulation.

20.4. Suppose that $A \in \mathsf{IP}$ via a verifier V and a prover P, who is responsible for $x \in A$. The prover can be regarded as a function $P : (x, y_1, \ldots, y_k) \mapsto z$, where x is the input, y_i is the communication between the prover and the verifier that occurred during (a previous) round i, and z is the the communication from the prover in the next round. We want to show that A is provable by an oracle.

In place of the prover, we use the oracle language

$$B = \{\langle x, y_1, \ldots, y_k, z' \rangle \mid P(x, y_1, \ldots, y_k) = z \text{ and } z' \text{ is an initial segment of } z\} .$$

In place of of the verifier, we have to describe oracle Turing machine M. M will behave exactly like the verifier, except that instead of writing a string y on the communication tape, M systematically writes strings of the form $\langle x, y_1, \ldots, y_l, y, z' \rangle$ (where the y_i's are the previous communications) on the oracle tape and uses the oracle B to obtain the information z. If $x \in A$, then it is clear that M^B exhibits the same probabilistic behavior as (P, V), and therefore accepts with probability $> 2/3$. Now suppose $x \notin A$ and let B be an arbitrary oracle. This corresponds to some prover P_B, and since M^B behaves just like (P_B, V), it will accept with probability at most $1/3$.

Now we will try to prove the reverse direction. Suppose A is provable by an oracle A via the machine M and the oracle language B. We want to show that $A \in \mathsf{IP}$. In place of M we use a verifier V that behaves exactly like M, except that instead of querying the oracle about a string w, w is communicated to the prover. The prover associated with the oracle B is defined by the function $P(x, y_1, \ldots, y_k, w) \in \{0, 1\}$ where $P(x, y_1, \ldots, y_k, w) = 1$ if and only if $w \in B$. That is, the prover ignores the input x and all previous communication and simply tells the verifier whether or not the last string written on the communication tape was a string in B (a single bit).

If $x \in A$, then it is clear that (P, V) exhibits exactly the same probabilistic behavior as M^B, and so accepts with probability $> 2/3$. If $x \notin A$, however, there is a problem. Let P be an arbitrary prover, that is, a function $P : (x, y_1, \ldots, y_k) \mapsto z$. It is not clear how the prover can be coded up into an oracle. The reason is that an oracle, unlike a prover, has no "memory" and, therefore, cannot make its answers dependent upon the previous communication. It has in fact been shown in

- L. Fortnow, J. Rompel, M. Sipser: On the power of multi-prover interactive protocols, *Proceedings of the 8th Structure in Complexity Theory Conference*, IEEE, 1988, 156–161.

that a language A is provable by an oracle if and only if $A \in \mathsf{NEXPTIME}$. This is potentially a bigger class than $\mathsf{IP} = \mathsf{PSPACE}$ (cf. Topic 21).

20.5. The probability is exactly $1/2$ if the prover always chooses $j \in \{0, 1\}$. Otherwise the probability is $p/2$, where p is the probability that the prover chooses $j \in \{0, 1\}$.

20.6. Change the line "Accept if i = j" to "Randomly select $k \in \{1,2,3,4\}$. Accept if $i = j$ and $k \leq 3$." This has the effect of translating the probabilities to 3/4 and $(1/2) \cdot (3/4) = 3/8$.

20.7. Instead of computing one "random copy" of one of the graphs, H, the verifier generates k independent random copies, $H_1, \ldots, H_k$, and communicates these to the prover. The verifier expects to receive k correct answers $j_1, \ldots j_k$ back from the prover and only accepts if this is the case. If the graphs are isomorphic, then the prover can evoke acceptance with probability at most 2^{-k}.

20.8. If the input graphs G_1 and G_2 are isomorphic, then the graph H generated by the prover is also isomorphic to both graphs and the prover (using his unlimited computational power) is able to compute the isomorphism σ. So in this case and with this prover, the probability of acceptance is 1.

But if the graphs G_1 and G_2 are not isomorphic, then no prover can produce the required isomorphism more than 1/2 of the time, since in half the cases, no such isomorphism will exist. By means of the usual techniques, this probability of 1/2 can be further reduced to fulfill the definition of IP.

20.9. The desired machine M works as follows:

INPUT (G_1, G_2);
GUESS RANDOMLY $j \in \{1,2\}$;
GUESS RANDOMLY $\pi \in S_n$;
(* S_n is the set of permutations of $\{1, \ldots, n\}$ *)
OUTPUT $(\pi(G_j), j, \pi)$;

The distribution of triples generated by this program is the same as the distribution that can be observed in the given protocol on an input $(G_1, G_2) \in GI$. The first component of this triple is a graph H isomorphic to G_1 or G_2, chosen under the uniform distribution; the second component is a number $j \in \{1,2\}$ that is uniformly distributed and independent of the first component; and the third component is an isomorphism between G_j and H.

20.10. The protocol can be followed word for word, except that at the point where the prover is required to "determine σ so that $\sigma(G_j) = H$," instead the prover uses the extra information (namely, φ with $\varphi(G_1) = G_2$) to compute σ in polynomial time as follows:

$$\sigma = \begin{cases} \pi & \text{if } i = 1,\ j = 1, \\ \pi\varphi^{-1} & \text{if } i = 1,\ j = 2, \\ \pi\varphi & \text{if } i = 2,\ j = 1, \\ \pi & \text{if } i = 2,\ j = 2. \end{cases}$$

21.1. By DeMorgan's laws one can systematically push all of the negation symbols to the inside until they are all in front of variables:

$$\neg(F \wedge G) = (\neg F \vee \neg G) ,$$
$$\neg(F \vee G) = (\neg F \wedge \neg G) ,$$
$$\neg\forall x\, F = \exists x\, \neg F ,$$
$$\neg\exists x\, F = \forall x\, \neg F .$$

21.2. For the variables this is true since only the values 0 and 1 are substituted. The use of $1 - x_i$ for negation turns a 0 into a 1 and vice versa, so this is also correct. (This is why it is important that negation only occurs at variables.) Now consider two formulas F and G, for which the claim is true. Then one can easily check that multiplication and addition behave correctly for $F \wedge G$ and $F \vee G$. Similarly, if we have a formula of the form $Qx\, F$, $Q \in \{\exists, \forall\}$, and substituting a 1 or 0 into F for x produces a correct arithmetic value for the corresponding formulas with the variable x replaced by TRUE or FALSE, then multiplication will correctly evaluate $\forall$ and addition will correctly evaluate $\exists$.

21.3. Since the variables x_i do not occur in the in the subformula $\exists y\, \exists z\, (y \vee z)$, this subformula can be evaluated directly: its value is 4. Each application of a universal quantifier squares the value, so in the end the value is 4^{2^m}.

21.4. We use induction on the length of formulas. The largest value that can be assigned to a variable or negated variable is $1 \le 2^{2^1}$. For a formula of length $n > 1$ of the form $(F \circ G)$, $\circ \in \{\vee, \wedge\}$, the formulas F and G will (by the inductive hypothesis) be assigned values $\le 2^{2^l}$ and $\le 2^{2^r}$ with $r + l \le n$. The value for $F \circ G$ is then at most $2^{2^l} * 2^{2^r} = 2^{2^l + 2^r} \le 2^{2^n}$. In the case of a formula $Qx\, F$, $Q \in \{\exists, \forall\}$, if the value of F is at most 2^{2^m} with $m < n$, then value for F is at most $2^{2^m} * 2^{2^m} = 2^{2 * 2^m} = 2^{2^{m+1}} \le 2^{2^n}$.

21.5. In the interval in question there are at least $\sqrt{2^{3n}} - 2^n > 2^n$ prime numbers. Let these be $p_1, p_2, \ldots, p_k$, $k > 2^n$. If for all $i \le k$, $a \equiv 0 \pmod{p_i}$, then by the Chinese Remainder Theorem, $a \equiv 0 \pmod{\prod_{i=1}^k p_i}$. Since $\prod_{i=1}^k p_i > \prod_{i=1}^k 2^n > 2^{2^n}$, and since $a \le 2^{2^n}$, it follows that $a = 0$. Contradiction.

21.6. Consider the set of numbers from 1 to n. Half of them are not prime, since they are divisible by 2. Of the rest, 2/3 remain if we strike the third that are divisible by 3. After the next step, 1/5 of the remaining prime number "candidates" are stricken because they are divisible by 5. If we continue this process until we reach the largest prime number less than $\sqrt{n}$, then only the prime numbers between 1 and n will remain. The number of candidates remaining is thus exactly $\pi(n)$. If we express this in formulas, letting p run over prime numbers, we get

$$\pi(n) \ge n \prod_{p \le \sqrt{n}} \frac{p-1}{p} \ge n \prod_{i=2}^{\lfloor \sqrt{n} \rfloor} \frac{i-1}{i} = n / \lfloor \sqrt{n} \rfloor \ge \sqrt{n} .$$

21.7. By the argument above (in Exercise 21.5), it follows that there are at most 2^n prime numbers p with $p \geq 2^n$ for which $a \equiv 0 \pmod{p}$. This means that in order to arrive at the desired error probability of 2^{-n}, we need an interval starting at 2^n that contains at least $2^n 2^n = 2^{2n}$ primes. If we use the sharper approximation $\pi(n) \sim n/\ln n$ we see that it suffices to choose the same interval as before, namely $[2^n, 2^{3n}]$.

21.8. The polynomial $p(x) - p'(x)$ also has degree (at most) d. Since the polynomial is over a field, it can have at most d zeroes. The probability of randomly selecting one of these at most d zeroes from the set $z \in \{0, \ldots, k-1\}$ is, therefore, at most $d/k \leq d/2^n$.

21.9. Note that we can extend the definition of p_G to include the case where G has more than one free variable, in which case the polynomial p_G will also have additional variables. We are only interested, however, in the degree of one variable x. OR and $\exists$ operations correspond to addition so they don't increase the degree of x. If $F = H \wedge K$, then $p_F = p_H * p_K$, so the degree of x in p_F is at most the sum of the degrees of x in p_H and p_K. If $F = \forall y H$, then the degree of x in p_F is twice the degree of x in p_H, but this is nonzero only once for a given variable. Thus for subformulas H of G, the degree of x in p_H is bounded by $|H|$ if H does not contain the universal quantifier that doubles the degree, and and by $2|H|$ if it does.

21.10. Every subformula in F of the form $Qx \ldots \forall y\, H(x, \ldots)$ (where $Q \in \{\exists, \forall\}$) is replaced by the following equivalent formula

$$Qx \ldots \exists x' \left((x \leftrightarrow x') \wedge \forall y\, H(x', \ldots)\right) .$$

That is, a new variable x' is introduced, its equivalence to x is confirmed, and then it is used in place of x. (The equivalence symbol can, of course, be expressed using AND, OR and NOT.)

21.11.

$$\begin{aligned} Pr[\text{error}] &= 1 - Pr[\text{no error}] \\ &= 1 - \prod_{i=1}^{n} Pr[\text{no error in round } i] \\ &\leq 1 - (1 - 2n/2^n)^n . \end{aligned}$$

22.1. Let A be PSPACE-complete. Then PSPACE $\subseteq$ P^A $\subseteq$ PSPACE and by a Savitch's Theorem PSPACE $\subseteq$ NP^A $\subseteq$ NPSPACE $\subseteq$ PSPACE.

22.2. A fixed block contains only strings in A with probability $1/2^n$, so the probability is $(1-1/2^n)^{2^n}$ that *none* of the blocks consists solely of strings in A. Thus the probability of at least one such block is $1 - (1 - 1/2^n)^{2^n}$, which approaches $1 - 1/e = 0.632...$ as n gets large.

22.3. On input x, $|x| = n$, nondeterministically guess a number i in $\{1,\ldots,2^n\}$ and verify that all strings in the ith x-block are in the oracle.

22.4. The proof follows the line of argumentation used in the case of P versus NP. Let $N_1, N_2, \ldots$ be an enumeration of all NP oracle machines, then

$$\begin{aligned} Pr[\mathsf{NP}^A = \mathsf{coNP}^A] &\le Pr[\overline{L(A)} \in \mathsf{NP}] \\ &= Pr[\exists i\, \overline{L(A)} = L(N_i^A)] \\ &\le \sum_i Pr[\forall j\,(x_j \in L(A)\Delta L(N_i^A))] \\ &= \sum_i \prod_j Pr[x_j \in L(A)\Delta L(N_i^A) \mid \overline{C}]\,. \end{aligned}$$

So it suffices to show that for some $\varepsilon > 0$

$$Pr[x_j \in L(A)\Delta L(N_i^A) \mid \overline{C}] = (2) + (3) < 1 - \varepsilon\,,$$

or, equivalently, that $(1) + (4) > \varepsilon$.

Now consider the cases $(1) > 0.1$ and $(1) \le 0.1$. If $(1) > 0.1$, then we are done. If $(1) \le 0.1$, then from $\frac{(1)}{(1)+(3)} \ge 1/3$ we can conclude that $(3) \le 0.2$; and since $(3) + (4) > 0.3$, it follows that $(4) > 0.1$.

23.1. A 1-superconcentrator is given by the following graph:

An n-superconcentrator can be made by putting together 2 copies of an $n/2$-superconcentrator S':

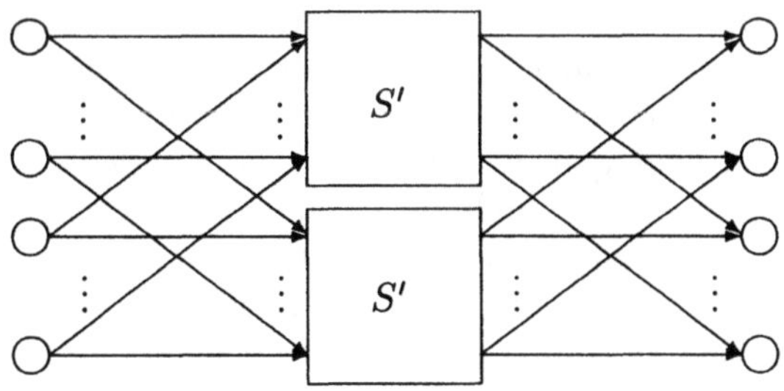

The size $g(n)$ of this graph satisfies $g(n) = 2g(n/2) + O(n)$, so $g(n) = O(n \log n)$.

This graph is a superconcentrator, in fact it is a *permutation network*, which means that for any arbitrary permutation of $\{1, 2, \ldots, n\}$, a node-disjoint connection can be found that realizes this permutation (between input and output nodes). Let $\pi : \{1, \ldots, n\} \to \{1, \ldots, n\}$ be a permutation. We can assign to π a bipartite graph G_π with n nodes (partitioned into two pieces of size $n/2$ each), such that for every (i, j) with $\pi(i) = j$ an (undirected) edge is drawn between the (i mod $n/2$)-th left node and the (j mod $n/2$)-th right node. In this way every node has degree 2 (multi-edges are possible). This bipartite graph consists of one or more disjoint cycles of even length. These can be colored red and blue in such a way that adjacent edges always receive different colors. We assign all red edges to the upper ($n/2$)-permutation network and all blue edges to the lower. These are each permutations of $n/2$, which by the induction hypothesis can be realized by the network S'.

23.2. For the size (number of edges) $g(n)$ of an n-superconcentrator we obtain the recursion $g(n) = g(2n/3) + dn$, where d is a constant and $g(2) = 4$. From this we get $g(n) = O(n)$.

23.3. Let $k \leq n$ input nodes S and k output nodes T be fixed. Let S' be those nodes in S that correspond to positions that also occur in T, so that they can be connected directly. Let T' be the set of corresponding positions in T. The inputs in $S - S'$ are routed through G. Since $k' = |S - S'| \leq n/2$, these k' inputs to G can be connected to some k' outputs of G (= inputs to S'). The size of $T - T'$ is also k', so for this set of outputs of G', there is some set of k' inputs that can be connected by node-disjoint paths. The superconcentrator S' connects these two sets of nodes. This shows that the sets S and T can be connected by node-disjoint paths.

23.4. If for some subset $S' \subseteq S$, $|S'| > |N(S')|$, then at least one node of S' cannot be connected.

In the other direction, suppose that $|S'| \leq |N(S')|$ and let M be a matching that does not match the node $u \in S$. Then $|N(\{u\})| \geq 1$ and the nodes in $N(\{u\})$ are already "blocked" by other nodes. Suppose $v_1 \in N(\{u\})$ and $(u_1, v_1) \in M$ for some node $u_1 \neq u$. Then $|N(\{u, u_1\})| \geq 2$. So there is at least one other node $v_2 \in N(\{u, u_1\})$, so that the matching M can perhaps be altered so that the edges (u, v_1), and (u_1, v_2) are in M instead. This will only fail if v_2 is already matched with some u_2 in M. But now $|N(\{u, u_1, u_2\})| \geq 3$, so we can proceed analogously, obtaining a new node v_3 and hoping to rearrange the edges of M so it includes (u, v_1), (u_1, v_2), and (u_2, v_3). This will only fail if M already matches some u_3 with v_3.

But we cannot fail forever. At the latest when we have used all the nodes in S, we must must find an unmatched node that allows for the rearrangement.

23.5. $(36m)!$

23.6. For $k = 2$ there are $6 \cdot 2 = 12$ edges to be connected on one side but only $9 \cdot 1 = 9$ possibilities on the other side, so such a matching can only happen if $k \geq 3$.

23.7. More generally, we can show that if $n = n_1 + n_2$, $k = k_1 + k_2$, $n_1 \geq k_1$, and $n_2 \geq k_2$, then $\binom{n_1}{k_1}\binom{n_2}{k_2} \leq \binom{n}{k}$. Note that $\binom{n}{k}$ is the number of ways to choose k of n people to occupy k available chairs. (We are only interested in who gets a chair and who doesn't, not who gets which chair.) Similarly,

$\binom{n_1}{k_1}\binom{n_2}{k_2}$ is the number of ways to seat k of n people with the added restriction that the first k_1 chairs are occupied by a subset of the first n_1 people, and the remaining k_2 chairs are occupied by a subset of the remaining n_2 people. Clearly, this is a smaller number.

23.8. We compute L_{k+1}/L_k, canceling redundant terms and grouping as follows:

$$\begin{aligned} L_{k+1}/L_k &= \frac{9k+9^{\underline{6k+6}}26m^{\underline{4k}}}{9k^{\underline{6k}}26m^{\underline{4k+4}}} \\ &= \frac{(9k+9)\cdots(9k+1)}{(3k+3)\cdots(3k+1)\cdot(26m-4k)\cdots(26m-4k-3)} \\ &= (9k+9)\cdots(9k+4)\cdot(\frac{9k+3}{3k+3})(\frac{9k+2}{3k+2})(\frac{9k+1}{3k+1}) \\ &\quad \cdot(\frac{1}{26m-4k})\cdots(\frac{1}{26m-4k-3})\,. \end{aligned}$$

Each of these factors is monotone increasing in k, so $\frac{L_{k+1}}{L_k}$ is monotone increasing in k, from which it follows that $L_{k-1}L_{k+1}/L_k^2 \geq 1$, so L_k is convex.

23.9. If we let $k=3$, then

$$\begin{aligned} 3m\cdot\frac{\binom{27}{18}}{\binom{26m}{12}} &= 3m\cdot\frac{\Theta(1)}{\Theta(m^{12})} \\ &= \Theta(m^{-11}) \;<\; 1\,. \end{aligned}$$

If we let $k=3m$, then

$$\begin{aligned} 3m\cdot\frac{\binom{27m}{18m}}{\binom{26m}{12m}} &= 3m\cdot\frac{\binom{27m}{9m}}{\binom{26m}{12m}} \\ &= 3m\cdot\frac{27m^{\underline{9m}}(12m)!}{(9m)!26m^{\underline{12m}}} \\ &= 3m\cdot\frac{27m^{\underline{9m}}12m^{\underline{3m}}}{26m^{\underline{12m}}} \\ &= 3m\cdot\frac{27m^{\underline{9m}}12m^{\underline{3m}}}{26m^{\underline{9m}}17m^{\underline{3m}}} \\ &\leq 3m\cdot(\frac{18}{17})^{9m}\cdot(\frac{12}{17})^{3m} \\ &\leq 3m\cdot(0.6)^m \;<\; 1\,. \end{aligned}$$

24.1. A pyramid can be pebbled level by level. For the lowest level, we need k pebbles. Then we need one more to begin the second level. From that point on, we can reuse pebbles to move up the graph.

24.2. We prove the following by induction on k:

> Every pebbling strategy, starting at any initial configuration of pebbles on P_k that leaves at least one path from the input nodes to the output node pebble-free requires at least $k+1$ pebbles.

The case $k = 2$ is clear. Now let $k > 2$ and let an arbitrary initial configuration with at least one pebble-free path be given. Without loss of generality, we may assume that there is a pebble-free path that passes through the node v_1:

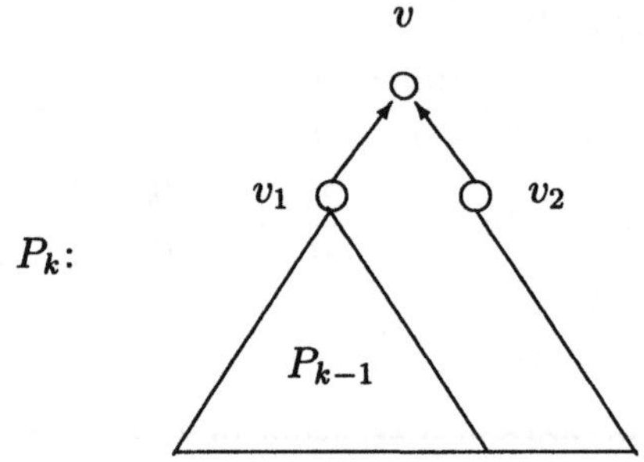

Now suppose there were a pebbling strategy for the output node v that used k or fewer pebbles. This strategy would include a strategy for pebbling v_1, which by induction would require the use of all k pebbles. At the point in the game where all k pebbles are on graph P_{k-1}, the path down the right edge of P_k is pebble-free. In particular, to pebble v_2 (in the copy of P_{k-1} at the right edge of P_k) will again require all k pebbles, which means that we must remove the pebble from v_1. Thus with k pebbles it will not be possible to cover v_1 and v_2 simultaneously, so we will need at least $k+1$ pebbles to cover v. (Only k pebbles would be necessary if we allowed "sliding" of pebbles, which would correspond to using only two registers to compute things like $x = x + y$.)

24.3. For every node u with in-degree $d > 2$, replace the subtree consisting of that node and its predecessors with a binary tree with d leaves (assigned to the original predecessors of u). The number of pebbles required to pebble the graph remains the same (it just takes more time), since once the d original predecessors of u have been pebbled, it takes only one additional pebble to cover u in the tree, just as in the original graph (see the previous exercises). Clearly the in-degree of each node will now be 2 and the number of edges will have at most doubled.

24.4. We start with $G_1 = \emptyset$ and $G_2 = G$ and successively move from G_2 to G_1 nodes (along with their in-coming edges) that already have all of their predecessors in G_2. In this way, there cannot be any "back-edges" in A. This process is continued until at least $n/2$ edges are in G_1. Since at each step at most 2 new edges enter G_1, the number of edges in G_1 will be at most $n/2 + 2$.

24.5. Case 1 is trivial since it only covers finitely many cases.

Case 2: $P(n) \leq P(n/2+2) \leq (n/2+2)/\log(n/2+2) \leq n/\log n$.

24.6. For case 3 we have:

$$\begin{aligned} P(n) &\leq \frac{2n}{\log n} + P(n/2+2) \\ &\leq \frac{2n}{\log n} + c \cdot \frac{n/2+2}{\log(n/2+2)} \\ &\leq \frac{2n}{\log n} + c \cdot \frac{0.6 \cdot n}{\log(n/2)} \\ &\leq \frac{2n}{\log n} + c \cdot \frac{0.6 \cdot n}{0.9 \cdot \log n} \\ &\leq c \cdot \frac{n}{\log n}, \end{aligned}$$

when $c \geq 9$ and n is large.

24.7. In case 4, apply $n/2 - 2n/\log n \geq n/4$ to get

$$\begin{aligned} P(n) &\leq P(n/2 - 2n/\log n) + P(n/2+2) + 1 \\ &\leq c \cdot \frac{n/2 - 2n/\log n}{\log(n/2 - 2n/\log n)} + c \cdot \frac{n/2+2}{\log(n/2+2)} + 1 \\ &\leq \frac{cn/2}{\log(n/4)} - \frac{2cn/\log n}{\log(n/4)} + \frac{cn/2}{\log(n/2)} + \frac{2c}{\log(n/2)} + 1 \\ &\leq \frac{cn/2}{\log n - 2} - \frac{2cn}{\log n(\log n - 2)} + \frac{cn/2}{\log n - 1} + 2\,. \end{aligned}$$

Now apply the equation $\dfrac{1}{x-a} = \dfrac{1}{x} + \dfrac{a}{x(x-a)}$ to get

$$\begin{aligned} P(n) &\leq \frac{cn/2}{\log n} + \frac{cn}{\log n(\log n - 2)} - \frac{2cn}{\log n(\log n - 2)} \\ &\quad + \frac{cn/2}{\log n} + \frac{cn/2}{\log n(\log n - 1)} + 2 \\ &\leq \frac{cn}{\log n} - \frac{cn/2}{\log n(\log n - 2)} + 2 \leq \frac{cn}{\log n}. \end{aligned}$$

24.8. Under the assumption that all context sensitive languages can be recognized in linear time we get

$$\begin{aligned} \mathsf{NSPACE}(n) &\subseteq \mathsf{DTIME}(n) \\ &\subsetneq \mathsf{DTIME}(n \log n) \qquad \text{(Time Hierarchy Theorem)} \\ &\subseteq \mathsf{DSPACE}(n) \\ &\subseteq \mathsf{NSPACE}(n)\,, \end{aligned}$$

which is a contradiction.

24.9. We build up a set of $n-j$ inputs with the desired property successively as follows: Let E_1 be an arbitrary $(j+1)$-element subset of the inputs. E_1 is connected to A via $j+1$ node-disjoint paths (by the definition of superconcentrator), of which at least one must be pebble-free. Let e_1 be the corresponding input node. Build $E_2 = (E_1 - \{e_1\}) \cup \{e\}$ for any input e that has not yet been considered. Once again there is at least one pebble free path with corresponding input $e_2 \in E_2$. Repeated application of this procedure leads to a set of $n-j$ inputs with the desired property.

24.10. $|C(n)| = \Theta(2^n)$, so $|G_{n+1}| = \Theta(2^n) + 2|G_n|$. This recursion relation has the solution $\Theta(n2^n)$.

24.11. G_n includes, among other things, direct connections between the inputs and outputs. If we just consider these edges, it is clear that the combination of G_n and $C(n)$ is at least as good as $C(n)$ alone, so it must also be a 2^n-superconcentrator.

24.12. Consider a strategy that takes a total of t steps on G_8, and – starting from a configuration in which at most 3 nodes are pebbled – pebbles 14 outputs. By Lemma 24.2, 4 of these outputs are connected with at least 253 outputs via pebble-free paths. So there must be one of these outputs that is connected to at least 64 of the inputs via pebble-free paths. Let a be this output and let t_1 be the last time at which all 64 of the inputs were still unpebbled. Then the statement of the theorem is satisfied for the interval $[t_1+1, t]$, since in this time interval $64 \geq 34$ inputs need to be pebbled and at least one pebble remains on the graph (otherwise t_1 would not have been the last time the inputs were all unpebbled).

24.13. We have a graph family $\{G_n\}$ with $|G_n| = \Theta(n2^n)$ edges. In order to pebble a certain subset of the outputs in any order, we need at least $c2^n$ pebbles, for some $c > 0$. So there must be an output that requires $c2^n$ pebbles (else one could pebble all the outputs with fewer pebbles by pebbling one after the other, each time removing all of the pebbles use.)

So $P(m)$, the required number of pebbles, satisfies

$$P(m) \geq c2^n = c\Theta(m)/n \geq c\Theta(m)/O(\log m) \geq \Omega(m/\log m)\ ,$$

where m is the size (number of edges) of G_n.

25.1. Consider the following P-computable distribution, defined on tuples $\langle x, a, b\rangle$, where x is a CNF formula, a an assignment to the variables in x, and b a bit:

$$\mu(\langle x, a, b\rangle) = \begin{cases} \frac{1}{|x|^2 \cdot 2^{|a|}} & \text{if } b \text{ is the truth value for } x \text{ under assignment } a, \\ 0 & \text{otherwise.} \end{cases}$$

Clearly this is P-computable. Furthermore, $\mu^*(x, \mathbf{1}, 1) - \mu^*(x, \mathbf{1}, 0) \neq 0$ if and only if there is a satisfying assignment for x. Thus if μ^* is P-computable, then $SAT \in$ NP, so P = NP.

25.2. $\dfrac{1}{m} - \dfrac{1}{m+1} = \dfrac{(m+1)-m}{m(m+1)} = \dfrac{1}{m(m+1)}$, so

$$\sum_{m=1}^{N} \frac{1}{m(m+1)} = 1 - \frac{1}{N+1} \to 1 \text{ as } N \to \infty \ .$$

More generally,

$$\begin{aligned}\sum_{m\geq 1}^{N} \frac{1}{m^k} &= \left(-\frac{1}{k}\right) \left(\frac{1}{m^{k-1}}\right)\Big|_1^N \\ &= \frac{1}{k!} - \frac{1}{kN^{k-1}}) \to \frac{1}{k!} \text{ as } N \to \infty \ .\end{aligned}$$

25.3. Let f be defined by

$$f(x) = \begin{cases} 2^n & \text{if } x = 0^n, \\ 0 & \text{otherwise.} \end{cases}$$

Then

$$\sum_{|x|=n} \frac{f(x)}{2^n} = \frac{2^n + 2^n - 1}{2^n} \leq 2 \ ,$$

but

$$\sum_{|x|=n} \frac{f(x)^2}{2^n} = \frac{2^{2n} + 2^n - 1}{2^n} \geq \frac{2^{2n}}{2^n} = 2^n \ .$$

25.4. Closure under maximum is demonstrated by

$$\begin{aligned}\sum_{|x|} \frac{\max^{\varepsilon}(f(x), g(x))}{|x|} \cdot \mu(x) &= \sum_{f(x)>g(x)} \frac{f^{\varepsilon}(x)}{|x|} \cdot \mu(x) + \sum_{f(x)\leq g(x)} \frac{g^{\varepsilon}(x)}{|x|} \cdot \mu(x) \\ &\leq \sum_{x} \frac{f^{\varepsilon}(x)}{|x|} \cdot \mu(x) + \sum_{x} \frac{g^{\varepsilon}(x)}{|x|} \cdot \mu(x) < \infty \ .\end{aligned}$$

Clearly we have closure under $\leq$. Closure under sum is then obtained by noticing that $f+g \leq 2\max(f,g)$. Closure under exponentiation is obtained by choosing an appropriately adjusted value for ε. Closure under multiplication then follows because $f \cdot g \leq f^2 + g^2$.

25.5. Suppose the expected value of f is polynomially-bounded with respect to some distribution μ. Then there are constants $c > 0$ and $k > 1$ such that for all n, $\sum_{|x|=n} f(x)\mu_n(x) \leq cn^k$. Let $\varepsilon = 1/k$, then

$$\sum_{|x|=n} \frac{f^\varepsilon(x)}{|x|}\mu_n(x) < \sum_{|x|=n} 1 + \left(\frac{f^\varepsilon(x)}{|x|}\right)^k \mu_n(x)$$
$$\leq \sum_{|x|=n} 1 + \frac{f(x)}{n^k}\mu_n(x)$$
$$= 1 + \frac{1}{n^k}\sum_{|x|=n} f(x)\mu_n(x)$$
$$\leq 1 + c\,.$$

So

$$\sum_{|x|\geq 1} \frac{f^\varepsilon(x)}{|x|}\mu(x) \leq \sum_{n\geq 1}\sum_{|x|=n} \frac{f^\varepsilon(x)}{|x|}\mu(x) \leq \sum_{n\geq 1}(1+c)\mu(\Sigma^{=n}) = 1 + c < \infty\,.$$

25.6. Consider the following algorithm:

1. Input a graph G.
2. Search G for a copy of K_4 (by checking each set of four vertices to see whether all six edges are present in the graph). If a copy of K_4 is found, reject.
3. Search for a 3-coloring by assigning each possible coloring to the nodes and checking if two adjacent nodes have the same color. If a 3-coloring is found, accept; else, reject.

The running time of this algorithm is polynomially bounded on instances that contain a copy of K_4, since there are only $\binom{n}{4} < n^4$ potential copies of K_4, and each can be checked in polynomial time. Let the polynomial bound in this case be $p(n)$.

If there are no copies of K_4 in G, then the algorithm must perform step 3. There are 3^n potential colorings, so this step takes at most $3^n q(n)$ time, for some polynomial q.

Now we need a bound on the probability of finding a copy of K_4 in G. Given any set of four nodes, the probability that they form a copy of K_4 is $(1/2)^6 = 1/64$. Thus we can give the following rough approximation for the probability that *no* K_4 is found:

$$Pr(G \text{ contains no } K_4) \leq \left(\frac{63}{64}\right)^{n/4}\,.$$

Let $c > 1$ and $k > 1$ be integer constants such that $cn^k > \max(p(n), q(n))$ and $(3^{1/k})(\frac{63}{64})^{1/4} = \alpha < 1$. Let A be the set of graphs that contain no copy of K_4. By the closure properties of polynomial on μ-average, it is sufficient to show that $g(x) = f(x) - c|x|^k$ is polynomial on μ-average. The following sequence of inequalities shows this to be the case:

$$\begin{aligned}
\sum_x \frac{g(x)^{1/k}}{|x|}\mu(x) &\le \sum_{x\notin A} 0\cdot\mu(x) + \sum_{x\in A}\frac{\left(3^{|x|}\right)^{1/k}}{|x|}\mu(x)\\
&\le 0 + \sum_n 3^{n/k}\mu(A^{=n})\\
&\le \sum_n 3^{n/k}\cdot(63/64)^{n/4}\\
&\le \sum_n \left(3^{1/k}\cdot(63/64)^{1/4}\right)^n\\
&\le \sum_n \alpha^n < \infty\,.
\end{aligned}$$

25.7. Suppose $f : (A,\mu) \le_{\mathrm{m}}^{\mathsf{P}} (B,\nu)$, and $g : (B,\mu) \le_{\mathrm{m}}^{\mathsf{P}} (C,\xi)$. Clearly $h = g\circ f : A \le_{\mathrm{m}}^{\mathsf{P}} C$, so it suffices to show that $\mu \preceq_h \xi$. Let p be a polynomial and let μ_1 and ν_1 be distributions such that

- $|f(x)| \le p(|x|)$,
- $|g(y)| \le p(|y|)$,
- $\mu(x) \le p(|x|)\mu_1(x)$,
- $\nu(y) \le p(|y|)\nu_1(y)$,
- $\nu(y) = \sum_{f(x)=y}\mu_1(x)$, and
- $\xi(z) = \sum_{g(y)=z}\nu_1(x)$,

as guaranteed by the definition of $\le_{\mathrm{m}}^{\mathsf{P}}$. (For ease of notation we are assuming $\nu(\mathrm{range}(f)) = 1$ and $\xi(\mathrm{range}(g)) = 1$, so no scaling is needed. The argument can be easily modified if this is not the case.) It follows that

$$\begin{aligned}
\xi(z) &= \sum_{g(y)=z}\nu_1(y)\\
&\le \sum_{g(y)=z} p(|y|)\nu(y)\\
&\le \sum_{g(y)=z}\sum_{f(x)=y} p(p(|x|))\mu_1(x)\\
&\le \sum_{h(x)=z} p(|x|)p(p(|x|))\mu(x)\,,
\end{aligned}$$

so we can define a distribution μ_2 such that $\xi(z) = \sum_{h(x)=z}\mu_2(x)$ and $\mu(x) \le p(p(|x|))p(|x)\mu(x)$, thus $\mu \preceq_h \xi$.

25.8. Suppose $f : (A,\mu) \le_{\mathrm{m}}^{\mathsf{P}} (B,\nu)$, and $(B,\nu) \in \mathsf{AP}$. As in the previous exercise, for ease of notation, assume that $\nu(\mathrm{range}(f)) = 1$. The obvious algorithm for determining whether $x \in A$ proceeds by first computing $f(x)$ and then checking whether $f(x) \in B$. Since f is computable in polynomial time, there are constants $c > 1$ and $k > 1$ such that $|f(x)| \leq c|x|^k$. Since $(B, \nu) \in \mathsf{AP}$, there is an algorithm for B that runs in time t, where t is polynomial on ν-average (witnessed by some exponent ε). The running of our algorithm for A is at most $c|x|^k + t(c|x|^k)$. By the closure properties of polynomial on average, it suffices to show that $h = t(c|x|^k)$ is polynomial on μ-average.

First we consider $h^{\varepsilon/k}$:

$$\begin{aligned}
\sum_x \frac{h^{\varepsilon/k}(x)}{|x|}\mu_1(x) &\leq \sum_y \sum_{f(x)=y} \frac{t^{\varepsilon/k}(y)}{|y|^{1/k}}\mu_1(x) \\
&\leq \sum_y \frac{t^{\varepsilon/k}(y)}{|y|^{1/k}}\nu(y) \\
&\leq \sum_y \left(1 + \frac{t^{\varepsilon}(y)}{|y|}\right)\nu(y) \\
&= \nu(\Sigma^*) + \sum_y \frac{t^{\varepsilon}(y)}{|y|}\nu(y) < \infty ,
\end{aligned}$$

so $h^{\varepsilon/k}$ is polynomial on μ_1-average. This implies that h is polynomial on μ_1-average, which implies that h/p is polynomial on μ-average, and thus $h = (h/p)p$ is polynomial on μ-average. So $(A, \mu) \in \mathsf{AP}$.

25.9. If $\mu(x) > 2^{-n}$, then the first difference in the binary representations of $\mu^*(x)$ and $\mu^*(x-1)$ must come at or before the nth digit. So let z_x be the longest common prefix of the binary representations of $\mu^*(x)$ and $\mu^*(x-1)$, and define $\mathrm{code}_\mu(x)$ by

$$\mathrm{code}_\mu(x) = \begin{cases} 0x & \text{if } \mu(x) \leq 2^{-|x|}, \\ 1z_x & \text{otherwise.} \end{cases}$$

Now we verify the three properties code_μ is required to have.

- *Efficiency.* Since μ^* is polynomial-time computable, so is code_μ.
- *Uniqueness.* If $\mu(x) \neq 0$, then

$$0.z_x \leq \mu^*(x-1) < 0.z_x1 \leq \mu^*(x) \leq 0.z_x\overline{1} .$$

  So x is uniquely determined by either $0x$ or $1z_x$.
- *Compression.* If $\mu(x) \leq 2^{-|x|}$, then $|0x| = 1 + |x| \leq 1 + \log(\frac{1}{\mu(x)})$. On the other hand, if $\mu(x) > 2^{-|x|}$, then $|z_x| < |x|$ and

$$\mu(x) \leq 0.z_x\overline{1} - 0.z_x = 2^{-|z_x|} ,$$

  so $|z_x| \leq \min(|x|, \log(\frac{1}{\mu(x)}))$.

25.10. By the definition of *D-HALT*,

$$\nu((M_{A,\mu}, \text{code}_\mu(x), 1^{q(|x|)}) = \frac{c}{q(|x|)^2 \cdot |\text{code}_\mu(x)|^2 \cdot 2^{|\text{code}_\mu(x)|}},$$

where c is a constant depending only on A and code_μ. By Lemma 25.11, $|\text{code}_\mu(x)| \leq 1 - \log(\mu(x))$, so $-|\text{code}_\mu(x)| \geq \log(\mu(x)) - 1$, which means that

$$2^{-|\text{code}_\mu(x)|} \geq \frac{\mu(x)}{2}.$$

Thus

$$\begin{aligned}\nu((M_{A,\mu}, \text{code}_\mu(x), 1^{q(|x|)})) &\leq \frac{c\mu(x)}{2q(|x|)^2 \cdot |\text{code}_\mu(x)|} \\ &< \frac{c}{2|(M_{A,\mu}, \text{code}_\mu(x), 1^{q(|x|)})|^2} \cdot |\text{code}_\mu(x)|,\end{aligned}$$

from which it follows that $\mu \preceq_f \nu$.

25.11. Suppose that a graph G with n nodes is encoded using an adjacency matrix. Then the size of the encoding x for G is n^2. The weight of such a graph is given by $n^{-2}2^{-n^2} < 2^{-|x|}$.

25.12. The following is a sketch of a solution, but it can be easily formalized. The encoding of $\langle M, x, 1^k \rangle$ takes about $|M| + |x| + k$ bits. So if we fix M and x and let k vary, the encoding takes $\Theta(k)$ bits and the weight is $\Theta(k^{-2})$. But for every ε, $\Theta(k^{-2}) > 2^{-\Theta(k)^\varepsilon}$ when k is large enough.

25.13. $x' \in B_0$ can be determined nondeterministically in time $2^{p(|x|)} = |x'|$.

26.1. $\dfrac{1}{N}(1 + 2 + \ldots + N) = \dfrac{N(N+1)}{2N} = \dfrac{N+1}{2}$.

26.2. m/N.

26.3. For ease of notation we will assume that each node in the tree has only two children; the general case follows by a similar argument. For any node v in the tree, let p_v be the probability labeling the edge to the first child; $(1 - p_v)$ is then the probability labeling the edge to the other child.

We prove that the sum of the probabilities at any level k is 1 by induction on k. When $k = 1$, there is only one node, and it has probability 1, since the empty product is 1. Now suppose that the sum of the probabilities at level k is 1. Let q_v be the probability of a node v on level k. Then the sum of the probabilities of the nodes on level $k + 1$ is

$$\sum_v q_v p_v + q_v(1 - p_v) = \sum_v q_v(p_v + (1 - p_v)) = \sum_v q_v = 1,$$

where the sums are over all nodes on level k.

26.4. If the entries in M are real, $M^t = M^*$. The fact that the rows (columns) are orthonormal is just another way of expressing that $MM^t = M^tM = I$, since the values in MM^t are just the dot product of two columns, and the values of M^tM are the dot product of two rows. This implies the stated equivalence.

26.5. Note that in the following example, the probability is 0 for *every* state after two steps, even though the probability of going from any parent node to either of its children is 1/2 .

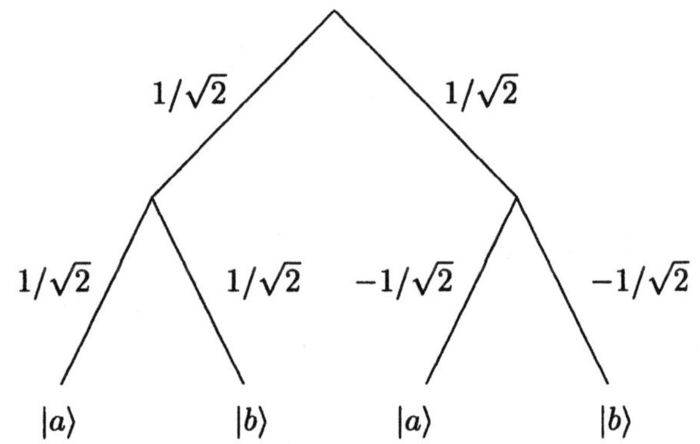

With an appropriate labeling of the internal nodes of this tree, this corresponds to a matrix $\frac{1}{\sqrt{2}}\begin{bmatrix} 0 & 1 & 1 \\ 0 & 1 & 1 \\ 0 & -1 & -1 \end{bmatrix}$, which is not unitary.

26.6. $M = \frac{1}{\sqrt{2}}\begin{bmatrix} 1 & 1 \\ 1 & -1 \end{bmatrix}$ will work.

26.7. $W : |c_0\rangle \mapsto \sum_i (\frac{1}{\sqrt{2}})^n |c_i\rangle$.

26.8. $W : |c_i\rangle \mapsto \sum_j (\frac{1}{\sqrt{2}})^n (-1)^{i\cdot j} |c_i\rangle$, where $i \cdot j$ is the dot product of the strings i and j. This is because a negative sign is introduced exactly when a bit is 1 both before and after the transformation.

26.9. Since $D = W\hat{F}W$, the effect of D on $|c_i\rangle$ is

$$\begin{aligned}
|c_i\rangle &\overset{W}{\mapsto} \sum_a (\frac{1}{\sqrt{2}})^n (-1)^{i\cdot a} |c_i\rangle \\
&\overset{\hat{F}}{\mapsto} |c_0\rangle + \sum_{a\neq 0} (\frac{1}{\sqrt{2}})^n (-1)^{1+i\cdot a} |c_a\rangle \\
&\overset{W}{\mapsto} \sum_j (\frac{1}{2})^n |c_j\rangle + \sum_{a\neq 0} \sum_j (\frac{1}{2})^n (-1)^{1+i\cdot a + a\cdot j} |c_j\rangle \,,
\end{aligned}$$

so

$$\begin{aligned}
D_{ii} &= \frac{1}{N} + \sum_{a\neq 0} \frac{1}{N}(-1)^{1+i\cdot a+a\cdot i} \\
&= \frac{1}{N}\left(1 + \sum_{a\neq 0} -1\right) \\
&= \frac{1-(N-1)}{N} = \frac{2-N}{N} ,
\end{aligned}$$

and

$$\begin{aligned}
D_{ij} &= \frac{1}{N} + \sum_{a\neq 0} \frac{1}{N}(-1)^{1+i\cdot a+a\cdot j} \\
&= \frac{1}{N}\left(1 + 1^{i\cdot 0+0\cdot i} + \sum_{a}(-1)^{1+i\cdot a+a\cdot j}\right) \\
&= \frac{1}{N}(2+0) = \frac{2}{N} .
\end{aligned}$$

26.10. Note that $D^t = D$, so it suffices to show that $D^2 = I$. Clearly, $I^2 = I$, and $P = P^2$ since $P^2_{ij} = \sum_{i=0}^{N-1}(1/N)(1/N) = \frac{N}{N^2} = \frac{1}{N}$. So

$$D^2 = (-I+2P)^2 = I^2 - 4P + 4P^2 = I - 4P + 4P = I .$$

26.11. For any vector $x = [x_0, x_1, \ldots, x_{N-1}]^t$, Px is a row vector, each component of which is equal to $\sum_{i=0}^{n-1}(x_i/N)$, so each component of Px is the average of the values in x. Thus $Dx = (-I+2P)x = -x+2Px = Px-(x-Px)$ is the inversion about the average.

26.12. The base case is trivial using $\sin(\theta) = 1/\sqrt{N}$ and $\cos(\theta) = \frac{\sqrt{N-1}}{\sqrt{N}}$.

Now suppose that we have shown that the equation is correct for k_j and l_j. It is perhaps most natural to verify the values of k_{j+1} and l_{j+1} are as stated by working backwards. Let $\alpha = (2j+1)\theta$. Then using $\sin(2\theta) = \frac{2\sqrt{N-1}}{N}$ and $\cos(2\theta) = \frac{N-2}{N}$, and a tirgonometric identity for $\sin(\alpha + 2\theta)$, we see that

$$\begin{aligned}
\sin((2(j+1)+1)\theta) &= \sin(\alpha + 2\theta) \\
&= \sin(\alpha)\cos(2\theta) + \cos(\alpha)\sin(2\theta) \\
&= k_j\frac{N-2}{N} + l_j\sqrt{N-1}\frac{2\sqrt{N-1}}{N} \\
&= k_j\frac{N-2}{N} + l_j\frac{2(N-1)}{N} .
\end{aligned}$$

The argument for k_{j+1} is similar.

26.13. If $a = |T|/N$, and the algorithm randomly picks an element to query repeatedly until a target is found, then the expected number of queries is

$$\begin{aligned}
a + 2a(1-a) + 3a(1-a)^2 + \cdots + (i+1)a(1-a)^i + \cdots \\
&= a\sum_{i=0}^{\infty}(i+1)(1-a)^i \\
&= a\sum_{i=0}^{\infty}\sum_{j=0}^{i}(1-a)^i \\
&= a\sum_{j=0}^{\infty}\sum_{i=j}^{\infty}(1-a)^i \\
&= a\sum_{j=0}^{\infty}\frac{(1-a)^j}{a} \\
&= \sum_{j=0}^{\infty}(1-a)^j \\
&= 1/a\,.
\end{aligned}$$

So if $|T|/N = 1/4$, the expected number of queries is 4. Even if the algorithm is modified so that no query is made more than once, the expected number of queries is nearly 4 when N is large.

26.14. Assuming the algorithm makes a new query each time, it could take $N - |T| + 1 > (3/4)2^n$ queries.

Bibliography

M. Aigner. *Combinatorial Search.* Wiley-Teubner, 1988.

N. Alon, J.H. Spencer. *The Probabilistic Method.* Wiley, 1992.

K. Ambos-Spies, S. Homer, U. Schöning, ed. *Complexity Theory: current research.* Cambridge University Press, 1993.

M. Anthony, N. Biggs. *Computational Learning Theory.* Cambridge University Press, 1992.

J.L. Balcázar, J. Diaz, J. Gabarró. *Structural Complexity I, 2nd edition.* Springer, 1995.

J.L. Balcázar, J. Diaz, J. Gabarró. *Structural Complexity II.* Springer, 1990.

L. Banachowski, A. Kreczmar, W. Rytter. *Analysis of Algorithms and Data Structures.* Addison-Wesley, 1991.

J.P. Barthélemy, G. Cohen, A. Lobstein. *Complexité Algorithmique et problèmes de communications.* Masson, Paris 1992.

R. Beigel. Class Notes on Interactive Proof Systems. Yale University Technical Report, YALEU/DCS/TR-947, 1993.

R. Book, ed. *Studies in Complexity Theory.* Pitman, 1986.

D.P. Bovet, P. Crescenzi. *Introduction to the Theory of Complexity.* Prentice-Hall, 1994.

W.S. Brainerd, L.H. Landweber. *Theory of Computation.* Wiley, 1974.

G. Brassard, P. Bratley. *Algorithmics: Theory & Practice.* Prentice Hall, 1988.

T.H. Cormen, C.E. Leiserson, R.L. Rivest. *Introduction to Algorithms.* MIT Press, McGraw-Hill, 1990.

F.R. Drake, S.S. Wainer, ed. *Recursion Theory: its Generalizations and Applications.* Cambridge University Press, 1980.

P. Dunne. *The Complexity of Boolean Networks.* Academic Press, 1988.

P. Dunne. *Computability Theory: concepts and applications.* Ellis Horwood, 1991.

R.W. Floyd, R. Beigel. *The Language of Machines: An Introduction to Computability and Formal Languages.* Computer Science Press, 1994.

M.R. Garey, D.S. Johnson. *Computers and Intractability: A Guide to the Theory of NP-Completeness.* Freeman, 1979.

A. Gibbons, W. Rytter. *Efficient Parallel Algorithms.* Cambridge University Press, 1988.

A. Gibbons, P. Spirakis, ed. *Lectures on Parallel Computation.* Cambridge University Press, 1993.

E.M. Gurari. *An Introduction to the Theory of Computation.* Computer Science Press, 1989.

J. Hartmanis. *Feasible Computations and Provable Complexity Properties.* Society for Industrial and Appl. Math., 1978.

J. Hartmanis, ed. *Computational Complexity Theory.* American Math. Society, 1989.

L. Hemaspaandra, A. Selman, ed. *Complexity Theory Retrospective II.* Springer, 1997.

R. Herken, ed. *The Universal Turing Machine: A Half Century Survey.* Kammerer & Unverzagt und Oxford University Press, 1988.

J. Hertz, A. Krogh, R.G. Palmer. *Introduction to the Theory of Neural Computation.* Addison-Wesley, 1991.

J. Kilian. *Uses of Randomness in Algorithms and Protocols.* MIT Press, 1990.

D.E. Knuth. *The Art of Computer Programming. Vol 2: Semi-Numerical Algorithms.* Addison-Wesley, 1981^2.

R.L. Graham, D.E. Knuth, O. Patashnik. *Concrete Mathematics: A Foundation for Computer Science, 2nd edition.* Addison-Wesley, 1994.

J. Köbler, U. Schöning, J. Torán. *The Graph Isomorphism Problem: Its Structural Complexity.* Birkhäuser, 1993.

D. Kozen. *The Design and Analysis of Algorithms.* Springer, 1992.

E. Kranakis. *Primality and Cryptography.* Wiley-Teubner, 1986.

L. Kučera. *Combinatorial Algorithms.* Adam Hilger, 1990.

J. van Leeuwen, ed. *Handbook of Theoretical Computer Science.* Volumes A & B. Elsevier, MIT Press, 1990.

H.R. Lewis, C.H. Papadimitriou. *Elements of the Theory of Computation.* Prentice-Hall, 1981.

M. Li, P. Vitányi. *An Introduction to Kolmogorov Complexity and its Applications, 2nd edition.* Springer, 1997.

C. Lund. *The Power of Interaction.* MIT Press, 1992.

M. Machtey, P. Young. *An Introduction to the General Theory of Algorithms.* North-Holland, 1978.

C. Meinel. *Modified Branching Programs and Their Computational Power.* Springer, Lecture Notes in Computer Science 370, 1989.

S. Micali, ed. *Advances in Computing Research.* Vol 5: Randomness and Computation. JAI Press, 1989.

M.L. Minsky, S.A. Papert. *Perceptrons.* MIT Press, 1969.

B.K. Natarajan. *Machine Learning: A Theoretical Approach.* Morgan Kaufmann, 1991.

P. Odifreddi. *Classical Recursion Theory.* North-Holland, 1989.

C. Papadimitriou. *Computational Complexity.* Addison-Wesley, 1994.

J. Parberry. *Parallel Complexity Theory.* Pitman-Wiley, 1987.

M.S. Paterson, ed. *Boolean Function Complexity.* Cambridge University Press, 1992.

H. Rogers. *Theory of Recursive Functions and Effective Computability.* McGraw-Hill, 1967. (Reprint by MIT Press, 1993).

G. Rozenberg, A. Salomaa, ed. *Current Trends in Theoretical Computer Science.* World Scientific, 1993.

G. Rozenberg, A. Salomaa. *Cornerstones of Undecidability.* Prentice-Hall, 1994.

A. Salomaa. *Computation and Automata.* Cambridge University Press, 1985.

A. Salomaa. *Public Key Cryptography.* Springer-Verlag, 1990.

C.P. Schnorr. *Rekursive Funktionen und ihre Komplexitt.* Teubner, 1974.

U. Schöning. *Complexity and Structure.* Lecture Notes in Computer Science 211, Springer, 1986.

A.L. Selman, ed. *Complexity Theory Retrospective.* Springer, 1990.

J.R. Shoenfield. *Mathematical Logic.* Addison-Wesley, 1967.

A. Sinclair. *Algorithms for Random Generation and Counting.* Birkhäuser, 1993.

M. Sipser. Lecture Notes 18.428: Computation by Automata. MIT, 1985.

R.I. Soare. *Recursively Enumerable Sets and Degrees.* Springer, 1987.

R. Sommerhalder, S.C. van Westrhenen. *The Theory of Computability: Programs, Machines, Effectiveness and Feasibility.* Addison-Wesley, 1988.

H. Straubing. *Finite Automata, Formal Logic, and Circuit Complexity.* Birkhäuser, 1994.

K. Wagner, G. Wechsung. *Computational Complexity.* VEB Deutscher Verlag der Wissenschaften und Reidel-Verlag, 1986.

O. Watanabe, ed. *Kolmogorov Complexity and Computational Complexity.* Springer, 1992.

I. Wegener. *The Complexity of Boolean Functions.* Wiley-Teubner, 1987.

D. Welsh. *Codes and Cryptography.* Oxford University Press, 1988.

D. Welsh. *Complexity: Knots, Colourings and Counting.* Cambridge University Press, 1993.

A. Wigderson. *Lecture Notes*, Barbados Workshop on Complexity, 1994.

Index

$\leq_{\mathrm{T}}^{\mathsf{P}}$ *see* Turing reduction
$\leq_{\mathrm{m}}^{\mathsf{P}}$ *see* many-one reduction
$\equiv_T$ *see* Turing reduction
$\leq_{\mathrm{T}}$ *see* Turing reduction
$\exists$ 61, 154
$\forall$ 61, 154
λ 1
$\mu \preceq_f \nu$ 218
μ' 214
μ^* 214
$\pi(n)$ *see* Prime Number Theorem
$a^{\overline{b}}$ (rising power) 200
$a^{\underline{b}}$ (falling power) 200
P^A 7
NP^A 7
Π_i^P 131
Σ_i^P 131
$\mathbb{N}$ 1
$\mathbb{R}$ 1
$\mathbb{Z}$ 1
1-1 reducibility 125

abacus 13
AC^0 101
AC^0-reducible 105
acc_M 168
acyclic graph 2, 115, 197, 203
Adleman 22, 235
advice 137, 145
Aho 197, 201
Aigner 309
Aleliunas 47
Allender 173
Alon 109, 282, 309
alphabet 1
Ambos-Spies 129, 309
amplitude amplification 228, 233
AND-function 16, 101, 102, 165
Angluin 90
Anthony 90, 309
AP 217
arithmetic formula 3, 16
arithmetic hierarchy 132
arithmetization of a formula 184
Arthur 178
Arthur-Merlin game 160, 178, 189
Arvind 129
Aspnes 109
Asser 62
atomic formula 61
automaton 26
average-case complexity 71, 213

Babai 160, 178, 181, 183, 189
back-tracking 290
Baker 191, 195
Balcázar 40, 151, 309
Banachowski 309
Barthélemy 309
Barwise 22
basis 104
BDD *see* binary decision tree
Beigel 109, 174, 309
Bell 22
Benioff 223, 234
Bennett 69, 151, 195, 235
Berman 123, 126, 129
Berman-Hartmanis Conjecture 123, 126, 134
Bernoulli experiment 144
Bernoulli trial 282
Bernstein 144, 234, 235
Berry Paradox 254
Berthiaume 235
Bhatt 201
Biggs 90, 309
Biham 233, 234
binary decision tree 115
binomial coefficients 21, 164, 239
binomial distribution 4, 94
Binomial Theorem 21, 255
bipartite graph 2, 198
Biron 233, 234

Blum 121
Blumer 88–90
Board 90
Book 253, 309
boolean circuit 88
boolean formula 2
boolean function 2, 79
boolean hierarchy 135
Boolos 267
Boppana 161
bound variable 61
Bovet 151, 181, 189, 309
Boyer 230, 233, 234
BP· operator *see* counting classes
BQP 226, 227
Brainerd 14, 309
branching program 2, 115
Brassard 151, 180, 182, 233–235, 309
Bratley 151, 309
Bshouty 138
Buntrock vi
bus 279

Cai 138, 173
Celoni 203, 212
Chaitin 75
Chandra 121
Chang 139, 195
Chebyshev's inequality 4, 94, 96
Chernoff 144, 262, 282
Chinese Remainder Theorem 185, 186, 244, 293
chip 133
Chor 195
Christen 70
Chung 201
circuit
– boolean, 2
– polynomial size, *see* polynomial-size circuits
– size of, 3, 92
circuit complexity 79, 133
circuit depth 92
Claus vi, 36
clause 49
Cleve 138
CNF *see* conjunctive normal form
Cohen 309
Coles viii
collapse 38, 142
– of BH, 135
– of PH, 132, 142, 145, 153, 158
collapsing degree 124
collision probability 147
communication tape 176
comparable 33
complement
– closure under, 6, 38
complete graph (K_n) 217
complete language 6, 41
– for BP·⊕P, 168, 289
– for coNP, 119
– for DistNP, 218, 219
– for ∃·⊕P, 288
– for NL, 41
– for NP, 6, 29, 52, 115, 116, 123, 126, 133, 153, 155, 159, 165, 213, 217
– for ⊕P, 165, 168, 289
– for PSPACE, 6
completeness 50
complex clause 55
compressible 77
computably isomorphic 123
computation node 115
computation tree 224
concept 86
conditional Kolmogorov complexity 72
conditional probability 4
configuration 4, 28, 40, 224, 290
conjunctive normal form 259, 269, 272
connected graph 2, 45, 46
coNP *see* counting classes
consistent 86
constant-depth circuits 93
context sensitive language 37, 207, 299
context-free language 119
convex function 201
Cook 59, 66, 165
Cook Hypothesis 132
Cook's Theorem 112, 113
Cormen 151, 186, 189, 282, 309
counting argument 159
counting classes 163–174
– BP·NP, 153, 155, 178
– BP· operator, 153, 165
– BPP, 142, 153, 159, 177, 227
– $C_=P$, 227
– FewP, 164
– MOD-classes, 174
– NP, 111, 163, 165, 173
– coNP, 111
– #P, 168
– ⊕P, 163–166, 173

- PP, 141, 171, 173
- ZPP, 138, 142
$C_=P$ *see* counting classes
Craig 113
Craig Interpolation Theorem 111
Crescenzi 151, 181, 189, 309
critical 274
critical assignment 53
crossing sequence 80
cryptology 181
cut-and-paste 122
cycle 2

D-3COL 215, 217
Dahlhaus 113
Davis 15, 22, 23
decidable 10, 27
degree
- of a language, 124
- of a node in a graph, 44
- of a node in graph, 2
- of a polynomial, 1, 95, 103, 106, 187, 188, 294
- total, 1, 107
Demarrais 235
DeMorgan's laws 101, 166, 259, 264, 280, 292
density function 214
depth
- of a circuit, 92
depth-first 290
descriptive complexity 61, 65
Deutsch 223, 234
D-HALT 215, 218
D-HAM 216
diagonalization 279
Diaz 40, 151, 309
diffusion transformation 229
dimension
- of a vector space, 104
Diophantine equation 15
Diophantus 15
directed graph 115, 197, 203
disjunctive normal form 49, 89, 259, 266
DistNP 214
distribution function 213
distributional problem 214, 215
divide-and-conquer 197
DNF *see* disjunctive normal form
$DNF_{n,k}$ 89
dot product 225
downward separation 132
Drake 309
Dunne 309
Dykstra-Pruim viii

e-mail 183
easy formula 136
easy-hard argument 136
Ehrenfeucht 88–90
Ekert 235
Emde Boas, van 22
Enderton 69
entropy 145, 256, 258
equivalence problem 26
- for branching programs, 119
- for circuits, 115
- for context-free languages, 119
- for LOOP-programs, 26
- for tournaments, 164
equivalence relation 33
evaluation vector 79
example set 86
expected value 4, 42, 143
exponential running-time 42
expression tree 33

factoring 77, 223
Fagin 68–70
failure 94
falling power 200
fan-in 91
Feigenbaum 181
Fenner 235
FewP *see* counting classes
Feynman 234
Fiat 181
Fibonacci sequence 238
finite field 120, 146, 185, 187
finite injury 13
finitely presented group 219
first-order 63
flat distribution 220
Floyd 22, 309
formal language 37
formula 61, 80
- arithmetic, 3
- boolean, 2
- predicate logic, 3
- quantified boolean, 3
- satisfiable, 3
- size, 3
Fortnow 227, 235, 291
Fortune 121, 126, 129
Fourier representation 103
Fourier transformation 228

free variable 61
Friedberg 9, 11
Furst 91, 99, 101, 109

Gödel 15
Gabarró 40, 151, 309
GAP 41
Garey 22, 42, 47, 113, 155, 310
generalized spectrum 64
Gergov 122
GF(n) 120, 146, 185, 187
GI *see* graph isomorphism
Gibbons 310
Gill 151, 191, 195
Goldreich 160, 177, 179, 181, 182, 195, 222
Goldsmith viii
Goldwasser 160, 175, 177–180, 182
GOTO-program 27
Grädel 70
Graham 310
grammar 39
graph 2
– acyclic, 2
– bipartite, 2
– connected, 2
graph accessibility *see GAP*
graph coloring 215, 217
graph isomorphism 42, 153, 155, 158–160, 177, 179
Grassl 233, 234
greedy algorithm 55
Green viii, 235
Grover viii, 223, 234
Gundermann 138
Gurari 40, 151, 310
Gurevich 70, 113, 222

Høyer 230, 233, 234
Hack 23
Hagerup 282
Haken 49, 59
halting problem 5, 9, 17, 18, 26, 27, 215, 218, 222
Hamiltonian circuit 42, 216
hard formula 136
Hartmanis 37, 40, 70, 123, 138, 310
hash function 146, 150, 156, 157
Hausdorff 281
Haussler 88–90
Hemachandra 138, 173
Hemaspaandra 310
Herken 181, 310
Hertrampf vi
Hertz 310
Hilbert 15
– Tenth Problem, 15
Hoffmann 160
Homer viii, 126, 129, 235, 309
Hopcroft 121, 197, 201, 212
Horn formula 65, 68, 69
Huang 235
Hunt 37, 40
hypothesis 86
hypothesis space 86
Håstad 99, 161

Immerman 37, 40, 63, 70
Impagliazzo 150, 151, 222
in-degree 205
inclusion problem 119
inclusion-exclusion principle 4, 157
Incompleteness Theorem *see* Gödel
independent events 4
index (of an equivalence relation) 33
inductive counting 39
initial configuration 209
input node 203
interactive proof systems 153, 160, 176
interpolant 111
interpolant complexity 111
Interpolation Theorem 2, 33, 120, 121, 275
interpreter 72
inversion about the average 229
IP 178, 183
isomorphic
– computably, 123
Isomorphism Conjecture 123, 125, 126
isomorphism degree 124
Israeli 113

Jeffrey 267
Johnson 22, 42, 47, 113, 155, 310
Jones 23, 69, 70
Jozsa 234, 235

Köbler vi, 42, 47, 151, 160, 165, 174, 181, 279, 283, 310
Kadin 135, 138, 139
Kannan 138
Karg vi
Karp 40, 47, 70, 126, 129
Kautz viii
Keisler 69

Kilian 310
Knuth 189, 310
Ko 151
Kolmogorov 75, 192
Kolmogorov complexity 71, 72, 75, 77, 86, 88
Kolmogorov random 74, 77
Kozen 121, 310
Kranakis 189, 282, 310
Krause 122
Kreczmar 309
Krogh 310
Kučera 310
Kuroda 37, 40
Kurtz 195

L 41
Lagrange 17
Landweber 14, 309
language 1
Lautemann 160
law of large numbers 44, 144
LBA *see* linear bounded automoton
LBA problem
- first, 37
- second, 38
learning 85, 107
learning algorithm 86
Leeuwen, van 202, 310
Leftover Hash Lemma 145, 147, 149
Leiserson 151, 186, 189, 282, 309
Levin 75, 213, 216, 222
Lewis 310
lexicographical order 1
Li 75, 83, 90, 310
Lidar 233, 234
linear bounded automaton 37
linearly independent 105
Lipton 47, 126, 129
literal 49, 89, 108
Lobstein 309
log-reducible ($\leq_{\log}$) 41
Lolli 70, 113
Longo 113
Longpré viii, 126, 129
loop-depth 26
LOOP-program 25
Lorenzen 175
Lovász 47
lower bounds
- for branching programs, 115
- for circuits, 91, 101
- for resolution proofs, 49
- via Kolmogorov complexity, 77
Lund 189, 310

Machtey 128, 254, 310
Mahaney 129
majority 105
majority vote 145, 148
Makowsky 113
Manders 22
many-one degree 124
many-one reduction 6
- for distributional problems ($\leq_m^{\mathrm{P}}$), 218
- polynomial time ($\leq_m^{\mathrm{P}}$), 6, 125
Marja 113
Markov chain 44
Markov's inequality 4, 45, 94, 248, 261, 282
Marriage Theorem 199
matching 198
Matijasevič 15, 23
McCulloch-Pitts neuron 106
Meinel vi, 122, 310
memory 204
Merlin 178, 189
Meyer 36
Micali 160, 175, 177, 179, 180, 182, 311
Milterson 76
Minsky 106, 107, 109, 311
MOD-classes *see* counting classes
model 3, 62
monomial 89, 101, 104, 108
monotone reduction 285
move 203
Muchnik 9, 11
multi-linear polynomial 104, 118
Mundici 111, 113
museum 45

Natarajan 90, 311
NC^1, NC^k 261
neural net 107
neuron 107
Nisan 122, 183
NL 41
nondeterminism 51
NOR 244
NOR-function 35
NOT-function 101, 165
NP *see* counting classes
(NP,P-computable) *see* DistNP
(NP-search, P-samplable) 222
NQP 226, 227

observation 226
Occam algorithm 88
Occam's Razor 85
Odifreddi 128, 311
Ogiwara 126, 129
one-one reduction
– polynomial time, 125
one-time-only 116
one-way function
– cryptographic, 221
OR-function 16, 101, 165
oracle results 183, 191
oracle Turing Machine 9
oracle Turing machine 5, 138, 192
orthonormal 225, 306
output node 203

P 173
#P *see* counting classes
P-computable distribution 214
P-isomorphic 123, 125
P-samplable distribution 221
PAC (probabilistically approximately correct 86
PAC-learnable 86
padding 124
padding function 124
Palmer, E.M. 282
Palmer, R.G. 310
Papadimitriou 40, 70, 173, 181, 189, 282, 310, 311
Papert 106, 107, 109, 311
Parberry 311
parity function 90, 91
⊕P *see* counting classes
partial assignment 55
Patashnik 310
Paterson 311
PATH 41
path 2
Paul 82, 203, 212
pebble 203
pebbling strategy 205
perceptron 106
permutation network 295
Petri net 23
Pfeiffer 282
PH 68, 131, 142, 153, 165, 173
PHP_n 52
pigeonhole principle 52
pipe 246
Pippenger 201, 202
Pitassi 59
Pitt 90
$\mathcal{POL}$ 120
$\mathcal{POL}$ 104
Polish notation 80
Pollett viii
polynomial 101
polynomial on μ-average 216
polynomial-size circuits 3, 93, 111, 133, 134, 145
polynomial-time hierarchy *see* PH
Pos *see* positive reduction
positive reduction 158, 285
Post correspondence problem 219
Post's Problem 9
Pratt 186, 189
predicate logic 61
predicate symbol 61
prime factorization 77
prime number 146, 185
prime number problem 165
prime number sieve 293
Prime Number Theorem 77, 78, 185
primitive recursive 25
priority method 9, 11
probabilistic method 46, 95, 159, 191, 200
probability amplification 46, 143, 154, 158, 166, 177, 283
probability amplitude 225
probability distribution 146
probability gap 141, 153
proof 134
proof calculus 175
property P 124
provable by an oracle 177
prover 175
Pruim 235
pseudo-random number 146, 148, 151
PSPACE 6, 168, 172, 177, 178, 183
public coins 178
Putnam 15
pyramid 205

QBF 3, 183
quantified boolean formula 3, 183, 188
quantifier 3, 16, 61, 64
quantum mechanics 223
quantum state 226
quantum Turing machine 225
QuickSort 71, 74, 75

Rödding 69
Rüb 282

Rackoff 47, 175, 177, 179, 180, 182
random bits 156
random oracle 192
Random Oracle Hypothesis 192
random polynomial 101
random restriction 95
random sequence 71
random variable 4, 141
random walk 43
random, Kolmogorov *see* Kolmogorov random
Razborov 101, 109
Reckhow 59
reducibility 123
refutation 50
register machine 5, 17, 25, 204
regular graph 46
relativization principle 191
resolution 49
resolvent 49
reversible computation 226, 228
Richter 70, 113
Ritchie 36
Rivest 151, 186, 189, 282, 309
RL 42
Robbin 69
Robinson 15
Rogers, H. 14, 129, 311
Rogers, J. 227, 235
Rompel 291
round 176
Rozenberg 23, 311
Rudich 109
Rytter 309

Salomaa 311
SAT 2, 6, 35, 115, 116, 124, 164
⊕*SAT* 165
Savitch 40, 294
Savitch's Theorem 37
Saxe 91, 99, 101
Schöning viii, 38, 40, 42, 47, 113, 129, 151, 160, 161, 165, 173, 181, 279, 283, 309, 310
Schaefer viii
Schmidt 121
Schnorr 311
scholastics 85
Schuler vi
Schulz 62
Schwichtenberg 69
search algorithm 223
Second Berman-Hartmanis Conjecture 126
second-order existential 64
second-order predicate logic 64
Seiferas 82
self-reducible 134, 145, 279, 283
self-terminating code 78, 79
Selman 40, 69, 70, 310, 311
sentences 61
set of examples 86
Sewelson 138
Shamir 178, 181, 183
Shoenfield 311
Shor viii, 223, 235
sieve of Eratosthenes 293
similar probability distributions 147
Simmons 181
Simon 82, 234
simple formula 188
Sinclair 311
sink 2
Sipser 47, 91, 99, 101, 160, 177, 178, 182, 291, 311
size
- of a circuit, 3, 92
- of a formula, 3
Smolensky 101, 109
SO∃ 64
Soare 311
Solomonoff 75
Solovay 191, 195
Sommerhalder 40, 311
soundness 50
source 2
sparse 125, 133
Specker 70
spectral problem 61, 62, 68
Spencer 109, 282, 309
Spirakis 310
start node 115
statistical test 151
Stirling's formula 255, 264
Stockmeyer 68, 70
Strassen 70
strategy 203
Straubing 311
Strauss viii
string 1
structure 61
subspace 104
success 94
SUPER proof system 51
super-duper-concentrator 208
superconcentrator 197
superconcentrators 203

superposition 226
Swapping Lemma 154
symmetric boolean function 105, 108, 261
Szelepcsényi 37, 40

Tamon 138
Tapp 230, 233, 234
Tarjan 203, 212
Tarui 174
tautology 3
teacher 85
terminal node 115
Thierauf vi
threshold function 265
threshold gate 106
threshold value 106, 153
Thue system 219
tiling 219
Time Hierarchy Theorem 299
time interval 209
time-space trade-off 205
Toda 165, 167, 174, 183
topological ordering 54
Torán vi, 42, 47, 113, 151, 160, 165, 181, 279, 283, 310
total degree 1, 22, 107, 108, 240
total ordering 69
truth table 49, 79
Tsichritzis 36
Turing machine 4, 26, 27, 175, 224
Turing reduction 9, 126, 133, 154

Ullman 197, 201
unbounded fan-in 91
undecidable 15, 27
uniform distribution 43, 146
unitary 225
universal hash functions 145, 146, 151, 156, 157
universal probability distribution 73, 75, 214, 222
universal traversal sequence 45, 46
universal Turing machine 72
universe 61
UNIX 246

Valiant 86, 89, 90, 101, 109, 165, 174, 212
valid formula 183
variance 4
Vazirani 101, 109, 165, 174, 234, 235
vector space 104
vector space homomorphism 104
verifier 175
Vitányi 75, 83, 90, 310

Waack 122
Wagner 138, 212, 311
Wainer 309
Walsh-Hadamard 228
Wang 222
Warmuth 88–90
Watanabe 126, 129, 311
Watrous 235
Wechsung 138, 212, 311
Wegener 279, 311
Wegman 121
Welsh 151, 256, 311
Westrhenen, van 40, 311
Wigderson 122, 160, 179, 182, 311
witness 10, 113, 134
witness circuit 134
WLOG 81
word problem 219
worst-case complexity 71
Wrathall 138

XOR 158

Young 11, 125, 128, 129, 254, 310

Zachos 160, 161, 173
Žák 122
zero-knowledge 179, 180
ZPP *see* counting classes
Zuckerman 150, 151

MIX
Papier aus verantwortungsvollen Quellen
Paper from responsible sources
FSC® C105338

If you have any concerns about our products,
you can contact us on
ProductSafety@springernature.com

In case Publisher is established outside the EU,
the EU authorized representative is:
Springer Nature Customer Service Center GmbH
Europaplatz 3, 69115 Heidelberg, Germany

Printed by Libri Plureos GmbH
in Hamburg, Germany